Cases on Effective Destination Management

Romina Alkier
University of Rijeka, Croatia

Giuseppe Catenazzo
American Institute of Applied Sciences in Switzerland, Switzerland

Vedran Milojica
University of Rijeka, Croatia

Aleksandra Zając
American Institute of Applied Sciences in Switzerland, Switzerland

Vice President of Editorial	Melissa Wagner
Managing Editor of Acquisitions	Mikaela Felty
Managing Editor of Book Development	Jocelynn Hessler
Production Manager	Mike Brehm
Cover Design	Phillip Shickler

Published in the United States of America by
IGI Global Scientific Publishing
701 East Chocolate Avenue
Hershey, PA, 17033, USA
Tel: 717-533-8845
Fax: 717-533-8661
E-mail: cust@igi-global.com
Website: https://www.igi-global.com

Copyright © 2025 by IGI Global Scientific Publishing. All rights reserved. No part of this publication may be reproduced, stored or distributed in any form or by any means, electronic or mechanical, including photocopying, without written permission from the publisher.
Product or company names used in this set are for identification purposes only. Inclusion of the names of the products or companies does not indicate a claim of ownership by IGI Global Scientific Publishing of the trademark or registered trademark.

Library of Congress Cataloging-in-Publication Data

Names: Alkier, Romina, 1974- editor. | Catenazzo, Giuseppe, 1982- editor. |
   Milojica, Vedran, 1984- editor. | Zając, Aleksandra, 1985- editor.
Title: Cases on effective destination management / edited by Romina Alkier,
   Giuseppe Catenazzo, Vedran Milojica, Aleksandra Zając.
Description: Hershey, PA : Business Science Reference, [2025] | Includes
   bibliographical references and index. | Summary: "Devising methodologies
   to help decision-makers handle destinations effectively is paramount in
   a post-COVID world where travelers are seemingly more numerous than
   ever. This methodological book showcases a selection of research-based
   case studies to illustrate how to design research beneficial for
   destination management"-- Provided by publisher.
Identifiers: LCCN 2023055012 (print) | LCCN 2023055013 (ebook) | ISBN
   9798369315484 (hardcover) | ISBN 9798369315491 (ebook)
Subjects: LCSH: Tourism--Marketing. | Hospitality industry--Marketing. |
   Branding (Marketing) | Place marketing.
Classification: LCC G155.A1 C316 2024 (print) | LCC G155.A1 (ebook) | DDC
   910.68/8--dc23/eng/20240102
LC record available at https://lccn.loc.gov/2023055012
LC ebook record available at https://lccn.loc.gov/2023055013

British Cataloguing in Publication Data
A Cataloguing in Publication record for this book is available from the British Library.

All work contributed to this book is new, previously-unpublished material.
The views expressed in this book are those of the authors, but not necessarily of the publisher.
This book contains information sourced from authentic and highly regarded references, with reasonable efforts made to ensure the reliability of the data and information presented. The authors, editors, and publisher believe the information in this book to be accurate and true as of the date of publication. Every effort has been made to trace and credit the copyright holders of all materials included. However, the authors, editors, and publisher cannot assume responsibility for the validity of all materials or the consequences of their use. Should any copyright material be found unacknowledged, please inform the publisher so that corrections may be made in future reprints.

Editorial Advisory Board

Suja A. Alex, *St. Xavier's Catholic College of Engineering, India*
Luzia Arantes, *Polytechnic University of Cávado and Ave, University of Aveiro, Portugal*
Debjani Banerjee, *VES Business School, India*
Mélanie Florence Boninsegni, *IPAG Business School, France*
Ljupcho Efremov, *Liberal Arts Department, American University of the Middle East, Kuwait*
Giovana Goretti Feijó Almeida, *CiTUR - Polytechnic University of Leiria, Portugal*
Sajal Kabiraj, *Häme University of Applied Sciences Ltd., Finland*
Marie Kerekes, *ESSEC Business School, France*
Maximiliano E. Korstanje, *University of Palermo, Argentina*
Mounia Moumen, *Ecole des Hautes Etudes d'Ingénierie of Oujda, Morocco*
Milena Podovac, *Faculty of Hotel Management and Tourism in Vrnjačka Banja, University of Kragujevac, Serbia*
Rafael Perez Pena, *Colorado Mountain College, USA*
Danka Milojkovic, *Singidunum University, Serbia*

Table of Contents

Preface xv

Acknowledgement xix

Chapter 1
The Shortest Form of Storytelling in Destination Marketing: Tourism Slogans of the European Capitals 1
    Árpád Ferenc Papp-Váry, Budapest Business University, Hungary
    Ahmad Hajeer, Budapest Business University, Hungary

Chapter 2
Destination Competitiveness, Culture and Heritage Tourism, and Regional Clusters: Case of Macedonia 27
    Marija Lazarev Zivanovic, Glion Institute of Higher Education, Switzerland

Chapter 3
Tourist Awareness in Tourism Development: Case Study of the City of Veria, Greece 57
    Ioannis Valachis, Hellenic Open University, Greece
    Nikolaos Trihas, Hellenic Mediterranean University, Heraklion, Greece

Chapter 4
Perspectives for the Potential and Future of Marine Tourism in Bangladesh 83
    Mohammad Badruddoza Talukder, International University of Business Agriculture and Technology, Bangladesh
    Firoj Kabir, Daffodil Institute of IT, Bangladesh
    Fahmida Kaiser, Daffodil Institute of IT, Bangladesh
    Mushfika Hoque, Daffodil Institute of IT, Bangladesh

Chapter 5
Special Forms of Tourism as a Territorial Management Tool: An Exploratory Study in the Context of Geocaching 105
 Júlio Sousa Silva, Polytechnic Institute of Cávado and Ave (IPCA), Portugal
 Bruno Barbosa Sousa, Polytechnic Institute of Cávado and Ave, Portugal & Applied Management Research Unit (UNIAG), Portugal & Centro de Investigação, Desenvolvimento e Inovação em Turismo (CiTUR), Portugal

Chapter 6
Film-Induced Tourism and Promotion of Tourist Destinations: An Exploratory Approach.. 125
 Bruno Barbosa Sousa, Polytechnic Institute of Cávado and Ave, Portugal & Applied Management Research Unit (UNIAG), Portugal & Centro de Investigação, Desenvolvimento e Inovação em Turismo (CiTUR), Portugal
 João Abreu, Polytechnic Institute of Cávado and Ave, Portugal & ISCET, Portugal
 Lara Marisa Santos, Universidade Lusófona, Portugal & CETRAD, Portugal
 Vítor Silva, Polytechnic Institute of Cávado and Ave, Portugal & Universidade de Vigo, Spain
 Ana Paula Figueira, Polytechnic Institute of Beja, Portugal

Chapter 7
Marketing Plan and Territorial Management: Vila Nova das Taipas (Portugal) 141
 Pedro Ruben Gonçalves, Polytechnic Institute of Cávado and Ave, Portugal
 Bruno Barbosa Sousa, Polytechnic Institute of Cávado and Ave, Portugal & Applied Management Research Unit (UNIAG), Portugal & Centro de Investigação, Desenvolvimento e Inovação em Turismo (CiTUR), Portugal
 João Abreu, Polytechnic Institute of Cávado and Ave, Portugal & ISCET, Portugal
 Manuel Sousa Pereira, Polytechnic Institute of Viana do Castelo, Portugal

Chapter 8
Destination Marketing and Sport: A Bibliometric Review................................ 165
 Jiyoon An, Fayetteville State University, USA

Chapter 9
Summer Olympic Villages as Catalysts for Accessible and Inclusive Places: Between Experiences and Reflections in the Places and Society of the Host Cities 185
> Valerio della Sala, Department of Geography, Universitat Autonoma of Barcelona, Spain & Sport Research Institute IRE-UAB, Spain & Interdepartmental Research Centre for Urban and Mega-Events Studies (OMERO), Italy

Chapter 10
Addressing and Overcoming Destination Rejection From a Destination Management Perspective 205
> Ali Inanir, Burdur Mehmet Akif Ersoy University, Turkey
> Yusuf Karakuş, Recep Tayyip Erdoğan University, Turkey

Chapter 11
Tourism and Destination Positioning Through Territorial Branding: The Case of Brazil 227
> Giovana Goretti Feijó de Almeida, CiTUR, Portugal
> Sarah Minasi, University of Vale do Itajaí, Brazil

Chapter 12
Tourists' Expectations-Based Countryside Walking Tourism Management 255
> Danka Milojković, Singidunum University, Belgrade, Serbia
> Snežana Štetić, The College of Tourism, Belgrade, Serbia & Balkan Network of Tourism Experts, Belgrade, Serbia
> Igor Trišić, Faculty of Geography, University of Belgrade, Serbia

Chapter 13
Heritage-Led Destination Management: Strategies for Competitive Advantage 285
> Aditi Nag, Birla Institute of Technology, Mesra, India
> Smriti Mishra, Birla Institute of Technology, Mesra, India

Compilation of References 325

About the Contributors 391

Index 399

Detailed Table of Contents

Preface xv

Acknowledgement xix

Chapter 1
The Shortest Form of Storytelling in Destination Marketing: Tourism
Slogans of the European Capitals 1
    Árpád Ferenc Papp-Váry, Budapest Business University, Hungary
    Ahmad Hajeer, Budapest Business University, Hungary

This chapter explores the role of storytelling in destination marketing and management, focusing on the utilization of slogans to enhance distinctiveness of tourist destinations, particularly European capitals. It discusses the application of narrative techniques in marketing to distinguish places in tourism market. The research identifies a gap in current understandings of how slogans can be employed in creating compelling destination brands that resonate with potential visitors. Through qualitative analysis of various slogans, the study highlights the importance of unique brand identities for destinations, which establish emotional connections with the audience. The findings suggest that storytelling transcends traditional advertising, offering a branding tool that can impact a destination's appeal and competitiveness. The chapter concludes by emphasizing the strategic value of narrative in destination marketing, proposing that effective storytelling can lead to more successful branding efforts and a stronger connection with target audiences.

Chapter 2
Destination Competitiveness, Culture and Heritage Tourism, and Regional
Clusters: Case of Macedonia 27
    Marija Lazarev Zivanovic, Glion Institute of Higher Education,
        Switzerland

In recent decades, research on cultural identity, state dynamics, and destination competitiveness has gained significant importance in the field of Cultural and Heritage Tourism. Specifically, in Macedonia, a region shared between two states—North Macedonia and Greece—tourism development occurs within a unique political and economic context. Does dissonant heritage hinder or promote destination development? This chapter aims to assess the destination competitiveness of Culture and (dissonant) Heritage tourism, focusing on the development of regional clusters. Perspectives from various stakeholders—academics, state officials, and tourism strategy developers—are essential. Bridging the gap in service provision and policy-making processes within this demand-led industry requires a shared doctrine. Notably, this introduces an additional perspective to the existing Competitiveness theory. While Culture and Heritage are recognized as core attractors, the dissonant aspect remains unexplored. Balkan states offer opportunities for further research in culture and heritage clusters.

Chapter 3
Tourist Awareness in Tourism Development: Case Study of the City of Veria, Greece 57
    Ioannis Valachis, Hellenic Open University, Greece
    Nikolaos Trihas, Hellenic Mediterranean University, Heraklion, Greece

The aim of this chapter is by focusing on the emerging tourism destination of Veria in Greece, to emphasize the importance of tourism awareness of the local community in achieving sustainable tourism development. In order to achieve this aim, the initiatives of the Tourism Department of the Municipality of Veria to raise tourism awareness of the local community are presented. The goal of these initiatives was to turn local residents into ambassadors for their city. Better knowledge of local points of interest and their importance, and greater familiarity with the concepts of hospitality and sustainability can lead to a behavior towards visitors that will meet their expectations and maximize their positive experiences from the destination. Findings and discussion of this case study are useful to academic researchers and organizations (DMOs, tourism bodies, community stakeholders) interested in sustainable tourism development.

Chapter 4
Perspectives for the Potential and Future of Marine Tourism in Bangladesh 83
    Mohammad Badruddoza Talukder, International University of Business
        Agriculture and Technology, Bangladesh
    Firoj Kabir, Daffodil Institute of IT, Bangladesh
    Fahmida Kaiser, Daffodil Institute of IT, Bangladesh
    Mushfika Hoque, Daffodil Institute of IT, Bangladesh

The marine tourism industry encompasses activities like water sports, coastal cruises, and marine biodiversity investigation, showing great potential for global economic growth and cultural advancement. This study examines the future of marine tourism in Bangladesh, a nation blessed with a rich maritime legacy, various coastal ecosystems, and its unrealized potential. The study also evaluates the present condition of marine tourism in Bangladesh by extensively analyzing extant literature, governmental directives, and case studies. To support the expansion of maritime tourism in Bangladesh, the study finds that integrated regulatory frameworks, public-private partnerships, and sustainable practices are necessary. This study suggests fully utilizing the nation's maritime resources for local communities, industry stakeholders, and legislators. Bangladesh can establish itself as a viable and alluring maritime tourist destination in the coming years by embracing a comprehensive strategy that will balance environmental preservation and economic growth.

Chapter 5
Special Forms of Tourism as a Territorial Management Tool: An Exploratory Study in the Context of Geocaching 105
    Júlio Sousa Silva, Polytechnic Institute of Cávado and Ave (IPCA),
        Portugal
    Bruno Barbosa Sousa, Polytechnic Institute of Cávado and Ave,
        Portugal & Applied Management Research Unit (UNIAG), Portugal
        & Centro de Investigação, Desenvolvimento e Inovação em Turismo
        (CiTUR), Portugal

Some Special Forms of Tourism (SFT) are the result of technological developments (e.g. virtual tourism, e-tourism, or emotional intelligence) or using highly developed specialist systems that can provide a greater variety of tourism products and tourism services. Geocaching is an outdoor recreational activity, in which participants use a Global Positioning System (GPS) receiver or mobile device and other navigational techniques to hide and seek containers, called geocaches or caches, at specific locations marked by coordinates all over the world. Apparently, this tourist practice could be an important tool in the dissemination and notoriety of tourist destinations (i.e. territorial management), as well as in regional and local development. This chapter aims to present some illustrative cases of geocaching as a territorial management tool. From an interdisciplinary perspective, the chapter presents insights for marketing (territorial) and tourism (niches and segments with specific motivations). At the end, lines of future research will be presented.

Chapter 6
Film-Induced Tourism and Promotion of Tourist Destinations: An
Exploratory Approach... 125
>   *Bruno Barbosa Sousa, Polytechnic Institute of Cávado and Ave,*
>   *Portugal & Applied Management Research Unit (UNIAG), Portugal*
>   *& Centro de Investigação, Desenvolvimento e Inovação em Turismo*
>   *(CiTUR), Portugal*
>   *João Abreu, Polytechnic Institute of Cávado and Ave, Portugal &*
>   *ISCET, Portugal*
>   *Lara Marisa Santos, Universidade Lusófona, Portugal & CETRAD,*
>   *Portugal*
>   *Vítor Silva, Polytechnic Institute of Cávado and Ave, Portugal &*
>   *Universidade de Vigo, Spain*
>   *Ana Paula Figueira, Polytechnic Institute of Beja, Portugal*

The film tourism business incorporates a series of activities. The development of destination marketing campaigns to promote films, while, increasingly, common initiatives between DMOs and filmmakers to promote films and tourist destinations. In several situations, a film or a documentary can prove to be a crucial element of communica-tion and dissemination of a country, a city or a territory. These cinematographic imag-es can influence consumers' decisions regarding their motivations to visit the places where the films were recorded. Tourism and cinema may represent a common element in favour of regional development and community feeling (e.g. a film about the histo-ry or culture of a population). The present study, in an exploratory approach, intends to understand the phenomenon and the importance of film tourism as a preponderant element in the management of territories (i.e. tourist destinations). Therefore, semi-structured interviews were carried out to define the object of study. Future studies, through a quantitative approach, should allow a greater generalization of results.

Chapter 7
Marketing Plan and Territorial Management: Vila Nova das Taipas (Portugal) 141
    Pedro Ruben Gonçalves, Polytechnic Institute of Cávado and Ave,
        Portugal
    Bruno Barbosa Sousa, Polytechnic Institute of Cávado and Ave,
        Portugal & Applied Management Research Unit (UNIAG), Portugal
        & Centro de Investigação, Desenvolvimento e Inovação em Turismo
        (CiTUR), Portugal
    João Abreu, Polytechnic Institute of Cávado and Ave, Portugal &
        ISCET, Portugal
    Manuel Sousa Pereira, Polytechnic Institute of Viana do Castelo,
        Portugal

The territorial development strategies constitute an important instrument for the adequate growth and pursuit of development mechanisms transversal to different local dynamics. Territorial Marketing has assumed, in addition to Strategic Planning, a relevant importance in view of the high competitiveness between territories. Territorial Marketing assumes itself as an important working tool in the strategic planning of territories, regardless of its magnitude and typology, enhancing the promotion and development of regions taking into account existing needs and potential. The present chapter is based on an analysis of a very specific territory – Vila de Caldas das Taipas, where gaps and substantial resources are recognized that allow us to develop a plan of action and sustainable strategic development that accompanies general growth. In this sense, an intervention strategy is developed that seeks above all to provide the socio-cultural and economic well-being of the resident population, visitors, and private agents.

Chapter 8
Destination Marketing and Sport: A Bibliometric Review............................... 165
    Jiyoon An, Fayetteville State University, USA

Sport is crucial to understanding destination marketing due to local/international, one-off/continual, and vacation-centric natures. This chapter summarizes the scholarship of sport and destination marketing using the domain-specific bibliometric review. This method allows us to evaluate thematic evolution in addition to backward-looking and forward-looking impacts across the disciplines. The findings revealed that destination marketing is transitioning from professional-driven sports event tourism to amateur-driven active sport tourism and is open to service innovation with emerging technologies. This research synthesis helps practitioners and academics assess research progress and suggest future research directions that may facilitate the inclusion of emerging technologies to service innovation at the intersection of sport and destination marketing.

Chapter 9
Summer Olympic Villages as Catalysts for Accessible and Inclusive Places: Between Experiences and Reflections in the Places and Society of the Host Cities 185

    Valerio della Sala, Department of Geography, Universitat Autonoma of Barcelona, Spain & Sport Research Institute IRE-UAB, Spain & Interdepartmental Research Centre for Urban and Mega-Events Studies (OMERO), Italy

The aim of this chapter is to examine the different use of the Summer Olympic Village over the years. Initially, the article will observe the temporal evolution of the built Olympic villages, establishing significant patterns that have followed over time. The evolution of Olympic Village models implies a critical reflection on how host communities experiment with collaborative forms and practices aimed at decreasing the phenomena of social exclusion. The composition of new housing units in central areas of metropolises may foment the emergence of new forms of gentrification or segregation within host cities.

Chapter 10
Addressing and Overcoming Destination Rejection From a Destination Management Perspective 205

    Ali Inanir, Burdur Mehmet Akif Ersoy University, Turkey
    Yusuf Karakuş, Recep Tayyip Erdoğan University, Turkey

Factors such as the development of technological possibilities, the growth of economies, social changes and the disappearance of borders have led individuals to travel to more distant regions. Depending on this situation, individuals have had to choose among multiple destinations. As a matter of fact, some destinations may be rejected for different reasons. Effective plans and policies should be developed to reduce the rejection of destinations. However, plans and policies to be developed for destination preference will not work in case of destination rejection. Because the consumer will remain a tourism product that is not even involved in the purchase decision process. This book chapter makes some inferences to contribute to the destination management process to eliminate this negative situation.

Chapter 11
Tourism and Destination Positioning Through Territorial Branding: The Case of Brazil 227

    Giovana Goretti Feijó de Almeida, CiTUR, Portugal
    Sarah Minasi, University of Vale do Itajaí, Brazil

Purpose The purpose is to examine how a territorial brand positions a tourism destination. Design/methodology/approach The strategy used a case study using a qualitative approach. Findings/Conclusion The results highlight the use of the territorial brand and scope-creating local events in urban areas. Studying the territorial brand in the context of cultural studies also extends to the study of tourism. Research limitations The study's shortcoming was that it was limited to cities in the interior. We propose broadening the study to include the realities of other small towns. Practical and Theoretical Implications The contributions address the complexity of the investigated themes, destination branding, place branding, and territorial brand. Originality There are certain places, such as Brazil, where the brand of the place is still embryonic. The territorial brand led from the feeling of local belonging. The reality of the city of Pelotas can reflect the existence of other territorial brands, and this study contributes to exposing this.

Chapter 12
Tourists' Expectations-Based Countryside Walking Tourism Management 255
    Danka Milojković, Singidunum University, Belgrade, Serbia
    Snežana Štetić, The College of Tourism, Belgrade, Serbia & Balkan
        Network of Tourism Experts, Belgrade, Serbia
    Igor Trišić, Faculty of Geography, University of Belgrade, Serbia

Countryside walking tourism contributes to sustainable rural socio-economic development. The purpose of the research is to observe the possibility of managing countryside walking tourism in a village according to the expectations of tourists during their travel and vacation in rural destinations. The research methodology was based on a descriptive statistical analysis using the survey for gathering data from the rural tourism demand market, and the VICE model for sustainable tourism for getting conclusions. The key result indicated that countryside walking tourism management should consider the tourists' expectations related to the clean environment. It preserved nature as the most influencing factor in the choice of a walking tour in rural destinations, and at the same time, it is more important to the female than to the male population. The authors recommend incorporating countryside walking tourism into walking strategies as a part of rural and tourism development policies.

Chapter 13
Heritage-Led Destination Management: Strategies for Competitive Advantage 285
    Aditi Nag, Birla Institute of Technology, Mesra, India
    Smriti Mishra, Birla Institute of Technology, Mesra, India

Heritage-led destination management is crucial for gaining a competitive edge in the global tourism industry. This paper explores the link between heritage assets and destination competitiveness, emphasizing their role in attracting visitors, generating economic benefits, and distinguishing a destination. It delves into factors enabling differentiation, including heritage preservation, effective interpretation, infrastructure, cultural events, and community collaboration. Case studies illustrate how these strategies boost visitor numbers, revenue, and destination image. Challenges like balancing conservation and tourism, over-tourism, and community involvement are discussed. The paper advocates sustainable heritage-led tourism to ensure long-term success and heritage preservation. It serves as a guide for destinations aiming to leverage their heritage for competitive advantage.

Compilation of References 325

About the Contributors 391

Index 399

Preface

A Snapshot of Cases on Effective Destination Management

In an era when tourists' preferences and behaviours continuously evolve, the complexities of effective destination management have never been more apparent. Today's destinations are tasked with leveraging their natural, cultural, and historical resources and include sustainability principles to thrive. The spectre of overtourism further complicates these challenges, exerting pressure on the environment, local populations, and infrastructures. In such a setting, robust methodologies are needed to help decision-makers manage destinations efficiently. In this regard, *Cases on Effective Destination Management* emerges as a valuable resource, offering a selection of research-based case studies. These case studies serve as a practical guide for designing and conducting research that can significantly benefit destination management. Whether literature-based, empirical, or a blend of both, each case study presented in this book delves into one or more methodologies pertinent to the field, highlighting the practical implications and potential impacts of the results obtained.

Readers of this book will gain a hands-on understanding of how to collect and interpret data and formulate and implement effective destination management strategies. Each chapter should be considered a standalone study; readers can easily cherry-pick their sections of interest without feeling stuck or lost. We envisage three primary audiences for this book:

1. **Students**: This book will be invaluable to undergraduate and postgraduate students specialising in management, business administration, tourism, transportation, and hospitality management.
2. **Scholars**: Academics can use these case studies to inspire and guide their research.

3. **Practitioners**: Professionals in tourism and related fields can use the insights provided to inform their analyses and decision-making processes.

We trust that *Cases on Effective Destination Management* will serve as an academic and professional reference to inspire innovative approaches and strategies in the dynamic field of destination management. The first chapter, "The Shortest Form of Storytelling in Destination Marketing - Tourism Slogans of the European Capitals", is authored by Árpád Ferenc Papp-Váry and Ahmad Hajeer, Budapest Business University, Hungary. They delve into the significance of storytelling in destination marketing, focusing on the role of slogans in enhancing the distinctiveness of tourist destinations, specifically European capitals. The second chapter, "Destination Competitiveness, Culture and Heritage Tourism, and Regional Clusters: The Case of Macedonia", by Marija Lazarev Zivanovic, Glion Institute of Higher Education, Switzerland, concerns the intersection of cultural identity, state dynamics, and destination competitiveness in the realm of cultural and heritage tourism, focusing on Macedonia. This region's unique political and economic context, shared between North Macedonia and Greece, presents challenges and opportunities for tourism development.

In chapter 3, "Tourist Awareness in Tourism Development: Case Study of the City of Veria, Greece", Ioannis Valachis, Hellenic Open University, and Nikolaos Trihas, the Hellenic Mediterranean University, Heraklion, Greece, highlight the importance of tourism awareness in the local community for achieving sustainable tourism development. They examine the case of the emerging tourism destination of Veria, Greece. Chapter 4 is "Perspectives for the Potential and Future of Marine Tourism in Bangladesh". Mohammad Talukder, International University of Business Agriculture and Technology, and Firoj Kabir, Fahmida Kaiser, and Mushfika Hoque, all from the Daffodil Institute of IT in Bangladesh, explore the potential and future of marine tourism in Bangladesh, a country rich in maritime heritage and diverse coastal ecosystems.

The three following chapters report cases from Portugal. Chapter 5, "Special Forms of Tourism as a Territorial Management Tool: An Exploratory Study in the Context of Geocaching", was authored by Júlio Silva, the Polytechnic Institute of Cávado and Ave (IPCA), and Bruno Sousa, IPCA and CiTUR, Portugal. They investigate the use of geocaching as a territorial management tool and its potential to enhance regional and local development. Geocaching, an outdoor recreational activity involving GPS technology to hide and seek containers, is explored to increase tourist destinations' notoriety. The next chapter (chapter 6) is titled "Film-Induced Tourism and Promotion of Tourist Destinations: An Approach", by Bruno Sousa, IPCA and CiTUR, Portugal; João Abreu, IPCA and ISCET; Lara Santos, Universidade Lusófona and CETRAD; Vítor Silva, IPCA, Portugal, and Universidade de

Vigo, Spain; and Ana Figueira, Polytechnic Institute of Beja, Portugal. This chapter concerns film-induced tourism and how film tourism can serve as a crucial element in destination marketing and regional development. Pedro Gonçalves, IPCA; Bruno Sousa, IPCA and CiTUR; João Abreu, IPCA and ISCET; and Manuel Pereira, Polytechnic Institute of Viana do Castelo, Portugal, discuss in Chapter 7 the importance of territorial development strategies for the growth and development of local dynamics, focusing on the specific case of Vila de Caldas das Taipas in Portugal. They highlight the role of territorial marketing in strategic planning, emphasising its relevance in promoting and developing regions.

Two chapters focus specifically on the relationship between destination management and sport: Chapter 8, "Destination Marketing and Sport: A Bibliometric Review", by Jiyoon An, Fayetteville State University in the United States of America, summarises the scholarship of sport and destination marketing. The findings reveal that marketing is transitioning from professional-driven sports event tourism to amateur-driven active sport tourism and is open to service innovation with emerging technologies. Valerio della Sala, Universitat Autonoma of Barcelona in Spain, examines in Chapter 9, "Summer Olympic Villages as catalysts for accessible and inclusive places: Between experiences and reflections in the places and society of the host cities", the different uses of the Olympic Village over the years. The takeaways from this analysis can make the Olympic Games leave a positive legacy far beyond the excitement of competition, creating more inclusive and equitable cities for future generations.

Ali Inanir, Burdur Mehmet Akif Ersoy University, and Yusuf Karakus, Recep Tayyip Erdogan University in Turkey, authored Chapter 10. In "Addressing and Overcoming Destination Rejection from a Destination Management Perspective", the authors address the issue of destination rejection, which arises when individuals choose not to travel to certain destinations for various reasons. They highlight the need for effective plans and policies to reduce destination rejection and boost destination preference. Chapter 11, "Tourism and the Positioning of Destinations Through Territorial Brand: The Case of Brazil", is a case study authored by Giovana Goretti Feijó de Almeida, CiTUR Leiria, Portugal, and Sarah Minasi, University of Vale do Itajaí, Brazil. They examine how territorial branding can position tourism destinations using a case study approach focused on Brazil. They highlight using territorial brands and local events in urban areas to create a sense of local belonging and enhance destination appeal.

In Chapter 12, "Tourists' Expectations-Based Countryside Walking Tourism Management", Danka Milojkovic, Singidunum University; Snežana Štetic, The College of Tourism Belgrade; and Igor Trišic, Faculty of Geography, University of Belgrade, study the management of countryside walking tourism based on tourists' expectations, focusing on rural socioeconomic development. They use descriptive statistical analysis and the VICE model for sustainable tourism to gather data and draw conclusions. Chapter 13, "Heritage-Led Destination Management: Strategies for Competitive Advantage", by Aditi Nag, Birla Institute of Technology Mesra, and Smriti Mishra, Birla Institute of Technology, India, concerns the role of heritage-led destination management in gaining a competitive edge in the global tourism industry. The authors examine the link between heritage assets and destination competitiveness, highlighting their importance in attracting visitors, generating economic benefits, and distinguishing a destination. They also discuss factors that enable differentiation, such as heritage preservation, effective interpretation, infrastructure, cultural events, and community collaboration.

We hope this book informs readers and inspires them to adopt innovative and sustainable approaches to destination management, ensuring that tourism remains a force for positive growth and development.

Romina Alkier
University of Rijeka, Croatia

Giuseppe Catenazzo
American Institute of Applied Sciences (AUS), Switzerland

Vedran Milojica
University of Rijeka, Croatia

Aleksandra Zając
American Institute of Applied Sciences (AUS), Switzerland

Acknowledgement

Our first thank you goes to all the authors who contributed to this work. It is fantastic to have gathered several scholars worldwide for this collective effort. Without their contributions, this book would not have been possible.

We are also profoundly grateful for the extensive help of the editorial board members and the additional reviewers in reading all submissions and providing all authors with timely and constructive feedback. Their efforts and sharing of knowledge and expertise were much appreciated.

We hope this work will be the first of a long-lasting, rewarding and fruitful research collaboration. We would be delighted to continue working together on passionate projects such as this one.

Thank you very much.

Chapter 1
The Shortest Form of Storytelling in Destination Marketing:
Tourism Slogans of the European Capitals

Árpád Ferenc Papp-Váry
https://orcid.org/0000-0002-0395-4315
Budapest Business University, Hungary

Ahmad Hajeer
https://orcid.org/0000-0002-4045-7289
Budapest Business University, Hungary

EXECUTIVE SUMMARY

This chapter explores the role of storytelling in destination marketing and management, focusing on the utilization of slogans to enhance distinctiveness of tourist destinations, particularly European capitals. It discusses the application of narrative techniques in marketing to distinguish places in tourism market. The research identifies a gap in current understandings of how slogans can be employed in creating compelling destination brands that resonate with potential visitors. Through qualitative analysis of various slogans, the study highlights the importance of unique brand identities for destinations, which establish emotional connections with the audience. The findings suggest that storytelling transcends traditional advertising, offering a branding tool that can impact a destination's appeal and competitiveness. The chapter concludes by emphasizing the strategic value of narrative in destination marketing, proposing that effective storytelling can lead to more successful branding efforts and a stronger connection with target audiences.

DOI: 10.4018/979-8-3693-1548-4.ch001

1. INTRODUCTION

The significance of storytelling in destination marketing is increasingly acknowledged within scholarly circles. Defined as a rapid and influential method for capturing interest, storytelling facilitates a connection with consumers, influencing their perceptions and decisions through brand narratives (Aaker et al., 2010; Rose, 2011). Kvítková and Petrů (2021) highlights storytelling adoption by destination marketing organizations to foster emotions and empathy and to cultivate positive behavioral intentions. Narratives, when enclosed in slogans, are instrumental in distinguishing tourist destinations within a competitive marketplace (Ferreira, 2022). Kotler and Keller (2006) claim that slogans serve as cues or reference points for customers, elucidating the essence and uniqueness of brands. Aleksandrova (2019) examines slogans as pivotal communication tools for tourist destinations, analyzing their influence on visitation intensity through a literature review and statistical analysis of slogans, emphasizing their critical role in brand communication. Furthermore, Reinhold et al. (2023) advocate for a narrative perspective in marketing and destination management, focusing on stewardship, collaboration, and enriched experiences.

While existing studies (Adamus-Matuszyńska, 2021; Cooper & Buckley, 2021) have delved into the visual and informational components of destination marketing, the strategic use of narrative within slogans – especially its impact on destination perception and choice – in Europe remains underexplored. This oversight represents a theoretical and practical gap in communicating the effectiveness of destination marketing strategies. Therefore, this study seeks to fill this gap by systematically examining the role of storytelling in destination marketing slogans in Europe. It aims to investigate the narrative techniques employed in successful slogans and their possible impact on the audience. By integrating insights from literature with an analysis of exemplary slogans, this research aspires to delineate the storytelling functions that significantly enhance destination appeal. Besides, this book chapter attempts to provide the readers with a unique European perspective, analyzing the slogans of European capitals. Throughout history, these major cities have usually been considered the 'gems' of their countries, and the word "capital" itself stems from "caput", a Latin word meaning "head". As a result, capital cities have been considered not only as the cultural, governmental and economic centers of their countries, but also as the flagship cities of their national tourism.

This attempt is timely as the tourism industry faces increasing challenges from global competition, digital marketing evolution, and shifting consumer preferences (Ojha, 2022). Understanding the role of storytelling in shaping destination images can provide critical insights for destination marketers and managers aiming to navigate these complexities. Besides, this study aims to contribute to the academic literature by providing a deeper understanding of narrative effectiveness in destination marketing and offering actionable insights for practitioners to craft more compelling marketing messages. By highlighting the strategic importance of narrative elements in slogans, this research underscores the potential for storytelling to elevate destination marketing beyond conventional approaches, fostering a more profound connection with potential visitors.

This chapter explores how storytelling impacts destination marketing. First, we set the scene by discussing storytelling's role in tourism. Next, we review existing research to show what's already known and where gaps lie. After that, our methodology section explains how we studied slogans. Then, we share our findings on how storytelling makes destinations stand out. The discussion connects these findings with broader marketing theories. Finally, we wrap up with a conclusion that highlights our main points and suggests future research directions.

2. LITERATURE REVIEW

The literature review section of this chapter examines various scholarly contributions and theoretical frameworks surrounding the utilization of storytelling in destination marketing, particularly focusing on the crafting and effectiveness of slogans in enhancing the appeal of tourist destinations. This analysis aims to delineate the role of storytelling in shaping consumer perceptions and behaviors towards tourism destinations in an attempt to bridge gaps identified in existing research. The purpose of this literature review is not only to map the current state of knowledge on the subject but also to identify potential avenues for future research, thereby setting the scene for the empirical investigation conducted in the subsequent sections of this chapter.

2.1 The Roots of Storytelling: A Cultural and Historical Perspective

The American Indian proverb, "Those who tell the stories rule the world" (Johnson, 2018), encapsulates the profound influence of storytelling throughout human history, stressing its important role in shaping human evolution (Moin, 2020). Multidisciplinary research highlights the capacity of stories to captivate and engage audiences both intellectually and emotionally (McKee & Gerace, 2018). This narrative power has attracted extensive scholarly interest across fields such as management (McKee, 2003), psychology (Wyer, 1995), sociology (Polletta et al., 2011), and marketing (Pera et al., 2016). The contributions of Pellowski (1990) on the "nature of storytelling" and Aaker et al. (2010) on its compelling force have led to storytelling's definition within communication studies as "sharing and combining of knowledge and experiences through narrative and anecdotes in order to communicate complex ideas, concepts, and causal connections and build connections and associations" (Keskin, Akgun, Zehir & Ayan, 2016, p. 32). Another explanation of storytelling was provided by Rodriguez (2020) in which he defines storytelling as a process of emotionally transferring information, including opinions, data, and arguments, via the introduction of characters and narratives, culminating in a resolution. These insights are expected to prove invaluable for analyzing the application of storytelling and slogans within the tourism sector.

Given its reputation as a leading marketing trend, paralleling the impact of influencer marketing, storytelling's application extends beyond mere promotional tactics (Rodriguez, 2020). Moin (2020) emphasizes the ethical imperative of brand storytelling to transcend manipulative narratives, advocating instead for authentic engagement that ensures memorable customer experiences across all points of interaction. Thus, Storytelling becomes a tool with many layers, essential for its practical uses, its strategic importance, and its ability to touch our hearts and connect with us on a deeply human level (Rodriguez, 2020). Fundamentally, storytelling is narrowed down into the essence of connection and engagement (Mathews & Wacker, 2007). According to Mathews and Wacker (2007), storytelling has ten functions:

- Explaining Origins: Stories often serve to explain the origins of natural phenomena, cultural practices, or societal structures. They offer narratives that ground abstract concepts in relatable and coherent explanations. For example, creation myths in various cultures explain the origin of the world and humanity, providing cultural and cosmological context.
- Defining Individual and Group Identity: Stories help individuals and groups define their identities by reinforcing shared values, beliefs, and experiences. For instance, national epics such as the Iliad or the Ramayana reinforce cultural identity and historical narratives for entire civilizations.
- Communicating Tradition and Delineating Taboo: Through storytelling, traditions are passed down, and taboos are outlined, guiding societal behavior and preserving cultural norms. For example, folktales and folklore often convey societal norms and taboos, teaching moral lessons and reinforcing cultural values.
- Simplifying and Providing Perspective: Stories simplify complex problems or situations, offering perspective and understanding through narrative structures. For instance, allegorical tales like George Orwell's "Animal Farm" simplify complex political ideologies, providing accessible commentary on power and corruption.
- Illustrating the Natural Order of Things: Narratives elucidate the natural order of the world, explaining natural phenomena or societal hierarchies. For

example, ancient myths explaining the movement of celestial bodies or the cycle of seasons provide early attempts to understand natural phenomena.
- Concisely Communicating Complex History: Stories distill complex historical events or eras into narrative form, capturing the essence of pivotal moments. To give an example, historical fiction novels like Hilary Mantel's "Wolf Hall" vividly depict the Tudor era, offering insights into the political intrigues of the time.
- Communicating Moral and Ethical Positions: Stories convey moral and ethical lessons, teaching readers about right and wrong through narrative examples. For instance, Aesop's fables teach moral lessons through animal characters, illustrating virtues such as honesty, kindness, and perseverance.
- Illustrating Relationships to and with Authority: Narratives explore power dynamics and relationships with authority figures, reflecting societal attitudes towards governance and authority. An example about this might be Shakespeare's plays that often depict the complexities of power and authority, exploring themes of kingship, ambition, and loyalty.
- Describing Appropriate Responses to Life or Modeling Behaviors: Stories model appropriate social behaviors and responses to life situations, offering readers guidance and inspiration. For example, heroic myths like the tale of Odysseus exemplify traits such as courage, resilience, and cunning, providing models for navigating life's challenges.
- Defining Reward and Detailing the Paths to Salvation and Damnation: Many stories outline the rewards for virtuous behavior and the consequences of vice, shaping moral and ethical frameworks. For instance, religious parables often illustrate the rewards of righteousness and the consequences of sin, guiding believers towards spiritual enlightenment.

Considering the literature delineated within this segment, it seems plausible to assume that Storytelling and slogans play a crucial role in destination management by enriching tourism marketing with compelling narratives that captivate and connect with audiences on an emotional level. This approach enhances destination appeal, ensuring positive experiences and favorable engagement.

2.2 Storytelling's Role in Destination Management and Branding

The primary role of storytelling within marketing literature has increased over time, however, its application within the domain of travel and tourism marketing remains relatively understudied (Keskin, Akgun, Zehir, & Ayan, 2016). Research in the field of tourism storytelling has predominantly centered on its role in shaping destination image formation (Ramkissoon, Nunko, & Gursoy, 2009), facilitating destination development (Mossberg et al., 2010), and influencing travel intentions (Akgün, Keskin, Ayar, & Erdoğan, 2015). Martin and Woodside (2011) assert that storytelling offers a nuanced approach to positioning destinations in the hearts and minds of prospective visitors, utilizing creative narratives for distinctiveness and depth. Stories that inspire with attractive appeal have the potential to flourish through social media channels, fostering global virality (Clara & Barbosa, 2021). Empirical findings accentuate the positive impact of tourism storytelling on brand value, encompassing dimensions of understandability, interestingness, educability, uniqueness, and sensibility (Choi, 2016). Moreover, scholarly evidence supports the idea that a coherent brand narrative may serve as an effective instrument in building a robust place brand name compared to conventional marketing communication strategies (Dziedzic, 2019). As a result, storytelling becomes crucial for shaping a strong and unified identity for a place. It serves as a valuable tool for regions and cities aiming to increase visibility, effectively connect with target audiences, and create value for local stakeholders (Clara & Barbosa, 2021). In fact, storytelling has become essential in how locals communicate, playing a key role in promoting and distinguishing destination brands in the online world (Youssef, Leicht, & Marongiu, 2019). Moreover, aside from its importance in branding strategies, storytelling also plays a practical role in city branding, serving as a powerful tool for communication and engagement (Keskin, Akgun, Zehir, & Ayan, 2016). Seen from this perspective, storytelling about a place becomes crucial in fostering long-term competitive advantage (Bassano et al., 2019).

While existing research has shed light on storytelling's role in shaping destination image and brand perception, there remains vast uncharted potential for utilizing storytelling in destination management strategies. By harnessing stories to communicate unique destination attributes, foster emotional connections, and differentiate destinations in the increasingly competitive tourism landscape, destination managers can improve place identities and enhance destination competitiveness. Moreover, integrating social innovation strategies, as discussed by Alkier, Milojica and Roblek (2017), can further enrich storytelling by involving communities, leveraging digital technologies, and promoting sustainable tourism practices, thus ensuring a holistic approach to destination management and competitiveness.

2.3 Understanding the Impact of Slogans on Brand Perception

While seemingly straightforward, a brand comprises three main components: the brand name, logo, and slogan, each playing a crucial role in shaping the brand's identity and image. Unlike brand names and logos, slogans have a special ability to effectively convey a message (Galí, Camprubí, & Donaire, 2017). The term "slogan" originates from the Scottish Gaelic term "Slaugh gairm," which means "gathering cry" or "battle cry" (Healey, 2009). Although the context has shifted from warfare, slogans remain influential in building brand equity, as asserted by marketing experts Kotler and Keller in their foundational work "Marketing Management" (2006). Expanding on this idea, Kotler and Keller (2006) emphasize the crucial role of slogans in providing a reference point for customers to grasp the essence of a brand. Similarly, Kohli, Leuthesser, and Suri (2007) stress the importance of slogans in encapsulating a brand's essence. In contrast to brand names and logos, slogans offer flexibility and adaptability, allowing brands to evolve and resonate with changing consumer preferences (Kohli, Leuthesser, & Suri, 2007). Sárközy (2009) further defines a slogan as a concise statement that encapsulates a brand's message, articulating its unique selling proposition. Positioned as the cornerstone of brand communication, a slogan serves as the foundation for conveying the brand message. Echoing these perspectives, Ries (2015) underscores the importance of crafting a memorable slogan, highlighting techniques such as rhyme, alliteration, repetition, reversal, and double entendre to enhance recall. Rosengren and Dahlén (2006) extend the discussion by asserting that slogans significantly contribute to a brand's prestige by communicating its values through everyday language.

In spite of their importance, there are actually only a few slogans that we can recall. (Although almost everyone knows the slogan of Nike, only a few people know the slogan of Adidas). That is, finding the appropriate slogan poses a challenge even for the biggest companies. This does not mean that a good slogan is not greatly useful, but its influence should not be overestimated either. The slogan might not be a magic bullet, but it plays a pivotal role in brand building. A good slogan not only shapes the image but generates sales; still, a less elaborated message may undermine marketing and sales efforts.

Although the previously mentioned insights in the current section accentuate the importance of slogans in brand communication, still, defining the attributes of an effective slogan remains a challenging task. According to Papp-Váry (2020), a compelling slogan should clearly articulate the brand's narrative and competitive advantages, evoke positive sentiments, and prompt action from consumers. Additionally, it should be concise, distinctive, and memorable, aligning harmoniously with the brand's visual identity and resonating with stakeholders. Even though slogans are important, only a few become widely known. Making a good slogan is not an easy task, even for big brands. A catchy slogan can indeed help a brand get noticed and sell more products, but a boring one can hurt sales. In destination management, using slogans is really needed for making people want to visit a place. A good slogan can show what's special about a destination and make people feel connected to it. So, using smart slogan strategies in marketing can help a destination stand out and attract more tourists, which is good for long-term tourism growth (Papp-Váry, 2021).

2.4 Tourism Destination Slogans

Tourism slogans play an important role in marketing destinations. They can greatly impact a destination's appeal but can also reduce the effectiveness of destination branding if the slogan is not appropriate or is overused (Wang, Huang & Yang, 2019). According to Pike (2007), slogans are a crucial part of a destination's branding strategy, serving as a public expression of its unique qualities. In other words, slogans are used to communicate the most important aspects of the destination in the clearest way possible (Supphellen & Nygaardsvick, 2002). Slogans serve three main purposes: improving a brand's image, helping people recognize it, and making it stand out from others in people's minds (Kohli et al., 2007).

Some destinations manage to create dynamic, memorable slogans that help position them strategically on the international stage, while others struggle to have a similar impact (Lehto et al., 2014). It's widely agreed that slogans focusing on specific characteristics of a destination can help position it better, make it more distinctive, and help it be recognized more easily (Donaire & Galí, 2012). On the other hand, Slogans that are too general and lack originality can significantly hinder the distinctiveness and appeal of a destination. A linguistic analysis of tourism destination branding slogans emphasizes the use of rhetorical elements such as duality, analogy, and transferred epithet to convey messages effectively, suggesting that originality in slogan creation is essential for impactful destination branding (Dongrui Hao, 2022). Another study carried by Klenosky and Gitelson (1997) and Obiol (2002) shows that many tourism slogans are created without much planning or professionalism, and often don't fit into a well-thought-out destination marketing plan.

Creating slogans for destination marketing is more complicated than for products, because specialists have to consider many different factors that make up the tourist experience, like social, cultural, economic, and political conditions (Supphellen & Nygaardsvik, 2002). Even though it's important, effectively promoting tourism destinations through slogans is challenging (Klenosky & Gitelson, 1997; Lehto et al., 2014). Galí et al., (2017) list five specific challenges in this area. Firstly, avoiding using characteristics that many other destinations also have, which makes the message less unique. Secondly, not including too much information in the message, which can make the slogan seem generic. Thirdly, dealing with decision-making limitations influenced by politics, which can lead to inconsistency and inefficiency. Fourthly, adapting slogans to different market environments to make sure they are relevant to different groups of people. Lastly, creating slogans that appeal to a diverse range of people, even though there isn't much research on what makes a good tourism slogan.

International destinations face additional challenges because they have to use specific languages, primarily English, in their tourism slogans. However, effective slogans should ideally work in multiple languages, which makes it difficult to craft slogans that are universally appealing. As a result, tourism slogans often prioritize broad appeal over uniqueness, which can make them less effective in attracting tourists. Despite limited research, analysis of 120 tourism destination slogans (Galí, Camprubí, and Donaire, 2017) reveals some common features, including brevity, meaningfulness, focus on the supply side, and specific geographical references. These findings show a shift towards emotionally appealing slogans that connect with people on a personal level, moving away from purely descriptive strategies (Galí, Camprubí, and Donaire, 2017).

Tourism slogans are crucial for destination marketing, influencing a destination's appeal and recognition. While effective slogans enhance a destination's visibility, generic or overused ones can hinder its distinctiveness. Crafting slogans for destinations involves navigating various factors, including cultural and political contexts, and adapting to diverse market environments. Despite challenges, originality and emotional resonance are key for impactful slogans. Moving forward, destination management should prioritize developing authentic and engaging slogans to effectively communicate the essence of their destinations and attract tourists.

3. METHODS

The methodology of our study is designed to offer an analysis of storytelling as a pivotal element in destination management, focusing on how it is leveraged across various European capitals to enhance tourism marketing and destination branding. To make the analysis as extensive as possible, we have interpreted the concept of Europe as broadly as possible, significantly expanding the destination grouping of visiteurope.com, which is considered to be a benchmark in the tourism industry. Thus, the survey included the capitals of several countries which are geographically located in Asia but are often considered to belong to Europe, such as Turkey, Armenia, and Azerbaijan. However, Kazakhstan, for example, was not included, as its capital Astana is located in the center of Asia.

3.1 Data Collection

In this study on European capitals' tourism slogans, our data collection strategy was designed to encompass a wide range of sources, ensuring the depth and diversity of the data collected. Following Creswell and Creswell (2018), we emphasized the importance of utilizing diverse and reliable sources, including official tourism websites and social media platforms, to understand destination branding strategies effectively, as supported by Kietzmann et al. (2018). The selection of 52 European capitals for examination aimed to provide a comprehensive analysis of the varied tourism branding strategies across the continent. This choice of sample size, informed by Malterud et al's. (2016) concept of "information power" reflects the need for a broad sample to adequately cover the range of branding strategies, enabling an in-depth examination of the slogans used by European capitals. This approach, in line with Patton (2015)'s recommendation for diverse sample selection, allows our study to document how capitals present their identity to tourists and utilize their unique features in branding effort.

3.2 Data Analysis

Incorporating the principles advocated by Eriksson and Kovalainen (2016) into the analysis of slogans within the tourism branding context, our qualitative content analysis was designed to not only investigate the core narratives and branding strategies from the collected data but also to delve deeper into the nature of brand identity as conveyed through these marketing tools. Hajeer and Toptsi (2022) emphasize the importance of understanding the context and meanings behind data in qualitative research, which guided our approach to examine the slogans beyond their surface value.

Following this methodological framework, we sought to interpret the slogans not just as promotional materials but as reflections of the cities' cultural, historical, and social ethos. This approach aligns with Eriksson and Kovalainen's (2016) assertion that qualitative analysis should move beyond descriptive findings to interpretative insights that reveal the underlying dynamics and meanings. Our analysis was thus aimed at uncovering how these branding elements communicate a city's unique appeal and promise to tourists, contributing to a city's strategic positioning in the global tourism market. By integrating Eriksson and Kovalainen's (2016) principles into our analytical methods, we attempted to ensure that our inquiry was rich in interpretative depth. This helped explore the multifaceted roles slogans play in shaping and conveying the brand identity of cities.

4. RESULTS: ANALYTICAL OVERVIEW OF EUROPEAN CAPITALS' SLOGANS

During the analysis of the capitals' tourism slogans, we encountered a specific challenge: for 16 out of 52 capitals, it was not feasible to clearly identify a central, international, English-language tourism slogan. These cities are Ankara, Baku, Bern,

Bucharest, Helsinki, Lisbon, Ljubljana, London, Madrid, Moscow, Oslo, Podgorica, Pristina, San Marino, Tallinn, and Tórshavn, showcasing a wide geographical diversity.

The analysis method for table 1 focuses on evaluating the slogans of European capitals across several dimensions: Origin & Creation, Intended Message, Cultural/Historical Relevance, and Effectiveness. This structured approach allows for a comprehensive understanding of how each slogan serves as a strategic tool for urban branding and tourism promotion. The Origin & Creation dimension uncovers the background and motivations behind each slogan's development. Intended Message examines the core message cities aim to communicate. Cultural/Historical Relevance explores the connection between the slogan and the city's identity, while Effectiveness assesses the slogan's possible impact on enhancing the city's image and attracting tourists (see Table 1).

Table 1. The Slogans of European Capitals: Origins, Messages, Relevance, and Effectiveness

Capital City	Slogan	Origin & Creation	Intended Message	Cultural/Historical Relevance
Amsterdam	I amsterdam	Created in 2004, originating from a neighborhood protest.	Encourages identification with the city, promoting unity.	Reflects the city's open, inclusive culture.
Andorra la Vella	Capital dél Pireneus	Based on its geographical location in the Pyrenees.	Highlights its status as a prime location for tourism and shopping.	Emphasizes its natural beauty and strategic location.
Athens	This is Athens!	Inspired by the iconic battle cry from the movie "300".	Creates an authentic impression of Athens, beyond clichés.	Connects with the city's ancient history and modern culture.
Belgrade	#gobelgrade	A modern call to action using social media conventions.	Encourages visitors to explore the city.	Reflects the city's adaptability to modern trends.
Berlin	The City of Freedom	Stemming from the fall of the Berlin Wall in 1989.	Represents freedom, open-mindedness, and creativity.	Deeply connected to its recent history of unity and diversity.
Bratislava	The City Where You Find Real Life	Reflects the city's genuine lifestyle.	Suggests authenticity and real-life experiences.	Highlights the blend of past and present.
Brussels	BXL Moves for You	Less information available, associated with lively city imagery.	Promotes Brussels as dynamic and welcoming.	Emphasizes the city's vibrancy.

continued on following page

Table 1. Continued

Capital City	Slogan	Origin & Creation	Intended Message	Cultural/Historical Relevance
Budapest	Spice of Europe	Highlights cultural and gastronomical diversity.	Suggests a mix of attractions and uniqueness.	Ties to Hungary's culinary reputation and cultural richness.
Chisinau	Discover The Routes of Life	Focuses on wine tradition and cultural diversity.	Invites exploration of the city's traditions and history.	Reflects the city's deep-rooted wine culture.
Copenhagen	Wonderful Copenhagen	Shifts from marketing to enabling cultural promotion.	Involves cultural institutions in storytelling.	Highlights Copenhagen's cultural richness.
Dublin	A Breath of Fresh Air	Highlights the city's access to nature and vibrant culture.	Promotes Dublin's unique blend of city life and nature.	Reflects the city's geographical and cultural diversity.
Gibraltar	A Year of Culture	Part of a new campaign evolving from previous themes.	Emphasizes cultural richness and diversity.	Builds on Gibraltar's history of cultural campaigns.
Kyiv	Everything Starts in Kyiv	Introduced in 2012 during the UEFA European Championship.	Positions Kyiv as a starting point for experiences.	Reflects the city's historical significance and renewal.
Luxembourg	Let's make it happen!	Illustrated through an animation showcasing the city's dynamism.	Conveys a spirit of action and multiculturalism.	Represents Luxembourg's forward-thinking and diversity.
Minsk	Think Minsk!	Developed by a London-based think tank to boost identity.	Promotes Minsk as a city of forward-thinking and innovation	Captures Minsk's cultural vibrancy, reflecting its journey from a historical settlement to a modern metropolis.
Monaco	Wild Beauty	Highlights luxury and natural beauty.	Combines nature's and human-made luxuries.	Contrasts with Monaco's known luxury, adding a natural dimension.
Nicosia	The Brightest Capital of Europe	Focuses on sunny weather and opportunities.	Emphasizes sunlight and city's potential in various fields.	Reflects the city's climate and growth in education and innovation.
Paris	Paris Je t'aime (Paris I love you)	Evolves from "City of love" to include the city's name.	Emphasizes romance and love associated with Paris.	Deeply tied to Paris's image as the capital of romance.
Prague	Prague:emotions	Designed to show Prague as more than historical sights.	Invites experiencing a range of emotions in Prague.	Connects contemporary experiences with historical backdrop.

continued on following page

Table 1. Continued

Capital City	Slogan	Origin & Creation	Intended Message	Cultural/Historical Relevance
Reykjavík	This is Reykjavík	Changed from "Reykjavík Loves Visitors" to present title.	Highlights the city's unique small-big city charm.	Emphasizes Reykjavík's diverse attractions in a compact area.
Riga	Live Riga!	Aims to attract investment and tourism since April 2021.	Appeals to tourists, potential residents, and locals alike.	Represents Riga's investment-friendly environment and tourism appeal.
Rome	The Eternal City	A nickname given by a poet, not an advertising campaign.	Reinforces Rome's timeless appeal.	Connects with Rome's enduring historical and cultural significance.
Sarajevo	A City of Thousand Tales	Portrays the city as a place where historical challenges enrich its narrative and identity.	Offers an authentic path to understanding the city's past.	Ties to Sarajevo's complex history and resilience.
Sofia	Grows, But Does Not Age	References the city's ability to modernize while preserving tradition.	Emphasizes Sofia's dynamic yet timeless nature.	Highlights Sofia's long history and cultural preservation.
Skopje	Feel Love Feel Skopje	Lacks direct reference to 'love' and 'feel' on official platforms.	Aims to portray Skopje as a city of energy and memories.	Reflects the personal connections and history of its residents.
Stockholm	The Capital of Scandinavia	Result of extensive research for a comprehensive city positioning.	Positions Stockholm as a key destination for business and tourism in Scandinavia.	Asserts Stockholm's leadership in the region.
Tbilisi	The City That Loves You	Unclear origin, suggesting warmth towards visitors.	Aims to make visitors feel welcome and loved.	May reflect Georgian hospitality.
Tirana	A Colorful Place	Initiated by Mayor Edi Rama's transformation of the cityscape.	Highlights the vibrant and artistic makeover of Tirana.	Represents a break from the city's grey communist past.
Vaduz	Centre of Culture	Highlights Vaduz's rich cultural offerings in a compact area.	Promotes Vaduz as a cultural hub with much to explore in a small space.	Showcases the city's modern and traditional cultural assets.

continued on following page

Table 1. Continued

Capital City	Slogan	Origin & Creation	Intended Message	Cultural/Historical Relevance
Valletta	European Capital of Culture	Retained from Valletta's designation as the European Capital of Culture in 2018.	Emphasizes Valletta's rich cultural heritage and diversity.	Celebrates the city's historical significance and cultural contributions.
Vatican	Miserando atque eligendo	Based on the city's spiritual and historic significance, using Latin.	Conveys the spiritual and cultural depth of the Vatican.	Rooted in the papal motto, emphasizing the Vatican's religious importance.
Vienna	Now! Forever	Developed to overcome the passive image of "Vienna waits for you".	Invites immediate and repeated visits to Vienna.	Aligns with Vienna's historic charm and modern appeal.
Vilnius	The G-spot of Europe	Emerged from a student project and gained viral attention.	Suggests Vilnius as an exciting, yet undiscovered destination.	A bold move to differentiate Vilnius in a crowded tourism market.
Warsaw	Fall in Love With Warsaw	Little information available on the slogan's origin.	Aims to evoke emotional connections with the city.	Leverages the universal appeal of love to attract visitors.
Yerevan	Feel the Warmness	Used for a decade, emphasizing the city's climate and hospitality.	Highlights the warmth of both weather and people in Yerevan.	Reflects the welcoming nature of the city and its residents.
Zagreb	Full of Experiences	Aligns with the national slogan "Full of Life".	Promotes Zagreb as a vibrant, activity-rich destination.	Ties into the broader branding of Croatia as an adventurous location.

Source: Official English-Language Tourism Slogans of European Capitals, Compiled by the Authors of the Book Chapter

What is interesting is that the capitals above made a conscious decision to equip themselves with a slogan that positions them within the tourism market. However though, many of them tend to use identical, almost clichéd expressions that any of the other capitals could also utilize, and the whole process loses its original value. Still, it is interesting to see the most common solutions and the key findings.

Following the evaluation of European capitals' tourism slogans as presented in Table 1, this study stresses the interplay between creativity, cultural significance, and the strategic messaging inherent in slogan development. The analysis shows the different approaches cities adopt to project their unique identities and appeal through brief, memorable phrases. Notably, the effective slogans are those that not only appealing on an emotional level but also reflect the cultural and historical richness of their destinations, thereby maintaining a deeper connection with potential tourists. This analysis reveals the critical role of originality and emotional resonance in creating slogans that go beyond mere promotional tools to become pivotal elements in the narrative construction of destination brands. As we move forward, it becomes imperative for destination management to prioritize the development of authentic and engaging slogans that adeptly communicate the essence of their locales, thereby enhancing their attractiveness and competitive edge in the global tourism marketplace.

5. DISCUSSION AND RECOMMENDATIONS

The "Discussion and Recommendations" section synthesizes the findings from the analysis of European capitals' tourism slogans and presents insights for enhancing destination branding. This section articulates the alignment between brand name and slogans, emphasizing their role in brand recognition and association. It discusses the strategic use of geographical markers and emotive language in slogans to increase brand appeal.

5.1 The Integration of Brand Name in Slogans

Several experts point out the significance of aligning the brand name with its corresponding slogan. Garrido (2005), Kohli et al. (2007), Obiol (2002), and Ortega et al. (2006) state that embedding the brand within the slogan enhances brand's recognition and association. While this integration may impose constraints on creativity, the potential benefits are substantial (Kohli et al., 2007). This practice finds ample demonstration across various industries. Gösser's slogan, "Gut, Besser, Gösser", and Calgon's iconic phrase, "Washing machines live longer with Calgon", exemplify how brands are seamlessly incorporated into slogans, fostering immediate brand recognition and reinforcing brand attributes. Similarly, automotive giant Toyota employs the slogan "Today, Tomorrow, Toyota", employing triple alliteration to enhance memorability while underscoring the brand's enduring reliability.

Similarly, slogans employed by airlines, such as United's "Fly the friendly skies of United", and car rental companies like Hertz's "There's Hertz and not exactly", capitalize on brand integration to reinforce unique selling propositions and market dominance. The tourism industry equally embraces this practice, with numerous European capitals adopting slogans that incorporate their names, occurring in 13 out of 36 cases: Amsterdam (Netherlands): I amsterdam; Athens (Greece): This is Athens!; Belgrade (Serbia): #gobelgrade; Brussels (Belgium): BXL Moves for you; Copenhagen (Denmark): Wonderful Copenhagen; Kyiv (Ukraine): Everything Starts in Kyiv; Minsk (Belarus): Think Minsk!; Paris (France): Paris Je t'aime (Paris I love you); Prague (The Czech Republic): Prague:emotion; Reykjavík (Iceland): This is Reykjavík; Riga (Latvia): Live Riga!; Skopje (North Macedonia): Feel Love Feel Skopje; Warsaw (Poland): Fall in Love With Warsaw.

This strategic integration of brand names within slogans serves to reinforce brand identity, enhance brand recall, and establish a distinctive market presence, as emphasized by Pike (2004). Particularly for lesser-known destinations, this approach aids in brand identification and differentiation (Ortega et al., 2006). In summary, the pervasive use of brand name integration within slogans across various sectors underscores its effectiveness in fostering brand recognition, enhancing consumer engagement, and amplifying brand messaging.

5.2 Layer in Destination Slogans

5.2.1 Geographical layers

Deliberating on whether to include the term 'city' in a slogan is crucial, while it might seem unnecessary for cities, it becomes vital for European capitals where awareness among potential tourists varies. Out of the European capital slogans analyzed, five out of thirty-six include the term 'city', such as Berlin (Germany): "The City of Freedom" and Bratislava (Slovakia): "The City Where You Find Real Life." This strategic choice aims to position the destination brand geographically, leveraging the existing recognition of the broader concept of a city (Caldwell and Freire, 2004). Furthermore, using 'capital' in slogans serves a dual purpose of indicating the city's status as the capital of its respective country and emphasizing its significance within a particular region. Examples include Andorra la Vella (Andorra): "Capital south of the Pyrenees" and Stockholm (Sweden): "The Capital of Scandinavia." This deliberate framing aligns with the hierarchical structure of brand association and aids in anchoring the destination's identity within the minds of tourists. Additionally, the term 'Europe' features prominently in four slogans, underscoring not only the geographical location of these destinations within the European continent but also highlighting their distinctive contributions. For instance, Budapest (Hungary): "Spice of Europe" and Vilnius (Lithuania): "The G-spot of Europe" evoke a sense of uniqueness and allure associated with their European heritage.

The strategic incorporation of terms like 'city,' 'capital,' and 'Europe' in the slogans of European capitals serves not only to geographically position and elevate the destination's brand but also to imbue it with a sense of identity and importance. The analysis reveals an approach to slogan creation, where geographical markers are leveraged to resonate with potential tourists' awareness and expectations.

5.2.2 Emotional & Cultural layers

To expand on the influence of emotional appeal and cultural significance in city slogans, it is essential to delve into how these elements not only attract tourists but also forge a deeper connection between the destination and its visitors. Emotional appeal, particularly through the use of 'love', serves as a powerful tool in marketing destinations. This strategy is not merely about attracting visitors; it's about creating an emotional narrative that resonates on a personal level. The slogan "Paris Je t'aime" is a prime example, as it encapsulates the romantic allure of Paris, often considered the city of love. This emotive phrasing is designed to evoke feelings of affection and belongingness, promising an unforgettable experience steeped in romance (Pike, 2004). Similarly, "Feel Love Feel Skopje" employs a direct emotional appeal, inviting visitors to experience the warmth and hospitality of Skopje through a personal emotional journey. Such slogans are adept at creating a narrative that visitors are not just traveling to a location but are embarking on a journey to experience love and connection.

The theme of 'culture' in city slogans, on the other hand, emphasizes the unique cultural heritage of a destination. This approach is significant for several reasons. Firstly, it highlights the city's commitment to preserving and celebrating its cultural identity, as seen in slogans like "A Year of Culture" for Gibraltar and "Centre of Culture" for Vaduz. These slogans suggest that visitors will have the opportunity to immerse themselves in a rich cultural experience, differentiating the destination from others (Richards, 2011). Valletta's slogan, "European Capital of Culture", not only signifies its cultural richness but also aligns with the city's recognition by a prestigious European Union initiative, further validating its cultural significance. This recognition plays a crucial role in attracting culturally inclined tourists, offering them a promise of enriching cultural encounters (Quinn, 2005).

The emphasis on emotional connections and cultural heritage through slogans underscores the diverse strategies employed to attract and engage visitors, reflecting the cities' aspirations to offer unique, memorable experiences. This nuanced use of language in destination branding highlights the complexity and creativity involved in crafting slogans that capture the essence of a place, ensuring they stand out in the competitive tourism market.

5.3 Call for action

Another aspect to consider when analyzing destination slogans is their use of a call to action. Whether prompting a visit or encouraging engagement in local experiences, these slogans often adopt a direct and informal tone, either abstractly or concretely. It can be inferred that these destinations aim to underscore their unique qualities and prompt visitor engagement primarily through their slogans. Essentially, they seek to influence tourists' decision-making processes and encourage travel to the destination. In the context of European capitals, several cities employ this strategy, such as Belgrade (Serbia) with its slogan "#gobelgrade", Chisinau (Moldova) with "Discover The Routes of Life", and Vienna (Austria) with "Now! Forever ".

Furthermore, research stresses the importance of slogan length. Effective slogans should succinctly convey the key message in a few words (Garrido & Ramos, 2006). Donaire and Galí (2012) suggest that, given the primary aim of retention, slogans tend to prioritize simplicity. Consequently, shorter slogans are generally more memorable than longer ones (Ortega et al., 2006; Pike, 2004). Remarkably, with the exception of Bratislava's "The City Where You Find Real Life", the slogans of European capitals typically consist of no more than five words.

The strategic use of calls to action within destination slogans represents a deliberate effort to engage potential tourists, highlighting the destinations' unique attributes and experiences. This approach, characterized by direct and sometimes informal language, serves as a tool in influencing tourists' decision-making and enhancing their inclination towards travel. Additionally, the emphasis on slogan brevity underscores the importance of conciseness in message delivery, with most effective slogans achieving memorable impact through minimal word use. This balance between prompt engagement and succinct communication is crucial in the competitive landscape of destination marketing, particularly for European capitals aiming to capture the essence of their appeal in a few, impactful words.

6. CONCLUSION

This study sets out to explore the significant role that storytelling, specifically through slogans, plays in marketing tourist destinations in Europe. It aimed to uncover how narrative techniques used in slogans can enhance the appeal of these destinations. Through an analysis of various European capitals' tourism slogans, the research sought to fill a gap in understanding how storytelling can be strategically used in destination marketing to make a place stand out. The findings highlight the importance of storytelling in creating unique brand identities for destinations, connecting emotionally with potential tourists, and differentiating these destinations in a crowded market. The outcomes of this study offer valuable insights for marketing professionals, showing how well-designed slogans can deeply influence tourists' perceptions and inclinations towards visiting a place. However, this research has its limitations, mainly its focus on European capitals, which might not fully represent global marketing practices. Moreover, interpreting the impact of slogans involves a degree of subjectivity, which could influence the study's conclusions. There's room for further research to broaden the scope beyond Europe, delve into the tangible effects of slogans on tourist behavior, and explore how storytelling integrates with various marketing channels. Investigating the role of digital media in enhancing the storytelling impact could also provide a deeper understanding of current trends in destination marketing. Ultimately, this study reaffirms the critical role of storytelling in the context of destination marketing, highlighting its strategic value beyond just advertising. By crafting compelling stories, destinations can not only boost their attractiveness but also establish meaningful connections with their audience, leading to a more sophisticated and effective branding strategy in the competitive tourism industry.

ACKNOWLEDGMENT

The authors would like to thank their students for their work in the phase collecting the slogans of European capitals.

REFERENCES

Aaker, J., & Smith, A. (2010). *The dragonfly effect: Quick, effective, and powerful ways to use social media to drive social change*. John Wiley & Sons.

Adamus-Matuszyńska, A., Dzik, P., Michnik, J., & Polok, G. (2021). Visual component of destination brands as a tool for communicating sustainable tourism offers. Retrieved from https://dx.doi.org/DOI: 10.3390/su13020731

Akgün, A. E., Keskin, H., Ayar, H., & Erdogan, E. (2015). The influence of storytelling approach in travel writings on readers' empathy and travel intentions. *Procedia: Social and Behavioral Sciences*, 207, 577–586. DOI: 10.1016/j.sbspro.2015.10.129

Aleksandrova, M. (2019). Importance of the slogans as a brand communication tool of tourist destinations. Retrieved from https://dx.doi.org/DOI: 10.36997/IJUSV-ESS/2019.8.3.154

Alkier, R., Milojica, V., & Roblek, V. (2017). Challenges of the social innovation in tourism. *Tourism in Southern and Eastern Europe.*, 4, 1–13. DOI: 10.20867/tosee.04.24

Bassano, C., Barile, S., Piciocchi, P., Spohrer, J. C., Iandolo, F., & Fisk, R. (2019). Storytelling about places: Tourism marketing in the digital age. *Cities (London, England)*, 87, 10–20. DOI: 10.1016/j.cities.2018.12.025

Caldwell, N., & Freire, J. R. (2004). The differences between branding a country, a region and a city: Applying the Brand box model. *Journal of Brand Management*, 12(1), 50–61. DOI: 10.1057/palgrave.bm.2540201

Choi, S. S. (2016). A study on effect of tourism storytelling of tourism destination brand value and tourist behavioral intentions. *Indian Journal of Science and Technology*, 9(46). https://sciresol.s3.us-east-2.amazonaws.com/IJST/Articles/2016/Issue-46/Article89.pdf

Clara, S., & Barbosa, B. (2021). People make places, what do stories do? Applying digital storytelling strategies to communicate the identity of cities and regions. In Handbook of Research on Contemporary Storytelling Methods Across New Media and Disciplines. DOI: DOI: 10.4018/978-1-7998-6605-3.ch005

Cooper, M., & Buckley, R. (2021). Tourist mental health drives destination choice, marketing, and matching. Retrieved from https://dx.doi.org/DOI: 10.1177/00472875211011548

Creswell, J. W., & Creswell, J. D. (2018). *Research design: Qualitative, quantitative, and mixed methods approach* (5th ed.). Sage Publications.

Donaire, J. A., & Galí, N. (2012). Eslóganes turísticos: Un análisis de los eslóganes de los destinos catalanes. *Boletín de la Asociación de Geógrafos Españoles*, 60, 521–533.

Dziedzic, E. (2019). Storytelling as a tool of the place identity formation. *Przedsiębiorczość i Zarządzanie*, 2(1), 109–119.

Eriksson, P., & Kovalainen, A. (2016). *Qualitative methods in business research* (2nd ed.). SAGE Publications.

Ferreira, A. (2022). Literary routes as a successful tourist offer in Porto. *International Conference on Tourism Research*, 15(1), 126–134. https://doi.org/DOI: 10.34190/ictr.15.1.279

Galí, N., Camprubí, R., & Donaire, J. A. (2017). Analysing tourism slogans in top tourism destinations. *Journal of Destination Marketing & Management*, 3(6), 243–251. DOI: 10.1016/j.jdmm.2016.04.004

Garrido, M. (2005). La publicidad turística en Andalucía (2002–2005): Andalucía sólo hay una, la tuya vs. Andalucía te quiere. *Questiones publicitarias*, 1(10), 77–97.

Garrido, M., & Ramos, M. (2006). *La evolución del eslogan en la publicidad gráfica española. III Simposium de profesores universitarios de creatividad publicitaria.* Universidad Ramón Llull. Barcelona: Trípodos.

Hajeer, A., & Toptsi, J. (2022). Piloting a semi-structured interview schedule: The influence of MOOC descriptions on potential students. *Journal of Adult Learning. Knowledge and Innovation*, 5(1), 36–45. DOI: 10.1556/2059.2021.00043

Healey, M. (2009). *Mi az a branding? (What is Branding?)*. Scolar Kiadó.

Hsieh, H.-F., & Shannon, S. E. (2005). Three approaches to qualitative content analysis. *Qualitative Health Research*, 15(9), 1277–1288. DOI: 10.1177/1049732305276687 PMID: 16204405

Johnson, C. (2018). The 10 functions of storytelling. Retrieved January 9, 2022, from https://www.carlajohnson.co/the-10-functions-of-storytelling/

Keskin, H., Akgun, A. E., Zehir, C., & Ayar, H. (2016). Tales of cities: City branding through storytelling. *Journal of Global Strategic Management, 1*(10), 2016 June, 31–41. https://www.researchgate.net/profile/Hayat-Ayar-Sentuerk/publication/309465697_TALES_OF_CITIES_CITY_BRANDING_THROUGH_STORYTELLING/links/581b0c0d08ae3c82664d5098/TALES-OF-CITIES-CITY-BRANDING-THROUGH-STORYTELLING.pdf

Kietzmann, J. H., Hermkens, K., McCarthy, I. P., & Silvestre, B. S. (2011). Social media? Get serious! Understanding the functional building blocks of social media. *Business Horizons, 54*(3), 241–251. DOI: 10.1016/j.bushor.2011.01.005

Klenosky, D. B., & Gitelson, R. E. (1997). Characteristics of effective tourism promotion slogans. *Annals of Tourism Research, 24*(1), 235–238. DOI: 10.1016/S0160-7383(96)00038-2

Kohli, C., Leuthesser, L., & Suri, R. (2007). Got slogan? Guidelines for creating effective slogans. *Business Horizons, 50*(5), 415–422. DOI: 10.1016/j.bushor.2007.05.002

Kotler, P., & Keller, K. L. (2006). *Marketing Management*. Akadémiai Kiadó.

Kvítková, Z., & Petrů, Z. (2021). Approaches to storytelling and narrative structures in destination marketing. Retrieved from https://dx.doi.org/DOI: 10.20867/tosee.06.28

Lehto, X., Lee, G., & Ismail, J. (2014). Measuring congruence of affective images of destinations and their slogans. *International Journal of Tourism Research, 16*(3), 250–260. DOI: 10.1002/jtr.1923

Malterud, K., Siersma, V. D., & Guassora, A. D. (2016). Sample size in qualitative interview studies: Guided by information power. *Qualitative Health Research, 26*(13), 1753–1760. DOI: 10.1177/1049732315617444 PMID: 26613970

Martin, D., & Woodside, A. G. (2011). Storytelling research on international visitors: Interpreting own experiences in Tokyo. *Qualitative Market Research, 14*(1), 27–54. DOI: 10.1108/13522751111099319

Mathews, R., & Wacker, W. (2007). *What's your story? Storytelling to move markets, audiences, people and brands*. Pearson Education.

McKee, R. (2003). Storytelling that moves people. A conversation with screenwriting coach Robert McKee. *Harvard Business Review, 81*(6), 51–55, 136. PMID: 12800716

McKee, R., & Gerace, T. (2018). *Storynomics: story-driven marketing in the post-advertising world*. Methuen.

Moin, S. M. A. (2020). *Brand storytelling in the digital age – theories, practice and application*. Palgrave-Macmillan. DOI: 10.1007/978-3-030-59085-7

Morgan, N., & Pritchard, A. (1998). *Tourism promotion and power: creating images, creating identities*. John Wiley & Sons.

Mossberg, L., Therkelsen, A., Huijbens, E., Björk, P., & Olsson, A. K. (2010). Storytelling and destination development - Possibilities and drawbacks of using storytelling as a means of developing and marketing Nordic tourism destinations. Nordic Innovation Centre (NICe) Project. Retrieved January 11, 2022, from http://www.nordicinnovation.org/Global/_Publications/Reports/2010/201012_StorytellingAndDestinationDevelopment_report.pdf

Obiol, E. (2002). Marcas turísticas y territorio: Un análisis geográfico del turismo valenciano. *Cuadernos de Turismo*, 9, 85–101.

Ojha, A. K. (2022). Strategies for sustainable tourism business development: A comprehensive analysis. Retrieved from https://dx.doi.org/DOI: 10.55529/jsrth.24.25.30

Ortega, E., Mora, P., & Rauld, L. (2006). El eslogan en el sector turístico español. *Cuadernos de Turismo*, 17, 127–146.

Papp-Váry, Á. (2021). Mitől jó egy szlogen? 2. rész – A legfontosabb marketingszempontok, amiket aztán mégis mindig elfelejtenek a marketingesek (What makes a good slogan? Part 2 – The most important marketing aspects that marketers always forget). *Márkamonitor Magazin*, 2021(3-4), 46–50.

Papp-Váry, Á. F. (2020). *A márkanév ereje – A sikeres brandépítés alapjai (The power of brand names – the basics of powerful brand building)*. Dialóg-Campus Kiadó.

Patton, M. Q. (2015). *Qualitative research & evaluation methods: Integrating theory and practice* (4th ed.). Sage Publications.

Pellowski, A. (1990). *The World of Storytelling*. Wilson.

Pera, R., Viglia, G., & Furlan, R. (2016). Who am I? How compelling self-storytelling builds digital personal reputation. *Journal of Interactive Marketing*, 35(1), 44–55. DOI: 10.1016/j.intmar.2015.11.002

Pike, S. (2004). Destination brand positioning slogan: Towards the development of a set of accountability criteria. *Acta Turística*, 16(2), 102–124.

Pike, S. (2007). *Destination marketing organizations and destination marketing: A narrative analysis of the literature*. Elsevier Science Publishers. DOI: 10.4324/9780080494463

Polletta, F., Chen, P., Gardner, B. G., & Motes, A. (2011). The sociology of storytelling. *Annual Review of Sociology*, 37(1), 109–130. DOI: 10.1146/annurev-soc-081309-150106

Quinn, B. (2005). Arts Festivals and the City. *Urban Studies (Edinburgh, Scotland)*, 42(5-6), 927–943. DOI: 10.1080/00420980500107250

Ramkissoon, H., Nunkoo, R., & Gursoy, D. (2009). How consumption values affect destination image formation. In: Woodside, A. G., Megehee, C. M., & Ogle, A. (eds.), Perspectives on Cross-Cultural, Ethnographic, Brand Image, Storytelling, Unconscious Needs, and Hospitality Guest Research (Advances in Culture, Tourism and Hospitality Research, Volume 3). Emerald, 143–168. DOI: 10.1108/S1871-3173(2009)0000003008

Reinhold, S., Beritelli, P., Fyall, A., Choi, H.-S. C., Laesser, C., & Joppe, M. (2023). State-of-the-art review on destination marketing and destination management. Retrieved from https://dx.doi.org/DOI: 10.3390/tourhosp4040036

Richards, G. (2011). Creativity and Tourism: The State of the Art. *Annals of Tourism Research*, 38(4), 1225–1253. DOI: 10.1016/j.annals.2011.07.008

Ries, L. (2015). *Battlecry – Winning the battle for the mind with a slogan that kills.* Ries Pieces.

Rodriguez, M. (2020). *Brand storytelling: Put customers in the heart of your brand story*. Kogan Page.

Rose, F. (2011). The art of immersion: How the digital generation is remaking Hollywood, Madison Avenue, and the way we tell stories. *International Journal of Advertising*, 30(5), 915–919. https://www.academia.edu/download/35025431/Resena_The_art_of_inmersion.pdf. DOI: 10.2501/IJA-30-5-915-916

Rosengren, S., & Dahlén, M. (2006). Brand–slogan matching in a cluttered environment. *Journal of Marketing Communications*, 12(4), 263–269. DOI: 10.1080/13527260600714700

Sárközy, I. (2009). Szlogenmeghatározások (Slogan definitions). Retrieved November 10, 2017, from www.szlogenek.hu/szlogenmeghat.php

Supphellen, M., & Nygaardsvik, I. (2002). Testing country brand slogans: Conceptual development and empirical illustration of a simple normative model. *Brand Management*, 9(4–5), 384–395. https://link.springer.com/article/10.1057/palgrave.bm.2540085

Wang, Y., Huang, L., Li, J., & Yang, Y. (2019). The mechanism of tourism slogans on travel intention based on Unique Selling Proposition (USP) theory. *Journal of Travel & Tourism Marketing*, 36(4), 415–427. DOI: 10.1080/10548408.2019.1568950

Wyer, R. S. (1995). *Knowledge and memory: The real story*. Lawrence Erlbaum Associates.

Youssef, K. B., Leicht, T., & Marongiu, L. (2019). Storytelling in the context of destination marketing: An analysis of conceptualisations and impact measurement. *Journal of Strategic Marketing*, 27(8), 696–713. DOI: 10.1080/0965254X.2018.1464498

KEY TERMS AND DEFINITIONS

Capital: The word "capital" originates from the Latin word "caput", that is "head", and they are hence regarded not only as the economic, governmental and cultural center of a country, but also its flagship in tourism.

Place Branding: A marketing strategy that is based on the premise that cities, regions, and countries can be branded. Place branding is largely linked to the characteristics of its native people, the characteristics of the region, the culture, the gastronomy, the organizations, and its history.

Storytelling: Sharing and combining of knowledge and experiences through narrative and anecdotes in order to communicate complex ideas, concepts and causal connections, and to build connections and associations.

Storytelling Strategies: Strategies designed to persuade through stories. The main objective of storytelling strategies is to create emotion and cognition through a story, in order to persuade and engage an audience.

Tourism Slogan: A short and catchy phrase, easy to memorize, staying in the consumers' minds, which characterizes the destination and makes it attractive for visitors.

Chapter 2
Destination Competitiveness, Culture and Heritage Tourism, and Regional Clusters:
Case of Macedonia

Marija Lazarev Zivanovic
https://orcid.org/0009-0004-1295-9945
Glion Institute of Higher Education, Switzerland

EXECUTIVE SUMMARY

In recent decades, research on cultural identity, state dynamics, and destination competitiveness has gained significant importance in the field of Cultural and Heritage Tourism. Specifically, in Macedonia, a region shared between two states—North Macedonia and Greece—tourism development occurs within a unique political and economic context. Does dissonant heritage hinder or promote destination development? This chapter aims to assess the destination competitiveness of Culture and (dissonant) Heritage tourism, focusing on the development of regional clusters. Perspectives from various stakeholders—academics, state officials, and tourism strategy developers—are essential. Bridging the gap in service provision and policy-making processes within this demand-led industry requires a shared doctrine. Notably, this introduces an additional perspective to the existing Competitiveness theory. While Culture and Heritage are recognized as core attractors, the dissonant aspect remains unexplored. Balkan states offer opportunities for further research in culture and heritage clusters.

DOI: 10.4018/979-8-3693-1548-4.ch002

CULTURE AND INTERPRETATION, STATE PERSPECTIVE AND CLUSTER DEVELOPMENT

Since not all heritage necessarily bears developmental potential, cultural values with developmental potential have been defined as follows to facilitate a better understanding of the terms: *"Cultural values are various tangible and intangible elements and individual natural elements of cultural significance and local origin that are identified by the stakeholders and have economic, social, ecological, or cultural developmental potential"* (Hribar et al, 2012). The importance of the development of a *"specific cultural value co-depends on the utility, compatibility, and the scope of developmental potential"* (Hribar et al., 2012, p.19). As Light (2007) stated in his research on cultural identity and state, the latter has an important role in defining cultural meanings, interpretations, and identities. It is essential to select the forms of tourism that the country wishes to develop and that correspond to the cultural and political identities. However, these go beyond control at certain points (Dracula tourism in Romania). With the image of the Balkan countries rather discordant to the markets outside of the region and with a rich heritage dissonance, what are the existing and preferred clusters that the tourism authorities create, co-create, and join in the current context?

Culture and Heritage Tourism in Balkan States

In research presented by Armenski, Gomezelj, Djurdjev, Djeri and Dragin (2011), Serbia received high ratings for Inherited resources (historic sites, heritage, traditional arts) however the lowest-rated indicator was for destination management and policy. According to Metodijeski and Temelkov (2014), all the Balkan countries have established national tourism organizations, for example the Tourist Organization of Serbia or government agencies for tourism, as exemplified by the Agency for Promotion and Support of Tourism of Macedonia (it will be further referred to as Macedonia, North Macedonia or FYROM (Former Yugoslav Republic of Macedonia)). These bodies have developed official websites and perform the function of promoting the tourism potential of a given country at the international level. (Metodijeski and Temelkov (2014))

Undoubtedly, the most important tourism destination of North Macedonia is Ohrid. The first written findings of the name Ohrid (previously Lichnidos) date from 879. In the 10th and 11th centuries, it was the capital and an important center of the medieval Macedonian state under the emperor Samoil, as well as the Patriarchate chair. With its early orthodox churches and basilicas, the unique beauty of nature and art, it still unites the mix of many civilizations with more than 100 square meters of fresco memoirs, a rich gallery of icons, manuscripts, and other rarities.

Although the sector is considered as vigorously subsidized and not highly productive, only 1.7% of EU Funding Research is provided. Nevertheless, the state-supported and subsidized heritage sites and Cultural heritage institutions, such as museums are not very strong and rapid in providing a package with a value propositions and business models that meet the current demands and profiles of the lifestyles. To fill this gap, it would be necessary to confront three key challenges:

1. Cultural heritage supply side fragmentation
2. Cultural communication
3. Value innovation

In the Balkan region, historical and political tensions between neighboring countries limit the recognition of cultural and historical heritage tourism potential. Cross-border cooperation between Macedonia and Greece faces complexity due to unique political and interstate issues, including the constitutional name dispute (Karadjoski, 2013). Efforts to harmonize collaboration continue within European Union programs.

Seven regions have been included, in the cross-border area, as these areas are often considered as periphery, especially in tourism development. The regions are Florina, Pella, Kilkis, and Serres in Greece and Pelagonija, Vardar, and Southeast in North Macedonia. This further gives an opportunity to the adjacent regions, such as Thessaloniki, as their size and functional role are important in the program area. The inclusion of Thessaloniki is based on the fact that the region is a geomorphological extension of the Pelagonija massif and geologically located on the west end of the Serbo-Macedonian massif (Greece-Macedonia IPA Cross-border Programme 2007-2013, pp. 10-11).

Ambiguity in Literature on Heritage: Case of Macedonia

In the book Transformational tourism: Host perspectives, a chapter provided by Ashworth assesses the regional issues under the Ethnic conflict: Is Heritage Tourism Part of the Solution or Part of the Problem? He proposes a discussion on competitive heritage tourism and the case of Macedonia. As argued in his latter book "Building a Heritage" (in this chapter under 1.8 and 1.9), heritage has contemporary usage including the national and political goals. He further referred to the presence and retreat of the Ottoman Empire, along with other important historical events that shaped the destiny and the heritage of Macedonia. He also discussed the more recent activity of Greece, successfully blocking the membership of FYROM (the name for Macedonia since Yugoslavia does not exist as a state) in the European Union or NATO. The building programme "Skopje 2014" was deemed extremely provocative by the Greek neighbours for its style and content (the monument of Alexander the Great, the Archaeological Museum).

What is particularly intriguing is the following statement *"The heritage tourism product sold in both the Republic of Macedonia and the Greek region of the same name, is almost exclusively Hellenistic"*. It further provides the data on the number of tourists in Greek Macedonia and the historical sites and allusions. The number of visitors is certainly more modest in North Macedonia, with a steady increase from 2006-2011, mostly focused on the Ohrid lake area and some other localities but there is no clear link to any particular Hellenistic related heritage in these areas. This might be due to the fact that Philip the Macedonian and Alexander the Great have conquered the rest of Greece. Hellenistic Greece represents the Greece from the death of Alexander the Great in 323 B.C until 146 B.C. The instauration of the Roman hegemony did not end the continuity of Hellenistic society and culture, which persisted until the arrival of Christianity.

Cross-Border Tourism Development: FYROM, Albania and Greece

One of the crucial projects concerning the development and implementation of cross-border long term tourism and economic development, was financially supported by the Global Environment Facility (GEF). The implementation of the project The Integrated Ecosystem Management in the Prespa Lakes Basin was overseen by the UNDP. The international agreement was ratified in 2010 by the Ministries of Environment in three countries: North Macedonia (in this document the country was still internationally recognized as the Former Yugoslav Republic of Macedonia), Albania, and Greece. This commitment obligated all three ratifying parties to establish mutual permanent structures and platforms for collaboration and cooperation as a long-term strategy whilst making sure that the protection of the natural environment and human activities remains preserved.

The Tourism Strategy and Action Plan aim to secure sustainable funds for local initiatives and environmental restorations. Despite challenges like insufficient market profiling and declining domestic tourism, community-based tourism in FYROM and grant-supported growth in Greece show promise. Trans-boundary tourism is emerging, with a vision of achieving World Heritage Site status.

The main goal is to establish a strategy for the future tourism development in the Prespa Lakes Basin. This is essential to strengthen public-private partnerships, attract potential investment, and manage the ecosystem with principles aligned with benchmarking best practices from the international scene.

In order to better understand the current market segmentation for the three countries, the table below provides an overview of the visitors in Prespa Lake Basin (2012-2016):

Table 1. Major tourism market segments for three countries

Albania	The former Yugoslav Republic of Macedonia	Greece
• Domestic tourists (mostly for restaurants);	• Domestic (mostly from Bitola, Skopje, Prilep), excursions and family trips;	• Domestic tourists from Western Macedonia (day trips)
• Ethnic Macedonians (mostly for restaurants);	• Foreign (mainly diaspora), above 35 years old guests, one-day weekend visits;	• Domestic tourists from Central Macedonia and Thessaloniki (day trips or one-or two-night stays);
• Hunters (domestic);	• Dutch tourists using homestay (from new Ohrid charters);	• Domestic tourists from all over the Greece (mainly for short breaks, families, and small groups (25- to 50-year-olds);
• Some foreign tourists taking boat trips;	• Israeli tourists using homestay and seeking value for money.	• Diaspora people (mainly from Canada, Australia, Germany);
• Some seminars and workshop participants, and other study/ work-related visitors, such as archaeologists.		• Foreigner holiday visitors (mainly from Western Europe and Israel);
		• Foreign special interest groups (birdwatching, dendrology, hiking, etc.);
		• Students and other volunteers (voluntourism).

Currently there are six main organisations responsible for developing marketing budgets to promote and enhance the profile of Prespa region. These are as follows:

- Albanian National Tourism Agency
- Agency for Tourism Promotion, the former Yugoslav Republic of Macedonia
- Greek Tourism Organisation
- Korcë DMO
- Pelagonija region, and
- The Ohrid-Prespa Euroregion.

"Rather than trying to develop Prespa's own "stand alone" campaign which would be very expensive to administer and unlikely to be sustained with so small an industry to fund it, it will be more effective to incentivize other organisations to feature Prespa Lakes basin more prominently." (https://www.undp.org)

Cultural Heritage Management: Tangible and Intangible Assets

According to McKercher, Ho, and du Cross (2005), cultural heritage assets form the building blocks for cultural tourism and their management is falls under the broadly defined Cultural Heritage Management sector. As such, the perspective of the asset manager is one of the significant viewpoints and not necessarily aligned with the views of other instances involved (government, tourism strategy planners, or Destination managers). Heritage is defined as a broad concept that includes tangible assets, such as natural and cultural environments, covering landscapes, historic places, sites and built environments as well as intangible assets such as collections, past and ongoing cultural practices knowledge, and living experiences.

The World Economic Forum (WEF) uses the Composite Global Competitiveness Index (GCI) to assess tourism sector competitiveness (Krstic, Jovanic & Stanisic, 2015). This index considers factors like openness to tourism, hospitality, and environmental attractiveness, including UNESCO World Heritage sites.

The World Heritage Committee adopted in 2008 a standard list of factors affecting the Outstanding Universal Value of World Heritage properties. Designed with the input of experts in both natural and cultural heritage; the list includes 14 factors with numerous sub-factors for each category. Efforts have been made to make these reports as site-specific as possible (as seen in the case of the Djoudj National Bird Sanctuary in Senegal). One of the factors refers to Social/Cultural uses of Heritage with a sub-factor on the Impacts of tourism/visitor/recreation:

- Inappropriate/non-existent interpretation (not an impact)
- High level of visitation
- Increase of vendors inside/outside site
- Building community support, sustainable livelihoods

According to McKercher, Ho and du Cross (2005) the "odd" relationship between tourism sector and cultural heritage management of the assets has been raised and discussed from the perspective of the tourism and cultural heritage management (CHM). They argue that historically, CHM has primarily focused on the conservation and protection of the cultural heritage assets while the tourism sector has taken on promotional and developmental roles. These two entities have often been in an opposition, with differing views and conflicts in understanding and cooperation.

On the one hand, many authors have suggested that tourism and CHM are incompatible (Berry, 1994; Boniface, 1998; Jacobs & Gale, 1994; Jansen-Verbeke, 1998 as cited in McKercher et al. (2004)), and that due to this incompatibility, a conflict relationship is inevitable. Culture and heritage asset managers argue that the original values should not be standardized or commercialized. Tourism developers find that the negative attitude towards "tourismification" increases the conflict and needs an alternative. The positive sides of the tourism development are that the local find the cultural roots, or rather rediscover them due to the interest shown by the visitors. It increases local pride and interest in cultural and historical values. Tourism can also play a vital role in conservation, raising awareness, and generating funds for the restoration or preservation of the past.

The Competitiveness of the Destination and Modelling

Competitive advantage is not a natural phenomenon but rather a combination of innovative driven competitive strategies coupled with visitors' aspirations (Fernando, 2015). Ritchie and Crouch's (2003) study on modelling Destination competitiveness, which identifies 36 attributes of competitiveness grouped into five main factors, found that *Culture and History* were the second most determinant attribute. Whereas *Physiography and Climate* represent the "natural" qualities of a destination, *Culture and History*, symbolize the primary touristic attractiveness of a destination stemming from the "human" rather than "natural" processes.

Crouch (2007) argues that competitiveness must be associated with sustainability. Following Bruntlandt's report on the definition of sustainability, which provides four separate pillars (human, physical, environmental, and socio-cultural), but a holistic approach is emphasized on economic and social development, particularly in places with a low standard of living. These pillars must be mutually supportive and not exclusive, as improvements in one should not come at the expense of another. Intergenerational solidarity plays a vital role: all development efforts must consider their impact on opportunities for future generations.

Hribar, Smid and Bole (2012) introduced environmental potential, recognizing that sustainable heritage management is linked to maintaining the complexity and stability of ecosystems – for instance, certain types of traditional farming activities can contribute to the prevention of soil erosion.

The competitive success of a tourism destination thus relies on its ability to bring to market a package of functional, psycho-social, experiential, and value-based benefits (Walls & Wang, 2011 as cited in Iazzi, Rosato, Gravili, 2012). It must ensure the potential user a level of satisfaction at least equal to what other rival destinations are can provide and it needs to be sustainable over time, considering into account economic, social, and cultural aspects (Caroli, 2006 as cited in Iazzi, Rosato, Gravili, 2012).

Tourism destination competitiveness is crucial for success. Models like Ritchie and Crouch or the Dwyer model highlight key factors affecting competitiveness. Sustainable tourism policies contribute significantly to competitiveness, considering environmental preservation and socio-cultural balance (Goffi, 2013). TDC matters beyond academia, drawing attention from various sectors.

Despite being the birthplace and residence of Philip the Macedonian and Alexander the Great, this region is seldom explored in case study research and there are no recent comparative studies between the two regions with the same name and shared history. Like in many other cases, majority of tourists gravitate towards big cities and coastal areas, often overlooking smaller destination and cross-border areas like Macedonia. Despite challenges in policy, legal frameworks, infrastructure, and political instability (with the recent agreement on the name of North Macedonia), coupled with European funds for regional development, this region still holds great potential to become more competitive, visible, and attractive.

In the last two years leading up to the 2019 report, North Macedonia's tourism has experienced a decrease in competitiveness, as indicated in Travel & Tourism Competitiveness Report 2019 released by the World Economic Forum. This biannual report, focusing more on investment potential factors than on the country's attractiveness as a tourist destination, saw North Macedonia decline by 12 positions, ranking 101st out of the 140 participating countries.

According to Macedonia News (17.9.19), several aspects of the nation's performance experienced significant deterioration:

1. **Business Environment**: The ranking dropped from 40th to 84th
2. **Human Resources and Labor Market**: A decline from 83rd to 108th
3. **Safety and Security:** A substantial decrease from 56th to 95th
4. **T&T Prioritization**: A decline from 85th to 114th
5. **International Openness**: A drop from 93rd to 119th
6. **Ground Infrastructure**: A notable decrease from 62nd to 104th

In comparison, neighbouring countries and the broader region fared better:

- **Greece** secured the 25th position with a score of 4.5 points
- **Croatia** ranked 27th with the same score of 4.5 points
- **Montenegro** achieved the 67th position with 3.9 points
- **Serbia** stood at 83rd place with 3.6 points.

Interestingly, Greece's ranking declined since 2017. In the Europe-Eurasia ranking, Greece currently holds the 15th position, with a score of 4.5, while Spain leads with 5.4 points.

Let's delve into specific aspects of Greece's travel and tourism sector:

- **Policy and Enabling Conditions**: Greece ranks 26th

- **Infrastructure**: it also excels, securing the 26th position
- **Natural and Cultural Resources**: Greece shines at 25th, showcasing its rich heritage
- **Health and Hygiene**: an impressive 13th position
- **Effective Prioritization**: Greece ranks 13th in this category
- **Air Transport Infrastructure**: it stands out at 18th

Areas for improvement:

- **Environmental Sustainability**: Greece ranks 37th
- **Ground and Port Infrastructure**: a 49th position
- **Natural Resources**: it stands at 45th
  Strengths:
- **Tourist Services**: an excellent 18th position
- **Cultural Resources and Business Travel**: both rank 21st

Overall, Greece's tourism sector demonstrates a mix of strengths and areas for enhancement, making it a fascinating destination for travelers.

In less positive news, according to GTP headlines (6.9.19), Greece faces challenges in certain aspects of its tourism sector. The country is ranked 119th for business environment, indicating room for improvement in this area. Safety and security are areas of concern, with Greece positioned at 61st, and the human resources and labor market ranking at 59th. In terms of Information and Communication Technology (ICT) readiness, Greece holds the 51st position. Price competitiveness is an area that requires attention, as Greece ranks 111th, highlighting potential concerns for cost-related competitiveness. Additionally, the country stands at 58th in terms of enabling the environment, indicating aspects that may impact overall tourism.

"As international connectedness continues to rise, we see travel and tourism competitiveness continue to grow," says Christoph Wolff, head of mobility at World Economic Forum. *"Increased tourism is bringing great benefits to many economies but must be managed properly by both policymakers and businesses for a sustainable future."*

For economies where tourism represents the largest source of income, studies of this kind are crucial. In the case of North Macedonia, such research serves to support and justify to the local stakeholders the necessity to further investment and involvement in its development, aiding in a better understanding of appropriate strategies and vision. One of the contributions of this thesis is to provide insights for the practitioners in the tourism policymaking and destination management, attempting to contribute to the body of knowledge on destination competitiveness, culture and heritage tourism and regional clusters.

Clusters: Classifications in European and World Context

Clusters can be classified by specialization and geography (Micic, 2010). Examples include export-import-oriented, local industry, and local affiliates of competitors. Virtual or internet clusters offer advantages like faster development and efficient communication.

The concept of an industrial district refers to the aggregation of many clusters in a region, interconnected into specific sectors. In the EU, nearly 40% of the employees work for a company that is a part of a cluster. The most successful ones are in Italy, Spain, Germany, Switzerland, and Belgium though the tourism clusters are not as prevalent. In the USA, the cluster development involves close collaboration between the entrepreneurs, regional and local governments as well as the universities and research and service centres. In England, the initiative begins with regional development agencies, and in Austria, collaboration occurs between research centres and the private sector.

Regional Clusters: Motor Valley Cluster, Italy

Alberti and Giusti (2012) argue that clusters can enhance the regional competitiveness, foster innovation, efficiently address customer needs, and contribute to the relations with other organizations and institutions. Micic (2010) suggests that a strict definition of clusters may be detrimental from a competitiveness standpoint, as the borders of clusters seldom align with standard market and industrial classifications.

Recognizing the influence of heritage and culture on regional competitiveness (Sasaki, 2004, as cited in Alberti and Giusti, 2012) marks a departure from historical rejection and neglect (Florida, 2002; Hesmonhalgh, 2002; Scott, 2002, as cited in Alberti and Giusti, 2012). However, determining destination competitiveness is not solely reliant on rigid determinants (man-made, natural, and cultural) but should also consider an "overall appeal" (Cracolici, Nijkamp, 2009, as cited in Armenski et al., 2011).

Additionally, tourism is being used by government agencies to justify the conservation of tangible heritage, but it has been done so without a demonstrated market demand for these assets by tourists. Likewise, the local Destination Marketing Organization (DMO) promotes all listed heritage structures as potential cultural tourism attractions, again without demonstrating market interest in visiting these places (McKercher, Ho and du Cross (2005)).

The Motor Valley in Italy, an inter-regional cluster blending history, culture, and heritage rich industrial tradition (Alberti and Giusti, 2012), stands in contrast to the still embryonic stages of such clusters in Serbia and Macedonia (Micic, 2010). The creation and development of clusters, alongside increased innovation, and start-ups growth of the innovation, undoubtedly impact overall productivity, regional promotion, and its competitiveness, and influence corporate organisations, educational institutions, and government entities.

In the findings of Iazzi, Rosato and Gravili's study, a key section focuses on developing networks in the implementation of projects in the Destination Cities. The concept of culture integration as a community developmental source is recognized by other studies. The level of frequency of contacts between the culture asset managers and DMO representatives is lower than with the entrepreneurs, institutions, professional associations, or trade unions. From a technical standpoint, cultural values in this context represent developmental or territorial capital. The critical challenge lies in the fact that both locals and visitors own and consume the destination and its culture, emphasizing the need to contribute to positive impacts from socio-cultural, economic, and environmental perspectives.

Due to the similarities among countries situated on the Balkan Peninsula, as outlined in Metodijeski and Temelkov (2014), the creation of a common regional - Balkan tourist product is crucial. Following the establishment of this product After the formation of this product, the next step should involve joint presence on the international tourism market as well as mutual promotion. In Motor Valley Cluster case, the initiatives of the industrial cluster and its entrepreneurs helped in creating new tourism themes. These themes, packages and activities for the tourists are created under the umbrella of the Motor Valley brand, contributing both to the volume and the value of tourism (Alberti & Giusti, 2012).

South Africa Cluster: Tourism Collaborative Action Analysis

In South Africa, post-Apartheid, tourism faced challenges like security perceptions, inadequate marketing, and skilled workforce shortages. National Clustering involved 650 participants, while Thematic Clustering focused on ecotourism and heritage tourism. Ecotourism success improved international representation and attracted investments. Heritage tourism offered unique experiences. Stakeholders established a National Heritage Association, fostering public-private partnerships. Practical guidelines emerged from local cluster pilots.

Although the results were positive at all the levels, it appears that the most immediate motivation for local participants was the clear benefit on a personal level. This empowers them in making decisions and helps them in measuring the outcomes. On a national level, collaboration was considered as necessary, given the systemic nature of tourism, and ideally governed by a small group of decision-makers.

The Critical Issues in Proposed Theoretical Framework and Empirical Studies: The Ritchie and Crouch (2003) and Dwyer's Model (2003)

According to Armenski et al. (2011), Dwyer's Integrated model introduced the element of the mutual dependence between the various attributes of the destination since the Destination Competitiveness model lacked this connection and was more linear and unidirectional.

The Integrated model also distinguishes natural from cultural and historical sources, whereas in Ritchie and Crouch's model they were placed in one core attribute group. A variety of studies has attempted to apply and discuss the destination competitiveness concept. One of the key identified limitations is the single-aspect approach in majority of these researches. According to Goffi (2013), there was a lack of holistic approach and comprehensive framework with various elements and components crosschecked. Nevertheless, Ritchie & Crouch's model (2000, 2003), applied in this study, is the most renowned conceptual model, empirically tested on more than 80 destinations worldwide (excluding North or Greek Macedonia). This model consists of 36 distinguished nodes that classify the competitiveness into seven key levels and factors. According to Dwyer and Kim (2003) this model can be translated into specific indicators, including new key factors demand and situational conditions which contribute the competitiveness of the destination.

For example, "tourism policy, planning and development" and "destination management", though grouped together in a larger context, are also interlinked. This reflects that the "destination management" ensures the economic sustainability, short term actions, and strives to maintain the competitiveness of the destination.

For a destination to achieve success, it must adopt a coordinated approach to policymaking, planning, management, and development (Ritchie & Crouch, 2003). While tourism policy establishes a framework for long-term competitive destination development, destination management focuses on various factors within a shorter time horizon. The goal is to ensure economic profitability while safeguarding the elements that constitute the destination's competitive position (Crouch & Ritchie, 1999).

There is a critical comparison and contrast exist between the two proposed models in Goffi's (2013) study. The main elements are presented here and further used in the research design and discussion, particularly Destination Management and Destination Policy, Planning, and Development for coding and themes in the analysis. Depending on the source, the Ritchie and Crouch model is sometimes referred to as Crouch and Ritchie, and there are several versions in different years of publication.

Review of Models, Definitions, and Determinants of Tourism Destination Competitiveness

In the article by Andrades-Caldito, Sanchez-Rivero, and Pulido-Fernandez (2014), the determinants of tourism destination competitiveness are examined from the demand perspective point of view and how these determinants influence tourists' choices. The rationale is that, ultimately, tourists make the decision about whether to choose a destination or not. While many studies (Gnoth & Knobloch, 2012; Leask, 2010; Tung & Ritchie, 2011; Buhalis, 2000; Crouch, 2007; Dwyer & Kim, 2003; Hu & Ritchie, 1993; Song & Witt, 2000) have explored attributes and their impact on the tourism destination competitiveness from the supply side (DMO, experts, service providers), there is a need to understand and empirically test the models from the demand perspective. This article establishes links between the model determinants and the influence of their relationship within tourism destination competitiveness. The methodology used was the Structural Equation Model, and the study was conducted in Andalusia. The survey distributed 19,423 questionnaires.

In a similar study, Cvelbar, Dwyer, Koman and Mihalic (2016) discuss the lack of common agreement on the definition of destination competitiveness. Various definitions have been proposed, including the one by Ritchie and Crouch (2007) stating that *"what makes a tourism destination truly competitive is its ability to increase tourism expenditure to increasingly attract visitors, while providing them with satisfying, memorable experiences, and to do so in a profitable way, while enhancing the well-being of destination residents and preserving the natural capital of the destination for future generations."* Dwyer, Forsythe, and Rao (2000) refer to it as *"a general concept that encompasses price differentials coupled with exchange rate movements, productivity levels of various components of the tourist industry, and qualitative factors affecting the attractiveness or otherwise of a destination."*

In the article by Goffi and Cucculelli (2014), the case of small destinations in Italy was investigated using the sets of indicators from the conceptual model of Ritchie and Crouch (2000). The study tested these indicators on 610 small destinations in Italy. The research adds value to the original model by identifying a set of nine indicators that enhance the analysis process. Notably, these indicators predominantly focus on sustainability, as emphasized by the statement that sustainability is *"illusory without sustainability"* (Ritchie and Crouch, 2000). Interestingly, while the model has primarily been tested on well-established and developed destinations (such as countries and regions), it has not been extensively applied to smaller destinations. In countries with rich cultural heritage, especially those with fragmented landscapes, many small places receive a significant influx of visitors. Surprisingly, this pattern has not received sufficient attention in the existing literature. The study sheds light on the importance of considering sustainability and the unique characteristics of smaller destinations in the context of tourism competitiveness.

Theoretical and conceptual models have been developed to assess the destination competitiveness, with empirical models such as those proposed by Sirse and Mihalic (1999), Dwyer et al (2003), Enright and Newton (2004), Gomezelj and Mihalic (2008). Despite the unanimous recognition of sustainability as a crucial issue, its measurement has not been fully addressed from all perspectives and dimensions.

Another important study by Mihalic and Aramberri (2015) highlights the differences between the WEF report, which includes 14 pillars, and the study by Goffi and Cucculelli (2014), which proposed nine pillars. The latter study utilized the PCA method. Additionally, Torres-Delgado and Palomeque (2014) conducted a multiple case study involving municipalities. They applied an indicator system to measure the level of sustainability at the destination. A total of 26 indicators were used and applied to over 20 municipalities in Catalonia, Spain. The data collection method employed was a Delphi survey. The findings demonstrate that this approach was an effective tool for planning and managing tourism at the municipal level.

Destination Branding in Central and Eastern European Countries

According to Morgan and Pritchard (1998), there are at least three major barriers in Central and Eastern European countries concerning destination branding and the development of well-focused and efficient communication strategy. These barriers include a lack of appropriate financial support and effective marketing research and campaigns due to inexperience in different markets and a shortage of educated experts. Another challenge is the pressure on the marketers and the destination to deliver short-term results in a context that requires long-term investment. Long-term strategies are essential for designing and maintaining brand consistency. Lastly, the difference between centralized communist regimes and the market economies lies in the level of control and coherence over the multitude of parts and elements that constitute a destination's product, image, and environments.

Critics of this paper might focus on the broad categorization Central and Eastern European countries, which spans from Slovenia and the Czech Republic in the West to the post-Soviet countries like Dagestan, Kyrgyzstan, and Kazakhstan. Although the political climate and the communist regime created similar tourism environments and influenced planning and policies, the differences lie in the competitive and comparative advantages of these now independent countries, which remain extremely varied.

New opportunities for the segmentation and marketing of Central and Eastern European tourism have emerged. At the national level, some mutual mainstream lines have been adopted to establish a brand image through uniqueness, accessibility, security, and ecological friendliness (Morgan, Pritchard, and Pride 2004). On the destination level, the focus has largely been on cultural and heritage tourism destinations to align with European heritage standards, as noted by Blonski (1998). In the late 80s and early 90s, branding across Central and Eastern Europe (CEE) was a significant endeavour. This branding aimed to establish new brand requirements for countries in transition, including Yugoslavia and Albania. The focus was on creating a "more European image", fostering customer loyalty, achieving market differentiation, and most importantly, dissociating from the communist past and the regional instability that characterized past era. During this period, special interest tourism in the entire Central and Eastern Europe became immensely popular among Western Europeans. Guides and operators encouraged the construction of an image of the socialist past as something exotic and romantic for the Western gaze. Meanwhile, the local populations grappled with the challenge of dissociating from their communist heritage while navigating economic realities. This dilemma is defined as "identity versus economy" (Light 2000; Tunbridge 1994 as cited in Light, 2007).

Internationally renowned groups such as S Team Bates Saatchi & Saatchi Advertising Balkans, along with Western organizations like Millennium PR of London, played significant roles in Serbia's tourism marketing campaigns. Considerable effort went into creating modern and imaginative websites, establishing an online presence, and developing effective marketing messages and logos as branding tools, as exemplified by the Slovenian Tourist Board in 2003.

Morgan, Pritchard, and Pride (2004) elaborate on the evolving market demands and the positioning of the Balkans. Unfortunately, the region often carries a pejorative image in the Western world due to its location on the western edge of the Islamic world. This perception emphasizes diversity, fractures, and conflict. The aftermath of the war in the ex-Yugoslav republics during the 1990s and their subsequent independence perpetuated this image. However, certain countries, such as Slovenia and Croatia, actively sought to dissociate themselves from the common past shared with neighboring countries. Their goal was to create a new national image — a crucial step for both tourism development and the formulation of a national tourism strategy.

Themes and Codes: Theory Based Key Words and Factors

The thematic codes for the analysis segment of the thesis are based on 15 factors (keywords) that are not directly mentioned in the questions posed to the respondents.

These themes were derived from the findings of Loulanski and Loulanski's (2011) paper. Their cross-disciplinary thematic investigation explored the intricate relationship between cultural heritage and tourism. The study systematically examined theories, concepts, strategies, and policies related to this dynamic interplay. The research covered 483 reviews of the studies using the same data analysis software

(NVivo). Employing meta-ethnography as the approach, the findings were grouped into categories, resulting in 15 synthesis factors that emerged as particularly important for the sustainable development of heritage and tourism. It systematically compiles evidence on concepts, policies, and strategies, offering an interpretive synthesis that sheds light on the critical factors identified by researchers for the sustainable integration of heritage and tourism. The ultimate goal is to achieve consilience—a convergence of knowledge—ushering in a 'new age of synthesis". These factors include local involvement, education and training, authenticity and interpretation, sustainability-centered tourism management, integrated planning, incorporation into a broader sustainable development framework, controlled growth, governance and stakeholder participation, market and product diversification, suitable funding provision, international governance and support systems, a heritage capital approach, effective site management, destination management and a sound theoretical/methodological base. These 15 factors are proposed as the fundamental components for a more effective theoretical framework, and evidence-based policy in the fields of cultural heritage and tourism, with the goal of achieving sustainability. The four overarching themes selected from these factors are presented in the Table 2 below. The codes are mostly named after the nodes in the Ritchie and Crouch (2003) Model, with the only addition being the dissonant heritage as found in the literature review.

Table 2. Codes and overarching themes in this thesis

Culture/Historical and cultural resources	Incorporation of heritage and tourism into a wider sustainable development framework
Clusters/competitive and collaborative analysis/Organization/Vision	Governance and stakeholder participation
Dissonant heritage/heritage	A heritage capital approach
Destination management/destination policy, planning and development/destination competitiveness/efficiency/infrastructure and tourism superstructure	Destination Management

The criteria for keyword search included terms related to sustainability, heritage, heritage and cultural tourism, as well as destination management, addressing over 600 sources from all top tier academic journals (Annals of Tourism Research, Journal of Sustainable Tourism, International Journal of Heritage Studies, Journal of Travel Research, Current Issues in Tourism, Tourism Management, International Journal of Tourism Research, Journal of Cultural Heritage, Planning and Research, Cities, Journal of Heritage Tourism, Progress in Tourism and Hospitality Research, Tourism Geographies and Journal of Ecotourism). Considering the factors derived from this extensive search, the Overarching themes for the thesis were formulated, incorporating both tangible and intangible heritage.

In the Tables 3, 4, 5, 6 below, there are four key factors that were used as Parent codes (Overarching themes): A heritage Capital approach, Destination Management, Incorporation of CH and tourism in the Sustainable development framework and policy and Integrated governance and stakeholder participation.

Table 3. Adapted from Loulanski and Loulanski's – Heritage Capital approach (Overarching theme)

Factors for the sustainable integration of cultural heritage and tourism: principles and tools	Unsustainable features and practices
12. "Heritage Capital" approach	
Shift to a capital approach in heritage management (recognition of heritage as integrative capital intrinsic to SD, focus on conservation and sustainable use, local resource management	Exploitation of resources; lack of conservation economics knowledge and its application; lack of protective legislation; seasonal, short-termed development
Planning and management for heritage sustainability (sustainability criteria, capacity and impact assessment, precautionary principle, etc.)	
Valuation and valorization of heritage assets (holistic approach: cultural and economic values, benefits, and costs; tangible and intangible aspects)	

Table 4. Adapted from Loulanski and Loulanski's – Destination Management (Overarching theme)

14. Destination management	Unsustainable features and practices
Destination management principles (priority of destination management over tourism management, place-specific approach, functional diversity, etc.)	Lack of financial viability; lack of administrative transparency; land fragmentation; miscalculation of real costs borne by the community; conflict over use
Employment of destination management tools (carrying capacities assessment – physical, economic, social, cultural, ecological, political; cultural landscape approach. Destination development scenario planning, area self-reliance and profitability management, integrated transportation and infra network, zoning of managed destinations, aggregate indicators measurement, accountable annual evaluation and monitoring, authority control, etc.)	

Table 5. Incorporation of CH and tourism in the Sustainable development framework and policy (Overarching theme)

6. Incorporation of CH and tourism in the SD framework and policy	Unsustainable features and practices
Commitment to the principles of SD: ecologically responsible, socially compatible, culturally appropriate, politically equitable, technologically supportive, and economically viable for community	Dominance of the old "modernization" paradigm and ineffective development patterns; growth-oriented policies; weak cross-sectoral linkages (economy-society-culture-environment)
Integration of both tourism and cultural heritage as part of destination and resource planning	
Employment of SD planning tools (long-term vision, holistic planning, synergy of TD goals and development vision, complementary and integrated policies, resource management and sustainable use of resources, localization of benefits, local capacity-building, best scenario approach, etc.)	

Table 6. Integrated governance ad stakeholder participation (Overarching theme)

8. Integrated governance and stakeholder participation	Unsustainable features and practices
Government leadership, management, and support (institution building, strategy and policymaking, legislation, planning, financing, regulation, etc.)	Peripherality of both heritage and tourism governing bodies; overreliance on market mechanisms; lack of collaboration and responsibilities delineation; lack of leadership and governance skills; low feasibility regulations; fuzzy legislation, poor intervention on negative impacts.
Radical rethinking of planning priorities, commitment to SD vision and framework	
Synchronized national, regional, and local governance and legislation, enforcement and delineation of responsibility	
Government – industry – community communication, negotiation, and partnership schemes (consensus-building, independent managerial structures like partnerships, trusts, community councils, cooperatives, taskforces, etc.)	
Inter-ministerial cooperation and harmonization of objectives, policies, substrategies, and plans for long-term viability (formal agreements on TD and cross-sectoral linkages, collaboration between national and local authorities)	

UNESCO, much like many heritage practitioners, proposes a very detailed categorization of cultural heritage types. The controversy lies in its dual nature, encompassing both cultural and economic values and functions. "*Heritage is understood as "culture and landscape that are cared for by the community" and "passed on to the future to serve people's need for a sense of identity and belonging;" however, on the negative side, heritage is considered equal to the "heritage industry," which has become "synonymous with the manipulation (or even invention) and exploitation of the past for commercial ends.""*

Dissonant Heritage in Balkan States

In Tomka's study (2015), seven research articles were published in a single issue of a special magazine, addressing various aspects of destination and cultural tourism development in the Balkan region. The contributors include authors from both within ((Bosnia and Herzegovina, Montenegro, Serbia) and outside the Balkans, providing diverse perspectives on the historical context and its consequences on the region today. While the conclusions and recommendations were similar across the different states, the consensus is that the consequences need to be overcome, and tourism can play a positive role in this regard. Some of the papers explored the potential of wine tourism development (e.g, John Hundelson's "Eastern Promises: The Potential Future for Wine Tourism in the Balkans") and preservation of the natural environment and ecology ("Responsible Community Based Ecotourism Initiatives in Protected Rural Areas of the Balkans: Case Studies from Serbia and Croatia" by Đukić, Volić, Tišma and Jelinčić). Others took more philosophical and anthropological approach. One of the key papers, by Šešić-Dragičević, M. and Rogač-Mijatović, Lj., titled "Balkan Dissonant Heritage Narratives (and Their Attractiveness) for Tourism", addresses the different tools and solutions of dissonant heritage restoration in the Balkan countries. The authors emphasize: *"Cultural heritage is often seen as an important factor in explaining the post-socialist landscape of the Balkans. In terms of symbolic geography, the Balkans has been and still remains inserted in the long-standing binary oppositions East - West, Europe - Asia, Christianity - Islam, Centre - Periphery, etc. These are in variations present also in travel writing through the dominant negative label of Western travel accounts. In investigating the historical heritage of the Balkans and its dissonant narratives, we put focus on those that left the deepest imprint on the region's multilayered identity: the Byzantine, the Ottoman and the communist / socialist."*

A diverse array of narratives and themes emerge in the context of the Balkan dissonant legacy. It is conclusively recognized that when creating new tourist products, these stories must be thoughtfully taken into consideration.

The researchers state: *"Only tourism might contribute to overcoming barriers – contemporary borders of nation-states, lack of mediated information, and deliberate manipulation through school manuals, memory site recognition and narrative creation. Raising the collective consciousness throughout the Balkans for the most important cultural sites and their incorporation into tourist routes as common products, is imposed as the first task in creating attractiveness for tourists outside the Balkan region. By mapping specific points related to Balkan cultural heritage we tried to point out numerous possibilities which exist for cultural tourism beyond border development (through cultural routes as an instrument)."* This research provides recommendations concerning the diverse range of interpretative possibilities. It highlights recently developed themed routes and collaborative efforts at various levels involving narratives, content development, and the promotion of the Balkans as a distinctive cultural area and a complex social and political region. Is this the *"very way it should be presented to tourists"*?

In his exploration of Dracula tourism in Romania, cultural identity, and state Light (2007) explains how Stoker made the lasting myth of the place in the East (Transylvania) as "social and spatial Other". It refers to a place that is on the periphery, devoid of modernity and lacking in Western progress. Using the term "Balkanism," Todorova (1995), as cited in Light (2007), addresses the understanding and analysis from a colonial context, wherein the West generates discourses and myths about people as Others. Balkanism encapsulate the ambiguous bridge or crossroad in Southeast Europe. *"Therefore, Dracula is clearly an early expression of the Balkanist discourse. The novel is insistent on the opposition between 'Western progress and Eastern stasis, between Western science and Eastern superstition, between Western reason and Eastern emotion, between Western civilization and Eastern barbarism''* (Arata 1990, p. 637 as cited in Light, 2007)

Literature on Heritage

During the late 1980s and early 1990s, European unity and identity emerged as significant topics, contrasting with individual state identities and nationalisms (Ashworth, 1994). Countries in the former Soviet bloc, as well as the Balkan countries, entered an era where they sought to strengthen their statehood while diminishing the lingering memories of communist control. This shift was partly driven by the desire to access the perceived material benefits and consumerism associated with Western European countries.

One of the key questions for the new Europe in the 1990s was whether the trend of fragmentation would persist and whether interpretations of national heritages would further divide the community. In 1992, some researchers and conferences examined the popularity of these themes and explored their potential positive impact on the identification and awareness of heritage, as well as the planning and understanding of their scale and nature. *"The likely exploitation of heritage in creating identity in the emerging small states is under-researched. There is a variety of conservation/ heritage ethics, without a common doctrine or a single approach. "*

Ashworth's book contends that history, representing the events of the past, is frequently harnessed to shape socio-cultural place-identities in alignment with specific state structures. This thesis examines European-related cases, although this situation is not strictly confined to Europe. However, the unique timing in the 1990s presents a challenge: using European history to shape these new entities. In this specific research, the supranational scale was chosen for state-building, as opposed to other scales such as local, regional, or national, which are typically more established and advanced.

Other major modern functions of history, apart from the socio-cultural ones, include psychological, individual, and collective needs, "so that the comfort of the past may anchor the excitement of the future" (Lynch, 1972 as cited in Ashworth, 2003). The transmission of societal norms and standards to younger generations is a fundamental purpose of museums, integral to their existence. Museums serve as educational institutions, playing a pivotal role in imparting cultural values, historical perspectives, and ethical principles to the youth. In political science research, past events are narrated to the present to reinforce current political ideologies and their power, justifying them in an appealing fashion. Economic reasons and interests have been recently joined this consideration.

For modern purposes and functions, it is not history but "heritage" that used to examine, define, and understand processes to achieve specific objectives. The relationship between locality (destination) and identity, as well as the connection between heritage and locality, is significant. From this understanding, the need arises to develop strategies for shaping destination identities and enhancing their competitiveness by leveraging heritage.

Approaches in heritage

There are three different approaches focused upon buildings as monuments, marking an evolutionary process in European concerns for preserving artifacts and historical structures (Ashworth, 2003). These approaches include preservation, predominantly during the first hundred years of European history, followed by conservation in the 1960s, and, most recently, a shift towards a market-oriented perspective that treats historical relics as products. This approach is demand-driven and managed within the market. The necessity of process model research arises to elucidate this phenomenon through the lens of marketing discipline.

According to McKercher et al. (2005), there is an almost unlimited range of potential cultural heritage assets. As they all have very particular group of stakeholders there are also many potential relationships between them. The differences between tangible and intangible heritage range from individual buildings to towns, cities, and countries to the languages, traditions, art, performances, events. and culture of the local communities. These categories of assets may have private, public, or mixed, community-based ownership, leading to variations in consumption from private to public. Trends have also evolved in terms of definition but also with regards to the contemporary role of heritage in societies, decision-making process, the involvement of from different sectors as well as its significance and interpretation.

The Commodification Process, Resources, Interpretation Process and Heritage Product

"History is the remembered record of the past: heritage is a contemporary commodity purposefully created to satisfy contemporary consumption". With commodification, one becomes the other. The main hypothesis is that heritage becomes a tradable product like in any other industry.

The mixture of events, historical facts, popular art, mythologies, poetry, and places is associated with symbolic meaning to be utilized as resources.

Transformation of historical resources into tourism products involves interpretation, storytelling, packaging, and selection. However, design, selection, and presentation of history-derived products are viewed from a marketing perspective, emphasizing a demand-led approach.

After undergoing various processes and stages, the final heritage product implies a different meaning from the ones in Oxford Dictionary (*Valued objects and qualities such as historic buildings and cultural traditions that have been passed down from previous generations*). Heritage is defined not only in relation to a single user but also as a rich palette encompassing many existing heritages. These heritage experiences can be tailored for various groups or customer segments (for instance: Turks visiting Macedonia after films and series, birthplace of Ataturk, Serbians visiting monasteries, US visiting the birthplace of Alexander the Great). In the end, heritage products are distinct and personalized, forging a meaningful connection at the very instant of consumption.

Ashworth (2003) highlights two crucial characteristics that define this model of heritage product development. The first one is a demand-led approach, meaning it is shaped by the requests and expectations of tourists rather than being solely resource-based. Instead of focusing solely on available resources, the emphasis is on creating experiences that align with what tourists desire. Another important aspect is the careful selection process, which depends on a variety of factors. Some heritage may have been physically damaged, nonexistent, or erased from national memory. Therefore, the range of heritage products is deliberately preselected, and the decision-making power lies with those who plan and execute, considering dimensions beyond the purely economic, such as political and social aspects.

CONCLUSION - HOMOGENOUS VS HETEROGENOUS TOURISM PRODUCTS

Creating a uniform tourism product within a destination as a state significantly reduces a range of marketing endeavors. These include branding, shaping the destination's image, and minimizing interpretive ambiguities. Simultaneously, it satisfies the domestic target market and other main groups of tourists. A few easily recognizable elements of the local culture and heritage, including some personalities, myths, and qualities, simplify the process, especially in the early development phases when the destination is still relatively unknown to the foreign travelers.

However, this is impossible in the Balkan region and more specifically in North Macedonia, Greece, and neighbouring countries. This would mean that certain minority groups would be ignored on a small or large scale while history is hijacked by the predominant ethnicity or social class. Assessing the sustainability of such an approach is challenging as it depends on the value of national unity and the competitiveness of the national image compared to other states. Even more concerning is the degradation and impoverishment of a country's heritage, product range, and product differentiation. It is crucial to diversify the product geographically and reduce concentration to promote dispersal. This shift is especially relevant during the current pandemic, where physical distancing is imperative. Tourism, in this context, has the potential to enhance cross-border collaboration, improve the political climate, and support regional development while fostering cultural tolerance.

REFERENCES

(2018, May 15). Récupéré sur economy.gov.mk: http://economy.gov.mk/Upload/Documents/Kohl%20&%20Partner_Tourism%20Strategy%20Macedonia_DRAFT%20FINAL%20REPORT_16%2002%2023_E.pdf

(2020, August 20). Récupéré sur https://travel2macedonia.com: https://travel2macedonia.com/destinations/ohrid/history-culture

https://ec.europa.eu/regional_policy/en/atlas/programmes/2007-2013/crossborder/greece-the-former-yugoslav-republic-of-macedonia-ipa-cross-border-co-operation-programme-2007-2013. (2020, October 1). Récupéré sur https://ec.europa.eu: https://ec.europa.eu/regional_policy/en/atlas/programmes/2007-2013/crossborder/greece-the-former-yugoslav-republic-of-macedonia-ipa-cross-border-co-operation-programme-2007-2013

(2020, September 13). Récupéré sur https://www.undp.org: https://www.undp.org/content/dam/the_former_yugoslav_republic_of_macedonia/docs/Tourism%20Strategy.pdf

Abreu-Novais, M., Ruhanen, L., & Arcodia, C. (2016, May 11). Destination competitiveness: What we know, what we know but shouldn't and what we don't know but should. *Current Issues in Tourism*, 19(6), 492–512. DOI: 10.1080/13683500.2015.1091443

Alberti, F., & Giusti, J. (2012). Cultural heritage, tourism and regional competitiveness: The Motor Valley cluster. *City Culture and Society*, 3(4), 261–273. DOI: 10.1016/j.ccs.2012.11.003

Andreopolou, Z., Leandros, N., Quaranta, G., & Salvia, R. (2016). *Tourism and New Media* (Zacharoula Andreopoulou, N. L., Ed.). Vol. 2). FrancoAngeli.

Arber, A. (2006). Reflexivity: A challenge for the researcher as practitioner? *Journal of Research in Nursing*, 11(2), 147–157. DOI: 10.1177/1744987106056956

Armenski, T., Gomezelj, D., Djurdjev, B., Djeri, L., & Dragin, A. (2011). Destination competitiveness: a challenging process for Serbia. Human Geographies -Journal of studies and research in Human Geography, 19-33.

Ashworth, G. J., & Larkham, P. J. (1994). Building a new heritage: tourism, culture, and identity in the new Europe. London; New York: Routledge.

Babbie, E. (2007). The practice of social research (éd. 11). Belmont: Thompson Wadsworth.

BBC. (2019, January 25). https://www.bbc.com/news/world-europe-46971182. Consulté le 2020, sur www.bbc.com

Blonski, K. (1998). *Krakow 2000: European City of Culture*. Voivodship.

Crouch, G. (2010). Destination Competitiveness: An Analysis of Determinant Attributes. *Journal of Travel Research*.

Cvelbar, L., Dwyer, L., Koman, M., & Mihalic, T. (2016). Drivers of destination competitiveness in tourism: A global investigation. *Journal of Travel Research*, 55(8), 1041–1050. DOI: 10.1177/0047287515617299

Cvelbar, L. K., Dwyer, L., & Mihalic, T. (2015, December). Drivers of Destination Competitiveness in Tourism: A Global Investigation. *Journal of Travel Research*, 55(8), 1041–1050. Advance online publication. DOI: 10.1177/0047287515617299

Denscombe, M. (2008). Communities of Practice: A Research Paradigm for the Mixed Methods Approach. *Journal of Mixed Methods Research*, 2(3), 270–283. DOI: 10.1177/1558689808316807

Denzin, N., & Lincoln, Y. (2011). *The SAGE Handbook of Qualitative Research*. SAGE Publisher.

Emden, M. S. (1998). Qualitative metasynthesis: Issues and techniques. *Research in Nursing & Health*.

Fallery, B. R. (2007). *Quatre approches pour l'analyse de données textuelles: lexicale, linguistique, cognitive, thématique. Conference: Actes de la XVIème Conférence Internationale de l'Association Internationale de Management Stratégique*. AIMS.

Fernando, I. (2015). What competitive strategies way forward the regional competitiveness, A comparative economic approach to Sri Lankan tourism. *International Journal of Business and Management*, 10(4), 178–186. DOI: 10.5539/ijbm.v10n4p178

Fernando, I. L. (2012). New Conceptual Model on Cluster Competitiveness: A New Paradigm for Tourism? *International Journal of Biometrics*.

Georgiev, G., & Vasileva, M. (2012). Tangible and intangible cultural heritage in the Western Balkan countries and tourism development. Tourism and Hospitality Management Conference proceedings, (pp. 501-506).

G.I., C. (2007). Modelling destination competitiveness, A survey and analysis of the impacts of competitiveness attributes. Sustainable tourism cooperative Research centre report.

Goffi, G. (2013, November). A Model of Tourism Destination Competitiveness: The case of the Italian Destinations of Excellence. *Anuario Turismo y Sociedad*, 14, 121–147.

Goffi, G., & Cucculelli, M. (2014, December). Components of Destination Competitiveness. The case of Small Tourism Destinations in Italy. *International Journal of Tourism Policy*, 5(4), 296–326. DOI: 10.1504/IJTP.2014.068035

Hakim, C. (2000). *Research Design: Successful Designs for Social and Economic Research*. Psychology Press.

Hribar, M. B. (2017). Participatory research in community development: A case study of creating cultural tourism products. (U. Karlova, Éd.) Acta Universitatis Carolinae. Geographica, 52(2), 1-12. DOI: 10.14712/23361980.2017.13

Iazzi, A., Rosato, P., & Gravili, S. (2015). Competitive processes in tourism destinations: The role of intangible assets. *International Journal of Management*.

Jankowicz, A. (2005). *Business Research Projects*. Thomson Learning.

Karadjoski, M. (2013). *Cross-border Cooperation between Macedonia and Greece as an Instrument for Good Neighbourhood Relations*. The Balkans Dialogue Conference 2013. Institute for Cultural Relations Policy.

Kolehmainen, J., Irvine, J., Stewart, L., Karacsonyi, Z., Szabo, T., Alarinta, J., & Norberg, A. (2015). Quadruple Helix, Innovation and the Knowledge-Based Development: Lessons from Remote, Rural and Less-Favoured Regions. *Journal of the Knowledge Economy*.

Krstic, B., Jovanovic, S., & Stanisic, T. (2015). Central and East European countries' tourism competitiveness as a factor of their national competitiveness level. Journal of tourism studies and research in tourism, 18, 61-68.

Lewis, J. R. (2006). Qualitative Research Practice: A Guide for Social Science Students and Researchers (éd. 2). SAGE Publications.

Light, D. (2007). Dracula tourism in Romania: Cultural identity and the state. *Annals of Tourism Research*, 34(3), 746–765. DOI: 10.1016/j.annals.2007.03.004

Loulanski, T. (2006, May). Revising the Concept for Cultural Heritage: The Argument for a Functional Approach. *International Journal of Cultural Property*, 13(2). Advance online publication. DOI: 10.1017/S0940739106060085

Loulanski, V. L., & Loulanski, V. (2011). The sustainable integration of cultural heritage and tourism: A meta-study. *Journal of Sustainable Tourism*, 19(7), 837–862. DOI: 10.1080/09669582.2011.553286

Mason, J. (1996). *Qualitative Researching*. SAGE Publications.

Mckercher, B., Ho, P., & du Cros, H. (2004, April). Attributes of popular cultural attractions in Hong Kong. *Annals of Tourism Research*, 31(2), 393–407. DOI: 10.1016/j.annals.2003.12.008

McKercher, B., Ho, P., & du Cross, H. (2005, August). Relationship between tourism and cultural heritage management: Evidence from Hong Kong. *Tourism Management*, 26(4), 539–548. DOI: 10.1016/j.tourman.2004.02.018

Metodijeski, D., & Temelkov, Z. (2014). Tourism policy of Balkan countries: Review of national tourism development strategies. *UTMS Journal of Economics (Skopje)*, 5(2), 231–239.

Micic, V. (2010). Klasteri-Faktor unapredjenja konkurentnosti industrije Srbije. *Ekonomski Horizont*, 12(2), 57–74.

Mihalic, T., & Aramberri, J. (2015, November 13-16). Myths of top tourism countries, tourism contribution and competitiveness. *Tourism Review*, 70(4), 276–288. DOI: 10.1108/TR-08-2014-0048

Morgan, N., & Pritchard, A. (1998). *Tourism Promotion and Power: Creating Images, Creating Identities*. Wiley.

Morgan, N., Pritchard, A., & Pride, R. (2014). *Destination Branding: Creating the Unique Destination Proposition*. Elsevier Butterworth-Heinemann.

Palomeque, A. T.-D. (2014). Measuring sustainable tourism at the municipal level. *Annals of Tourism Research*, 49(C), 122–137.

Peräkylä, A. (2010). Two traditions of interaction research. *British Journal of Social Psychology*. PMID: 15035695

Pulido-Fernández, J. I., Andrades, L., & Marcelino Sánchez, R. (2014, November). Is sustainable tourism an obstacle to the economic performance of the tourism industry? Evidence from an international empirical study. *Journal of Sustainable Tourism*, 23(1), 47–64. DOI: 10.1080/09669582.2014.909447

Reisinger, Y. (2015). *Transformational tourism: host perspectives*. CAB International. DOI: 10.1079/9781780643922.0000

Richards, G. (2018). Cultural tourism: A review of recent research and trends. *Journal of Hospitality and Tourism Management*, 36, 12–21. DOI: 10.1016/j.jhtm.2018.03.005

Richards, L. (2014). *Handling Qualitative Data.* SAGE Publications. Ritchie, B., & Crouch, G. (2003). *The Competitive Destination: A Sustainable Tourism Perspective.* CABI.

Ritchie, B., & Crouch, G. (2011). A model of destination competitiveness and sustainability.

Roberts, K. D.-B. (n.d.). Attempting rigour and replicability in thematic analysis of qualitative research data; a case study of codebook development . BMC Medical Research Methodology.

Saunders, M. L. (2009). *Research Methods for Business Students.* Pearson.

Shah, S., & Corley, K. (2006). Building Better Theory by Bridging the Quantitative–Qualitative Divide. *Journal of Management Studies*, 43(8), 1821–1835. DOI: 10.1111/j.1467-6486.2006.00662.x

Sharrock, W., Anderson, B., & Anderson, R. (1986). The ethnomethodologists. Taylor & Francis.

Silverman, D. (2006). Interpreting Qualitative Data: Methods for Analysing Talk, Text and Interaction (éd. 3). Sage.

Silverman, D. (2010). Doing Qualitative Research: A Practical Handbook (éd. 3rd). London: Sage Publication.

Smith, M. (2003). *Issues in Cultural Tourism studies.* Routledge. DOI: 10.4324/9780203402825

Tight, M. (2017). *Understanding Case Study Research-Small-scale Research with Meaning.* SAGE Publications. DOI: 10.4135/9781473920118

Tomka, D. (2014). On the Balkans – History, Nature, Tourism and Dilemmas Faced by Researchers. *American Journal of Tourism Management*, 3(1B).

Veal, A. (2018). *Research Methods for Leisure and Tourism.* Pearson.

World Economic Forum. (2019). The travel and tourism competitiveness report. Consulté le June 26, 2020, sur https://www.weforum.org/reports/the-travel-tourism-competitiveness-report-2019

Yin, R. (2009). Case study research: Design and methods (éd. 4). Thousand Oaks, CA: SAGE.

Zhou, Y., Maumbe, K., Deng, J., & Selin, W. (2015, July). Resource-based destination competitiveness evaluation using a hybrid analytic hierarchy process (AHP): The case study of West Virginia. *Tourism Management Perspectives*, 15, 72–80. DOI: 10.1016/j.tmp.2015.03.007

Chapter 3
Tourist Awareness in Tourism Development:
Case Study of the City of Veria, Greece

Ioannis Valachis
Hellenic Open University, Greece

Nikolaos Trihas
Hellenic Mediterranean University, Heraklion, Greece

EXECUTIVE SUMMARY

The aim of this chapter is by focusing on the emerging tourism destination of Veria in Greece, to emphasize the importance of tourism awareness of the local community in achieving sustainable tourism development. In order to achieve this aim, the initiatives of the Tourism Department of the Municipality of Veria to raise tourism awareness of the local community are presented. The goal of these initiatives was to turn local residents into ambassadors for their city. Better knowledge of local points of interest and their importance, and greater familiarity with the concepts of hospitality and sustainability can lead to a behavior towards visitors that will meet their expectations and maximize their positive experiences from the destination. Findings and discussion of this case study are useful to academic researchers and organizations (DMOs, tourism bodies, community stakeholders) interested in sustainable tourism development.

DOI: 10.4018/979-8-3693-1548-4.ch003

INTRODUCTION

The active involvement of the local community is inherently regarded as indispensable in every endeavor aimed at fostering sustainable tourism development (Tosun, 2006). The benefits (social and economic) of tourism development should be fairly distributed to all the stakeholders involved, and should primarily be directed to local communities, contributing to the gradual eradication of poverty (Jeelani et al., 2022; Ndivo and Cantoni, 2016). Furthermore, these advantages for local communities are clearly described within the Sustainable Development Goals (SDGs) of 2030 Agenda for Sustainable Development (Alieva and Usmonova, 2021; Pasanchay and Schott, 2021; Taliouris and Trihas, 2017; UNWTO, 2017). However, there is little evidence indicating progress in its implementation (Sharpley, 2020). Hence, the involvement of local communities in tourism planning and development process is crucial in a bottom-up process (Mak et al., 2017; Zouganeli et al., 2012). Local residents should be involved in the decision-making process for their place, as they are the ones who will primarily experience the future positive and negative impacts of tourism development in their area (Dogra et al., 2022). Over the last twenty years, there has been a powerful acknowledgment of the significance of community-based tourism within the framework of sustainable tourism development (Yanes et al., 2019).

By focusing on the tourism destination of Veria in Greece, the aim of this chapter is to analyze the role of tourism awareness as the cornerstone of local community involvement in tourism development and thus, to achieve sustainability within an emerging tourism destination in Greece. In this chapter the initiatives of the Tourism Department of the Municipality of Veria are presented in order to raise tourism awareness in the local community. The ideas of hospitality, tourism, sustainability and codes of ethics in tourism are of great importance when developing tourism in a sustainable way. The implementation of a training program for school students, teachers and residents in a destination, which is in its early stages in terms of tourism development, intends to educate the local community by introducing the concepts of hospitality ("Philoxenia") and sustainability, while at the same time makes them aware of the local attractions. The ultimate goal of the program was to turn local residents into ambassadors for their city (Sammy, 2008). Better knowledge of local points of interest and their importance, greater familiarisation with the concepts of hospitality and sustainability can lead to a behavior that will meet the visitors' expectations and maximize their positive experiences from the destination. The chapter describes the planning of the program, the schedule, the budget, the different phases of implementation, the actions taken and the degree of local participation.

Literature Review

The broadly acknowledged beneficial impacts of tourism on enhancing economic activity, notably within the context of regional economic development, are widely acknowledged within academia (Dodds et al., 2018; Wani et al., 2022; García-Villaverde et al., 2020). According to Holland et al. (2022), the involvement of local community in sustainable tourism development is related to the familiarity and the ability to manage tourism resources. Some argue that tourism activity might reduce resource consumption and environmental pollution levels (Matarrita-Cascante et al., 2020). Chirikure et al. (2010) argue that the level of the community involvement depends on the local individual characteristics. The more the local community participates in any developmental phase, the more supportive it will be in any tourism development activity or initiative reducing any negative impacts that may arise on the local community (Lee and Park, 2019).

However, in order for locals to be motivated to actively participate in this process they must first be informed and convinced of the potential benefits that tourism development will bring to their community (Peterson et al., 2022; Saarinen, 2019). According to Eusébio et al. (2018) and Dada et al. (2022), the perceptions of local people towards tourism development play an important role in promoting sustainable development. Lack of interest and knowledge from local people are noteworthy obstacles to the sustainability of any developmental initiative (Moghavvemi et al., 2021; Šegota et al., 2024).

Tourism has an impact on every part of life. It is very important for every local stakeholder to understand tourism, its determinants and the impacts resulting from this activity (Pearce, 2008). Encouraging active participation from locals in tourism planning can lead to higher community satisfaction and it will thus contribute to the promotion of sustainable tourism development (Wani et al., 2024). Moreover, the level of locals' involvement in tourism depends on the opportunities provided by both private and public sector stakeholders (Pham et al., 2024). It is of great importance the local stakeholders to cooperate with each other in order to effectively manage tourism destinations (Jamal and Stronza, 2009). The dynamic involvement of local community is the basis of social and economic development (Huong et al., 2021).

Subsequently, the interaction between hosts and guests will impact not only on the views of local residents regarding tourism activity, but also on the impressions formed by tourists regarding the destination itself (Lehto et al., 2020; Tung et al., 2021). Tourists now seek authentic experiences in destinations, so interaction with locals will shape these experiences (Engeset and Elvekrok, 2015; Ramkissoon and Uysal, 2018). If the outcome of this encounter is positive, then this will likely lead (along with other factors) to satisfaction, positive feelings about the destination and a desire to visit it again in the future (Nguyen et al., 2024). Conversely, if the quality of this encounter is low, visitors will be dissatisfied, discredit the destination and probably will not visit it again in the future. However, in order for locals to fulfil their role as hosts, it is necessary for them to have developed what in the literature is called 'tourism awareness' (Porter et al., 2018).

Tourism awareness entails firstly the attitude, secondly the behavior and thirdly the implementation of actions, as all those contribute to provide the best possible service and satisfaction of visitors - tourists, not only within tourism businesses, but also within the destination. This will not only affect those directly employed in tourism, but all local residents in tourist destinations as well. Moreover, the development of environmental awareness for both locals and tourists successively makes them eco-friendlier (Valachis and Giouzepas, 2006). The tourism awareness group constitutes an integral component of societal dynamics, uniquely positioned to exert influence and make substantial contributions towards the advancement of tourism within its locality (Ochieng et al., 2018). This tourism awareness or consciousness can shape the local residents' perceptions about tourism and increase their participation in the developmental process (Musavengane, 2019).

The visitor-tourist is perhaps the most important factor for many destinations and their economy respectively. The focus should be on how that visitor will leave satisfied, happy and willing to pass on their positive experiences to others and promote the destination. In general, when the community is satisfied, it tends to lend support to tourism initiatives (Wani et al., 2024; Kanwal et al., 2020). A simple smile or a greeting from a local to a visitor they meet can significantly contribute to this positive experience. According to Zamani-Farahani and Musa (2012), a happy community creates positive word of mouth. This tourism consciousness can be passed on to local people, a process which is considered crucial especially for destinations in their early stages of the tourism developmental process, in order to enhance the positive (Gyan, 2021) and reduce the negative impacts concerning tourism (Gannon et al., 2021).

TOURISM AWARENESS: THE CASE OF VERIA

The Destination Veria

Veria is located in the northern Greece at the Region of Central Macedonia and it is the capital of the Regional Unit of Imathia. It is built on the foothills of Mount Vermion and surrounded in the northeast by Pieria Mountains and the Aliakmonas River. The Municipality of Veria has a population of 62,064 inhabitants (Hellenic Statistical Authority, 2023). The city is located 511 km away from Athens, the capital city of Greece and 73 km away from Thessaloniki, which is the second biggest

Greek city. Veria is widely known for its rich, long history. Several important cultural monuments are located in the area, such as: (a) the UNESCO World Heritage Site Vergina (Aigai), which was the first capital in the Kingdom of Macedonia, the place where Alexander the Great was crowned King, (b) the Apostle Paul's Tribune, "a global monument of religious heritage", the place where 2,000 years ago Apostle Paul conveyed the message of Jesus to the people of Veria, (c) 48 Byzantine and post-Byzantine churches, (d) Ottoman religious monuments, and (e) the oldest Jewish Synagogue in Northern Greece.

Tourism Highlights of Veria

The economy of Veria is mainly based on fruit and vegetable cultivation, remaking and livestock farming (70% of Greek beef production and large milk production) and to a small extent on tourism. Compared to other popular tourist destinations in Greece, Veria is one of the least known destinations in the country. For many years the economy of Veria was based on primary production, while tourism was not even on the agenda of local economic activities, making the active participation of the homegrown community in tourism initiatives particularly important. Despite its great environmental and cultural potential, the tourism development of Veria is still at an early stage, with a small number of tourism infrastructures and visitors.

The city has a total of 10 hotels (one 4* hotel, eight 3* hotels and one 2* hotel) and 9 hostels with a total capacity of 687 beds. The accommodation infrastructure is complemented by a number of sharing economy accommodation (Airbnb). There are 5 local based travel agencies and 5 licensed tour guides. Moreover, there are 90 restaurants, tavernas and cafes in the city of Veria and a number of tavernas in nearby areas. Five wineries operate in the region, and a number of 'tsipouro' distilleries (local grape spirit). Regarding conference facilities, 5 conference/meeting venues are available, with a total capacity of 1,200 people. Finally, there is a number of sports and outdoor facilities, including Seli Ski Resort at 1,900 m – the first organized ski resort in Greece since 1934 –, a motocross track and 3 climbing fields with more than 23 routes.

The 'Discover Veria' Project

'Discover Veria' is the authorized tourism promotion and branding initiative of the Municipality of Veria aiming to establish and promote Veria as a tourism destination. 'Discover' was chosen as the most representative title without any bureaucratic definitions or titles that are common in municipality divisions (Trihas *et al.*, 2013a). The campaign was designed and implemented by the Tourism Department of Municipality of Veria, with the aim of enhancing awareness and creating positive perceptions within the potential markets. Starting practically from scratch, the newly established Tourism Department of Municipality of Veria had to formulate and follow four primary objectives or strategic axes (Figure 1).

Figure 1. Main tourism strategic axes of Municipality of Veria

Organization & Planning		Tourism Awareness
	Discover Veria	
Partnerships		Promotion

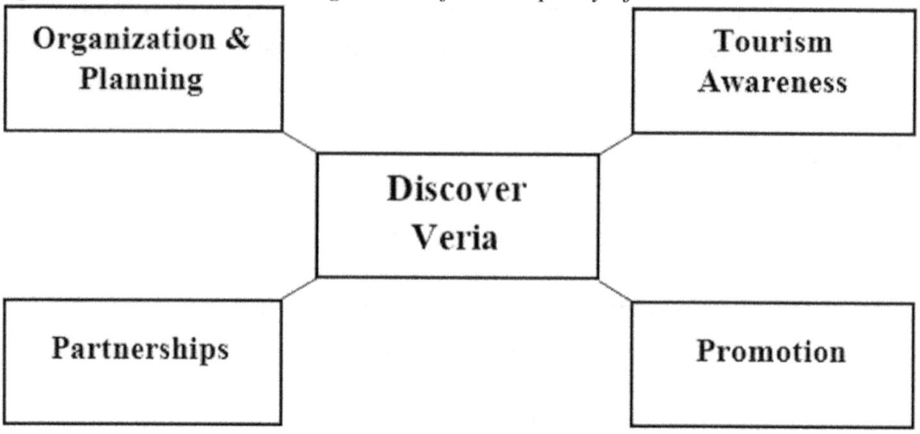

Source: *Municipality of Veria*

Planning and Programming Objectives

The objectives of tourism planning and programming are to organize an effective promotional campaign aiming to establish Veria as a primary tourism destination. Planning is directly connected with destination management as it endeavors to formulate policies and initiatives. Thus, it can implement essential alterations to social, environmental, and economic frameworks so as to attain sustainability objectives (Heslinga et al., 2019; dos Anjos and Kennell, 2019; Bhuiyan et al., 2023). In other words, the strategic aim of the program is to establish the Municipality of Veria on the tourist map and to promote it as a main tourist destination rather than as a complementary or secondary destination. Through these actions the Municipality aims to increase tourist arrivals, expand the average length of stay and gradually grow the per capita tourism product and service consumption.

In addition, the creation and 'cultivation' of tourism awareness and knowledge in the local community is an important strategic objective of the programme. Its design is consistent with the guidelines of the Ministry of Tourism and the Greek National Tourism Organization on "Procedure for the approval of the programmes and actions of tourism promotion of the regions and municipalities". Local community involvement in tourism is related to strategic planning and policy in a multi-stakeholder process in order to achieve long-term sustainability (Farsari, 2023; Saufi et al., 2014).

Main Strategic Tourism Axes

The main axes of the programme concern (Figure 1): (a) the organization and (b) the promotion of the tourism resources available in the Municipality of Veria and their design, so that they constitute either a single tourism product or individual products addressed to specific market segments; (c) the development of appropriate partnerships with the tourism industry and local stakeholders; as well as (d) the awareness, knowledge, consciousness, activation and organization of the local community for the achievement of the above objectives. All the above, both in the long and in the short term, contribute to the creation and consolidation of the destination's image as a key tourist destination. By exploiting the natural and cultural wealth of the municipality, emphasis is placed on the following target markets, relating mainly with special and alternative forms of tourism:

- Visitors from Thessaloniki and other close areas for short visits (urban tourism / city break),
- School tourism / student excursions,
- Visitors of religious interest,
- Visitors of archaeological and cultural interest,
- Visitors of culinary / wine interest,
- Conference and business events,
- Sports and cultural events.

All the above planning and programming initiatives lead to the formulation of the tourism vision of the Municipality of Veria: *"The emergence of the Municipality of Veria on the global tourism map through a sustainable tourism development model"*.

Tourism Reality to Challenge With

Based on the tourism highlights of Veria, the economy of the city is primarily reliant on agriculture and livestock farming, leading to limited tourism entrepreneurship. Additionally, it's commonly assumed that many local residents are unaware of the region's main attractions. Although Veria is not recognized as a prominent tourist destination in Greece, there has been a steady rise in visitor traffic; however, the expected economic benefits have not been materialized yet. This can be attributed to the city's economy which is predominantly based on primary production, while tourism-related entrepreneurship plays a minor role in the region's economic activities.

Initiatives of Veria's Tourism Department Related Tourism Awareness and Community Involvement

Local community knowledge and awareness of the cultural and historical monuments and other attractions of the area is considered very important, as through this, the reception, hospitality, and service of visitors can meet their expectations and maximize their positive experiences of the destination (Alaimo and Carman, 2022). The better the knowledge of residents about the monuments and attractions in the area, the better the results of promoting and protecting these attractions will be. Local community perceptions are directly related to the success or not of tourism development (Gannon et al., 2021). Similarly, Aref et al. (2010) argue that the role of the local community in the development and the provision of products and services is in every aspect of the sector crucial. Residents are a key component in a destination that is in its developmental phase.

Furthermore, each resident has the capacity to serve as an authentic "ambassador", guide and "custodian" of the local cultural heritage. It is very important for local communities to understand tourism and its impacts (Gani, 2022, Sammy, 2008). The lack of knowledge makes it difficult for local communities to participate in the tourism process. In many destinations, local communities face difficulties in managing the positive and negative impacts of tourism development (Moghavvemi et al., 2021; Moscardo, 2008). The Tourism Department of Municipality of Veria places great emphasis on the implementation of actions including publications in the local press; cooperation with local businesses, institutions and active citizens to organize tours and excursions aimed at the local community; attraction of more and more residents to the municipal social media; organization of local events; training; offer of entertainment and acquaintance with the main monuments and sites of the city; provision of a wide range of activities to the local community; as well as the implementation of conferences, seminars and other educational activities, in collaboration with the Directorate of Primary and Secondary Education and other public or private bodies.

The aforementioned initiatives seek to provide preliminary education to the local community on tourism-related matters and to engage and motivate them in the planning and developmental phases of tourism, giving this process characteristics of sustainability (Nugroho et al., 2023). For this reason, the involvement of local communities should be strengthened (Moghavvemi et al., 2021) and a bottom-up process should be followed in any tourism planning and developmental process (Zouganeli et al., 2012) to achieve the best possible outcome for the local community (Lamichhane, 2021).

Table 1. Initiative: 'I discover my city and its treasures' project

Period of Action	2016-2017
Cost of Action	0€
Targeted Group	Local community in total

In order to achieve the goal of developing tourism awareness in the local community, the Tourism Department of Municipality of Veria initially focused on introducing a number of famous tourist resources and attractions to the locals. This may seem like a simple matter, but it is worth mentioning that a large number of local people are even unaware of the existence of the main 'treasures' of their birthplace. However, even those who are familiar with these attractions cannot conceive their importance as a necessary resource for tourism development, due to the fact that the region is not the typical tourist destination and tourism is not the pioneer economic sector.

Under the title "Discovering my city and its treasures", the Tourism Department of Municipality of Veria has published a series of articles in the local press (Figure 2) in order to make citizens aware of the main tourist, archaeological and religious points of interest. The following main monuments of the city of Veria were presented in chronological order:

- The Old Metropolitan-Cathedral Church of Saint Apostles Paul and Petros
- The Apostle Paul's Tribune
- The Jewish District and the most ancient synagogue in Northern Greece
- The Byzantine Museum of Veria
- The Church and the archaeological site of Saint Patapios
- The Archaeological Museum of Veria.

In addition to the basic knowledge of tourist resources (historical and architectural), the publications provided a range of tourism-related information. This information is useful for local people firstly to acquire basic knowledge which they can then transfer to visitors of the area, and more importantly, to help them start thinking in a tourism-oriented way about their area and its resources. It is very important for local people to know basic tourist information of the monuments, such as opening hours, specific locations, ticketing, additional services in order to provide it to visitors. Better familiarisation of the citizens themselves with the monuments and attractions in the area can be particularly useful for the promotion and protection of the monuments, as each citizen can act as an actual 'ambassador' of the local cultural heritage.

Figure 2. Published articles in the local press

Source: *Municipality of Veria*

Table 2. Initiative: Social media as an educational tool

Period of Action	2015-to now
Cost of Action	0€
Targeted Group	Local community in total

In the same context of informing and familiarizing the local community with the tourist resources of the Municipality of Veria and the nearby area (surrounding settlements and natural environment), the role of social media is particularly important. Previous studies (Trihas et al., 2013b; Valachis, 2021) have shown that social media is increasingly being used by various Greek municipalities, both to promote them to tourists and visitors, and to inform the locals themselves. The Tourism Department of Municipality of Veria uses multiple social media where it frequently publishes photos, descriptions, historical data and tourist information about all points of interest and tourist resources throughout the territory of the Municipality and announces events of cultural and tourist interest. Within a short period of time the Tourism Department of Municipality of Veria managed to build an online community of people who follow the pages of the Municipality, are informed about its activities and receive useful information about the points of interest of the area.

Table 3. Initiative: Student photo competitions

Period of Action	March and May 2022
Cost of Action	300€ competition prizes
Targeted Group	Local Students

a) "On the move... With an eye on my place..."

The Tourism Department of the Municipality of Veria co-organized with the Directorate of Secondary Education of Imathia and the Environmental Team of the Evening Junior High School of Veria a student photography competition entitled: "On the move... With my eyes on my place..." during March and May 2022. The aim of the competition was for the students, using photography as a tool, to get to know the natural, historical and cultural wealth of their birthplace and to gain interest in its promotion and sustainable development.

Table 4. "Aspects of my place: yesterday, today, tomorrow..."

Period of Action	March and May 2018
Cost of Action	300€ competition prizes
Targeted Group	Local Students

The Tourism Department of the Municipality of Veria co-organized with the Directorate of Secondary Education Imathia, the Environmental Group 'Buildings and people in the slums of Veria' of the Evening Junior High School of Veria, the School Committee of the Municipality of Veria and the Photography Group of Veria 'Antithesis'. Its theme was the "Aspects of my place: yesterday, today, tomorrow..." for the students of the Directorate of Secondary Education of Imathia from March to May 2018. More specifically, the theme concerned the photographic capture of images from the following thematic categories: Tourism, Religion, Culture, Nature and Environment, Urban Environment and Architecture, Gastronomy, History. The aim of the competition was for the students to get to know their place in the light of tourism and sustainable development and to get closer to the elements of the natural and cultural wealth of the region that make up the mosaic of Imathia as a tourist destination. After the competition ended, there was an exhibition of the students' works that was open to the public (Figure 3).

Figure 3. Student photo competitions

Source: *Municipality of Veria*

Table 5. Initiative: "We get to know our city by walking!" Educational Walks

Period of Action	Since 2021, during the school period. One or two times in a week
Cost of Action	0€
Targeted Group	Local Students-Teachers / Adult groups - approximately 40 guided tours annually

As part of the European Mobility Week – the European Commission campaign on sustainable urban mobility which takes place every September – the Tourism Department of the Municipality of Veria and the Directorate of Secondary Education of Imathia in cooperation with the retired volunteer teacher Mr. Thomas Dimitrakis, conducts every year since 2021 more than 40 educational guided tours of primary and secondary classes and citizens in the traditional districts and historical monuments in the city of Veria (Figure 4). It proved to be a very successful initiative that brought schools, the educational community and residents very close together to get to know their place but also to seek and create cultural and tourist routes through the field tour.

The interest in the participation of schools and adults is very high, as through this walk they come into contact with unknown information about their place, very useful for the preservation of their cultural heritage and for the better service of visitors to the city. By actually following one or more of the proposed tourist routes drawn up by the Tourist Department, the citizens of Veria are able to take on the role of tourist-visitor, seeing first-hand, on a practical level, what a tourist route means, the places they visit, the times needed to get from one point to another and other information that is useful in order to better serve the visitor. At the same time, printed information material, provided by the Municipality of Veria, is distributed to them both for further study and for further familiarization with the tourism development of their city.

Figure 4. Educational walk in the city of Veria

Source: *Municipality of Veria*

Table 6. Initiative: Guided Tours of the elderly – pensioners

Period of Action	2023-to now
Cost of Action	0€
Targeted Group	Local elderly people – pensioners

The Tourism Department of Municipality of Veria in cooperation with the KAPI (Open Centres for the Protection of the Elderly), the Association of Friends of the Polycentric Museum of Aigai and the Ephorate of Antiquities of Imathia organized a tour for the elderly – retired residents of the Municipality of Veria to the New Central Museum Building of the Polycentric Museum of Aigai in Vergina. During this visit, the elderly residents of Veria had the opportunity to get to know and be guided through the brand-new Museum of Aigai. The role of the elderly residents is very important in informing, promoting and protecting the cultural wealth of a region. Due to the recent completion of the restoration works of the Palace of the Aigai, it is expected that additional educational visits will be made to the Palace as well.

Table 7. Initiative: Guided Tours of groups of local community

Period of Action	2023-to now
Cost of Action	150€ per tour/transfer costs
Targeted Group	Local seniors, cultural and professional groups, Municipal Councilors

The Tourism Department of the Municipality of Veria organized a total of 15 guided tours for various groups of local residents (senior groups, cultural and professional groups) to get closer to some very important tourist resources. The tours followed six thematic routes:

- Vergina: New Polycentric Museum of Aigai
- Pieria Mountains and Holy Monastery of Saint John the Baptist
- Vermio Mountain: The Holy Monastery of Panagia Kallipetras and the villages of Georgianoi, Santa and Leykopetra with the archaeological site of the Sanctuary of the Mother of the Gods
- The Holy Monastery of Panagia Dovra, the villages of Trilofo (Aristotles Cultural Center), Fytia, Kostochori (the church of Agios Athanasios)
- The villages of Palatitsia (the church of Agios Dimitrios), Sykea, Agia Varvara and Assomata.

Furthermore, the Tourism Department of the Municipality of Veria organized two guided tours for Municipal Councilors to the cultural and touristic assets of Veria. This engagement not only contributes to informed decision-making but also augments the effective representation of the area.

Table 8. Initiative: "The Little Tourist – A Suitcase Travels...to Veria"

Period of action	04-05/05/2018
Cost of Action	200€ - hosting costs and stationery
Targeted Group	Local school students and teachers, residents and entrepreneurs

The Tourism Department of the Municipality of Veria in cooperation with the Primary Education Directorate of Imathia and the Public Central Library of Veria organized two days of educational activities entitled "The little tourist – A suitcase travels...to Veria" (Figure 5). The actions were related to the development of tourism awareness of students, teachers and the local community and were carried out by Dr. Eleftheria Griba, an Executive of the Ministry of Tourism. It was a free, award-winning, innovative interdisciplinary activity supported by the Ministry of Tourism, the Hellenic Tourism Organization, the European Parliament Office in Greece, the UN Regional Information Centre and others. The following activities were included:

- *Experiential workshops for Primary School students*: As part of the two-day educational activities, experiential workshops were held for the students of the 4th, 5th and 6th grade of the Primary Schools of the Municipality of Veria. The aim of the workshops was for the students to understand, through experiential activities, the relationship between tourism and sustainable development. The experiential workshops had a duration of 2 teaching hours, and included a guided tour to the Apostle Paul's Tribune and the Barbouta neighborhood, as well as other related educational activities. Up to 25 students participated in each workshop.
- *Interactive seminar for teachers, students, residents and entrepreneurs*: The programme included an interactive seminar for teachers, residents and entrepreneurs, open to the public with free admission. The aim of the seminar was for participants to learn about the Sustainable Development Goals and develop active citizenship through sustainable education, travel and responsible consumption. The objective was achieved through case studies and practical exercises based on visual/artistic works, state-of-the-art audiovisual material and appropriate teaching material.
- *Educational programmes for students aged 8-12 years old*: The educational programs for students aged 8-12 years old took place in the Central Public Library of Veria. As stated in the invitation: *"What do you think? Does the future of humanity hinge upon children? Are we obliged to be responsible tourists and active citizens? Are you familiar with the concept of 'Sustainability'? How does it relate to the Sustainable Development Goals? Can we measure our ecological 'footprint'? How can we protect our tourist destinations? These and many other questions will be addressed through our forthcoming initiative, entitled "The Little Tourist – A Suitcase Travels...to Veria". It will be a creative and playful approach through visual and artistic presentations, as well as state-of-the-art audio-visual materials. Thus, we will engage in play, humor, exploration, and innovative endeavors, relishing flavors, aromas, discourse, and collaboration, all in pursuit of an enjoyable experience".*

It is worth to be mentioned that during the activities, children were given the opportunity to engage with real tourists, which they met by chance during the educational walk in the city center, thereby exercising, to a certain degree, the knowledge acquired during the workshop in a role playing and drama activity.

Figure 5. The Little Tourist – A Suitcase Travels...to Veria

Source: *Municipality of Veria*

Table 9. Initiative: Webinars during the period of Covid-19 pandemic

Period of Action	During the lock-down period of Covid-19
Cost of Action	0€
Targeted Group	Local residents and entrepreneurs. An average of 30-40 participants per webinar

The quarantine and lockdown measures during the pandemic period (Trihas et al., 2023) provided an excellent opportunity to implement web training seminars (webinars) for locals, residents and entrepreneurs. Consequently, the Tourism Department of the Municipality of Veria undertook a sequence of such webinars focusing on various aspects such as: sustainable tourism development, environmental consciousness, ethical conduct, customer service, digital marketing, food costing and promotional strategies, as well as effective hotel management. Due to the expected restart in tourism activities the framework of each thematic title centered on strategizing how the tourism industry could effectively adapt to the evolving conditions in preparation for the emerging post-Covid-19 economic landscape. Remarkably, participation in these webinars was notably robust.

CONCLUSION

Tourism is a multi-faced activity, in which several different stakeholders are potentially engaged or are affected by it, directly and indirectly. Among other stakeholders, the role of the local community is very important in achieving sustainability in tourism development. However, for this role to be exercised successfully, the local community must firstly be given the opportunity to participate in any tourism planning and developmental process in a bottom-up approach (Salma, et al., 2022). Secondly, the local community must be informed about the impacts (positive and negative) of tourism, so that they are motivated to take an active part in this process.

This interaction bears significant influence on the daily lives of the local population and more importantly shapes the visitor's experiences within the destination, thereby impacting on the overall satisfaction with the locals. Within this context, the significance of fostering tourism awareness among local residents proves paramount. Consequently, the objective of this chapter is to present the endeavors undertaken by the Municipality of Veria in Greece to enhance tourism awareness and gain residents' support for tourism initiatives. The ultimate goal was to engage them in the municipality's ongoing endeavors to position itself as a notable tourist destination in the forthcoming years.

Veria, as an emerging tourist destination, has as a strategic goal to achieve sustainable tourism development. The Tourism Department of the Municipality of Veria is aware that this goal cannot be achieved without the active local community participation. As a result, the development of tourism awareness and knowledge among local people has been set from the outset as a key priority of the whole project. The idea is that if the local people are first informed about the benefits that tourism can bring to their city, learn about their local heritage and are educated on how to treat visitors, they will then become 'ambassadors' of their city, ready to welcome visitors (Sammy, 2008).

As a result, visitors will experience a level of hospitality from locals that will meet or exceed their expectations leading to higher levels of satisfaction and possibly to a positive word-of-mouth and increased likelihood of further visits. In this context, the tourism committee organized and implemented a series of actions targeting different groups of the local population (students, teachers, residents, entrepreneurs): published articles in the local press with information of the main attractions of tourist, archaeological, religious, naturalistic interest in their area; used social media to build a community of locals who would be informed on a regular basis on tourism issues; organized photo competitions, educational walks, activities, seminars and webinars for the locals during the pandemic.

The great acceptance of community members, coupled with their interest and demand for involvement in these endeavors, is an indicator of accomplishing the initiative. One may assert that tourism is increasingly becoming the main focus among the residents as they are particularly interested in discussions related to proposals for tourism development, promotion and initiatives. Nevertheless, it is imperative to assess and quantitatively evaluate the outcomes of such initiatives. For instance, it is recommended to examine the participants' perceptions, alterations in local behaviors, increase in visitor numbers, length of stay and consumption, visitor satisfaction, and various other assessment indexes.

Findings and discussions of this case study are useful to academic researchers and organizations (DMOs, tourism bodies, community stakeholders) interested in sustainable tourism development. The results can be particularly useful for other destinations with similar characteristics to the city of Veria, which might want to enhance the tourism awareness and knowledge of the local community by introducing the three practical techniques of drama, drawing and field trips. The cultivation of tourism awareness and knowledge and the educational initiatives among local stakeholders constitutes an ongoing endeavor because of the continuous emergence of new and innovative concepts and the evolving needs within the field.

Future research could be done in order to measure with qualitative and quantitative indicators the results of this initiative of the Municipality of Veria. For example, interviews could be carried out with the stakeholders involved (local residents, entrepreneurs, tourism-related bodies, visitors) in order to examine their experiences and perceptions of these actions focusing on their economic, environmental and social impacts. In addition, it would be interesting to explore the role of emerging technologies, such as augmented reality and artificial intelligence, in supporting sustainable tourism development and to look for ways in which the Municipality of Veria can leverage them in this direction. Finally, a comparison of this initiative of the Municipality of Veria with other similar case studies of other destinations in order to seek good practices would be of particular interest.

REFERENCES

Alaimo, S. P., & Carman, J. G. (2022). Decisions, decisions, decisions: Community foundations and community well-being. *International Journal of Community Well-being*, 5(2), 213–239. DOI: 10.1007/s42413-021-00125-7

Alieva, D., & Usmonova, G. (2021). Sustainability perceptions of community based tourism by stakeholders in Central Asia. *Local Development & Society*, 2(2), 244–254. DOI: 10.1080/26883597.2021.1953944

Aref, F., Redzuan, M. R., Gill, S. S., & Aref, A. (2010). Community Capacity Building in Tourism Development in Local Communities. *Journal of Sustainable Development*, 3(1), 81–90. DOI: 10.5539/jsd.v3n1p81

Bhuiyan, M. A., Zhang, Q., Xuan, W., Rahman, M. K., & Khare, V. (2023). Does good governance promote sustainable tourism? A systematic review of PESTEL analysis. *SN Business & Economics*, 3(33), 33. Advance online publication. DOI: 10.1007/s43546-022-00408-x PMID: 36684689

Chirikure, S., Manyanga, M., Ndoro, W., & Pwiti, G. (2010). Unfulfilled promises? Heritage management and community participation at some of Africa's cultural heritage sites. *International Journal of Heritage Studies*, 16(1-2), 30–44. DOI: 10.1080/13527250903441739

Dada, Z. A., Batool, N., & Shah, S. A. (2022). GIS-based analysis of green space in urban Himalayas and modelling the effects on destination business performance. *International Journal of Tourism Cities*, 8(4), 1102–1126. DOI: 10.1108/IJTC-06-2021-0121

Dodds, R., Ali, A., & Galaski, K. (2018). Mobilizing knowledge: Determining key elements for success and pitfalls in developing community-based tourism. *Current Issues in Tourism*, 21(13), 1547–1568. DOI: 10.1080/13683500.2016.1150257

Dogra, N., Adil, M., Dhamija, A., Kumar, M., & Nasir, M. (2022). What makes a community sustainably developed? A review of 25 years of sustainable community tourism literature. *Community Development (Columbus, Ohio)*, 53(5), 585–606. DOI: 10.1080/15575330.2021.2015606

dos Anjos, F. A., & Kennell, J. (2019). Tourism, governance and sustainable development. *Sustainability (Basel)*, 11(16), 4257. DOI: 10.3390/su11164257

Engeset, M. G., & Elvekrok, I. (2015). Authentic Concepts: Effects on Tourist Satisfaction. *Journal of Travel Research*, 54(4), 456–466. DOI: 10.1177/0047287514522876

Eusébio, C., Vieira, A. L., & Lima, S. (2018). Place attachment, host–tourist interactions, and residents' attitudes towards tourism development: The case of Boa Vista Island in Cape Verde. *Journal of Sustainable Tourism*, 26(6), 890–909. DOI: 10.1080/09669582.2018.1425695

Farsari, I. (2023). Exploring the nexus between sustainable tourism governance, resilience and complexity research. *Tourism Recreation Research*, 48(3), 352–367. DOI: 10.1080/02508281.2021.1922828

Gani, A. (2022). Leveraging the community development approach to examine the natural capital effect on sustainable development goal 3-target 2. *Community Development (Columbus, Ohio)*, 53(5), 607–623. DOI: 10.1080/15575330.2021.2023601

Gannon, M., Rasoolmanesh, S. M., & Taheri, B. (2021). Assessing the mediating role of residents' perceptions toward tourism development. *Journal of Travel Research*, 60(1), 149–171. DOI: 10.1177/0047287519890926

García-Villaverde, P. M., Elche, D., & Martinez-Perez, A. (2020). Understanding Pioneering Orientation in Tourism Clusters: Market Dynamism and Social Capital. *Tourism Management*, 76, 103966. https://Doi.Org/Https://Doi.Org/10.1016/J.Tourman.2019.103966. DOI: 10.1016/j.tourman.2019.103966

Gyan, C. (2021). Community development participation scale: A development and validation study. *Community Development (Columbus, Ohio)*, 52(4), 459–472. DOI: 10.1080/15575330.2021.1885049

Hellenic Statistical Authority. (2023). *Census 2021*. https://elstat-outsourcers.statistics.gr/Census2022_GR.pdf

Heslinga, J., Groote, P., & Vanclay, F. (2019). Strengthening governance processes to improve benefit-sharing from tourism in protected areas by using stakeholder analysis. *Journal of Sustainable Tourism*, 27(6), 773–787. DOI: 10.1080/09669582.2017.1408635

Holland, K. K., Larson, L. R., Powell, R. B., Holland, W. H., Allen, L., Nabaala, M., Tome, S., Seno, S., & Nampushi, J. (2022). Impacts of tourism on support for conservation, local livelihoods, and community resilience around Maasai Mara National Reserve, Kenya. *Journal of Sustainable Tourism*, 30(11), 2526–2548. DOI: 10.1080/09669582.2021.1932927

Huong, L. T., Hang, N. T., Huy, D. T., Tinh, D. T., & Huyen, D. T. (2021). Educating Students in History and Geography Subjects through Visiting Historical Sites to Develop Local Economy and Community Tourism Services in Thai Nguyen and Ha Giang Provinces, Vietnam. *Revista Gestão Inovação e Tecnologias.*, 11(3), 1–12. DOI: 10.47059/revistageintec.v11i3.1911

Jamal, T., & Stronza, A. (2009). Collaboration theory and tourism practice in protected areas: Stakeholders, structuring and sustainability. *Journal of Sustainable Tourism*, 17(2), 169–190. DOI: 10.1080/09669580802495741

Jeelani, P., Shah, S. A., Dar, S. N., & Rashid, H. (2022). Sustainability constructs of mountain tourism development: The evaluation of stakeholders' perception using SUS-TAS. *Environment, Development and Sustainability*, 25(8), 8299–8317. DOI: 10.1007/s10668-022-02401-8 PMID: 35915719

Kanwal, S., Rasheed, M. I., Pitafi, A. H., Pitafi, A., & Ren, M. (2020). Road and transport infrastructure development and community support for tourism: The role of perceived benefits, and community satisfaction. *Tourism Management*, 77, 104014. DOI: 10.1016/j.tourman.2019.104014

Lamichhane, B. P. (2021). Good governance in Nepal: Legal provisions and judicial praxis. *Journal of Political Science*, 21, 19–30. DOI: 10.3126/jps.v21i0.35260

Lee, S., & Park, D. (2019). Community attachment formation and its influence on sustainable participation in a digitalized community: Focusing on content and social capital of an online community. *Sustainability (Basel)*, 11(10), 2935. DOI: 10.3390/su11102935

Lehto, X., Davari, D., & Park, S. (2020). Transforming the guest-host relationship: A convivial tourism approach. *International Journal of Tourism Cities*, 6(4), 1069–1088. DOI: 10.1108/IJTC-06-2020-0121

Mak, B. K. L., Cheung, L. T. O., and Hui, D. L. H. (2017). Community Participation in the Decision-Making Process for Sustainable Tourism Development in Rural Areas of Hong Kong, China. *Sustainability,* 9(10),1695, 1-13, DOI: 10.3390/su9101695

Matarrita-Cascante, D., Lee, J. H., & Nam, J. W. (2020). What elements should be present in any community development initiative? Distinguishing community development from local development. *Local Development & Society*, 1(2), 95–115. DOI: 10.1080/26883597.2020.1829986

Moghavvemi, S., Woosnam, K. M., Hamzah, A., & Hassani, A. (2021). Considering Residents' Personality and Community Factors in Explaining Satisfaction with Tourism and Support for Tourism Development. *Tourism Planning & Development*, 18(3), 267–293. DOI: 10.1080/21568316.2020.1768140

Moscardo, G. (2008). *Building community capacity for tourism development*. CABI. DOI: 10.1079/9781845934477.0000

Musavengane, R. (2019). Understanding tourism consciousness through habitus: Perspectives of 'poor' black South Africans. *Critical African Studies*, 11(3), 322–347. DOI: 10.1080/21681392.2019.1670702

Ndivo, R. M., & Cantoni, L. (2016). Rethinking local community involvement in tourism development. *Annals of Tourism Research*, 57, 275–278. DOI: 10.1016/j.annals.2015.11.014

Nguyen, K. T. T., Murphy, L., Chen, T., & Pearce, P. L. (2024). Let's listen: The voices of ethnic villagers in identifying host-tourist interaction issues in the Central Highlands, Vietnam. *Journal of Heritage Tourism*, 19(2), 263–286. DOI: 10.1080/1743873X.2023.2259512

Nugroho, A. W., Prasetyo, S. I., Candra, I. A., Saputra, R. A., & Putra, A. S. (2023). Community-Based Tourism: Strengthening understanding and assistance in establishing tourism awareness group. *Journal of Community Service and Empowerment*, 4(2), 271–282. DOI: 10.22219/jcse.v4i2.26389

Ochieng, J., Knerr, B., Owuor, G., & Ouma, E. (2018). Strengthening Collective Action to Improve Marketing Performance: Evidence from Farmer Groups in Central Africa. *Journal of Agricultural Education and Extension*, 24(2), 169–189. Https://Doi.Org/10.1080/1389224x.2018.1432493. DOI: 10.1080/1389224X.2018.1432493

Pasanchay, K., & Schott, C. (2021). Community-based tourism homestays' capacity to advance the sustainable development goals: A holistic sustainable livelihood perspective. *Tourism Management Perspectives*, 37, 100784. DOI: 10.1016/j.tmp.2020.100784

Pearce, P. L. (2008). Understanding how tourists can bring sociocultural benefits to destination communities. In Moscardo, G. (Ed.), *Building community capacity for tourism development* (pp. 29–40). CABI., DOI: 10.1079/9781845934477.0029

Peterson, C., Ortiz, R., & Rocconi, L. (2022). Community food security: The multi-level association between social capital, economic capital, and diet quality. *International Journal of Community Well-being*, 5(3), 571–585. DOI: 10.1007/s42413-022-00170-w

Pham, K., Andereck, K. L., & Vogt, C. (2024). Stakeholders' involvement in an evidence-based sustainable tourism plan. *Journal of Sustainable Tourism*, •••, 1–24. DOI: 10.1080/09669582.2023.2259117

Porter, B. A., Orams, M. B., & Lück, M. (2018). Sustainable Entrepreneurship Tourism: An Alternative Development Approach for Remote Coastal Communities Where Awareness of Tourism is Low. *Tourism Planning & Development*, 15(2), 149–165. DOI: 10.1080/21568316.2017.1312507

Ramkissoon, H., & Uysal, M. S. (2018). Authenticity as a value co-creator of tourism experiences. In Prebensen, N. K., Chen, J. S., & Uysal, M. S. (Eds.), *Creating experience value in tourism* (pp. 98–109). CABI., DOI: 10.1079/9781786395030.0098

Saarinen, J. (2019). Communities and sustainable tourism development: Community impacts and local benefit creation in tourism. In McCool, S. F., & Bosak, K. (Eds.), *A Research Agenda for Sustainable Tourism* (pp. 206–222). Edward Elgar Publishing Limited., DOI: 10.4337/9781788117104.00020

Salma, Wijaya, A. A. M., Basir, M. A., and Lawelai, H. (2022). Community Based Tourism in The Development of Sustainable Tourism in Baubau City. *APLIKATIF: Journal of Research Trends in Social Sciences and Humanities*, 1(1), 28–38. DOI: 10.59110/aplikatif.v1i1.32

Sammy, J. (2008). Examples of effective techniques for enhancing community understanding of tourism. In Moscardo, G. (Ed.), *Building community capacity for tourism development* (pp. 75–85). CABI. DOI: 10.1079/9781845934477.0075

Saufi, A., O' Brien, D., & Wilkins, H. (2014). Inhibitors to host community participation in sustainable tourism development in developing countries. *Journal of Sustainable Tourism*, 22(5), 801–820. DOI: 10.1080/09669582.2013.861468

Šegota, T., Mihalič, T., & Perdue, R. R. (2024). Resident perceptions and responses to tourism: Individual vs community level impacts. *Journal of Sustainable Tourism*, 32(2), 340–363. DOI: 10.1080/09669582.2022.2149759

Sharpley, R. (2020). Tourism, sustainable development and the theoretical divide: 20 years on. *Journal of Sustainable Tourism*, 28(11), 1932–1946. DOI: 10.1080/09669582.2020.1779732

Taliouris, E., & Trihas, N. (2017). Public Policy for Corporate Social Responsibility and Governance for Sustainable Tourism Development in Greece. *Business Ethics and Leadership*, 1(4), 49–57. DOI: 10.21272/bel.1(4).49-57.2017

Tosun, C. (2006). Expected nature of community participation in tourism development. *Tourism Management*, 27(3), 493–504. DOI: 10.1016/j.tourman.2004.12.004

Trihas, N., Perakakis, E., Venitourakis, M., Mastorakis, G., & Kopanakis, I. (2013a). Destination Marketing using Multiple Social Media: The Case of 'Visit Ierapetra'. *Tourism Today (Nicosia)*, 13, 114–126.

Trihas, N., Perakakis, E., Venitourakis, M., Mastorakis, G., & Kopanakis, I. (2013b). Social Media as a Marketing Tool for Tourism Destinations: The Case of Greek Municipalities. *Journal of Marketing Vistas*, 3(2), 38–48. DOI: 10.26215/tourismos.v11i3.486

Trihas, N., Vassakis, K., Kopanakis, I., Nikoloudakis, Y., Kefaloukos, I., Pallis, E., & Markakis, E. (2023). The impact of COVID-19 on travel behavior and holiday intentions. Evidence from Greece. In Sharp, B., Finkel, R., & Dashper, K. (Eds.), *Transforming Leisure in the Pandemic: Re-imagining Interaction and Activity during Crisis* (pp. 42–56). Routledge.

Tung, V. W. S., Tse, S., & Chan, D. C. F. (2021). Host-guest relations and destination image: Compensatory effects, impression management, and implications for tourism recovery. *Journal of Travel & Tourism Marketing*, 38(8), 833–844. DOI: 10.1080/10548408.2021.1883499

UNWTO. (2017). *Tourism and the Sustainable Development Goals – Journey to 2030*. UNWTO.

Valachis, I. (2021). Photographic Tourism. In Agarwal, S., Busby, G., & Huang, R. (Eds.), *Special interest tourism* (pp. 249–270). Broken Hill Publishers Ltd. (in Greek)

Valachis, I., & Giouzepas, D. (2006). Mould tourists into environmental friendly visitors: 'Interactive architecture' and eco-educating parks. *2nd International Scientific Conference Progress in Tourism and Hospitality: Present & Future Challenges*, Thessaloniki, Greece

Wani, M. D., Batool, N., Dada, Z. A., & Shah, S. A. (2024). Investigating the impact of community-based tourism on the residents' quality of life and their support for tourism. *Community Development (Columbus, Ohio)*, 55(1), 138–159. DOI: 10.1080/15575330.2023.2272271

Wani, M. D., Dada, Z. A., & Shah, S. A. (2022). Building peace through tourism: The analysis of an ongoing Siachen Glacier dispute between India and Pakistan. *Asian Journal of Comparative Politics*, 7(4), 836–848. DOI: 10.1177/20578911221118730

Wani, M. D., Dada, Z. A., & Shah, S. A. (2024). The impact of community empowerment on sustainable tourism development and the mediation effect of local support: A structural equation modeling approach. *Community Development (Columbus, Ohio)*, 55(1), 50–66. DOI: 10.1080/15575330.2022.2109703

Yanes, A., Zielinski, S., Cano, M. D., & Kim, S. I. (2019). Community-based tourism in developing countries: A framework for policy evaluation. *Sustainability (Basel)*, 11(9), 2506. DOI: 10.3390/su11092506

Zamani-Farahani, H., & Musa, G. (2012). The relationship between Islamic religiosity and residents' perceptions of socio-cultural impacts of tourism in Iran: Case studies of Sare'in and Masooleh. *Tourism Management*, 33(4), 802–814. DOI: 10.1016/j.tourman.2011.09.003

Zouganeli, S., Trihas, N., Antonaki, M., & Kladou, S. (2012). Aspects of Sustainability in the Destination Branding Process: A Bottom-up Approach. *Journal of Hospitality Marketing & Management*, 21(7), 739–757. DOI: 10.1080/19368623.2012.624299

Chapter 4
Perspectives for the Potential and Future of Marine Tourism in Bangladesh

Mohammad Badruddoza Talukder
https://orcid.org/0009-0008-1662-9221
International University of Business Agriculture and Technology, Bangladesh

Firoj Kabir
https://orcid.org/0009-0001-3014-3163
Daffodil Institute of IT, Bangladesh

Fahmida Kaiser
https://orcid.org/0009-0002-4113-207X
Daffodil Institute of IT, Bangladesh

Mushfika Hoque
https://orcid.org/0009-0000-4645-5105
Daffodil Institute of IT, Bangladesh

EXECUTIVE SUMMARY

The marine tourism industry encompasses activities like water sports, coastal cruises, and marine biodiversity investigation, showing great potential for global economic growth and cultural advancement. This study examines the future of marine tourism in Bangladesh, a nation blessed with a rich maritime legacy, various coastal ecosystems, and its unrealized potential. The study also evaluates the present condition of marine tourism in Bangladesh by extensively analyzing extant literature, governmental directives, and case studies. To support the expansion of maritime tourism

DOI: 10.4018/979-8-3693-1548-4.ch004

in Bangladesh, the study finds that integrated regulatory frameworks, public-private partnerships, and sustainable practices are necessary. This study suggests fully utilizing the nation's maritime resources for local communities, industry stakeholders, and legislators. Bangladesh can establish itself as a viable and alluring maritime tourist destination in the coming years by embracing a comprehensive strategy that will balance environmental preservation and economic growth.

INTRODUCTION

The marine tourism business is a vibrant and lucrative sector within the travel industry worldwide. Marine tourism encompasses various activities, from relaxing beach cruises to in-depth marine biodiversity studies. Over the past few years, nations worldwide have begun understanding their coastal areas' economic and cultural potential (Das et al., 2024). This has increased the efforts to capitalize on the benefits of marine tourism. Bangladesh is a nation that is in a unique position with an extended coastline, diversified ecosystems, and a rich maritime heritage (Talukder, 2021). This chapter investigates the views, potential, and future trajectory of marine tourism in Bangladesh. The coastline of Bangladesh extends along the Bay of Bengal, passing through the Sundarbans, the most extensive mangrove forest in the world, and sketching the delicate contours of the largest delta in the world (Nurhayati et al., 2023). Despite these natural treasures, the marine tourism industry in Bangladesh is still largely unexplored, which presents an exciting possibility for expansion and development. This study aims to assess the existing condition of marine tourism in Bangladesh, determine the primary elements that contribute to the formation of its landscape, and conceive opportunities for sustainable expansion (Oh et al., 2024).

As we continue digging further into the topic, it is of the utmost importance to acknowledge the relevance of marine tourism outside the realm of economic concerns. Industry can catalyze cultural interchange, environmental awareness, community development, and the potential for generating money and creating jobs (Talukder et al., 2020). This chapter aims to provide comprehensive knowledge of the difficulties and possibilities that characterize the current landscape and to assist in forming a vision for the future of marine tourism in Bangladesh. This will be accomplished by reviewing global trends, existing policies, and case studies (Choi & Lim, 2024). The investigation of this subject is not only an academic exercise; it is an important activity that aims to give insights that can be put into action, which may facilitate the formation of policy choices, advise industrial stakeholders, and empower local communities. By imagining a future for marine tourism in Bangladesh that is both sustainable and responsible, we want to pave the way for a flourishing business that not only contributes to the nation's economy but also protects and honours the distinctive coastal legacy of this dynamic nation (Affatati et al., 2024).

There is tremendous potential for establishing a thriving marine tourism business in Bangladesh due to the country's extensive maritime heritage and a broad range of coastal scenery. Throughout Bangladesh's history, rivers and seas have played a significant part in building the country's cultural and economic fabric (Tait et al., 2024). However, the entire breadth of tourism opportunities along the country's broad coastline has not yet been exploited to its full potential. With its intricate network of mangrove forests, tidal rivers, and one-of-a-kind species, the Sundarbans, a UNESCO World Heritage Site, offers an unrivalled appeal for anyone interested in nature and ecotourism. In addition, the coastal sections of the nation are home to scenic beaches, traditional fishing settlements, and historical monuments that can accommodate a wide range of tourist interests (Talukder et al., 2021). Several problems, including poor infrastructure, restricted accessibility, and environmental concerns, have delayed the rise of maritime tourism in Bangladesh (Ma et al., 2024). These challenges have been present despite the intrinsic attractions that are there. The coastal communities, which are frequently marginalized, need to be actively included in the development process to guarantee the sustainability of tourist efforts and ensure that they remain inclusive. Across the world, the tourist industry is undergoing a paradigm shift toward more responsible and environmentally conscious practices. By incorporating eco-friendly policies, community-based tourism projects, and technology-driven solutions that enhance the overall visitor experience while preserving the natural beauty and cultural authenticity of its coastal regions, Bangladesh can position itself as a leader in this movement. This can be accomplished by integrating these elements (Thu Huong et al., 2024).

This article aims to provide an in-depth examination of the current situation of marine tourism in Bangladesh, focusing on the industry's socioeconomic, environmental, and cultural aspects. This study proposes actionable strategies for stakeholders, such as policymakers, industry players, and local communities, to unlock the vast potential of marine tourism in Bangladesh and ensure a sustainable, inclusive, and rewarding future (Talukder, 2020). These strategies will be derived from successful marine tourism models worldwide (Osogbo, 2023). With this intention, it hopes to contribute to the larger conversation on environmentally responsible tourism and economic growth in the context of coastal communities. There is a close connection between establishing comprehensive policies that balance economic growth and environmental protection and the success of maritime tourism in Bangladesh (Talukder et al.,2022). Implementing sustainable practices can reduce the adverse effects imposed on fragile ecosystems, guaranteeing the durability and resilience of the country's coastal regions (Kim & Kim, 2024).

Additionally, incorporating community-based tourism programs can empower local communities, generating a feeling of ownership and pride in preserving their cultural and natural heritage. It is impossible to overestimate the significance of digital platforms, data analytics, and communication tools in this age of constant technological advancement. Leveraging these technologies may improve the tourism experience in several ways, including making bookings more streamlined and delivering real-time information about the environment's state and the precautions that should be taken. Furthermore, incorporating intelligent technology can help efficiently administer and monitor tourist activities, lowering the danger of overexploitation and the accompanying environmental damage (Kwong, 2024).

It is not just domestic tourists that can benefit from Bangladesh's maritime tourism industry. A wide variety of tourists can be attracted to a destination by implementing international marketing strategies, partnerships with foreign travel companies, and participation in international tourism fairs (Talukder & Kumar, 2024). To present Bangladesh as an appealing and responsible option for tourists from all over the world looking for genuine, nature-centred experiences, it is possible to highlight the distinctive features offered by Bangladesh's maritime locations and demonstrate a commitment to environmentally responsible activities (Prokopenko et al., 2023).

The public and private sectors must work together to solve existing infrastructure constraints and foster sustainable growth. Improving the tourist ecosystem by investing in transportation infrastructure, lodging facilities, and educational programs for individuals living in the surrounding areas is possible (Mohammad et al., 2024a). Contributing to study and conservation efforts is possible by cultivating collaborations with environmental groups, non-governmental organizations (NGOs), and academic institutions. This will ensure that maritime tourism in Bangladesh develops congruent with its natural surroundings (Machado & De Andrés, 2023; Mohammad et al., 2024b).

It may be concluded that the future of marine tourism in Bangladesh is filled with chances, given that there is a coordinated effort to address obstacles and embrace opportunities. The purpose of this paper is to provide essential insights that will motivate educated decision-making, stimulate cooperation, and create the framework for a maritime tourism sector in Bangladesh that is both sustainable and prosperous (Talukder et al., 2024). With careful planning, community participation, and a dedication to environmental stewardship, Bangladesh can become a model of responsible maritime tourism, which would benefit the country's economy and the worldwide conservation agenda (Chan et al., 2022).

Objectives of the Study

a. To analyze and evaluate the landscape of marine tourism in Bangladesh, identifying key strengths, weaknesses, opportunities, and threats.
b. To assess the socioeconomic, environmental, and cultural factors influencing the growth of marine tourism in the country.
c. To provide actionable policy recommendations for governmental bodies, policymakers, and regulatory authorities to facilitate the growth of marine tourism in Bangladesh.

Review of the Relevant Literature

The literature review portion of a study on the potential and future of marine tourism in Bangladesh gives an overview of current studies, theories, and findings connected to marine tourism, mainly focusing on Bangladesh's setting. The study was conducted to investigate the prospective tourist industry in Bangladesh. The following is a summary of the relevant literature:

1. **Trends in Marine Tourism Around the World**: A study shows a growing interest in marine tourism worldwide. Several causes drive this interest, including an increased requirement for nature-based experiences, cruise tourism, and adventure travel (Mohammad et al., 2023). There is a growing awareness of the need for responsible tourism in coastal regions worldwide since sustainable and environmentally friendly methods are gaining popularity.
2. **The Association Between Coastal Tourism and Economic Development**: Coastal tourism has been acknowledged globally as an essential contributor to economic development. It creates job possibilities and generates cash for community economies (Zhang & Xing, 2023). To ensure long-term sustainability, studies highlight the significance of striking a balance between economic rewards and the preservation of the environment.
3. **Obstacles and Opportunities for Marine Tourists**: The literature illustrates the typical issues that marine tourist locations confront, such as the degradation of the environment, shortcomings in infrastructure, and the requirement for community engagement (Figueroa Jr, 2023). Opportunities may be found in the utilization of one-of-a-kind natural assets, the promotion of tourism based on community involvement, and the adoption of technical breakthroughs for the sake of sustainable development.

4. **Sustainable Tourism Practices**: Sustainable tourism practices have evolved as an essential component of the growth of maritime tourism. These practices limit tourism's adverse environmental effects, maintain biodiversity, and involve local people (People & Chan, 2023). Successful case studies highlight the beneficial effects that may be achieved by implementing sustainable practices in maritime tourism.
5. **Involvement of Local Communities in the Planning and Administration of Marine Tourism**: The study highlights the significance of integrating local communities in the planning and administration of marine tourism to guarantee their active involvement and ensure that they benefit from economic prospects. Community-based tourism models thrive in various settings, providing opportunities for social inclusion and preserving cultural traditions (Papageorgiou, 2016).
6. **Technology in Marine Tourism**: The use of technology, such as mobile applications, virtual reality, and data analytics, is becoming increasingly popular in the process of boosting the overall experience of tourists and supporting activities that are environmentally responsible. Intelligent technologies are essential for monitoring environmental conditions, controlling tourist flows, and assuring safety in maritime tourism locations (Talukder et al., 2022).
7. **Policy and Governance**: For the marine tourist industry to progress toward a sustainable future, it is essential to have clearly defined and effective governance policies. Using adequate policy frameworks that have fostered maritime tourism expansion while safeguarding natural resources is demonstrated via case studies from different nations.
8. **The Coastal Tourism Landscape of Bangladesh**: There has been a limited amount of study done on marine tourism in Bangladesh, with a particular emphasis on the distinctive characteristics of the country's coastal regions, such as the Sundarbans, Cox's Bazar, and Saint Martin's Island (Sohel Ahmed, 2019). Existing studies may highlight the issues and potential solutions for the Bangladeshi setting.
9. **Cultural and Heritage Tourism Along the Coastline**: Bangladesh's coastal areas, which are abundant in cultural and historical value, provide one-of-a-kind chances for tourism focusing on cultural and heritage tourism (Kudinova et al., 2023). There is a possibility that literature will investigate how the conservation of cultural heritage might be included in maritime tourism initiatives to attract tourists interested in genuine experiences.
10. **Environmental Conservation in Marine Tourism**: The Sundarbans, a UNESCO World Heritage Site, are an essential focal point for organizations concerned with environmental conservation. There is a possibility that the study may investigate the efforts and difficulties involved in striking a balance between

the development of tourism and the preservation of fragile ecosystems and endangered species inside the Sundarbans (Talukder et al., 2024a).

11. **Tourists and the Resilience to Climate Change**: The susceptibility of coastal regions to the effects of climate change, such as the escalation of sea levels and extreme weather events, is an essential component of marine tourism in Bangladesh. There is a possibility that studies may address adaptive techniques and policies to construct resilience in the face of climate change.
12. **The Influence of COVID-19 on Marine tourists**: Recent occurrences, such as the worldwide COVID-19 pandemic, have substantially influenced the tourist sector. A literature review might investigate the short-term and long-term consequences of similar crises on marine tourism in Bangladesh and the measures that can be used to recover from them (Bagchi, 2021).
13. **The Importance of Education and Awareness**: Educational programs and awareness campaigns are essential in promoting responsible tourism practices among tourists, tour operators, and the communities directly affected by tourism (Talukder et al., 2024b). The study may shed insight into the efficacy of educational programs in building a culture of responsible tourism in maritime areas.
14. **Collaboration and Partnerships among Stakeholders**: The successful development of maritime tourism frequently necessitates collaboration across a wide range of stakeholders, such as government agencies, entities from the corporate sector, non-governmental organizations (NGOs), and local communities. The literature may describe examples of successful collaboration and partnerships in other locations, which might provide Bangladesh with valuable information for the growth of its maritime tourist industry.
15. **Market Segmentation and Target Audience**: To design and implement successful marketing and development plans, it is vital to have a comprehensive understanding of the various interests of potential visitors. Market segmentation may be investigated during the study to identify distinct target audiences for marine tourism in Bangladesh (Zeydan & Gürbüz, 2023). This may involve taking into consideration elements such as demographics and travel preferences.
16. **Legal and Regulatory Frameworks**: It is necessary to thoroughly analyze the existing legal and regulatory frameworks that regulate maritime tourism. Literature can analyze the appropriateness and efficiency of existing rules, highlighting areas that require reform and adaptation to guarantee responsible and sustainable tourist operations.
17. **Health and Safety Precautions for Marine tourists**: Recent worries about world health, such as the COVID-19 pandemic, have brought to light the significance of health and safety precautions in the tourist industry. The literature may investigate the most effective methods and developing tendencies in im-

plementing health protocols to guarantee the health and safety of visitors and local populations participating in maritime tourism activities.
18. **Economic effect Assessments:** Economic effect assessments have the potential to offer insightful information on the financial contribution that maritime tourism makes to the economy as a whole. The study may investigate the approaches that can be used to evaluate the direct and indirect economic advantages, job creation, and income production related to marine tourism in Tanzania.
19. **Tourist Preferences and Behavior:** Understanding tourist behaviour and preferences to customize marine tourism services is essential. The literature can investigate study on the reasons for, expectations for, and levels of satisfaction of tourists who participate in maritime activities (Visuwasam et al., 2023). This has the potential to assist in creating experiences that are both targeted and appealing.
20. **Capacity Building and Training**: The development of capacity within local communities and the tourist sector is an essential component of the sustainable growth of maritime tourism.

There is a possibility that the study may investigate the efficacy of training programs that are designed to improve the capabilities of local inhabitants, tour operators, and hospitality providers to fulfil the ever-changing requirements of maritime tourism (Talukder et al.,2023).

21. **Cross-Cultural Tourism Experiences**: The coastal areas of Bangladesh offer a one-of-a-kind chance for visitors to engage in cross-cultural interactions with the communities they visit. Literature can examine effective forms of cross-cultural tourism that encourage tourists and hosts to develop mutual knowledge, respect, and admiration for one another.
22. **Marketing and Branding Strategies**: To successfully promote marine tourist areas, it is necessary to employ strategic branding and promotion. Studies could investigate the marketing campaigns and branding methods that have been effective in other coastal locations (Masengu et al., 2023). These studies will provide insights into how Bangladesh might improve its visibility and desirability in international tourism.
23. **Lessons Learned from Successful Models of Marine Tourism**: Comparative studies of successful models of marine tourism from other nations might lead to discovering essential lessons. The literature may investigate case studies demonstrating how sustainable practices, community participation, and good governance have contributed to the growth of maritime tourism, which would provide insights that apply to Bangladesh.

24. **Accessible tourists in Coastal Areas**: The tourist sector is increasingly taking into consideration the need to ensure accessibility for all persons, including those who have impairments. Through study, it may be possible to investigate how marine tourist locations might be created and changed to meet the varied requirements of visitors, therefore fostering an inclusive environment.
25. **Monitoring and Assessment Over the Long Term**: Establishing continuous monitoring and assessment procedures is essential to adaptive management and continuous improvement. Frameworks for long-term evaluations of the impacts of marine tourism may be discussed in the literature. These frameworks allow dynamic modifications to be made in response to shifting conditions and stakeholder feedback (Kumar et al., 2024).
26. **The Resilience of the Tourism Industry**: Tourism is becoming increasingly important in various crises, including natural catastrophes and global events. Crisis management is also essential to tourism resilience (Sanfilippo et al., 2023). By examining the measures other coastal destinations have implemented to create stability in their tourist sectors, the literature may provide Bangladesh with valuable insights to develop effective crisis management plans.
27. **Ecotourism and the Conservation of Biodiversity**: The Sundarbans, well-known for their rich biodiversity, are a primary target for ecotourism activities. Studies may investigate effective ecotourism models that balance visitors' participation and conservation efforts (De Zoysa, 2022). This will highlight the significance of maintaining and presenting the region's distinctive flora and wildlife.
28. **Digital Marketing and Online Platforms**: Digital marketing and online platforms are significant factors to consider when promoting tourist locations. To increase the exposure and attractiveness of Bangladesh's maritime tourist offers, an investigation may be conducted to investigate efficient digital marketing tactics (Gurunathan & Lakshmi, 2023). These strategies may include social media, virtual tours, and online travel agencies.
29. **The Preservation of Culture Through Tourism**: The success of maritime tourism and the preservation of culture can be closely connected. Literature may dive into instances of tourist projects that have helped preserve local cultures, customs, and legacy along coastal areas. These examples may indicate methods in which Bangladesh might use its cultural assets.
30. **Providing chances for Responsible Wildlife Tourism**: The Sundarbans, which are home to several different species, including the Bengal tiger, offer opportunities for responsible wildlife tourism. The world's best practices for managing wildlife interactions, limiting disruptions, and assuring the ethical treatment of animals in marine tourism contexts may be investigated by examining global best practices.

31. **Water-based Activities and Nautical Tourism:** Nautical tourism, which includes activities such as sailing, yachting, and water sports, is a subset of marine tourism that provides a specialized market (Cardoso et al., 2023). There is a possibility that literature may investigate the development potential, obstacles, and best practices in creating nautical tourist options along Bangladesh's coastline.
32. **Multi-stakeholder Collaboration for Sustainable Tourism**: An effective multi-stakeholder collaboration requires coordination between government agencies, entities from the corporate sector, local communities, and non-governmental organizations from the tourism industry (Chan, 2023). Several studies might be conducted to investigate effective forms of collaborative governance in the marine tourist industry. These studies highlight essential concepts and tactics for promoting synergy among various stakeholders.
33. **Tourism Education and Skill Development**: For marine tourism projects to be successful, it is essential to cultivate a qualified workforce. Education and skill development in the tourist industry are also significant (Rumiantseva, 2023). Literature may explore the role of education and skill development programs in training individuals for professions in the marine tourism sector, contributing to economic growth and the empowerment of local communities.
34. **The Influence of Cultural Events and Festivals**: Cultural events and festivals that take place along the shore have the potential to attract individuals to the area. The study may investigate how events of this nature add to the overall attraction of maritime tourist sites, promoting a sense of celebration and getting the community involved.
35. **Long-Term Socioeconomic Implications:** To achieve sustainable development, it is imperative to have a comprehensive understanding of the long-term socio-economic implications of marine tourism (Roem, 2023). In the literature, there may be discussions of case studies that illustrate how marine tourism has been responsible for bringing about good social and economic changes in coastal towns over an extended period.

This study aims to provide a complete knowledge of the varied nature of marine tourism in Bangladesh. This will be accomplished by expanding the literature review to include these new elements. This broad study will enrich the ensuing analysis and suggestions, contributing to a nuanced and well-informed view of maritime tourism's potential and future trajectory in the country.

Figure 1. Conceptual Framework (Authors compilation)

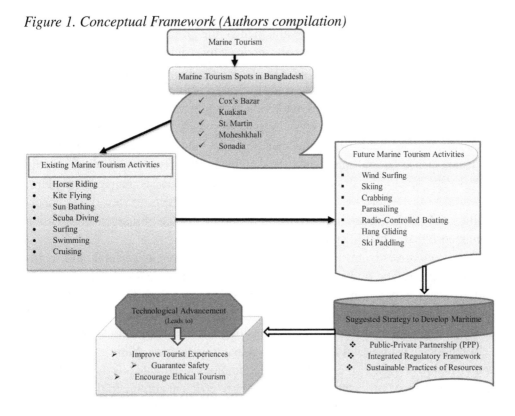

Findings of the Study

The study on the potential and future of marine tourism in Bangladesh revealed a landscape filled with unexplored opportunities and one-of-a-kind attractions throughout the nation's coastline. With its untouched beaches, the Sundarbans mangrove forest, which is known all over the globe, and its extensive cultural history, Bangladesh is well-positioned to become a significant participant in the marine tourism industry worldwide. On the other hand, the necessity of strategic planning is highlighted by obstacles such as poor infrastructure, environmental worries, and limited accessibility. According to the study's findings, there are economic benefits, such as large money production and employment development, particularly for coastal villages in the immediate area. Environmental sustainability emerges as a fundamental principle, highlighting the importance of responsible actions to protect delicate ecosystems, particularly in environmentally vulnerable regions such as the Sundarbans. In addition, the significance of community involvement and empowerment is emphasized, with the emphasis being placed on the fact that the success of maritime tourism is dependent on the active participation of local communities. Additional characteristics of the results include the protection of cultural heritage through maritime tourism activities, the incorporation of technical advancements to improve tourists' experiences, and particular policy suggestions for achieving sustainable growth. The findings of the study indicate that international cooperation and the implementation of successful marketing strategies are essential elements in the process of attracting a wide variety of tourists. The study highlights the significance of constructing resilience within the marine tourist industry to successfully traverse obstacles such as natural catastrophes and global health crises. It also highlights the necessity of developing strategies that are adaptable and crisis management plans. When taken as a whole, these findings provide a comprehensive view of the opportunities and obstacles, providing a road map for the growth of maritime tourism in Bangladesh that is both sustainable and inclusive.

This study investigates marine tourism's economic, environmental, and sociocultural aspects. The findings highlight Bangladesh's potential to become a destination of choice for marine tourism on a worldwide scale. Specifically, it highlights the one-of-a-kind function that maritime tourism plays in helping preserve cultural heritage along the coast, therefore establishing a mutually beneficial interaction between local customs and the experiences that tourists have. Mobile applications and virtual reality are two examples of technologies highlighted as having the potential to enhance participation and enable more efficient administration of tourist operations. Incorporating technology has been seen as a driver for transforming visitor experiences. The study highlights the significance of striking a balance between economic growth and environmental conservation, and the findings are highly significant since they argue for a paradigm shift toward sustainable practices. Maintaining this equilibrium is considered of utmost importance, particularly in environmentally delicate regions such as the Sundarbans, where responsible tourist practices are of the utmost importance for the long-term condition of the area. According to the study's findings, the active participation of local communities is essential for overcoming obstacles and cultivating a feeling of ownership and pride in maritime tourist efforts.

In addition, the study is accompanied by several policy suggestions intended to direct governmental entities and stakeholders in enabling sustainable growth. These ideas include legal frameworks, incentives for ethical activities, and strategies for creating specifically targeted infrastructure. The international aspect is brought to the forefront, and solid marketing techniques and collaborative efforts are anticipated to be the primary drivers in growing Bangladesh's footprint in the worldwide marine tourism sector. The study highlights the significance of resilience in the face of unpredictability, such as natural catastrophes and global health crises. It suggests adaptive techniques and crisis management plans to guarantee the marine tourist industry's continued success in the long run. The study's findings weave a narrative that acknowledges the obstacles and gives a forward-looking vision, defining concrete actions for Bangladesh's sustainable, culturally rich, and commercially viable maritime tourism sector.

The study's findings shed light on the interconnection of several elements contributing to Bangladesh's diverse character of maritime tourism. The economic effect is not limited to generating immediate money. However, it emphasizes establishing various job possibilities to bolster the towns along the shore. When combined with environmentally responsible behaviours, this economic empowerment is hypothesized to work as a catalyst for social transformation, strengthening the resilience and well-being of communities.

Cultural preservation develops as more than a result of marine tourism; it becomes a dynamic force that shapes the experience that visitors have. The study highlights the significance of cultural events and festivals in improving maritime tourism locations' appeal. These events and festivals create a dynamic tapestry that attracts travellers seeking genuine, immersive adventure experiences. In addition, the study acknowledges the dynamic nature of the tourism industry, recognizing that incorporating technology improves tourists' experiences and serves as a tool for efficiently administrating destinations. In today's technologically advanced world, the focus placed on digital marketing techniques and online platforms reflects the changing nature of how travellers interact with and learn about places.

In recognition that sustainable growth necessitates coordinated efforts from various stakeholders, the policy recommendations of the study call for an all-encompassing approach. It advocates for regulatory frameworks that incentivize responsible behaviours, infrastructure development that aligns with environmental concerns, and strategic interventions to address difficulties unique to the maritime tourist industry. In a nutshell, the findings portray a multifaceted image of marine tourism in Bangladesh, not just as an economic enterprise but also as a transformational force that has the potential to positively influence local people, protect cultural heritage, and highlight the natural beauty of the country on the international stage. The suggestions of the study offer stakeholders a road map that can be used to manage problems, capitalize on opportunities, and collaboratively drive the marine tourism sector in Bangladesh towards a future that is both sustainable and successful.

The study's findings show the necessity of international collaboration and robust marketing methods in bringing Bangladesh's maritime tourism to the forefront of the world. The country has the potential to attract a wide variety of tourists by tapping into the global tourism industry. This would create opportunities for cultural interaction and increase the country's attractiveness as a one-of-a-kind destination. According to the study, a coordinated effort to communicate with the international community, travel agencies, and potential tourists is required for marine tourism to be booming. The report acknowledges that the success of marine tourism is not limited to the borders of individual nations.

Furthermore, the study highlights the necessity of continuous monitoring and evaluation systems, highlighting the significance of adaptive management in reacting to emerging trends, stakeholder input, and changing environmental circumstances. This iterative approach is vital for fine-tuning plans, ensuring that marine tourism projects remain dynamic and sensitive to the ever-changing needs and expectations of visitors and the communities they visit. In addition, the data support the idea that maritime tourism has a significant socioeconomic influence across the long distance. The study investigates how prolonged involvement with marine tourism might spark beneficial reforms in local economies, education, and infrastructure. These opportunities extend beyond the immediate economic gains that marine tourism provides. Additionally, it anticipates a future in which the advantages of marine tourism extend well beyond the profits realized in the near term, contributing to the general growth and well-being of coastal communities.

The study emphasizes the significance of resilience in assuring the continued viability of the maritime tourist industry for the long term. The sector can traverse obstacles more successfully, displaying agility and a commitment to sustainability, if it anticipates and prepares for future crises. According to the study, Bangladesh's maritime tourism industry is envisioned as a resilient and forward-looking sector that flourishes under favourable conditions and exhibits resilience in the face of adversity.

In conclusion, the findings of the study help to weave together a narrative that conceives of marine tourism in Bangladesh as a transformational force that has the potential to reach everywhere in the world. To establish a sustainable and prosperous future for maritime tourism in the country, it argues for a strategy that incorporates sustainability and cultural preservation, technical innovation, and international collaboration.

Recommendations

I. Create and carry out all-encompassing policies that prioritize sustainable maritime tourist practices. Guidelines for community involvement, environmental preservation, and efforts promoting responsible tourism should be part of this.
II. Invest funds in the construction and renovation of coastal infrastructure. This comprises entertainment, lodging, and transportation amenities to improve the traveller experience.

III. To guarantee that the local communities actively engage in and profit from maritime tourism, promote and assist community-based tourist projects. Programs for training, ways to share earnings, and chances for cross-cultural interaction can all be part of this.
IV. Accept technology to improve the experience for guests. Create mobile apps, virtual reality experiences, and other digital tools that give travellers information, guarantee their safety, and give them engaging travel experiences.
V. Put effective environmental protection initiatives in place, especially in regions like the Sundarbans, which are environmentally delicate. This might involve programs for sustainable wildlife tourism, habitat protection, and waste management.
VI. To maintain and preserve maritime tourist sites' many habitats and species, develop and implement responsible wildlife tourism principles. This entails limiting disruptions and establishing guidelines for interactions with wildlife.
VII. Start training initiatives to improve the local labour force's abilities, including tour operators, guides, and hospitality employees. This guarantees that they have all they need to meet visitors' expectations and maintain excellent service.
VIII. Encourage cooperation between the public and private sectors to use their combined resources, know-how, and inventiveness. Sustainable practices may be promoted, and maritime tourist development projects may be made more efficient through public-private partnerships.
IX. Create focused marketing initiatives to raise Bangladesh's profile in the world travel industry. Draw a broad spectrum of foreign visitors by emphasizing distinctive attractions, cultural events, and environmentally friendly activities.
X. Create thorough crisis management strategies to handle future obstacles like natural catastrophes and international health emergencies. To enhance resilience in the face of unanticipated disasters, these plans should include methods for communication, safety precautions, and industry-wide collaboration.

By implementing these suggestions, we can support economic growth, cultural preservation, environmental protection, and the sustainable, inclusive, and resilient development of maritime tourism in Bangladesh.

CONCLUSION AND FUTURE STUDY

In conclusion, the study on the potential and future of marine tourism in Bangladesh sheds light on the transformational possibilities inherent in the country's broad coastal regions. Bangladesh is positioned to become a worldwide player in marine tourism because it possesses the necessary foundations. Some of the distinctive attractions that Bangladesh boasts are the Sundarbans mangrove forest, virgin beaches, and a rich cultural legacy. The findings highlight the significance of environmentally responsible practices, active participation in the community, and progressive technical advancement as essential elements for the industry's success. The ideas that have been put up, which include the establishment of comprehensive policies, the investment of infrastructure, and international collaboration, combined provide a road map for guiding maritime tourism towards a resilient, inclusive, and ecologically conscientious future. By putting these plans into action, Bangladesh has the chance to realize the economic potential of its coastal regions and highlight and conserve the natural and cultural assets that make it a unique destination on the map of the world's tourism destinations. In the envisioned future, marine tourism is seen as a driver for good socioeconomic development, celebrating cultural variety and contributing to the general well-being of coastal communities in Bangladesh.

While the environment of maritime tourism in Bangladesh is constantly shifting, future studies may go more deeply into particular components to deepen and broaden our understanding. An in-depth examination of the socioeconomic effects of marine tourism on local communities, considering the distribution of revenue and the empowerment of the community, will provide valuable insights for realizing sustainable development. A detailed evaluation of the success of the policies that have been adopted and the incorporation of new technologies in improving the overall experience of visitors will provide significant input for projects that are currently being undertaken and those that will be undertaken in the future. Examining the long-term environmental effects and adaptation tactics in response to climate change and extensive market assessments for specific tourist segments might guide implementing focused initiatives. In addition, a comparison study with successful models from other countries might reveal subtle insights pertinent to Bangladesh's particular circumstances. These future studies have the potential to contribute to a dynamic and adaptable strategy, which will ensure the sector's resilience, sustainability, and good influence on both the economy and the environment. Marine tourism continues to play a crucial role in the country's development.

REFERENCES

Affatati, A., Scaini, C., & Scaini, A. (2024). The role of operators in sustainable whale-watching tourism: Proposing a continuous training framework. *PLoS One*, 19(1), e0296241. DOI: 10.1371/journal.pone.0296241 PMID: 38166106

Bagchi, S. (2021). Exploring the impact of covid-19 on tourism industry of Bangladesh: an empirical study. *International Journal of Study -Granthaalayah*, 9(8), 42–58. DOI: 10.29121/granthaalayah.v9.i8.2021.4141

Cardoso, L., Lopes, E., Almeida, G. G. F. D., Lima Santos, L., Sousa, B., Simões, J., & Perna, F. (2023). Features of Nautical Tourism in Portugal—Projected Destination Image with a Sustainability Marketing Approach. *Sustainability (Basel)*, 15(11), 8805. DOI: 10.3390/su15118805

Chan, C.-S., Chang, T. C., & Liu, Y. (2022). Investigating Creative Experiences and Environmental Perception of Creative Tourism: The Case of PMQ (Police Married Quarters) in Hong Kong. *Journal of China Tourism Research*, 18(2), 223–244. DOI: 10.1080/19388160.2020.1812459

Chan, J. K. L. (2023). Sustainable Rural Tourism Practices From the Local Tourism Stakeholders' Perspectives. *Global business finance review*, 28(3), 136–149. DOI: 10.17549/gbfr.2023.28.3.136

Choi, J., & Lim, S. (2024). Establishing a Marine Protected Area in the Waters Surrounding Dokdo: Necessity and Legality. *Sustainability (Basel)*, 16(2), 611. DOI: 10.3390/su16020611

Das, I. R., Talukder, M. B., & Kumar, S. (2024). Implication of Artificial Intelligence in Hospitality Marketing. *Utilizing Smart Technology and AI in Hybrid Tourism and Hospitality*. IGI Global, USA. DOI: 10.4018/979-8-3693-1978-9.ch014

De Zoysa, M. (2022). Ecotourism Development and Biodiversity Conservation in Sri Lanka: Objectives, Conflicts and Resolutions. *Open Journal of Ecology*, 12(10), 638–666. DOI: 10.4236/oje.2022.1210037

Figueroa, R. B.Jr. (2023). Immersive capability and spatial presence in virtual reality photo-based tours: Implications for distance education. *Asian Association of Open Universities Journal*, 18(3), 201–217. DOI: 10.1108/AAOUJ-12-2022-0171

Gurunathan, A., & Lakshmi, K. S. (2023). Exploring the Perceptions of Generations X, Y and Z about Online Platforms and Digital Marketing Activities – A Focus-Group Discussion Based Study. *International Journal of Professional Business Review*, 8(5), e02122. DOI: 10.26668/businessreview/2023.v8i5.2122

Kim, H., & Kim, C. W. (2024). Limitations and Problems Associated with Marine Healing Tourism: An Examination of the Chungcheongnam-Do Marine Healing Pilot Program. *Journal of Coastal Research*, 116(sp1). Advance online publication. DOI: 10.2112/JCR-SI116-087.1

Kudinova, I., & Terzi, S. (2023). Cultural heritage - the tourism brand of ukraine. *Journal of Lviv Polytechnic National University.Series of Economics and Management Issues*, 7(2), 27–40. DOI: 10.23939/semi2023.02.027

Kumar, S., Talukder, M. B., Kabir, F., & Kaiser, F. (2024). Challenges and Sustainability of Green Finance in the Tourism Industry: Evidence from Bangladesh. In Taneja, S., Kumar, P., Grima, S., Ozen, E., & Sood, K. (Eds.), (pp. 97–111). Advances in Finance, Accounting, and Economics. IGI Global., DOI: 10.4018/979-8-3693-1388-6.ch006

Kumar, S., Talukder, M. B., & Kaiser, F. (2024). Artificial Intelligence in Business: Negative Social Impacts. In *Demystifying the Dark Side of AI in Business* (pp. 81-97). IGI Global. https://doi.org/ DOI: 10.4018/979-8-3693-0724-3.ch005

Kumar, S., Talukder, M. B., & Pego, A. (Eds.). (2024). *Utilizing Smart Technology and AI in Hybrid Tourism and Hospitality*. IGI Global., DOI: 10.4018/979-8-3693-1978-9

Kwong, Y. M. C. (2024). Engaging children's voices for tourism and marine futures through drawing in Gili Trawangan, Indonesia. *Frontiers in Sustainable Tourism*, 2, 1291142. DOI: 10.3389/frsut.2023.1291142

Ma, H.-Y., Kao, J.-C., Kao, R.-H., Chiang, N.-T., & Cho, C.-C. (2024). A study on transboundary governance of marine plastic debris—The case of an adjacent waters between China and Taiwan. *Environmental Science and Pollution Study*. DOI: 10.1007/s11356-024-31876-3

Machado, J. T. M., & De Andrés, M. (2023). Implications of offshore wind energy developments in coastal and maritime tourism and recreation areas: An analytical overview. *Environmental Impact Assessment Review*, 99, 106999. DOI: 10.1016/j.eiar.2022.106999

Masengu, R., Bigirimana, S., Chiwaridzo, O. T., Bensson, R., & Blossom, C. (Eds.). (2023). *Sustainable Marketing, Branding, and Reputation Management: Strategies for a Greener Future*. IGI Global., DOI: 10.4018/979-8-3693-0019-0

Mohammad Badruddoza Talukder, Firoj Kabir, K. M., & Das, I. R. (2023). Emerging Concepts of Artificial Intelligence in the Hotel Industry: A Conceptual Paper. *International Journal of Study Publication and Reviews, Vol 4, no,* pp 1765-1769. https://doi.org/DOI: 10.55248/gengpi.4.923.92451

Mohammad Badruddoza Talukder. Sanjeev Kumar, I. R. Das. (2024a). Implications of Blockchain Technology- Based Cryptocurrency in the cloud for the Hospitality Industry. In *Emerging Trends in Cloud Computing Analytics, Scalability, and Service Models* (p. 19). https://doi.org/DOI: 10.4018/979-8-3693-0900-1.ch018

Mohammad Badruddoza Talukder. Sanjeev Kumar, I. R. Das. (2024b). Perspectives of Digital Marketing for the Restaurant Industry. In *Advancements in Socialized and Digital Media Communications* (p. 17). https://doi.org/DOI: 10.4018/979-8-3693-0855-4.ch009

Nurhayati, A., Herawati, T., Handaka, A. A., Pamungkas, W., Akbarsyah, N., & Sudarmono, A. (2023). Sustainable marine ecotourism governance based on tourism preferences. *IOP Conference Series. Earth and Environmental Science,* 1289(1), 012012. DOI: 10.1088/1755-1315/1289/1/012012

Oh, C., Kim, K.-B., Lee, H., & Nam-Jo, S. K. (2024). Beaches for Everyone? World's First Water Wheelchair with Smart Safety Features for Barrier-Free Tourism. *Journal of Coastal Research,* 116(sp1). Advance online publication. DOI: 10.2112/JCR-SI116-097.1

Osogbo, Nigeria. (2023). The effect of informal economy on human capital development. *Izvestiya Journal of the University of Economics – Varna,* 67(3), 182–195. DOI: 10.56065/IJUEV2023.67.3.182

Papageorgiou, M. (2016). Coastal and marine tourism: A challenging factor in Marine Spatial Planning. *Ocean and Coastal Management,* 129, 44–48. DOI: 10.1016/j.ocecoaman.2016.05.006

Prokopenko, O., Järvis, M., Saichuk, V., Komarnitskyi, I., Glybovets, V., & Troian, M. (2023). International Marine Tourism: Trends and Prospects for Sustainable Development. *Pomorstvo,* 37(1), 23–31. DOI: 10.31217/p.37.1.3

Rumiantseva, I. (2023). Systematization of tourist market development factors. *Ukrainian Journal of Applied Economics and Technology,* 8(4), 250–257. DOI: 10.36887/2415-8453-2023-4-41

Sanfilippo, F., Pomeroy, C., & Bailey, D. N. (2023). Crisis Management. In F. Sanfilippo, C. Pomeroy, & D. N. Bailey, *Lead, Inspire, Thrive* (pp. 99–102). Springer Nature Switzerland. DOI: 10.1007/978-3-031-41177-9_16

Sohel Ahmed, S. M.Sohel Ahmed, S. M. (2019). Risks of Climate Change at Coastal Tourism in Bangladesh: A Study on Cox's Bazar. *Information Management and Business Review*, 11(3(I)), 1–12. DOI: 10.22610/imbr.v11i3(I).2942

Tait, M., Gaughen, K., Tsang, A., Walton, M., Marcoux, S., Kekoa, L., Kunz, M., & Vaughan, M. (2024). Holomua Marine Initiative: Community-generated sociocultural principles and indicators for marine conservation and management in Hawai'i. *Ecology and Society*, 29(1), art4. DOI: 10.5751/ES-13640-290104

Talukder, M., Kumar, S., Misra, L., & Kabir, F. (2024). Determining the role of ecotourism service quality, tourist satisfaction,and destination loyalty: A case study of Kuakata Beach. *Acta Scientiarum Polonorum. Administratio Locorum*, 23(1), 133–151. DOI: 10.31648/aspal.9275

Talukder, M., Shakhawat Hossain, M., & Kumar, S. (2022). Blue Ocean Strategies in Hotel Industry in Bangladesh: A Review of Present Literatures' Gap and Suggestions for Further Study. SSRN Electronic Journal. DOI: 10.2139/ssrn.4160709

Talukder, M. B. (2020). An Appraisal of the Economic Outlook for the Tourism Industry, Specially Cox's Bazar in Bangladesh. *i-manager's Journal on Economics & Commerce*, 2(1), 23-35. DOI: 10.26634/jecom.2.1.17285

Talukder, M. B. (2020b). The Future of Culinary Tourism: An Emerging Dimension for the Tourism Industry of Bangladesh. I-Manager's. *Journal of Management*, 15(1), 27. DOI: 10.26634/jmgt.15.1.17181

Talukder, M. B. (2021). An assessment of the roles of the social network in the development of the Tourism Industry in Bangladesh. *International Journal of Business, Law, and Education*, 2(3), 85–93. DOI: 10.56442/ijble.v2i3.21

Talukder, M. B. (2024). Implementing Artificial Intelligence and Virtual Experiences in Hospitality. In *Innovative Technologies for Increasing Service Productivity* (pp. 145–160). IGI Global., DOI: 10.4018/979-8-3693-2019-8.ch009

Talukder, M. B., & Hossain, M. M. (2021). Prospects of Future Tourism in Bangladesh: An Evaluative Study. I-Manager's. *Journal of Management*, 15(4), 1–8. DOI: 10.26634/jmgt.15.4.17495

Talukder, M. B., Kabir, F., Kaiser, F., & Lina, F. Y. (2024). Digital Detox Movement in the Tourism Industry: Traveler Perspective. In *Business Drivers in Promoting Digital Detoxification* (pp. 91-110). IGI Global. DOI: 10.4018/979-8-3693-1107-3.ch007

Talukder, M. B., & Kaiser, F. (2023). Economic Impact of River Tourism: Evidence of Bangladesh. *i-manager's. Journal of Management*, 18(2), 47–60. DOI: 10.26634/jmgt.18.2.20235

Talukder, M. B., & Kumar, S. "The Effect of Food Service Quality on Customer Satisfaction in the Hotel Industry: A Conceptual Paper," StudyGate, Jun.10, 2023. [Online]. Available: https://www.studygate.net/publication/371503829_The_Effect_of_Food_Service_Quality_on_Customer_Satisfaction_in_the_Hotel_Industry_A_Conceptual_Paper

Talukder, M.B., & Kumar, S. (2024). Revisiting intention in food service outlet of five-star hotels: A quantitative approach based on food service quality. Sport i Turystyka. Środkowoeuropejskie Czasopismo Naukowe, 7(1), 137–156. DOI: 10.16926/sit.2024.01.08

Talukder, M. B., Kumar, S., & Das, I. R. (2024). *Food Wastage on the Economic Outcome: Evidence From the Hotel Industry. Sustainable Disposal Methods of Food Wastes in Hospitality Operations*. IGI Global., DOI: 10.4018/979-8-3693-2181-2.ch005

Talukder, M. B., Kumar, S., & Das, I. R. (2024). Mindfulness of Digital Detoxification: Healthy Lifestyle in Tourism. In *Contemporary Management and Global Leadership for Sustainability* (pp. 56–71). IGI Global., DOI: 10.4018/979-8-3693-1273-5.ch004

Talukder, M. B., Kumar, S., Sood, K., & Grima, S. (2023). Information Technology, Food Service Quality and Restaurant Revisit Intention. *International Journal of Sustainable Development and Planning*, 18(1), 295–303. DOI: 10.18280/ijsdp.180131

Thu Huong, D. T., Lan, T. D., & Le, D. T. (2024). Environmental Conflicts with Tourist Beach Uses along the Northeastern Vietnam Coast. *Journal of Coastal Research*, 40(1). Advance online publication. DOI: 10.2112/JCOASTRES-D-23-00002.1

Visuwasam, L. M. M., Srinath, M., Raj, V. S. A., Sirajudeen, A., Sudhir Maharaaja, S., & Raja, D. (2023). Tourist Behaviour Analysis Using Data Analytics. In Singh, S., Rajest, S. S., Hadoussa, S., Obaid, A. J., & Regin, R. (Eds.), (pp. 343–355). Advances in Business Information Systems and Analytics. IGI Global., DOI: 10.4018/979-8-3693-2193-5.ch023

Zeydan, İ., & Gürbüz, A. (2023). Examining tourists' travel intentions in Türkiye during pandemic and post-pandemic period: The mediating effect of risk reduction behavior. *Journal of Multidisciplinary Academic Tourism*, 8(2), 171–183. DOI: 10.31822/jomat.2023-8-2-171

Zhang, G., & Xing, L. (2023). Study on tourism economic effect under the threshold of new-type urbanization in coastal cities of China: From the perspective of development economics. *Ocean and Coastal Management*, 239, 106587. DOI: 10.1016/j.ocecoaman.2023.106587

Chapter 5
Special Forms of Tourism as a Territorial Management Tool:
An Exploratory Study in the Context of Geocaching

Júlio Sousa Silva
Polytechnic Institute of Cávado and Ave (IPCA), Portugal

Bruno Barbosa Sousa
https://orcid.org/0000-0002-8588-2422
Polytechnic Institute of Cávado and Ave, Portugal & Applied Management Research Unit (UNIAG), Portugal & Centro de Investigação, Desenvolvimento e Inovação em Turismo (CiTUR), Portugal

EXECUTIVE SUMMARY

Some Special Forms of Tourism (SFT) are the result of technological developments (e.g. virtual tourism, e-tourism, or emotional intelligence) or using highly developed specialist systems that can provide a greater variety of tourism products and tourism services. Geocaching is an outdoor recreational activity, in which participants use a Global Positioning System (GPS) receiver or mobile device and other navigational techniques to hide and seek containers, called geocaches or caches, at specific locations marked by coordinates all over the world. Apparently, this tourist practice could be an important tool in the dissemination and notoriety of tourist destinations (i.e. territorial management), as well as in regional and local development. This chapter aims to present some illustrative cases of geocaching as a territorial management tool. From an interdisciplinary perspective, the chapter presents insights for marketing (territorial) and tourism (niches and segments with

DOI: 10.4018/979-8-3693-1548-4.ch005

specific motivations). At the end, lines of future research will be presented.

INTRODUCTION

Tourism, as an area of research, has expanded its scope, reflecting a growing recognition in the academic community, parallel to the application of interdisciplinary concepts and methods (Santos et al., 2021; 2022). In fact, tourism research has studied its various implications from a multitude of perspectives and with interdisciplinary perceptions (Aliperti et al., 2019; Okumus et al., 2018; Franch et al., 2008; Pradhan, Malik & Vishwakarma, 2023). For instance, niche tourism can be considered an alternative, almost the antithesis of modern mass tourism (for example, rural tourism products or services (Liu, Dou & Cai, 2020). In this context, geocaching is an activity that can be compared to traditional treasure hunting (Boulaire & Hervet, 2012; Martins, 2014; Lusa, 2015). However, unlike the usual physical maps, geocachers, the name given to those who practice this activity, use location coordinates through a GPS system (Global Positioning System). This chapter proposes a comprehensive review of the existing literature on the use of Geocaching as a strategic tool in city territorial promotion initiatives. This study aims to explore how cities that have adopted Geocaching as an effective strategy to publicize and highlight their points of cultural, historical and natural interest. The literature review analyzes how this practice has been implemented in different contexts, highlighting initiatives, strategies and success stories that reveal the impact of Geocaching on attracting visitors, strengthening local identity and valuing heritage, in addition to evaluating its contribution to the promotion of sustainable tourism.

1. NICHE TOURISM PERSPECTIVES

Competitiveness assumes as a growing phenomenon and quality and innovation are a priority in the business world. Therefore, organizations express the need to create mechanisms capable of providing added value to consumers and occupying a better position in their minds. It is in this perspective that relationship marketing emerges as a strategy of loyalty and creation of strong links between organizations and their consumers (Macedo et al., 2021; Duarte et al., 2021). Trends in global tourism demand suggest the emergence of sophisticated consumers looking for new, different, and specific tourist experiences (Soroker, Bergerv& Nebenzahl, 2023; Choe, Baek & Kim, 2023; Gaetjens et al., 2023). Niche marketing seems a relevant response to market dynamics (Wen, Goh & Yu, 2023). Although niche marketing has been successfully applied to a high number and many types of businesses, there is a shortage of research addressing the way niche marketing may be applied to (geochaching experiences) tourism. While mass tourism is homogeneous in nature (a standardized and uniform product for a large market segment), niche tourism is defined by its heterogeneous nature (greater demand for a more distinct and unique product) (Proos & Hattingh, 2022; Novelli et al., 2022).

2. GEOCACHING: SPECIAL INTEREST TOURISM

Geocaching is an activity that can be compared to traditional treasure hunting (Boulaire & Hervet, 2012; Martins, 2014; Lusa, 2015). However, unlike the usual physical maps, geocachers, the name given to those who practice this activity, use location coordinates through a GPS system (Global Positioning System). The first cache was placed in Portland, in the United States, in 2000, following the decision of the North American government that, on May 1 of the same year, released the GPS signal for civilian use (Fernandes, 2012; Gram-Hansen 2009). To test it, Dave Ulmer had the idea of creating the "Great American GPS Stash Hunt", and decided to hide, the next day, a black bucket in a forest near Beavercreek, Oregon, leaving, inside, a logbook (currently called a logbook), a pencil, a VHS cassette, a candy, among other small items (Gram-Hansen 2009; Pisula et al., 2023). He then shared the coordinates online and explained that the locator could only use the GPS receiver to reach the location (Boys et al., 2023). If he managed to find the bucket, he should take one of the objects and leave another in exchange (Kosmaczewska, 2022). In the first month, Mike Teague, the first person to find Dave Ulmer's bucket, decided to start collecting all the texts that indicated the coordinates of a container and shared them on his personal page: GPS Stash Hunt.

Geocaching practitioners have the objective and challenge of finding geocaches (or, in the common language of this community, caches) (Boulaire & Hervet, 2012; Martins, 2014; Pisula, 2021), which will allow them to record the moment of visiting the location in the logbook. Caches are, as a general rule, hidden in places of some type of interest, namely historical places, places with good landscapes and public monuments, with the aim of making these new places known or, if they are already known places to the geocacher, lead you to discover caches and thus have greater success in the game.

New caches are launched daily (designated by creators as owners), hiding them and then registering their information and geocache coordinates on the game's official website, www.geocaching.com, where the activity is organized (Boulaire & Hervet, 2012; Fernandes, 2012; Martins, 2014). When submitting a new geocache, the owner must include a generic description of the cache, the difficulty level of the cache and the terrain where it is hidden, and also several other attributes that will later be visible to other geocachers (Fernandes, 2012; Martins, 2014). When they find it, they leave their signature on a recording paper found inside, the logbook, as mentioned above (Fernandes, 2012; Martins, 2014). After searching for and discovering (or not) the cache, practitioners return to the official website and, on the cache page, record their visit, called a log (Fernandes, 2012; Martins, 2014). This record is associated with a geocache page and always includes the date it occurred, and may also have attached a more or less long comment and some photos about the experience (Martins, 2014).

There are several types of geocaches, each with its specific characteristics:

Traditional Cache: This is the most basic type of geocache. It consists of a physical container hidden at certain coordinates, which participants use a GPS to find. It usually contains a logbook to record the visit and sometimes small items to exchange.

Multi-Cache: This type of geocache involves several steps to find the final container. Participants solve clues or find coordinates in each step to reach the cache's final location.

Mystery or Puzzle Cache: These caches require you to solve a puzzle to obtain the real coordinates. There can be different types of challenges such as puzzles, encrypted codes, among others.

EarthCache: An EarthCache does not contain a physical container. These are places where participants learn about specific geological or natural phenomena, such as rock formations, reliefs, or other natural features, and answer questions related to the location.

Event Cache: These are meetings organized by geocachers in specific locations and dates. Generally, these are opportunities for participants to get together and exchange experiences, without necessarily looking for a physical cache during the event.

Virtual Cache: Virtual Caches, like Earth Cache, do not have a physical container. As a rule, they go to a place where they take a photo and answer questions about that same place.

The geocaching application is a fundamental tool for players and is available on mobile devices. The application offers access to a vast world of adventures and caches. With an intuitive interface, it allows users to find, register and even hide caches. Additionally, the application provides detailed information about each cache, including descriptions, tips, precise GPS coordinates and comments from other geocachers. The application has a premium option for players who pay an annual fee. Being a premium geocaching player offers a number of significant advantages over the basic account. Premium players have access to exclusive features like advanced searches, which allow you to filter caches based on specific criteria, making it easier to discover caches that are ideal for your search style or preferences. Additionally, premium players can view additional caches compared to basic accounts, expanding their exploration opportunities. Another important benefit is the ability to open maps offline, allowing players to plan and carry out their adventures even in places without an internet connection (figure 1).

Figure 1. Exemple of "cache"

3. GEOCACHING IN PORTUGAL

In Portugal, the history of geocaching began with the first cache launched, entitled AlfaRomeu Abandonado! (GC1DA), on February 2, 2001, revealing its content through the theme of the title. Unfortunately, this cache was not found, as the cache ended up disappearing. However, on May 15, 2001, "AZGTJ – Translant Chess Cache" (GC8EF9) appeared, the oldest cache that remains active to this day. Since then, interest in this activity has continued to grow, both in hidden caches and in participants, reaching a peak in recent years, mainly due to the popularization of smartphones.

With the advancement of geocaching, a dynamic community has blossomed. The first forum to be established was geocaching-pt.net. A few years later, geopt.org appeared. These forums have become excellent spaces for exchanging information and promoting this pastime, bringing together players who share experiences, tips and challenges, thus contributing to the continued growth and dissemination of geocaching in Portugal. In 2022, there were more than 50,000 players registered and more than 20,000 active caches.

3.1. Benefits of Practicing Geocaching

Geocaching is an activity that has some benefits. According to Geopt (2016), these benefits can be divided into three areas: social, pedagogical and physical.

In terms of social benefits, geocaching can be understood as a socialization practice (Fernandes, 2012), since, as it is an activity preferably practiced in groups, it fosters cohesion between families and practitioners and allows for meetings and social closer ties, exchanging information or even creating common projects to search for and place new caches (Fernandes, 2012), through the organization of events (with different themes - walks, coffees between geocachers, etc.). The practice of this activity is supported by a network of contacts in a web environment and in the field (Skinner et al., 2018).

With regard to pedagogical benefits, geocaching is an activity that allows the acquisition of new knowledge. The caches, located in strategic locations, enable practitioners to acquire historical, geographic and cultural knowledge. Furthermore, the process of creating and hiding a geocache is also a means of enrichment and personal knowledge, as it is necessary to do initial research on the place where we want to hide our treasure, which requires research on the Internet and in the place itself. that we keep an eye on (Geopt, 2016; Skinner et al., 2018). Due to the need to use GPS systems, which imply the use of geographic coordinates – latitude and longitude, geocaching promotes the acquisition of knowledge about geography and history (Geopt, 2016; Lebre, 2017).

Finally, the physical benefits, intrinsic to geochaching, are the most obvious benefits, given that the search for caches often involves long walks and journeys (Geopt, 2016). The physical benefits can also be subdivided into physiological and psychological benefits: the physiological ones are related to the benefits of physical exercise at a physiological level, while the psychological ones are associated with the challenge and success of finding the desired object, the geocache (Geopt, 2016).

3.2. Geocaching as a Tool for Promoting Territories

In Portugal, tourism plays a fundamental role in the economy, showing consistent growth over the years. Nature Tourism is recognized in the National Tourism Strategic Plan (PENT) as one of the main tourism products to be developed in the country, based on Portugal's distinctive natural resources and its potential for future growth. However, PENT also highlights certain gaps that the country faces, such as clear deficiencies in infrastructure, services, experiences and expertise of companies operating in this field. These challenges require the development of a tourist offer that is not only attractive to visitors, but also respectful of the environment and promotes the preservation of protected areas. Furthermore, in order for us to get to know different places, it is crucial to promote and enhance natural and scenic heritage. However, certain places of interest and significant value often lack marketing that promotes their potential.

In this context, geocaching presents itself as a tool for promoting a region or territory (Boulaire & Hervet, 2012; Mydłowska, 2023; Pisula, 2021; Pisula et al., 2023). In addition to being a type of technology-guided walk, geocaching can be presented as an innovative approach to exploring a place, be it a country, a region or a city, making them more captivating (Boulaire and Hervet, 2012; KC & Leung, 2022; Silva et al., 2023). In other words, this activity, by using online technology, not only offers an interactive and educational experience, but can also serve as a powerful vehicle to increase the visibility of natural, cultural and scenic areas, thus contributing to sustainable and conscious tourism. . Thus, practicing this activity combines the opportunity to wander and explore new places with learning about the history, culture, customs and traditions of a given place (Matherson et al. 2008; Pisula, 2021; MacBride-Stewart et al., 2021).

According to Ihamäki (2012), geocaching is a location-based experience, which has established and sustained itself over several years. As others such as (Harper et al., 2006; O'Hara et al., 2007; Palen et al., 2000) argue them studies, there has limited field trial studies are not designed to explore the emergent everyday practices with technologies, the factors creative tourism experience that shape these practices, and the social meaning they acquire as they become integrated into people's everyday lives. A study of geocaching affords us the opportunity to get this longer-term perspective on practices with a location-based experience Ihamäki (2012). The growing practice of geocaching is hide-and-seek game. Except the seeking is done by hand held GPS devices, and the hiding is done by geocachers on haring their favorite places with the world. The global game is a growing trend with families of all ages. Then adventurous geocachers, armed with GPS devices and co-ordinates found on the geocaching website, search for box, take a trinket and replace it, or record their visit, and meanwhile, enjoy someone's special spot. Although there is still no specific concept for Geocaching tourism, there are authors who are beginning to look at this activity as a form of tourism. In the opinion of Oliveira (2010), Geocaching has characteristics that make this game an eminently touristic activity, as it involves travel and/or short-term trips and motivation, the reasons for which are: discovery, knowledge, adventure, fun, contact with the outdoors and traveling to visit urban, rural or natural places, which can be carried out individually or in specific groups (family or friends). In order to facilitate this new type of search, tourist routes, called Geotours, were developed on the official Geocaching page. Geotours are one of the best examples of Geocaching activities as a promoter of tourism in the regions. They function as structured itineraries to guide the geocacher in a specific region or natural park, they allow you to discover interesting stopping points, such as a natural or built monument, a typical restaurant that showcases local gastronomy, a panoramic view or even even a place to stay overnight, thus allowing contact with the local population.

According to Boulaire and Hervet (2012), there is the possibility of combining Geocaching with tourism promotion in two ways. The first way is to promote Geocaching through existing geocaches in destinations or events taking place. The second way is to promote territories, using Geocaching as a way to explore what the destination has to offer, and in this second strategy, the best the destination has to offer can be promoted with Geocaching and can be done through the creation of new routes. to showcase lesser-known places. By placing caches in strategic locations, Geocaching provides a unique experience to participants, revealing distinctive aspects of a territory. Caches contain individual descriptions (called listings) of the place or monument where they are located, thus allowing the dissemination of precise information about places of interest. Authors such as Lebre (2017) state that the creation of elaborate caches, including historical details or local curiosities, offers a unique opportunity to transmit knowledge to practitioners, thus expanding awareness and understanding of the territory in question. Thus, geocaching offers the opportunity to make the location recognizable (Gram-Hansen 2009), as it is a practice that strengthens destinations, reinforces points of greatest interest, reinforces already established routes and/or promotes new routes and gives to get to know places, which, although less known, are publicized by geocachers whenever there is a record or placement of a new geocache (Fernandes, 2012).

3.3. Geocaching Initiatives of Portuguese Municipalities and Other Related Entities

3.3.1. Municipality of Águeda

In 2008, Águeda City Council presented the "Geocaching in Águeda" project. The president of the municipality at the time, Gil Nadais, and the Tourism councilor at the time, Elsa Corga, were present at the ceremony. This project's main purpose was to promote tourism in Águeda, through the dissemination of the municipality's historical, cultural and natural heritage, the promotion of tourist routes and itineraries, and the organization of environmental cleaning actions in specific locations. With this activity, the municipality of Águeda sought to place all parishes in the municipality on the "Geocaching" map. The "caches" were launched in the Geocaching Application by the municipality itself.

3.3.2. Mafra Municipality

The municipality of Mafra presents, on its website, five trails with a diverse selection of caches spread across Mafra and surrounding areas, providing geocachers with the opportunity to discover interesting places, historical riches and natural beauty while engaging in exciting cache hunting. This initiative by the municipality of Mafra highlights its commitment to promoting geocaching as an outdoor exploration activity and an exciting way to get to know the region.: https://www.cm-mafra.pt/p/turismo_geocaching

3.3.3. Municipality of Oliveira de Azeméis

The Municipal Council of Oliveira de Azeméis prepared a comprehensive project to create a municipal Geocaching network with the aim of promoting and highlighting the municipality's points of interest. The president of the City Council, Joaquim Jorge, emphasized the importance of these initiatives, stating that these geocaches will be promoted in several locations to attract those who practice this outdoor activity.

3.3.4. Municipality of Montemor-O-Velho

In Montemor-O-Velho, the "Caches Route through Montemor" was developed. This project arose with the aim of showing a little about each Montemorese parish, and presents itself as a current alternative in promoting local heritage. It is a differentiating tourist initiative in a municipality with great historical and cultural interest. It also allows you to promote the municipality in a creative and interactive way.

3.3.5. Municipality of Pampilhosa da Serra

In September 2021, the Pampilhosa da Serra City Council promoted the "GeoCa(t)che me" initiative, promoting the discovery of the territory through Geocaching.

Thus, in some of the 73 geocaches of the GeoPampilhosa project, distributed across the municipality's 9 walking routes, geocachers had the opportunity to find vouchers offering experiences and/or endogenous products. 3 trails were selected to host the awards, without the information having been disclosed. To claim the prize, the geocacher had to go to the Pampilhosa da Serra Tourism Office and hand in the form which, after instant validation, gave access to the prize defined for the month/route in question.

The "Geoca(t)che me" prizes were, for example, endogenous products, such as honey and brandy, stys in local accommodation or tourist entertainment experiences.

Participation was open, requiring only registration on the Geocaching platform.

In Pampilhosa da Serra, the Geocaching network was established in 2018 by the Municipality in partnership with the Department of Geography and Tourism of the University of Coimbra.

3.3.6. Municipality of Arruda dos Vinhos

In 2018, the Municipality launched the Municipal Geocaching Network, which has 100 caches. The main objective of this initiative was to "bring even more people to visit and discover our Municipality".

The launch was accompanied by an Initiation to Geocaching training course in the Municipality of Arruda dos Vinhos with the aim of promoting the municipality as a territory with great potential for the practice of outdoor recreational and sporting activities, promoting habits of healthy lives. In this action, participants had the opportunity to learn how it is practiced, the recommended equipment, the use of GPS and search and orientation techniques.

3.3.7. Municipality of Olhão

In 2013, the municipality of Olhão organized a "CITO" event. This type of event allows you to promote environmental quality and, at the same time, get to know the places where they take place, in this case the city of Olhão. CITO stands for "Cache In, Trash Out", that is, "We put in a Cache, we take out the Trash". This is an ecological event in which geocachers voluntarily contribute to cleaning public spaces. At these "CITO" events, geocachers and community groups work together to improve parks and other outdoor environments. They clean up trash, plant trees, remove invasive species, create trails and more.

3.3.8. Municipality of Oliveira de Frades

The International Geocaching Mega-Event, entitled 'Love Love… Oliveira de Frades', took place between the 11th and 13th of August 2023. Organized by the 100espinhos group in collaboration with the Workers' Association and the Municipal Council of Oliveira de Frades, This event brought together around 500 national and international geocachers of all ages for an exciting search for treasures through the streets, mountains, and other natural and cultural wonders of this Portuguese region.

For three days, Oliveira de Frades hosted this unique event, welcoming visitors from various parts of the world. The event program was extensive and, among the activities planned, were visits to the Municipal Museum, walking tours of the historic center and the municipality's trails, and tree planting. For the more adventurous, exploration included the Teixeira River and the Vouga Line.

This event aimed not only to uncover the hidden secrets of Oliveira de Frades, but also to create unforgettable memories for everyone involved, celebrating the passion for Geocaching and discovering the charms of this picturesque Portuguese region.

4. FINAL CONSIDERATIONS

Although niche marketing has been successfully applied to a high number and many types of businesses, there is a shortage of research addressing the way niche marketing may be applied to (geocaching) tourism. While mass tourism is homogeneous in nature (a standardized and uniform product for a large market segment), niche tourism is defined by its heterogeneous nature (greater demand for a more distinct and unique product) (Chen, Huang, Wu, Ip, & Wang, 2023; Sousa et al., 2023).

In this chapter the authors have argued that definitions and models of geocaching need to be more encompassing and include attachment perspective and guest experiences. With the change in demand and image for mass tourism, niche tourism products and markets have become more significant, both for the development of global tourism and for specific destinations. This preliminary chapter develops the existing research since it discusses the growing phenomena of geocaching experience with a relationship marketing perspective. A future study should include emotional factors. Geocaching has emerged as a strategic tool for municipalities to actively promote their territories. The growing recognition of the benefits of Geocaching in promoting tourist destinations has led local entities to embrace this practice as an integral part of their promotion strategies. Increasingly, municipalities recognize Geocaching's ability to attract visitors, highlight lesser-known spots, preserve cultural and natural heritage and encourage sustainable tourism.

The literature highlights successful examples of how carefully planned and attractive caches, located in strategic points, result not only in attracting tourists, but also in enhancing the cultural and natural heritage of the regions. Additionally, the flexibility and adaptability of Geocaching offers municipalities a dynamic platform to tell their stories and attract a global audience. By creating caches strategically located in areas of interest, municipalities have the opportunity to tell their own stories, promote their unique resources and celebrate the unique identity of their territories. The growing adoption of municipalities in Geocaching reflects the positive perception that this game not only attracts tourists, but also strengthens the regional economy and preserves cultural and natural heritage for future generations. Thus, Geocaching continues to consolidate itself as an effective and versatile tool in the promotion and preservation of territories. In an interdisciplinary perspective, the present manuscript represents an important contribution in relation to the management of tourist destinations and rural market segmentation. Future studies may lead to a greater generalization of the results.

REFERENCES

Aliperti, G., Sandholz, S., Hagenlocher, M., Rizzi, F., Frey, M., & Garschagen, M. (2019). Tourism, crisis, disaster: An interdisciplinary approach. *Annals of Tourism Research*, 79, 102808. DOI: 10.1016/j.annals.2019.102808

Boulaire, C., & Hervet, G. (2012). New Itinerancy: The Potential of Geocaching for Tourism. *International Journal of Management Cases*, 14(4), 210–218. DOI: 10.5848/APBJ.2012.00099

Boys, K. A., DuBreuil White, K., & Groover, G. (2017). Fostering rural and agricultural tourism: Exploring the potential of geocaching. *Journal of Sustainable Tourism*, 25(10), 1474–1493. DOI: 10.1080/09669582.2017.1291646

Brochado, A., Stoleriu, O., & Lupu, C. (2021). Wine tourism: A multisensory experience. *Current Issues in Tourism*, 24(5), 597–615. DOI: 10.1080/13683500.2019.1649373

Chen, J., Huang, Y., Wu, E. Q., Ip, R., & Wang, K. (2023). How does rural tourism experience affect green consumption in terms of memorable rural-based tourism experiences, connectedness to nature and environmental awareness? *Journal of Hospitality and Tourism Management*, 54, 166–177. DOI: 10.1016/j.jhtm.2022.12.006

Choe, Y., Baek, J., & Kim, H. (2023). Heterogeneity in consumer preference toward mega-sport event travel packages: Implications for smart tourism marketing strategy. *Information Processing & Management*, 60(3), 103302. DOI: 10.1016/j.ipm.2023.103302

Duarte, B. F., Vareiro, L. C., Sousa, B. B., & Figueira, V. (2021). The Influence of Tourist Characteristics on the Perceived Quality of Hostels in Portugal: An Exploratory Study. In *Rebuilding and Restructuring the Tourism Industry: Infusion of Happiness and Quality of Life* (pp. 221–240). IGI Global. DOI: 10.4018/978-1-7998-7239-9.ch011

Fernandes, J. L. (2012). Tecnologia, georreferenciação e novas territorialidades: o caso do geocaching. Cadernos de Geografia, 30/31 (2011/12), 171-180. Coimbra: Faculdade de Letras da Universidade de Coimbra. Disponível em http://hdl.handle.net/10316/23635

Franch, M., Martini, U., Buffa, F., & Parisi, G. (2008). 4L tourism (landscape, leisure, learning and limit): Responding to new motivations and expectations of tourists to improve the competitiveness of Alpine destinations in a sustainable way. *Tourism Review*, 63(1), 4–14. DOI: 10.1108/16605370810861008

Gaetjens, A., Corsi, A. M., & Plewa, C. (2023). Customer engagement in domestic wine tourism: The role of motivations. *Journal of Destination Marketing & Management*, 27, 100761. DOI: 10.1016/j.jdmm.2022.100761

Geopt. (2016, fevereiro). Benefícios de praticar Geocaching. Geopt. Consultado em dezembro 26, 2023 em: https://www.geopt.org/index.php/artigos/outros-artigos/geocaching/item/3390-beneficios-de-praticar-geocaching

Gram-Hansen, L. B. (2009), "Geocaching in a persuasive perspective", Conference: Persuasive Technology, Fourth International Conference, Persuasive 2009, California: Claremont, No. 34, pp. 1-8. https://doi.org/DOI: 10.1145/1541948.1541993

Ihamäki, P. (2012). Geocachers: The creative tourism experience. *Journal of Hospitality and Tourism Technology*, 3(3), 152–175. DOI: 10.1108/17579881211264468

Imamović, I., Azevedo, A. J., & Sousa, B. M. (2022). The Urban Sensescapes and Sensory Destination Branding. In Valeri, M. (Ed.), *New Governance and Management in Touristic Destinations* (pp. 276–293). IGI Global., DOI: 10.4018/978-1-6684-3889-3.ch017

Ivanovic, S., Milenkovski, A., & Milojica, V. (2015). Croatian tourism and hospitality industry: Current state and future development perspectives. *UTMS Journal of Economics (Skopje)*, 6(2), 293–305.

Kc, B., & Leung, X. Y.KC. (2022). Geocaching in Texas state parks: A technology readiness analysis. *Journal of Hospitality and Tourism Technology*, 13(1), 182–194. DOI: 10.1108/JHTT-09-2020-0240

Kosmaczewska, J. (2022). Should I stay or should I go out? Leisure and tourism consumption of geocachers under the existence of COVID restrictions and economic uncertainty in Poland. *Annals of Leisure Research*, ●●●, 1–19.

Kruger, M., & Viljoen, A. (2021). Terroir wine festival visitors: Uncorking the origin of behavioural intentions. *Current Issues in Tourism*, 24(5), 616–636. DOI: 10.1080/13683500.2019.1667310

Kumar, S., & Valeri, M. (2022). Understanding the relationship among factors influencing rural tourism: A hierarchical approach. *Journal of Organizational Change Management*, 35(2), 385–407.

Lebre, A. de F. da S. F. dos S. (2017). O Geocaching como estratégia competitiva para o Enoturismo da Bairrada. Dissertação de mestrado, Escola Superior de Educação – Instituto Politécnico de Coimbra, Coimbra, Portugal.

Liu, C., Dou, X., Li, J., & Cai, L. A. (2020). Analyzing government role in rural tourism development: An empirical investigation from China. *Journal of Rural Studies*, 79, 177–188. DOI: 10.1016/j.jrurstud.2020.08.046

Liu, J., Wang, C., & Zhang, T. C. (2024). Exploring social media affordances in tourist destination image formation: A study on China's rural tourism destination. *Tourism Management*, 101, 104843. DOI: 10.1016/j.tourman.2023.104843

Lusa (2015, agosto). "Geocaching", a caça ao tesouro "evoluída": o que é e os cuidados a ter. *Jornal Expresso*. Consultado em dezembro 23, 2023 em: https://expresso.pt/sociedade/2015-08-03-Geocaching-a-caca-ao-tesouro-evoluida-o-que-e-e-os-cuidados-a-ter

Ma, X., & Su, W. (2024). Local government intervention in tourism-driven rural gentrification: Types and interpretative framework. *Tourism Management*, 100, 104828. DOI: 10.1016/j.tourman.2023.104828

MacBride-Stewart, S., Parsons, C., & Carati, I. (2021). *Playfulness and game play: Using geocaching to engage young people's wellbeing in a National Park. Gamification in tourism. Aspects of Tourism Series*. Channel View Publications. DOI: 10.2307/jj.22730549.15

Martins, G. F. M. (2014). Caracterização da atividade de Geocaching no Parque Natural da Arrábida. Dissertação de mestrado, Universidade de Lisboa, Lisboa, Portugal.

Martins, J., Gonçalves, R., Branco, F., Barbosa, L., Melo, M., & Bessa, M. (2017). A multisensory virtual experience model for thematic tourism: A Port wine tourism application proposal. *Journal of Destination Marketing & Management*, 6(2), 103–109. DOI: 10.1016/j.jdmm.2017.02.002

Matherson, L., Wright, V. H., Inman, C. T., & Wilson, E. K. (2008). Get up, Get out with Geocaching: Engaging Technology for the Social Studies Classroom. *Social Studies Research & Practice*, 3(3), 80–85. DOI: 10.1108/SSRP-03-2008-B0006

McDonagh, P., & Prothero, A. (2014). Sustainability marketing research: Past, present and future. Journal of Marketing Management, 30(11 - 12), 1186 - 1219.

Mydłowska, E. (2023). Geocoaching Adventure Lab–The Innovative Tool for Exploring and Creating Tourism Space. *Studia Maritima*, 36(1), 1–22. DOI: 10.18276/sm.2023.36-02

Novelli, M., Cheer, J. M., Dolezal, C., Jones, A., & Milano, C. (Eds.). (2022). *Handbook of Niche Tourism*. Edward Elgar Publishing. DOI: 10.4337/9781839100185

Okumus, F., Van Niekerk, M., Koseoglu, M. A., & Bilgihan, A. (2018). Interdisciplinary research in tourism. *Tourism Management*, 69, 540–549. DOI: 10.1016/j.tourman.2018.05.016

Oliveira, S. (2007). O Turismo Gastronómico e o Enoturismo como Potenciadores do Desenvolvimento Regional. Comunicação apresentada no III Congresso Internacional de Turismo. Disponível em http://cassiopeia.ipleiria.pt/esel_eventos/files/3902_12_SimaoOliveira_ 4bf5103dd97f6.pdf)

Pan, S., & Ryan, C. (2009). Tourism Sense-Making: The Role Of The Senses And Travel Journalism. *Journal of Travel & Tourism Marketing*, 26(7), 625–639. DOI: 10.1080/10548400903276897

Park, D.-B., & Yoon, Y.-S. (2009). Segmentation by motivation in rural tourism: A Korean case study. *Tourism Management*, 30(1), 99–108. DOI: 10.1016/j.tourman.2008.03.011

Pisula, E. (2021). Informative, educational, and promotional role of geocaching in the region. *ToSEE – Tourism in Southern and Eastern Europe*, Vol. 6, pp. 623-635

Pisuła, E., Florek, M., & Homski, K. (2023). Marketing communication via geocaching–When and how it can be effective for places? *Journal of Outdoor Recreation and Tourism*, 42, 100622. DOI: 10.1016/j.jort.2023.100622

Popp, L., & McCole, D. (2016). Understanding tourists' itineraries in emerging rural tourism regions: The application of paper-based itinerary mapping methodology to a wine tourism region in Michigan. *Current Issues in Tourism*, 19(10), 988–1004. DOI: 10.1080/13683500.2014.942259

Pradhan, D., Malik, G., & Vishwakarma, P. (2023). Gamification in tourism research: A systematic review, current insights, and future research avenues. *Journal of Vacation Marketing*, •••, 13567667231188879. DOI: 10.1177/13567667231188879

Priatmoko, S., Kabil, M., Akaak, A., Lakner, Z., Gyuricza, C., & Dávid, L. D. (2023). Understanding the complexity of rural tourism business: Scholarly perspective. *Sustainability (Basel)*, 15(2), 1193. DOI: 10.3390/su15021193

Proos, E., & Hattingh, J. (2022). Dark tourism: Growth potential of niche tourism in the Free State Province, South Africa. *Development Southern Africa*, 39(3), 303–320. DOI: 10.1080/0376835X.2020.1847636

Rosalina, P. D., Dupre, K., Wang, Y., Putra, I. N. D., & Jin, X. (2023). Rural tourism resource management strategies: A case study of two tourism villages in Bali. *Tourism Management Perspectives*, 49, 101194. DOI: 10.1016/j.tmp.2023.101194

Santos, V., Sousa, B., Ramos, P., & Valeri, M. (2022). Emotions and involvement in tourism settings. *Current Issues in Tourism*, 25(10), 1526–1531. DOI: 10.1080/13683500.2021.1932769

Santos, V. R., Sousa, B. B., Ramos, P., Dias, Á., & Madeira, A. (2022). Encouraging wine storytelling in the tourist experience: a preliminary study. In *Advances in Tourism, Technology and Systems: Selected Papers from ICOTTS 2021* (Vol. 1, pp. 235–242). Springer Nature Singapore. DOI: 10.1007/978-981-19-1040-1_20

Saputro, K. E. A. (1835). Hasim, Karlinasari, L., & Beik, I. S. (2023). Evaluation of Sustainable Rural Tourism Development with an Integrated Approach Using MDS and ANP Methods: Case Study in Ciamis, West Java, Indonesia. *Sustainability (New Rochelle, N.Y.)*, 15(3).

Schneider, I. E., Silverberg, K. E., & Chavez, D. (2011). Geocachers: Benefits sought and environmental attitudes. *LARnet*, 14(1), 1–11.

Silva, J., Sousa, B., & Abreu, J. (2023). Place Marketing and Destination Management: A Study in the "Quadrilátero do Minho". In *Advances in Tourism, Technology and Systems: Selected Papers from ICOTTS 2022* (Vol. 2, pp. 567–577). Springer Nature Singapore. DOI: 10.1007/978-981-19-9960-4_49

Skinner, H., Sarpong, D., & White, G. R. (2018). Meeting the needs of the Millennials and Generation Z: gamification in tourism through geocaching. *Journal of tourism futures*, 4(1), 93-104.

Soroker, S., Berger, R., Levy, S., & Nebenzahl, I. D. (2023). Understanding consumer sophistication and the moderating role of culture in the tourism context. *International Journal of Hospitality & Tourism Administration*, 24(1), 29–64. DOI: 10.1080/15256480.2021.1938781

Sousa, B., Machado, A., de Oliveira, F. F., de Abreu Rocha, A. M., & Ribeiro, M. (2023). Promoting Favela Storytelling in the Tourist Visitation: An Exploratory Study. In *Advances in Tourism, Technology and Systems: Selected Papers from ICOTTS 2022, Volume 2* (pp. 343-351). Singapore: Springer Nature Singapore. Pisula, E., Florek, M., & Homski, K. (2023). Marketing communication via geocaching–When and how it can be effective for places? *Journal of Outdoor Recreation and Tourism*, 42, 100622.

Sousa, B., Machado, A., Gonçalves, M., Santos, L., & Catarino, A. (2023). Market Segmentation and Relationship Management of Fashion Tourism: An Exploratory Perspective. In *Advances in Tourism, Technology and Systems: Selected Papers from ICOTTS 2022* (Vol. 2, pp. 399–407). Springer Nature Singapore. DOI: 10.1007/978-981-19-9960-4_35

Wen, J., Goh, E., & Yu, C. E. (2023). Segmentation of physician-assisted suicide as a niche tourism market: An Initial Exploration. *Journal of Hospitality & Tourism Research (Washington, D.C.)*, 47(3), 574–589. DOI: 10.1177/10963480211011630

Wen, J., Wang, W., Kozak, M., Liu, X., & Hou, H. (2020). Many brains are better than one: The importance of interdisciplinary studies on COVID-19 in and beyond tourism. *Tourism Recreation Research*, 46(2), 310–313. DOI: 10.1080/02508281.2020.1761120

Wilson, S., Fesenmaier, D. R., Fesenmaier, J., & Van Es, J. C. (2001). Factors for success in rural tourism development. *Journal of Travel Research*, 40(2), 132–138. DOI: 10.1177/004728750104000203

Wu, M. Y., Tong, Y., Li, Q., Wall, G., & Wu, X. (2022). Interaction rituals and social relationships in a rural tourism destination. *Journal of Travel Research*, •••, 00472875221130495.

Yang, Y., Zhang, H., & Chen, X. (2020). Coronavirus pandemic and tourism: Dynamic stochastic general equilibrium modeling of infectious disease outbreak. *Annals of Tourism Research*, 83, 102–913. DOI: 10.1016/j.annals.2020.102913 PMID: 32292219

Zhao, C., Shang, Z., & Pan, Y. (2023). Beauty and tourists' sustainable behaviour in rural tourism: A self-transcendent emotions perspective. *Journal of Sustainable Tourism*, •••, 1–20.

KEY TERMS AND DEFINITIONS

Geocaching: is an outdoor recreational activity, in which participants use a Global Positioning System (GPS) receiver or mobile device and other navigational techniques to hide and seek containers, called geocaches or caches, at specific locations marked by coordinates all over the world

Experiencescapes: The purposeful places where experiences are produced, staged, and consumed by diverse groups in tourism industry

Niche Tourism: Niche Tourism refers to a specialized or unique form of tourism that caters to the interests and preferences of a particular group of travellers. This type of tourism often focuses on a specific activity, theme, or experience, and may appeal to a smaller, more specialized market than mainstream tourism.

Sensescapes: Sensory experience of the environment.

Territory management: - is the strategic process of organizing, managing, and expanding various groups of customers and potential customers. It's typically based on key market segments, which can be defined by using tools like sales territory mapping and territory alignment.

Chapter 6
Film-Induced Tourism and Promotion of Tourist Destinations:
An Exploratory Approach

Bruno Barbosa Sousa
https://orcid.org/0000-0002-8588-2422
Polytechnic Institute of Cávado and Ave, Portugal & Applied Management Research Unit (UNIAG), Portugal & Centro de Investigação, Desenvolvimento e Inovação em Turismo (CiTUR), Portugal

João Abreu
Polytechnic Institute of Cávado and Ave, Portugal & ISCET, Portugal

Lara Marisa Santos
https://orcid.org/0000-0001-6927-8906
Universidade Lusófona, Portugal & CETRAD, Portugal

Vítor Silva
https://orcid.org/0009-0008-9569-627X
Polytechnic Institute of Cávado and Ave, Portugal & Universidade de Vigo, Spain

Ana Paula Figueira
Polytechnic Institute of Beja, Portugal

EXECUTIVE SUMMARY

The film tourism business incorporates a series of activities. The development of destination marketing campaigns to promote films, while, increasingly, common initiatives between DMOs and filmmakers to promote films and tourist destinations.

DOI: 10.4018/979-8-3693-1548-4.ch006

In several situations, a film or a documentary can prove to be a crucial element of communica-tion and dissemination of a country, a city or a territory. These cinematographic imag-es can influence consumers' decisions regarding their motivations to visit the places where the films were recorded. Tourism and cinema may represent a common element in favour of regional development and community feeling (e.g. a film about the histo-ry or culture of a population). The present study, in an exploratory approach, intends to understand the phenomenon and the importance of film tourism as a preponderant element in the management of territories (i.e. tourist destinations). Therefore, semi-structured interviews were carried out to define the object of study. Future studies, through a quantitative approach, should allow a greater generalization of results.

INTRODUCTION

According to Tajeddini and Ratten (2017), in the last two decades, brand management has generated much interest both in academic and business circles and branding strategy has been widely recognised as a source of sustainable competitive advantage (Aaker, 2002; Kapferer, 2008; Keller, 2008). Segmentation and niche tourism have been asserting itself in recent decades and is strongly associated with the theory of niche marketing (Sousa et al., 2020). In this context, film-induced tourism has recently been considered a leisure activity, in a tourist variant promoted by individuals for whom the purchase of products outside their usual environment is a determining factor in their decision to travel and make decisions (Hsieh & Chang, 2006; Hao et al., 2024). Thus, there has been a notable growth in this activity, as it is a segment where tourists have higher expenditure and, consequently, deserving greater attention from businessmen, politicians, and academics (Jewell & McKinnon, 2008). However, combining the interests of several stakeholders is not an easy task, making it a very complex process (both for destination management and operational marketing), implying greater experience, knowledge, investment, and partnerships (Sousa et al., 2021). Film-induced tourism has assumed itself as a sector of strong growth and of an important nature in research in the tourism sector. Therefore, destination management is the vital element on which a city or region is defined (Liberato et al., 2018; Vieira et al., 2022; Liberato, 2020), and thus intends to measure, to manage and to develop a distinct image of the place in order to satisfy their interests by creating a positive international reputation. The present chapter, in an exploratory approach, intends to understand the phenomenon and the importance of film tourism as a preponderant element in the management of territories (i.e. tourist destinations).

Film-Induced Tourism

To set segmentation and special interest tourism (SIT) in a broader overall hospitality and tourism context, (Robinson & Novelli, 2005) suggest a "tourism interest continuum". Although they have similar characteristics, they differ to some extent (Dalgic & Leeuw, 1994). The keyword niche, in a marketing perspective, refers to two key interrelated ideas: that there is a place in the market for the product, and that there is an audience for that same product. This refers to a specific product capable of keeping up with the needs of a specific market segment (Liberato et al., 2018). According to Evans et al. (2003) and Hudson and Ritchie (2006), film tourism is a tourist activity induced by the visualization of a moving image, also seen as a comprehensive film, television, pre-recorded products and currently extends to digital media. Some distinction must be made between its shape, that is, a film or television program and the medium through which the image is transmitted, in which there are numerous ways of viewing cinematographic images and viewing can occur in an increasing multiplicity of environments (Liberato et al., 2018). This distinction may have implications for the way in which we perceive and relate to the outcome of a cinematic experience. Film tourism seems to be the generic term adopted in most studies and, although there are some debates about the differences in images perceived via film and television in the media literature, the term is undoubtedly more important than the concept. There is a variation in the terminology used to define the concept of film tourism. The most basic differentiation is cultural / geographical, that is, some countries tend to favor the term "movie tourism", while others use the term "film tourism". The two terms are used interchangeably in tourism research, but essentially the "film" refers to the vocabulary of early American cinema of the "moving image". In 1985, the Lumière brothers staged the world's first public screening of a film. From that moment on, cinematography captured the public imagination and films became the dominant art form of the 20th century, increasing the awareness, appeal and increased profit of venues through the power of the image and story they portray (Macionis, 2004). Film tourism can take many forms and activities, as identified, and discussed by some authors (e.g. Croy & Heitmann, 2011): Visits to locations portrayed in a specific film / television production; Visits to groups of studios; Visits to theme parks and specific film / TV attractions; Visits to themed attractions with a movie theme - the world's most popular tourist attractions and theme parks are directly related to films; Visits to locations where filming is taking place; Visits to locations that are marketed as cinematographic locations; Participation in excursions organized in the locations where the filming took place; Participation in tours organized to see the homes of celebrities; Visits to Film Festivals; Visits to destinations for film premieres.

The existence of units dedicated to the promotion of films is, in many places, well established (Edgerton, 1986; Leong et al., 2024) in order to promote the adaptation of places and spaces such as filming locations, as well as the provision of resources to provide or find studio spaces. Great cinematographic films can provide the locations, objects and people for the look and motivation of various people and, for some, films can induce these same people to travel specifically to the places where those same films were shot. Although some of these great films are not primarily intended to induce people to visit the sites in question, it appears that they can enhance the awareness, appeal and profitability of the sites through the power of the imagination, image and fantasy of films in question (Figueira et al., 2015).

According to Liberato et al. (2018), these cinematographic images can influence consumers' decisions regarding their motivations to visit the places where the films were recorded. However, it is necessary to ask the question: do films really have an impact with respect to consumer choice in relation to the tourist destination?

Cinema is also a form of visual language and has been one of the main vehicles for building and transmitting places with which people have no experience or knowledge (Kim & Richardson, 2003). This modern phenomenon in the tourism sector establishes a connection between emotions, ideas and images of a destination in the cinematographic context and the tourist destination itself, which can result in positive or negative consequences, depending on the image created by films in relation to destinations. The film industry has the power to create a powerful image around a specific tourist destination. This representation of reality has aroused the interest of authorities responsible for promoting tourism (Juškelytė, 2016).

First, the attributes intrinsic to the destination appear: scenario, icons, brand, background, sensitivity and set. Next, the group of factors related to the viability of the location emerge, such as resources offered, costs, taxes, local job offer and employee specialization. The third pillar is composed of government actions and film commissions (a government organization dedicated to attracting and encouraging the creation of audiovisual productions in its area of activity), including tax incentives, lobbying, active promotion, related websites and help in the search for filming locations. The fourth pillar encompasses factors specifically related to the film, such as success in selling cinema tickets, easily identifiable and accessible hotels, connection and relevance of the story with the location, length of exposure on screen, positive and stimulating image presented, connection emotional relationship with spectators, underexplored environments and the existence of factors that allow differentiation. The fifth pillar is related to the marketing actions carried out by the destinations. It is crucial that Destination Marketing Organizations (DMOs) work in partnership with film commissions in order to obtain maximized results from the activity (Hudson & Ritchie, 2006).

Films have the power to influence people's perceptions of tourist destinations. Through the media, cinema is able to convey ideas and change behaviours, which means that the representation of tourist destinations in films can allow the public to gain interest in places they have never visited before (Redondo, 2012). According to Redondo (2012), usually, for the recording of a film, only one country or region is chosen and during the two hours of the film (average duration), the viewer is reminded for a large amount of time about that destination, often having a crucial role in the plot. Another element of tourist promotion through films is the narrative. It is through this that the film communicates with the spectators, creating expectations and perceptions. It has the ability to mold imaginaries and create an emotional connection between the spectator and the destination, even before the tourist visits the place. Films that portray tourist destinations act as guides and create guidelines for anticipation and experience for tourists. The narrative, therefore, has the ability to induce and reinforce tourist imaginaries, transforming a tourist destination into a unique and differentiated place (Hao & Ryan, 2013). This work involves a deep knowledge of the places where filming takes place. There is always the risk of making mistakes that could distort the local culture and, in this case, the result could be compromised. Take the example of the mov-ie "Heart of Stone", in which Gal Gadot plays the main role, released by Netflix on August 11th. The film was recorded in several countries, including Lisbon, more specifically, in the neighborhoods of Chiado, Baixa, Mouraria and Estrela. However, there is an error that did not go unnoticed by the Portuguese! In a scene that is making waves, Rachel Stone and her team struggle with the question of how to find a missing 'hacker' in Lisbon. "What if she's not there?" asks the agent. "Eat tapas", replies her superior, played by Sophie Okonedo. Apparently, some-one confused tapas with Portuguese cuisine, causing a real gastronomic revolution.

Disney and New Zealand are the most successful spaces. Disney for the experience it gives visitors to feel like the characters in their films, and New Zealand for the contradiction between reality and fiction. Thus, it can be considered that the tourist's motivations result from the affinities created. "The mythology of the place, transformed and communicated through films, may be what attracts tourists, and not the destination itself" (Li et al., 2017, p. 179), thus being able to remember the feeling when are in place. The impact of marketing on the production and dissemination of the film must be very careful so that the tourist does not suffer any disappointment with the location as it is not identical to what is broadcast, as it is through the viewing of the films that tourists build their aspirations, desires and expectations about tourist destinations. All of this shows that "popular cultural forms of media can promote, confirm and reinforce images, views and specific identities of destinations in a powerful way" (Tkalec, Zilic & Recher, 2017, p. 706).

Great Britain is a highly developed and organized destination in the film tourism segment. VisitBritain, the national tourism agency, plays a key role in outreach across the world through elaborate marketing strategies aimed at boosting tourism economically. Funded by the UK Department for Culture, Media and Sport (DCMS), the agency works closely with a range of public and private bodies, both nationally and internationally. Among them, the official tourism bodies of England, Scotland and Wales stand out (Northern Ireland belongs only to the United Kingdom) (Guthrie, 2011). Furthermore, in these 3 nations belonging to Great Britain, renting properties for filming is also a very profitable business. The National Trust is the body dedicated to the preservation of historical, architectural and natural heritage and makes its iconic properties and beautiful landscapes available as backdrops for film productions. This organization is able to generate financial resources through this partnership with the film industry, not neglecting the maintenance and protection of cultural and natural treasures.

The success was such that other destinations, such as Seattle, New York, Australia and Mississippi, also developed their own movie-maps. inspired by this pioneering initiative by VisitBritain (Hudson & Ritchie, 2006). One of the most outstanding promotional actions conceived by the VisitBritain agency was the "Bond is GREAT Britain" campaign. The release of the film "007 – Operation Skyfall" from the 007 franchise in October 2012, which used iconic London filming locations, was the starting point for the campaign slogan, which aimed to convey the idea that there was no better time. to visit the homeland of the world's most famous secret agent. The film saga completed 50 years and as part of this campaign, an online adventure related to the film was also launched, with a trip to England as a prize. This initiative aimed to involve fans of the film and provide them with the opportunity to experience firsthand the British atmosphere portrayed in the 007 saga (Daines & Veitch, 2012). According to a survey carried out by VisitBritain, 39% of tourists in Britain said they had been influenced by films seen in cinemas or on television. Through strategic partnerships with studios, distributors, production companies, marketing and tourism companies, VisitBritain has achieved significant results in this regard. A notable example is the film "Elizabeth - The Golden Age" (2007), which features scenes recorded in various locations in England, with the aim of promoting the main cultural heritage of the country. This approach aims to meet the interest of potential visitors, since a survey revealed that 73% of them expressed an interest in seeing heritage associated with the royal family (Nascimento, 2009). According to Liberato et al. (2018), authenticity is one of the key factors for tourists and film tourism, on the one hand it allows people to live out the fantasies of their favorite films or actors in some mythical locations. Visitors associate personal meanings with certain places, and authenticity thus becomes a subjective experience, a combination of the visitors' experiences and the interactions inherent in them. Literature-related tourism is defined as an experience carried out by tourists as a way of celebrating associations with authors and books. This type of tourism is a desire to experience a version of the past or an attempt to experience a version of the future and make a connection between the past and the future, fact, and fiction. This tourism establishes a correlation between the images and the expectations of specific people, places, and historical periods. Indeed, literature tourism has focused on the main precursor of tourism mentioned above, cinema tourism.

Film tourism also has other negative impacts, namely congestion and environmental pollution, deterioration of natural attractions, overtourism, difficulty in maintaining and properly preserving destinations, theft of film-related souvenirs and can also result in the replacement of more lucrative local markets and previously established (Phomsiri, 2015; Tuclea & Nistoreanu, 2011).

Films can serve as an incentive for people to visit certain destinations, but it is important to consider that some cinematographic representations may differ from the authentic reality of the place. This can result in unrequited expectations when tourists visit the destination and fail to experience what has been promoted to them. It can be tricky for tourists to find exactly what they're looking for, especially when reality doesn't match the expectations created by the film. [26]. Maintaining the authenticity of a destination is essential for the effective development of the film tourism phenomenon (Yen & Croy, 2016).

Methodology

The methodology used to carry out this exploratory chapter was, firstly, a literature review study on important topics for the work, such as basic concepts about tourism, cinematographic tourism, marketing and tourist marketing and tourist promotion through films. The second stage adopted a quantitative approach, involving the creation of a questionnaire directed to the general population, carried out in Google Forms, having been disclosed on social networks such as Facebook, Instagram, WhatsApp and also via email. During the study, three interviews were carried out, namely with a tourism marketing company, a researcher in the area and a film director. This study, carried out through a questionnaire and three interviews, has as main objective to understand the impact that the cinema industry has on the visitor's motivation in choosing a tourist destination to visit and what were the factors that captivated and generated curiosity in the spectators. Another objective was to understand how tourist destinations promote tourism after being featured in a successful film production. The questionnaire was designed to be simple and concise, avoiding being excessively massive, but at the same time providing clear answers to the desired questions. The main questions are related to the motivation to know a tourist destination after its film exhibition. Respondents are also asked what the factors behind this interest were and what was the film or series and the respective tourist destination that they wanted to visit. The population covered by this study includes all people fluent in Portuguese. The theme to be developed was included in an open questionnaire, allowing anyone to share their opinion. Completing the questionnaire takes an average of about 2 minutes, which helps to increase interest in participating. After dissemination through social networks, 75 responses were obtained. In order to obtain concrete answers from professionals involved in the subject in question, I contacted the company "IPDT – Turismo e Consultoria", which is a specialist company in the development of strategic plans and tourism marketing, communication strategies and tourism promotion, certification processes of sustainability for tourism and production of tourist information. It is an Affiliate Member of the World Tourism Organization (UNWTO) and the Global Sustainable Tourism Council (GSTC) and is part of a worldwide network of public and private organizations in the sector.

Discussion

Of the 75 respondents who participated in this study, 73 (97.3%) referred they enjoyed watching movies, series or television programs. The remaining 2.7%, which corresponds to only 2 people, assume that they have no interest in watching cinematographic productions. For these two people, the questionnaire ended immediately, as they were not eligible for the study in question. 64 people (87.7%) responded that they had already felt motivated to visit a country or city under the influence of a film, series or television program. On the other hand, the remaining 12.3% never felt that motivation. Of the 64 people who reached this section of the survey, and more than one option could be selected, it can be concluded that the images of destinations present in film productions are the main motivating factor for respondents. The culture, traditions and customs of the country or city in question also seduce people, having obtained 46 responses. only 6 people selected the narrative as a motivational factor. 7 people said that the series "Emily in Paris" aroused their interest and curiosity in knowing the city of love.

The "Fast and Furious" saga follows in second place, with 5 answers, but without any concrete destination, since the various films take place in different parts of the globe. In turn, the recent Portuguese Netflix series "Rabo de Peixe" comes up with 3 responses, which means that it captivated people to visit the small village on the island of São Miguel, in the Azores (Portugal). the majority (67.2%) stated that they still have not been able to travel motivated by a cinematographic production, but that they are interested in doing so. Eleven people (17.2%) revealed that they had already done so and the remaining 15.6% did not show any kind of interest. The "Emily in Paris" series took the lead again, with 3 people saying they traveled to Paris because of this successful series. Another respondent also traveled to Paris, but this one was stimulated by the film "Midnight in Paris". Madrid and the respective production "La Casa de Papel" obtained 2 responses. Two respondents also revealed that they went to Greece encouraged by the films "Mamma Mia!" and "Percy Jackson". The Spanish island "Lanzarote" is also worth mentioning, after a participant visited it, induced by the film "Los Abrazos Rotos".

At the same time, three interviews were carried out, namely with a tourism marketing company, a researcher in the area and a film director. Regarding the first question, the IPDT company stated that cinematographic productions do not always stimulate the desire to visit a certain place, giving the example that sometimes there are films that portray political conflicts, signs of poverty, social injustices and problems associated with damn it. In these situations the impacts can obviously be reversed.

In turn, the academic researcher stated that film tourism can be an important factor in motivating an individual to visit a particular tourist destination. He went on to say that the decision-making process to travel is influenced by several factors and that there are variables such as 'destination image', 'place identity' and 'destination attributes' that arise when talking about cinema and its influence on the decision to travel. travel. She concluded by saying that the image and attributes of the place are key aspects to attract tourists and are present both in plans and in promotional campaigns.

The interviewed film director also expressed his opinion saying that the question in question is affirmative and gave the example of the city of Viana do Castelo, which has a significant audiovisual investment policy and that after being the scene of the filming of the television soap opera "A Heiress", revived dynamics that were forgotten in the city such as the riverside area and catapulted the local economy and business. The IPDT declared that there is no direct answer and that the strategies to be defined depend a lot on the market segments that are intended to be reached. The film director supported his position with a personal example. He said that in Brazil, at the reception of one of the awards that the film "A Lenda do Galo" collected, he dressed in the uniform of the band of the rooster and insisted on being the last to enter the ceremony. He also mentioned that when someone presents himself in a different way, he has an impact and that he managed to attract the attention of the entire press, thus promoting his film and his city. He believes that sometimes the best marketing strategies are not the ones that spend a lot of money, but the most creative ones. the company IPDT stated that the development of cinematographic productions alone does not combat seasonality, and that for this to happen it would be necessary to communicate the destinations in times of lower tourist influx, arguing the advantages of being visited in less busy times. They also added that the productions can be arguments for communication/promotion, but it is necessary to build a whole narrative around the destination so that people feel attracted and verify that it is worth traveling in low season to the detriment of high season. In turn, the academic researcher's opinion is that, overall, film tourism will not help to combat seasonality, but in conjunction with other factors and in certain geographical contexts, it may be able to mitigate this tourism problem. As far as the film director is concerned, he declares that there will probably always be a difference between the summer months and the rest, because the temperature is high and that is also when emigrants return to their origins, but he believes that the problem of seasonality will be gradually reduced, because each region has different tourist attractions and many of them are available every month of the year. Lastly, the film director stated that the film commissions play a fundamental and decisive role, given that they have an extensive and interesting network of contacts and are the ones who bridge the gap with major productions. He also mentioned that film commissions have the ability to show the most beautiful places in Portugal, thus contributing to issues of marketing and promotion of a territory.

FINAL CONSIDERATIONS

In recent years, tourism researchers are increasingly interested in examining the role of place attachment to evaluate local residents' attitudes toward tourism management and development. This increased interest, on the one hand, is due to the decisive attitude of local residents toward tourism in determining tourism development (Yuan et al., 2019; Ng & Feng, 2020). An increase in international travel and the development of the entertainment sector translated into growth for film tourism, which within a relatively short time became a rapidly growing sector of the tourism industry (Michopoulou, Siurnicka & Moisa, 2022; Vieira et al., 2022). The film tourism business incorporates a series of activities, such as Hudson and Ritchie (2006), the development of destination marketing campaigns to promote films, while, increasingly, common initiatives between DMOs and filmmakers to promote films and tourist destinations. The existence of units dedicated to the promotion of films is, in many places, well established in order to promote the adaptation of places and spaces such as filming locations, as well as the provision of resources to provide or find studio spaces. In addition to that, they provide incentives to filmmakers regarding tax benefits and incentives (Sousa & Liberato, 2022; Zhu et al., 2024). The companies took steps to continue the business because there is no knowledge of the end of the pandemic by Covid-19. They were forced to rethink strategies and processes to ensure that they have the necessary tools to remain open after the pandemic. The experience in the digital commerce process by some companies has proved to be a sustainable competitive advantage. In this context, and in specific, the film tourism business incorporates a series of activities, such as, the development of destination marketing campaigns to promote films, while, increasingly, common initiatives between DMOs and filmmakers to promote films and tourist destinations [5, 28-31]. The management of territories provides several advantages for the sustainable development of a tourist destination, stimulating exports and attracting more tourism and investment. Film tourism presents itself as an innovative way of traveling, providing tourists with the opportunity to immerse themselves in the settings of their films and series of choice. With proper strategy and planning, this type of tourism can become a driver of the tourism industry, offering authentic and enriching experiences for travelers. The present (preliminary) research confirmed the growing relevance of this niche market and its impact on the tourism sector. Through a detailed and comprehensive analysis, it was possible to verify that filming locations for films and series have the power to attract and captivate tourists. During the research, it was evident that the emotional connection of viewers with filming locations is a crucial factor for the success of film tourism. The possibility of visiting iconic scenarios awakens a feeling of proximity and belonging, thus increasing the level of involvement of tourists and making their trips even more memorable. In addition, the methodological approach adopted, which included the use of three interviews, and the analysis of primary data from the questionnaire carried out, allowed a deeper understanding of the desires and expectations of tourists induced by films. In order to boost this type of tourism, it is essential that governments, local authorities, companies and professionals in the sector are aware of this growing demand. It is essential to invest in infrastructure and preserve filming locations in order to guarantee the continued success of this tourist segment and contribute to the economic and cultural development of the regions involved. This study is a preliminary contribution; however it is expected that in the future a quantitative study will be developed with questionnaires among visitors to assess the impact of the television campaigns that have been developed. In an interdisciplinary perspective, the present manuscript presents inputs for tourism (film-induced tourism) and for territorial development (specifically, in the post-pandemic recovery period).

REFERENCES

Bolan, P., & Williams, L. (2008). The role of image in service promotion: Focusing on the influence of film on consumer choice within tourism. *International Journal of Consumer Studies*, 32(4), 382–390. DOI: 10.1111/j.1470-6431.2008.00672.x

Bornhorst, T., Ritchie, J. B., & Sheehan, L. (2010). Determinants of tourism success for DMOs & destinations: An empirical examination of stakeholders' perspectives. *Tourism Management*, 31(5), 572–589. DOI: 10.1016/j.tourman.2009.06.008

Croy, G., & Heitmann, S. (2011). Tourism and film. Research themes for tourism, 188-204.

Daines, A., & Veitch, C. (2012). 22 VisitBritain: Leading the World to Britain. *Best Practice in Accessible Tourism: Inclusion, Disability. Ageing Population and Tourism*, 53, 322.

Dalgic, T., & Leeuw, M. (1994). Niche marketing revisited: Concept, applications and some European cases. *European Journal of Marketing*, 28(4), 39–55. DOI: 10.1108/03090569410061178

Edgerton, G. (1986). The film bureau phenomenon in America and its relationship to independent filmmaking. *Journal of Film and Video*, •••, 40–48.

Evans, N., Campbell, D., & Stonehouse, G. (2003). *Strategic Management for Travel and Tourism*. Butterworth-Heinemann.

Figueira, A. P., Figueira, V., & Monteiro, S. (2015). Turismo e cinema: A importância de uma film commission na promoção do destino Alentejo. *Int. J. Sci. Manag. Tour*, 1, 29–37.

Guthrie, C. (2011). VisitBritain: satisfying the online market dynamics. In *eTourism case studies* (pp. 181-189). Routledge.

Hao, X., Jiang, E., & Chen, Y. (2024). The sign Avatar and tourists' practice at Pandora: A semiological perspective on a film related destination. *Tourism Management*, 101, 104856. DOI: 10.1016/j.tourman.2023.104856

Hao, X., & Ryan, C. (2013). Interpretation, film language and tourist destinations: A case study of Hibiscus Town, China. *Annals of Tourism Research*, 42, 334–358. DOI: 10.1016/j.annals.2013.02.016

Hsieh, A. T., & Chang, J. (2006). Shopping and tourist night markets in Taiwan. *Tourism Management*, 27(1), 138–145. DOI: 10.1016/j.tourman.2004.06.017

Hudson, S., & Ritchie, J. B. (2006). Promoting destinations via film tourism: An empirical identification of supporting marketing initiatives. *Journal of Travel Research*, 44(4), 387–396. DOI: 10.1177/0047287506286720

Jewell, B., & McKinnon, S. (2008). Movie tourism—A new form of cultural landscape? *Journal of Travel & Tourism Marketing*, 24(2-3), 153–162. DOI: 10.1080/10548400802092650

Juškelytė, D. (2016). Film induced tourism: Destination image formation and development. *Regional Formation and Development Studies*, 19(2), 54–67. DOI: 10.15181/rfds.v19i2.1283

Kim, H., & Richardson, S. L. (2003). Motion picture impacts on destination images. *Annals of Tourism Research*, 30(1), 216–237. DOI: 10.1016/S0160-7383(02)00062-2

Leong, A. M. W., Yeh, S. S., Zhou, Y., Hung, C. W., & Huan, T. C. (2024). Exploring the influence of historical storytelling on cultural heritage tourists' value co-creation using tour guide interaction and authentic place as mediators. *Tourism Management Perspectives*, 50, 101198. DOI: 10.1016/j.tmp.2023.101198

Li, S., Li, H., Song, H., Lundberg, C., & Shen, S. (2017). The economic impact of on-screen tourism: The case of Lord of the Rings and the Hobbit. *Tourism Management*, 60, 177–187. DOI: 10.1016/j.tourman.2016.11.023

Liberato, P. (2020). Movie Tourism and Attracting New Tourists in the Post-pandemic Period: A Niche Marketing Perspective. *Advances in Tourism, Technology and Systems: Selected Papers from ICOTTS20, Volume 1, 208*, 373.

Liberato, P., Alén, E., & Liberato, D. (2018). Smart tourism destination triggers consumer experience: The case of Porto. *European Journal of Management and Business Economics*, 27(1), 6–25. DOI: 10.1108/EJMBE-11-2017-0051

Macionis, N. (2004). Understanding the film-induced tourist. In *International tourism and media conference proceedings* (Vol. 24, pp. 86-97). Tourism Research Unit, Monash University: Melbourne, Australia

Michopoulou, E., Siurnicka, A., & Moisa, D. G. (2022). Experiencing the Story: The Role of Destination Image in Film-Induced Tourism. In *Global Perspectives on Literary Tourism and Film-Induced Tourism* (pp. 240-256). IGI Global.

Nascimento, F. M. (2009). *Cineturismo*. Aleph.

Ng, S. L., & Feng, X. (2020). Residents' sense of place, involvement, attitude, and support for tourism: A case study of Daming Palace, a Cultural World Heritage Site. *Asian Geographer*, 37(2), 189–207. DOI: 10.1080/10225706.2020.1729212

Özdemir, G., & Adan, Ö. (2014). Film tourism triangulation of destinations. *Procedia: Social and Behavioral Sciences*, 148, 625–633. DOI: 10.1016/j.sbspro.2014.07.090

Phomsiri, S. (2015). Film tourism and destination marketing: Case studies of inbound and out-bound in Thailand. *Review of Integrative Business and Economics Research*, 4(3), 241.

Redondo, I. (2012). Assessing the appropriateness of movies as vehicles for promoting tourist destinations. *Journal of Travel & Tourism Marketing*, 29(7), 714–729. DOI: 10.1080/10548408.2012.720156

Robinson, M., & Novelli, M. (2005). In Sheldon, P. J., Wöber, K. W., & Fesenmaier, D. R. (Eds.), *Niche Tourism: Contemporary issues, trends and cases. Elservier publishers* (pp. 294–302). Information and Communication Technologies in Tourism.

Sousa, B., & Liberato, D. (2022). Film induced Tourism. In *Encyclopedia of Tourism Management and Marketing* (pp. 1–3). Edward Elgar Publishing. DOI: 10.4337/9781800377486.film.induced.tourism

Sousa, B., Malheiro, A., Liberato, D., & Liberato, P. (2021). Movie tourism and attracting new tourists in the post-pandemic period: a niche marketing perspective. In *Advances in Tourism, Technology and Systems: Selected Papers from ICOTTS20, Volume 1* (pp. 373-384). Springer Singapore. DOI: 10.1007/978-981-33-4256-9_34

Sousa, B., Silva, A., & Malheiro, A. (2020). Differentiation and Market Loyalty: An Approach to Cultural Tourism in Northern Portugal. In Rocha, Á., Abreu, A., de Carvalho, J., Liberato, D., González, E., & Liberato, P. (Eds.), *Advances in Tourism, Technology and Smart Systems. Smart Innovation, Systems and Technologies* (Vol. 171, pp. 681–690). Springer., DOI: 10.1007/978-981-15-2024-2_58

Tajeddini, K., & Ratten, V. (2017). The moderating effect of brand orientation on inter-firm market orientation and performance. *Journal of Strategic Marketing*, •••, 1–31.

Tkalec, M., Zilic, I., & Recher, V. (2017). The effect of film industry on tourism: Game of Thrones and Dubrovnik. *International Journal of Tourism Research*, 19(6), 705–714. DOI: 10.1002/jtr.2142

Tuclea, C. E., & Nistoreanu, P. (2011). How film and television programs can promote tourism and increase the competitiveness of tourist destinations. *Cactus Tourism Journal*, 2(2), 25–30.

Vieira, J. S., Araújo, C. A., & Sousa, B. B. (2022). Film-Induced Tourism and Selling Storytelling in Destination Marketing: The Legend of the Rooster of Barcelos (Portugal). In J. Santos (Ed.), *Sales Management for Improved Organizational Competitiveness and Performance* (pp. 290-302). IGI Global. https://doi.org/DOI: 10.4018/978-1-6684-3430-7.ch015

Volo, S., & Irimias, A. (2016). Film tourism and post-release marketing initiatives: A longitudinal case study. *Journal of Travel & Tourism Marketing*, 33(8), 1071–1087. DOI: 10.1080/10548408.2015.1094000

Yen, C. H., & Croy, W. G. (2016). Film tourism: Celebrity involvement, celebrity worship and destination image. *Current Issues in Tourism*, 19(10), 1027–1044. DOI: 10.1080/13683500.2013.816270

Yuan, Q., Song, H. J., Chen, N., & Shang, W. (2019). Roles of tourism involvement and place attachment in determining residents' attitudes toward industrial heritage tourism in a resource-exhausted city in China. Sustainability (Switzerland), 11(19).

Zhu, C., Fong, L. H. N., Li, X., Buhalis, D., & Chen, H. (2024). Short video marketing in tourism: Telepresence, celebrity attachment, and travel intention. *International Journal of Tourism Research*, 26(1), e2599. DOI: 10.1002/jtr.2599

KEY TERMS AND DEFINITIONS

Film-induced tourism: is a kind of business that profits from attracting visitors inspired by beautiful sceneries of locations exposed in movie or drama and stories linked to the locations, through merchandising of filming sets or locations as a tour program.

Place Attachment: The affectivity a tourist develops to a place.

Place Dependence: Functional connection with a particular place or context.

Place Identity: Symbolic or emotional connection for a location or context.

Social Media: Social media are interactive computer-mediated technologies that facilitate the creation and sharing of information, ideas, career interests and other forms of expression via virtual communities and networks.

Social Networks: Is a social structure composed of persons or organizations, connected by one or several types of relationships, which share common values and goals.

Chapter 7
Marketing Plan and Territorial Management:
Vila Nova das Taipas (Portugal)

Pedro Ruben Gonçalves
Polytechnic Institute of Cávado and Ave, Portugal

Bruno Barbosa Sousa
https://orcid.org/0000-0002-8588-2422
Polytechnic Institute of Cávado and Ave, Portugal & Applied Management Research Unit (UNIAG), Portugal & Centro de Investigação, Desenvolvimento e Inovação em Turismo (CiTUR), Portugal

João Abreu
Polytechnic Institute of Cávado and Ave, Portugal & ISCET, Portugal

Manuel Sousa Pereira
https://orcid.org/0000-0002-6238-181X
Polytechnic Institute of Viana do Castelo, Portugal

EXECUTIVE SUMMARY

The territorial development strategies constitute an important instrument for the adequate growth and pursuit of development mechanisms transversal to different local dynamics. Territorial Marketing has assumed, in addition to Strategic Planning, a relevant importance in view of the high competitiveness between territories. Territorial Marketing assumes itself as an important working tool in the strategic planning of territories, regardless of its magnitude and typology, enhancing the promotion and development of regions taking into account existing needs and potential. The present chapter is based on an analysis of a very specific territory – Vila de Caldas das Taipas, where gaps and substantial resources are recognized that allow us to

DOI: 10.4018/979-8-3693-1548-4.ch007

develop a plan of action and sustainable strategic development that accompanies general growth. In this sense, an intervention strategy is developed that seeks above all to provide the socio-cultural and economic well-being of the resident population, visitors, and private agents.

INTRODUCTION

Territorial Marketing is one of the fundamental elements of the strategic planning of territories and appears as a process of territorial management and decentralization of power in search of local development, always reinforcing the competitive advantages of the location (Cidrais, 1998). When we talk about the development of a territory from an integrated and interest-compromising perspective, the objectives of this development are all combined with the purpose of attracting or creating opportunities for the territory. These opportunities result from several aspects, such as local attractiveness initiatives, business, tourist and visitor-oriented initiatives, as well as the creation or consolidation of export markets (Nunes, 1999).

Currently, the evolution of globalization favors growing competition for tourists, visitors, investors, new residents and workers, between different territories (Kotler & Gertner, 2002). The competitive environment, which leads to greater awareness of marketing strategies, which indicates the main competitive advantages of the territory (Popkova, 2013; Fernandes & Gama, 2006; Metaxas, 2010), cited in Santos (2017). Territorial marketing comprises a set of strategic actions to attract new activities to territories, with the aim of favoring the development of organizations that carry out their activity, and of the territories themselves, and promoting a favorable image at a global level (Almeida, 2004).

Since the end of the 19th century and the beginning of the 20th century, there have been records of competitiveness between the various territories (Ward, 1998), with the aim of creating distinction and preference. Recent years have brought changes to the economy, culture and social values of the territories, leading them to operate in order to adapt to constant challenges (Kavaratzis, 2005).

The detachment from territories by individuals, investments, companies and industry is increasingly visible, making it imperative to create favorable and attractive environments. In this way, bringing new challenges to territories, where the ability to attract investments, businesses, tourists and residents has become essential (Anholt, 2007; Hospers, 2003; Kavaratzis, 2005; Zenker, 2009; Kotler et al., 1999).

As a response to this need, marketing played an important role in valuing territories, in transferring its application, theoretical and practical, to unique and peculiar environments, characteristics and needs of territories (Rainisto, 2003; Barke, 1999), with a view to the satisfaction of all its stakeholders (Kavaratzis, 2005).

Similar to the world of companies, which compete with each other, there is also competition between territories, and marketing can also be applied to places, known as City Marketing, or in a broader term, Territorial Marketing. However, territories are more difficult entities to manage and sell due to the complexity of local stakeholder relationships (Sautter & Leisen, 1999).

It is necessary to explain the concept of territory, taking into account that, in this theme, territories are the places where marketing strategies are applied. Traditionally, territory is defined as a historically established geographic place, composed of unique characteristics, with available and potential resources for the needs of internal and external consumers (Bondarenko et al., 2018). The expression "place" is also used to name all types of places such as cities, regions, communities, areas, states and nations. There is currently consensus, among several authors, on the success of developing marketing strategies targeted at places for the success of marketing applied to products and services (Van Den Berg et al., 1990; Kotler & Gertner, 2002; Rainisto, 2003) and Therefore, the importance of designations of origin as a marketing tool has been observed.

Currently, territories are increasingly equated with products, with the former achieving differentiation through the construction of territorial brands, with their own characteristics and attributes. Therefore, countless countries, regions and cities, like many companies, have created marketing plans, thus becoming strong brands, managing to promote themselves to various target audiences (Costa, 2013).

The aforementioned advantages will also be felt, consequently, by residents, so the management of territories must be carried out in a rigorous and delicate manner with them, regularly communicating projects, cultural and artistic activities. At the same time, seek to develop a positive environment among residents, namely enhancing values, such as friendship, solidarity, security, respect, in a way that results in an increase in emotional commitment. This high affective commitment can be observed through the involvement of residents in city events, such as environmental projects or through volunteering in community spaces, which will culminate in the sustainable development of a city (Mcccunn & Gifford, 2014).

According to Azevedo, Magalhães & Pereira (2011), it is necessary for places to understand their potential and the dimensions in which they are inserted: economic, political, cultural and ecological. According to Kotler, Haider & Rein (1993), there are several reasons why certain territories fall into oblivion, but as a general rule, we can attribute these reasons to two main factors: internal forces and external forces.

Internal forces concern localized events that occur in the territory, such as the example of a large industry leaving the region, which leads to increased unemployment and unfavorable economic conditions (Kotler et al, 1993). The same authors state that the city's own environment, its culture and history, the way people interact and the infrastructure it has, represent factors that can be significant for the city's image and attractiveness, serving as aspects of differentiation. of competition. In line with this, (Gonzalez 2001) states that the past of territories, their history, identities, images, ethics, values, citizenship, participation, negotiation, contractualization, communication and information are immaterial dimensions now highly valued and considered as fundamental resources to face challenges, in order to affirm and emancipate territories in the World-System. One of the main objectives of Territorial Marketing is to position every type of territory (village, city or region) in the national and international market, promoting and reinforcing the attractiveness of places and attracting target audiences (visitors, tourists, residents and companies), satisfying them better than the competition. Territorial Marketing activity is carried out and managed by public authorities in partnership with agents from the private sector of the territories, more specifically with companies associated with various planning areas (economy, entrepreneurship, culture, etc.), (Megri & Bencherif, 2014; Dziembowska-Kowalska & Funck, 2000).

Territorial Marketing is a strategic tool with an increasingly significant influence on city management, and it is essential to develop a marketing strategy that is capable of positioning the city and giving it something differentiating (Lages et al., 2018).

Territorial Marketing practices are not limited to large cities and countries, they are inserted in a wide variety of small and medium-sized territories.

BACKGROUND

Strategic Territorial Marketing Planning for a Destination

The adoption of a strategic planning in the management of territories is easily understandable when comparing the administration of a given territory to business administration, since the former has, like a company, management skills with an increasing degree of complexity and subject to changes that are difficult to predict. Furthermore, at present, the strong dynamism of the geopolitical, social and economic, cultural, technological and administrative environment produces implications of great magnitude for urban development, which, in turn, require the transformation and renewal of traditional planning instruments, implying greater participation of local agents. This import of the methods used by companies for territorial management sought to "rationalize urban public action through the definition and implementation of a common project and objectives of valorization, affirmation and innovation framed by an organizational structure, participation, achievement of consensus and constant evaluation" (Cabral et al., 1996).

Fundamentally, strategic planning is a process suited to the complexity of modern systems, because it does not conceive the plan as a finished "product", but rather as a process in constant evaluation. Ferreira (2005) states that some authors even propose the designation of management or planification to replace the designation of "planning". This redefinition of the concept of strategic planning brings it closer to its origins, the business environment, and, at the same time, separates it from conventional planning methodologies.

The uniqueness of each territory has social, economic, political and cultural particularities, among others. In this sense, strategic marketing planning applied in a given location must take into account local singularities, not adopting models applied in other territories without first adapting them to local reality and characteristics (Minciotti & Silva, 2011).

Although there is no rigid scheme leading to the formalization of a strategic plan, a certain consensus prevails among some authors. In this way, it is possible to identify three major essential steps to structuring a strategic plan: the first is the diagnosis, the second corresponds to the formulation of the plan and the third concerns the formalization or implementation of the plan (Fonseca & Ramos, 2006). Strategic territorial marketing planning must be able to answer questions such as: Where are we? Where do we intend to get to? And how can we get there?

In the diagnostic phase, internal analysis was carried out, which allows the main strengths and weaknesses of the territory to be determined, and external analysis which identifies opportunities and threats external to the territory. In this initial phase, one must understand the current scenario of the territory, its characteristics, its dynamics and its regional insertion. The information collected must be known and shared by all local actors (public and private), where together, after the diagnosis, they will decide the best sustainable and well-founded development model (Fonseca & Ramos, 2006).

The formulation phase proceeds immediately after the diagnosis and begins with the definition of the model that is intended to be implemented for the territory. The participation of all local actors and the inclusion of the most differentiating and priority endogenous resources in the territory are essential. To formulate the plan, we begin by defining a central objective that we intend to achieve, which focuses on the critical situations diagnosed in the territory in order to resolve them. After identifying the main objective, strategies are defined that will allow it to be achieved. Each strategy designed has a set of objectives and, these, have a set of specific actions, planned and coordinated according to the expected result. In the feasibility of actions, the participation and identification of actors is decisive so that it is possible to establish contracts or partnerships. After formulating the plan, a public presentation is made to publicize all strategic planning and defined objectives and also to promote participation and local identity. (Fonseca & Ramos, 2006).

Implementation phase is when the application of the entire defined plan begins. It is at this stage that we begin to obtain results, with continuous monitoring of them, in which the implemented projects are evaluated, in which we verify whether the strategies are causing the expected effect, in which we analyze internal and external developments. and as well as the behavior of the actors involved. This phase is important, since the entire evaluation of strategies and actions allows adaptation depending on the results obtained and changes verified (Fonseca & Ramos, 2006).

However, despite the differences between both types of planning, strategic planning aims to complement and not replace traditional urban planning. In this way, strategic development plans and projects are flexible and more aimed at demonstrating the potential of a given place than an exact program, and more aimed at communicating ideas than regulating land use.

Strategic planning is a cyclical process, unlike traditional planning whose objective was to approve the definitive plan, which constituted a finished product. It is a continuous planning process, where development goals, action priorities and action programs must be defined, which requires the organization of an efficient monitoring and monitoring system (Alexandre, 2003).

Just like territories, companies are subject to competition in the market. Territorial marketing is concerned with issues of social and economic development. It reflects the territory, in the sense that, subsequently, in a logic of competitiveness, apply the necessary communication strategy. The objectives of territorial marketing must be in line with the stakeholders' vision for economic and social development. In effect, it is marketing that aims to develop the full potential of a region (Nunes, E., 2011).

According to Kotler et al., (1993) it is a process in five stages:

> **Site audit:** It is an orderly analysis of economic and demographic factors, to classify the strengths and weaknesses to compete and consequently indicate opportunities and threats;
> **Vision and objectives:** through the results of preparing the SWOT analysis, it is essential to describe priorities;
> **Elaboration of a strategy:** after defining the vision, goals and objectives and the remaining steps, you can move on to the identification stage, choosing strategies to achieve the goals;
> **Action plan:** preparation of your own action plan to achieve strategies;
> **Implementation and control:** "plans have no value until they are successfully implemented".

There are five fundamental fields of territorial Marketing, which are: brand, image, products and services, tourism and events. The image and brand allow the construction of identity, differentiation and culture and a positioning in the territory. Products and services belong to the supply capacity, that is, to the potential of that same territory. An efficient Territorial Marketing strategy allows you to consider what still needs to be done, what the next steps are, and what can be improved, taking into account past experiences (Pacheco, V., 2011).

Strategic planning based on territorial marketing becomes an added value for territories that wish to be competitive, because it allows the development of a cohesive, consistent and value-generating strategy for all stakeholders. Furthermore, the combination of these two tools encourages cooperation between the public and private sectors, facilitates communication between all actors and assigns the responsibilities of each agent so that the strategy is successful (Mendes, D. et al., 2023).

The Importance of an Identity for a Destination

A brand can be defined as a name, term, sign, symbol or design, or the combination of these elements that aim to identify products or services of a company or group and that are deferential. (Kotler, 1991). Due to the ease of a product's characteristics being easily replicated, brands emerge as tools that can offer differentiation between products (Kotler & Getner, 2002).

A brand is defined as a solid set of characters, emotions or images that consumers experience or observe and that are associated with a service, a product, an organization or a location (Simeon, 2006).

There are four main points of view in brand conceptualization, all of them related to each other (Hankinson, 2004).

At first glance, the brand is conceptualized as a "Communicator", that is, it is seen from a more graphic point of view, allowing the differentiation of a product through names, logos and registered trademarks. It also has an identity that is used by an organization to communicate its differentiation and positioning in relation to the competition.

In a second view, the brand is defined as a "perceptual entity", appealing to the consumer's senses, reason and emotions in which they associate the brand image with a set of associations or attributes to which they attribute personal value. Attributes are further categorized into functional and symbolic; functional or representative, appealing to emotion and reason. A third dimension is also added, which concerns the experience, appealing to the consumer's sensations. However, it is important to highlight that the image is defined as what the consumer perceives of the brand while the identity corresponds to what the organization intends to communicate.

In a third view, the brand is conceptualized as a "Value Adder", this idea is supported by the concept of brand equity, that is, brand value. The value of a brand includes dimensions such as brand image, brand awareness, brand associations, brand loyalty that the consumer has in relation to the brand (Haker & Cameron, 2008), and also the perception of its quality (Hankinson, 2004). Brand value also reflects the results obtained from the sales of a product or service due to a specific brand, which would not happen if the same product or service had the name of another brand (Kotler & Armstrong, 2015).

In the fourth vision, the brand is seen as a "Relationship", that is, it has its own personality and with which it establishes a relationship with the consumer. This relationship can result from the consumer's identification with the brand and also adjustment between the consumer's physical and psychological needs and the functional and symbolic values of the brand. Territorial branding consists of applying the brand concept to products and places, however territories are much more complex to be treated as mere products, since places have a greater variety of audiences, sakeholders and sectors than product companies. In addition, the places have a wide variety of offers/products, but the objectives of the territory's producers and the needs of consumers are varied (Kavaratzis & Ashworth, 2005).

In an attempt to define the concept of territorial brand, it is important to make a clear distinction between the concepts of image and brand. The image corresponds to a set of perceptions that the individual holds in their mind regarding a certain place, taking into account that this image can be constructed from interaction with the respective place (Tasci & Gatner, 2007). The brand, in turn, refers to the deliberate creation of an image designed and constructed by the "producer", which from the point of view of the territory can be several (local authorities, private sector, civil society) (Neacsu et al., 2016).

The image is the bridge between the product and consumers, and is reflected in the processes of personalization, identification and differentiation of the territory. The perception of the territory must be as close as possible to reality, which is translated by the policies and communication actions that are generated. Territory image management aims to ensure that any local element obtains rapid positive identification at regional and national level. And international, implying a complex communication process. (Azevedo et al., 2011).

In its great essence, the territorial brand aims to combine the unique attributes of the place, such as language, architecture, culture, heritage, among others and synthesizes these elements into a single brand identity, with the aim of influencing the value of the brand (brand equity) and make the target audience choose the place to visit, live or work over another (Zavattaro, 2014).

The connection established between the consumer and a brand has two components: one rational and the other symbolic. The first arises from the brand's ability to fulfill its promises in terms of functional attributes. The second comes from the emotional connection between the consumer and the brand (Brito, 2009).

Brito (2008), argues that there are three sources of brand value that deserve to be highlighted:

> **Notoriety** - It depends on the level of presence in the client's spirit, largely resulting from the feeling of familiarity it provides.
> **Image** - Or set of "perceptions that the consumer makes of it" (Keller, 1993), as cited by (Brito, 2008). The strength of the brand depends on both the quantity and quality of information about the brand that is given to the customer.
> **Loyalty or Involvement** - Happens with the attitude of connection. More than repeating the purchase, the customer reveals a positive attitude towards it.

For Aaker (2007), a brand's value proposition is an affirmation of the functional, emotional and self-expression benefits that are offered by the brand and that provide value to the customer. This value proposition must lead to a brand-customer relationship and drive choice decisions.

Managing a Brand

A brand is seen as a multidimensional construction in which the managers of entities or organizations add value to products and services and these values are easily recognized and valued by consumers. The limits of brand construction are, on the one hand, in the activities of entities or organizations and, on the other hand, in the perceptions of consumers, and it is on this interface that the brand focuses (Kavaratzis & Ashworth, 2005).

Kavaratzis & Ashworth (2005) understand branding as a process that interconnects the concepts of identity, positioning and brand image.

> **Brand identity** – How managers want the brand to be perceived.
> **Brand positioning** – The part of the value proposition communicated to a specific segment that demonstrates competitive advantage.
> **Brand image** – How the brand is perceived by consumers.

For (Anholt, 2008), the main axes that determine the positioning of a city or region are:

Presence - The international reputation of a region or city, be it cultural, historical or other, places it at the top of the preferences of cities to visit, live in or invest in. Cities like Paris, London or New York appear as privileged destinations in the collective imagination.
Potential - It is directly related to the opportunities that the city offers to those who visit or want to settle.
Pulse - this vertex is directly related to the lifestyle that the city can provide.
People - This axis evaluates the hospitality of residents and the feeling of security provided to visitors.
Prerequisites - Analyzes infrastructures that are directly linked to people's quality of life.

In this way, the Anholt hexagon is seen as a tool that measures the perception of different audiences about a given city or region. In other words, the way in which a given city brand is perceived by its "interpretants", with the value of the brand being in the response it obtains in its target markets (Lencastre, 2007).

Once the strategy is defined, the places must be presented to the outside in a clear, coordinated and communicative way, thus allowing to influence public opinion. For this, it is necessary, first of all, a partnership between local administrative officials, companies and civil society, in addition to institutions and structures to achieve and maintain this behavior in the long term.

Marketing agility in managing and maintaining the destination strategy, in which the brand is the main asset, is one of the ways to improve the attractiveness and competitiveness indexes of destinations. The new challenges caused by the pandemic crisis require responses that consider contextual change at a social, environmental and/or political level as well as market changes themselves. This process implies permanent collaboration between stakeholders through a lasting commitment, which encourages and combines, for example, the economic-financial perspective of business with the interests of the local community. The future will certainly be guided by this triangulation of interests and only then will the destination have truly sustainable development. (Moura A. & Morais J. 2021)

The creation of a territorial brand, more than communication, has to do with policies, attitudes and should not be seen as a tool that only the richest or most powerful can have access to (Anholt, 2008). It is therefore not surprising that, as happens in companies, the territorial brand has become a fundamental instrument for creating value between the administrative entities of a given territory and individuals (Ham, 2008), being used in a way of have a positive impact on the image of a place on its economy and its citizens.

The eight principles of place branding for complementary competitiveness are:

Objective and potential: Strategic, powerful and particular vision. Give the place a voice, highlight its international reputation;
Truth: Certify a genuine, complete and contemporary image. Conscious communication of the values and accessories of the place;
Ambitions and improvements: Announce a credible, appealing and sustainable vision for the future. A vision, built under these premises, is the basis for the political, economic, cultural and social well-being growth of the residents of that place;
Inclusion and common good: The method of branding a place must be used to achieve social, political and economic objectives;
Creativity and innovation: The brand description procedure must be capable of discovering, releasing and helping to guide talents and skills of communities. Only with creativity can you overcome the complexity of places and decide on a brand strategy that is authentic and effective in delivering your message.
Complexity and simplicity: The process of defining territorial brands is required to authorize communicating in a truthful, motivating (promoting), attractive and creative way the characteristics and attributes of territories;
Work, cooperation and connectivity networks (network): The way of building a brand for a place allows people and organizations to be connected. A good marketing strategy can strengthen public-private partnerships, stimulating involvement and participation in the community. Together, territorial branding must consolidate strong and positive relationships with external entities;
Long-term strategy: Explaining a brand to a place is a long-term endeavor, and short-term results should never be predicted. Defining a solid brand for a place requires commitment, tolerance, with investments adapted to the budgetary capabilities of the territory. This will define a robust brand with long-term advantages.

Territories can "sell" themselves as success as long as they have a representative and recognized brand, created and promoted by city marketing on a firm foundation of a territorial model, of a vision of the future defined through strategic planning.

Target

For marketing to fulfill the objective of its strategy, it must be directed to the needs of consumers or potential consumers (Braun, 2008).

Territorial marketing is segmented into two types of audiences: internal customers (resident citizens, workers and established organizations), whose loyalty is important, and external customers (non-resident citizens, organizations with the potential to establish themselves in the area, visitors of business and tourists), as there is an interest in attracting them to the region.

Kotler and collaborators (2002) state that through territorial marketing it is possible to satisfy the needs of different target market segments to attract new investors and companies, attract tourism revenue, improve the quality of life and well-being of its residents, in a sustainable way, and attract new residents as young, creative and qualified workers, thus increasing human capital.

In addition to adding analysis, planning and execution, territorial marketing provides the entire communication and promotion strategy, with the aim of enhancing the qualities of a territory, but also its promotion due to the dynamism of its guidelines, both worked on by local actors (Fonseca & Ramos, 2006).

Image, Identity and Positioning

Identity is seen as the understanding of the real characteristics of a region, which are necessary to describe, so that it is possible to "retain a city", such as communication, physical and "word of mouth" of the region (Zenker, 2011) . Identity influences the image perceived by the target audience through verbal, visual and behavioral factors that must be part of the brand of a region and, therefore, labeled as its identity (Zenker, 2011).

When individuals identify with social characteristics and feel integrated, the region presents a more positive image, creating meaning and belonging, which will subsequently facilitate decision-making and reduce uncertainty (Zenker et al., 2017).

The relationship between image and identity is reciprocal, the brand image plays a very relevant role in the construction of the brand's identity, but at the same time this image is a reflection of its identity (Qu, Hyunjung, L. & Hyunjung, H. 2011).

A term that cannot be dissociated from words such as image, identity and even value is the positioning of the brand in people's minds. The main objective is related to creating the desired perception in the mind of the target audience, which at the same time creates a differentiation that distinguishes itself from competitors with the same characteristics, thus managing to raise the expectations of this audience.

The Communication

For Kavaratzis (2004), what is carried out and processed in cities is what distinguishes them and thus their image is communicated through different types of communication: primary, secondary and tertiary.

The primary concerns the physical component of the city, such as infrastructure, places, heritage, etc. The secondary is advertising sponsored by basic marketing strategies, such as indoor and outdoor advertising, logos, graphic design, etc. Tertiary communication is part of that which is not controlled, structured or programmed, word-of-mouth.

If the communication of a city brand is carried out in the same way for all its targets and the complexity of the region is ignored, the probability of this communication failing is quite high (Braun & Zenker, 2010).

Logo and Slogan

Currently, there is a concern regarding the image of the city, this time, municipalities, in order to increase their attractiveness and uniqueness to their various audiences, be they investors, tourists, industries or even residents themselves, try to use different methods (Avraham, 2004). One of the mechanisms they use as a strategy to improve the image is changing the logo and slogan. This strategy's main objective is sometimes to remove a negative image of the city, if it exists, or to create a dynamic around it (Avraham, 2004).

The logo/slogan helps to characterize the equity of the city brand, it is not the symbol or phrase that helps create a reputation for the site in question, but it can be an icon for a reputation that has been built over time.

It is part of the role of those who design the graphic representation to make it new, desired, yet contemporary and capable of bringing a future dimension. It is part of the role of those who have the power to manage places to place design management among their governance priorities. The image of the city does not end with the brand that it graphically represents, but a coordinated image of a brand conducive to the needs and ambitions of that same city will be essential and therefore, the management of the 21st century city brand requires high levels of political competence, administrative and technical (Ribeiro M., 2021).

MAIN FOCUS OF THE CHAPTER

This methodological book showcases a selection of research-based case studies to illustrate how to design research beneficial for destination management. These cases will be literature-based, empirical, or both. Each will specifically address one or more methodologies for undertaking research in this field and the practical implications of the obtained results. Readers will find a hands-on methodological guide on collecting and interpreting data and building effective destination management strategies and operations. Each study elaborates on the used technique's advantages, drawbacks, and field applications.

Taking into account that the research focus involves the area of marketing, we adopted the perspective of a specialist in this specific area, Kotler et al. (2007), which explains what pillars are necessary for a territory to be able to prosper. In this way, the aforementioned author highlights four components that form the various ways in which a territory can improve its conditions, its attractiveness, as well as promote the appreciation of its residents and their companies. For this to become a reality, it is necessary to bring together four fundamental elements: a project, resources, services and attractions.

A territory needs a project and a solid development plan, which fully promotes its potential, qualities and aesthetic, cultural and economic values. Regarding resources, it is necessary to develop and maintain a basic infrastructure that is compatible with the natural environment. As for the services component, it is essential to provide good quality basic services to meet all the needs of companies and the population. Finally, the attraction component assumes that a territory needs a range of attractions for citizens, residents and visitors, such as natural features, emblematic people, shopping places, cultural attractions, entertainment, festivals, commemorative dates, monuments and all its history.

The development of tourism and the economy itself around this sector meant that cities and other territories began to see themselves as brands, focusing more on those who visit them and less on those who live in them. However, in recent years there has been an awareness of the impact that residents have on the distribution of services and positive experiences for those who visit the territory. Furthermore, the economic development that the territory can achieve, when its residents are satisfied, is much higher than that which occurs when the opposite happens. This means that the role of residents is increasingly valued, leading territories to seek experiences that meet the needs of those who live there, providing them with satisfaction. Consequently, a positive image of the territory on the part of its residents translates into the transmission of positive feedback that will be transmitted, thus also reducing the intention to abandon it.

According to Lencastre (2007), the brand is an essential instrument of economic activity in a market economy system. Without brands there is no possibility of choice for consumers, and without choice there is no competition. The identifying and distinctive function of products and services are the most important aspects of the brand.

Brandão (2011) refers to the brand as a "process of mobilizing identity resources to create value". To this end, the author explains that this process must include objectives, the definition of target audiences, and the assumption of a coherent position.

This work is developed according to a methodological structure divided into two distinct phases (analysis and interpretation of the place and an action plan), which follow a logic of strategic intervention in the village of Taipas. This strategy consists mainly of enhancing the various existing strengths and developing instruments and/or mechanisms that complement them.

The analysis and interpretation of this area results from a crossing of documented and collected information, semi-structured and exploratory interviews of a qualitative nature, which are fundamental to understanding the context of the study and also a literature search on the topics covered, on which this is based. case. To this end, interviews will be carried out with public and private agents (associations, residents, businesspeople, councilors...) in which several key elements fundamental to the community's needs will be highlighted.

In this sense, interaction with the various organisms allows us to establish a logic of action that seeks above all to boost this territory, using territorial marketing as the main intervention tool, in order to retain the population, attract more tourists and promote the local economic growth.

In this way, this interpretation is developed through a set of points, which are based on a careful analysis of the surrounding environment, establishing concrete guidelines according to the focus.

Given all the collection of information and issues identified and elements previously collected, the aim is to develop an action plan, which is based on an intervention strategy in this territory, with the purpose of promoting and developing the aspects with the greatest potential, differentiating the surrounding environments., but also the biggest gaps, which can give rise to new infrastructure and job creation.

This plan is based on:

- Carrying out an assessment of the specific territory and its surroundings;
- Transmit attractive and competitive factors to internal and external audiences;
- Maximize demand satisfaction from different target audiences to stimulate supply;
- Identify trends and anticipate opportunities;
- Define segmentation, targeting and positioning strategy;
- Develop the action plan;
- Main objectives of the action plan;
- Strengthen the visibility and attractiveness of Vila de Caldas das Taipas;
- Boosting investment in the forefront of the local economic base.

In short, the main aim is to reaffirm the importance of the existence of a territorial marketing plan, which reinforces the importance of convergence in a future, prospective vision, with the definition of strategic goals and objectives, which encourage the development and competitiveness of the town, mobilizing its main actors, in the selection and participation in key projects for its development.

ANALYSIS AND STRATEGY DEFINITION

The term SWOT (Strengths (S-Strengths), Weaknesses (W – Weaknesses), Opportunities (O – Opportunities) and Threats (T -Threats)) is a management tool widely used in companies to define strategy. This analysis makes it possible to distinguish the internal environment (internal factors and realities – strengths and weaknesses) and the external environment (future factors and aspects – opportunities and threats) of the organization.

It is essential to identify the internal and external environment to establish strategies and define priorities, as well as deciding which guidelines to take in order to achieve the objectives, always keeping threats under a critical eye. Strengths and weaknesses are a representation of the present moment. From another perspective, opportunities and threats represent what the company foresees in the future. Therefore, this analysis must relate strengths to opportunities and weaknesses to threats. The conclusions drawn from the analysis must be presented and subject to debate and analysis before the organization's decision-makers, so that they lead to the implementation of concrete measures, with well-established objectives, deadlines and responsibilities. (Ribeiro,2010)

SWOT analysis, as already mentioned, is a recommended technique for summarizing and clarifying the strengths, weaknesses, opportunities and threats to the development of a territory. Development and progress will not be achieved without prior work being done to diagnose the territory (Rainisto 2003). The territorial marketing process consists of analyzing opportunities, developing strategies and planning efficient and effective programs from the point of view of optimizing resources.

PROPOSALS PRESENTED

Development of Brand Image, Logo, Slogan

Brand image is the "perception of the brand in the minds of customers, it is a (perhaps inaccurate) reflection of the brand's personality or product. It is what people believe about a brand, thoughts, feelings and expectations" (Bennett, 1995).

The name of the city or territory is what is normally associated with the name of the brand, symbol or design or combination of these, which seeks to identify and interconnect the most relevant characteristics and attributes of the same.

When associated with a territory, the brand synthesizes the image that, to be successful, needs to establish emotional connections with its target audiences and awaken feelings. The image of a territory is a mental representation, a synthesis of its most important attributes, which makes it unique.

"Brand identity creates a relationship between the brand and customers with a value proposition that incorporates functional, emotional and self-expression benefits" (Kapferer, 1994).

The logo is the graphic representation of a brand, which thus identifies it and makes it unique, and together with the font, image and color, it constitutes the logo.

Means of Communication and Dissemination

The implementation of the marketing and promotion plan for Caldas das Taipas must involve a concentration of efforts from various actors involved (residents, potential residents, businesspeople/investors, the local authority and other public entities). It is proposed to create a communication and dissemination body for Caldas das Taipas and digital media, as explained in the following points.

The creation of a communication and dissemination body should be a small structure that does not involve high costs. This project envisages the creation of at least one job, through the hiring of a technician to manage it, with marketing and social communications skills.

The main purposes of this body are:

- Structure and communicate the territorial offer to the target audience;
- Provide information platforms with content and structured according to various market segments.

All of these purposes are inherent to various activities that can be carried out, such as:

- Dissemination of promotional material;
- Creation of an app, so that there is a concentration of information on a single platform;
- Recreate the village's existing website, in collaboration with the parish council;
- Collaboration with local partners to coordinate promotional activities;
- Monitoring of marketing activities.

Development of the Mobile Application (app)

A free application for mobile phones, as a means of communication, promotion and business for the town of Caldas das Taipas is the proposal that will bring the most varied advantages in order to boost and create involvement with the community, mainly:

- For residents who want to quickly consult useful contacts or access the events calendar;
- For tourists who want to consult maps, information about events, activities, accommodation, restaurants and see points of interest;
- For businesspeople/investors who want to identify potential business opportunities and partnerships;
- Guided tours and virtual tours;
- Exclusive discounts in partnerships with local stakeholders.

Creating an Event

Currently, events are very important and fundamental to the culture of a place, region or country. For this reason, events are used by various public and private entities, as part of the promotional and economic development strategy of a given destination.

At a social and cultural level, events enable the dissemination of traditions, an increase in the feeling of belonging, the participation of local communities and, also, the expansion of cultural projects. The physical and environmental impacts of events are essentially related to increased environmental awareness and new practices (Santos et al., 2012).

Gastronomic Tourism is considered an intangible heritage as it is associated with valuing the identity and unity of destinations (Henriques & Custódio, 2010).

The events also allow for urban regeneration and improvement of infrastructure, transport and means of communication. In the political sphere, events enable international prestige, publicity, as well as the promotion of investments and projects and, also, social cohesion (Santos et al., 2012).

Monitoring of Proposals Presented

The proposals presented that form part of the construction strategy of the territorial marketing plan for Caldas das Taipas will only be successful if the proposals are effectively implemented and their communication is well articulated with the target audiences.

An analysis of the needs of the various actors (residents, potential residents, tourists, businesspeople/investors, potential investors) will need to be carried out in order to ensure a relationship with competitive advantages between them, thus increasing the competitiveness and attractiveness of the territory .

In this context, some basic ideas are presented:

- Use of media, with a special focus on the internet, to implement a standout differentiated marketing strategy;
- Integration of identity/branding in all events and activities related to the village;
- Integration of information and brand image on platforms to support the target audience;
- Integration of the digital platform (app), as an essential mechanism for a more attractive dynamic for residents and visitors, creating greater interaction with the younger community;
- Permanently updating the website and information mechanisms with information in Portuguese, Spanish, English, French and German, thus guaranteeing universal access to information;
- Creation of the annual event, with the aim of promoting the image of the village - nature and stimulating the local economy;
- Carrying out training actions (seminars, meetings, etc.).

CONCLUSION AND FUTURE RESEARCH

The case under study must be qualified as the beginning of fieldwork, which must continue with future investigations and new fronts of action, always valuing the need for active participation of the local community, linked directly or indirectly to the academic community, in future actions that are developed.

In scientific terms, it seeks to contribute to the deepening of knowledge in the area of territorial marketing, mainly with regard to the creation and management of the territory brand, which is, like any other brand, the way in which it is exposed and made known to its audiences and the way they receive and interpret it.

In a context marked by increasing competition between territories and the unpredictability of their economies, there is a need to develop clear and concerted strategies that directly contribute to the sustainable development of territories. The growing competition between territories is essentially done by attracting and capturing resources, investments, companies, residents and tourists, capable of generating positive dynamics in the territories.

With the project under study, it is intended to justify that the lessons and experiences carried out by companies can be adapted to the territories, in a strategic planning logic, which, analyzing the characteristics and specificities of a territory with the participation and involvement of local actors, can formulate a long-term plan and development, projecting an effective and attractive image, always promoting your affirmation and development.

The development of a territorial marketing plan and a positioning strategy must guarantee the essential tools for creating strategic policies that make the territory more competitive and sustainable. In this sense, it is essential that all stakeholders are involved in task planning.

Cooperation and complementarity between territories have a strong impact on their development process, particularly due to the ability to articulate different sectors (economic, political and social) and to boost efficiency and sustainability.

REFERENCES

Ancarani, F. (2001). *Marketing Places. A Resource-Based Approach And Empirical Evidence From The European Experience*. SDA Bocconi, Research Division Working Paper No. 01/55.

Anholt, S. (2007). *Competitive Identity. The New Brand Management for Nations, Cities and Regions*. Palgrave Macmillan.

Anholt, S. (2008). *Place Branding: Is Marketing or Isn't? Place Branding and Public Diplomacy*, 4(1), 1–6. DOI: 10.1057/palgrave.pb.6000088

Avraham, E. (2004). *Media strategies for improving an unfavorable city image*. Elsevier Ltd, 21(6), 471–479.

Azevedo, A., Magalhães, D., & Pereira, J. (2011). *City Marketing: Myplace in XXI*. Vida Económica – Editorial SA.

Azevedo, A., Magalhães, D., & Pereira, J. (2011): City Marketing. Gestão estratégica e Marketing de cidades. Editor Vida Económica. ISBN: 9789727883738.

Bardin, L. (1977). *Análise de Conteúdo*. Edições 70. Lisboa. 9- 14, 31, 38- 45, 95-141. *Research*, 26(2), 312–328.

Barke, M. (1999). City Marketing as a Planning Tool. In Pacionae, M. (Ed.), *Applied Geography: Principles and Practice*. Routledge.

Bennett, D. (1995). *Dictionary of marketing terms*. American Marketing Association.

Bondarenko, V. A., K., O., & Pisareva, E. (2018). *Marketing management of the territory in the aspect of the regional brand formation*. European Research Studies Journal, Volume XXI, Special Issue 2, 72-78.

Braun, E., & Zenker, S. (2010). *Towards an Integrated Approach for Place Brand Management. In 50th Congress of the European Regional Science Association: "Sustainable Regional Growth and Development in the Creative Knowledge Economy"*, Jönköping, Sweden: Towards an Integrated Approach for Place Brand Management. 36 (pp. 1–12)

Cabral, J., & Marques, T. (1996). - *"Do planeamento estratégico ao desenvolvimento sustentável: experiência em Portugal"*, in Inforgeo, n°11. Lisboa.

Cidrais, Á. (1998), *O marketing territorial aplicado às cidades médias portuguesas: os casos de Évora e Portalegre*, Dissertação de mestrado apresentada à Faculdade de Letras da Universidade de Lisboa. 121 p.

Costa, A. (2013). *Destination Branding: o papel dos stakeholders na gestão de uma marca-destino – o caso da marca Douro* (Dissertação de mestrado). Universidade do Minho, Braga, Portugal.

Ferreira, A. (2005). Gestão *estratégica de cidades e regiões*. Fundação Calouste Gulbenkian, 2ª edição, Lisboa.

Fonseca, F., & Ramos, R. (2006) *O planeamento estratégico em busca de potenciar o território – o caso de Almeida*. In II Congresso Luso-Brasileiro 107 de Planeamento Urbano Regional Integrado Sustentável, 27 a 29 de Setembro, Universidade do Minho, Braga.

Gerhardt, T. E, R. & Silveira, D. T. (2009). *Metodos de Pesquisa. Universidade Aberta Do Brasil- UAB/UFRGS E Pelo Curso de Graduação Tecnológica – Planejamento e Gestão para o Desenvolvimento Rural da SEAD/UFEGS*,1º, 1-120.

González, X. (Dir.) (2001). *Planeamento Estratégico e Mecanotecnia Territorial*. EixoAtlântico do Noroeste Peninsular.

Ham, P. (2008). Place Branding: State of Art. *The Annals of the American Academy of Political and Social Science*, 616(1), 126–149. DOI: 10.1177/0002716207312274

Henriques, C., & Custódio, M. J. (2010). *Turismo e Gastronomia: A valorização do património gastronómico na região do Algarve*. Revista Encontros Científicos - Tourism & Management Studies, (6), 69-81. *HSM Management*, 3(44), 61–72.

Kapferer, J. N. (1994). *Strategic brand management, new approaches to creating and evaluating brand equity*. The Free Press.

Kavaratzis, M. (2004). From city marketing to city branding: Towards a theoretical framework for developing city brands. *Place Branding and Public Diplomacy*, 1(1), 58–73. DOI: 10.1057/palgrave.pb.5990005

Kavaratzis, M., & Ashworth, G. J. (2005). City Branding: An effective assertion of identity or a transitory marketing trick? *Tijdschrift voor Economische en Sociale Geografie*, 96(5), 506–514. DOI: 10.1111/j.1467-9663.2005.00482.x

Kotler, P., & Gertner, D. (2002, April). Country as brand, product, and beyond: A place marketing and brand management perspective. *Journal of Brand Management*, 9(4-5), 249–261. DOI: 10.1057/palgrave.bm.2540076

Kotler, P., Haider, D. H., & Rein, I. (1993). *Marketing Places*. The Free Press.

Lages, R. (2017). *O posicionamento e a imagem em contextos de marketing territorial: Estudo de caso aplicado à cidade de Braga*. Escola de Economia e Gestão da Universidade do Minho.

McCunn, L. J., & Gifford, R. (2012). Do green offices affect employee engagement and environmental motivation? *Architectural Science Review*, 55(2), 128–134. DOI: 10.1080/00038628.2012.667939

Megri, Z., & Bencherif, F. (2014). The Effect of Territorial Marketing on City Image Valuation: An Exploratory Study in Algeria. *International Journal of Marketing Studies*, 6(4), 145–156. DOI: 10.5539/ijms.v6n4p145

Minciotti, S., & Silva, E. (2011). Marketing de Localidades: Uma abordagem ampliada sobre o desenvolvimento da cidade ou região. *Revista Turismo Visão e Ação*, 13(3), 329–346.

Neacşu, M.-C., Neguţ, S., & Vlăsceanu, G. (2016). Place Branding – Geographical Approach. Case Study: Waterloo. *Amfiteatru Economic*, 18(10), 944–959.

Nunes, E. (2011). *Fatores de sucesso em marketing territorial: desafios de desenvolvimento na região Alentejo*. Instituto Superior de Ciências Sociais e Políticas.

Nunes, F. (1999), *Processo de Planeamento de Marketing Territorial Estratégico- Um instrumento de operacionalização de estratégias de política para Área Metropolitana do Porto*, Dissertação de Mestrado apresentada à Faculdade de Arquitetura e Engenharia do Porto, Porto. 160 p.

Qu, L., & Hyunjung, H. (2011). A model of destination branding : Integrating the concepts of the branding and destination image. *Tourism Management*, 32(3), 465–476. DOI: 10.1016/j.tourman.2010.03.014

Rainisto, S. (2003). *Sucess factores of Place Marketing: a Study of Place Marketing Practices in Northern Europe and Unite States*. Helsinki University of Technology, Finland: Institute of Strategy and International Business, Doctoral Dissertations.

Ribeiro, E. (2010). Análise financeira. Portal Gestão. Disponível em www.portal-gestao.com

Santos, A. C. S. C, M. J. & Eusébio, C. (2012). *Avaliação de festivais: O caso da Viagem Medieval de Santa Maria da Feira*. Revista Turismo e Desenvolvimento 1645- 9261. 1597-1609. https://www.ua.pt/file/30716

Sautter, E. T., & Leisen, B. (1999). *Managing stakeholders: A tourism planning model*. Annals of Tourism

Tasci, A., & Gartner, W. (2007). Destination image and its functional relationships. *Journal of Travel Research*, 45(4), 25–413. DOI: 10.1177/0047287507299569

Van Den Berg et al. (2002). *Sports and City Marketing in European Cities. European Institute for Comparative Urban Research*. Ashgate.

Ward, S. (1998). Selling places: the marketing and promotion of towns and cities, 1850-2000.

Zavattaro, S. (2014). *Place Branding through Phases of the Image* (1a Ed). New York: Palgrave Macmillan

Zenker, S. (2011). How to catch a city? *The concept and measurement of place brands.Journal of Place Management and Development*, 4(1), 40–52. DOI: 10.1108/17538331111117151

Zenker, S. B. E., & Petersen, S. (2017). Branding the destination versus the place : The effects of brand complexity and identification for residents and visitors. *Tourism Management*, 58, 15–27. DOI: 10.1016/j.tourman.2016.10.008

Chapter 8

Destination Marketing and Sport:
A Bibliometric Review

Jiyoon An
https://orcid.org/0000-0002-4394-148X
Fayetteville State University, USA

EXECUTIVE SUMMARY

Sport is crucial to understanding destination marketing due to local/international, one-off/continual, and vacation-centric natures. This chapter summarizes the scholarship of sport and destination marketing using the domain-specific bibliometric review. This method allows us to evaluate thematic evolution in addition to backward-looking and forward-looking impacts across the disciplines. The findings revealed that destination marketing is transitioning from professional-driven sports event tourism to amateur-driven active sport tourism and is open to service innovation with emerging technologies. This research synthesis helps practitioners and academics assess research progress and suggest future research directions that may facilitate the inclusion of emerging technologies to service innovation at the intersection of sport and destination marketing.

INTRODUCTION

Sport is important to destination management and marketing as sports initiatives help tourists engage with destinations for various value constellations: entertainment, education, esthetics, and escapism (Oh et al., 2007; Pine & Gilmore, 1999). 2014 Fédération Internationale de Football Association (FIFA) World Cup and 2016 Olympics have played central roles in destination marketing of Rio de Janeiro,

DOI: 10.4018/979-8-3693-1548-4.ch008

Brazil (Maiello and Pasquinelli, 2015). Pontevedra in the Galicia region of Spain has developed a strategic initiative to build a sports event portfolio to host small- or medium-sized sports events for destination marketing (Salgado-Barandela et al., 2021).

Herstein and Berger (2013) conceptualize sports initiatives with two main dimensions, such as local/international events and one-off/continual events. The authors suggest international (vs. local) events contribute to creating a significant economic transformation and urban redevelopment, transitioning to a global service economy. They underscore the important role of sport in destination marketing for city brands and sports league brands with host cities for one-off and continual events, respectively. The classification identifies the Seoul Marathon (local/one-off), Northern Athletics Collegiate Conference (NACC) (local/continual), FIFA World Cup (international/one-off), and U.S. Open (international/continual).

The scholarship at the intersection of sport and destination marketing has two camps: active sport tourism for amateur athletes at a vacation destination and mega sports tourism for professional athletes for the spectacles. Researchers in active sport tourism have investigated the risk and sustainability assessments for participating in amateur sports at vacation destinations and segmented marketing efforts from destination marketing organizations (Hugenberg et al., 2016; Johann et al., 2022). Mega sports tourism scholars have provided a taxonomy to examine the sports initiatives for destination marketing, such as sports venues (e.g., Olympic stadium) and mega event organizations (e.g., FIFA World Cup) (Higham & Hinch, 2018; Ramshaw, 2020).

Although existing literature in this area is informative, there is a noticeable lack of scholarly attention to the evolving scholarship of destination marketing and sport. This is because the literature fails to address the divide between amateur and professional sports in destination marketing. This study aims to fill this gap by examining the scholarship of destination marketing and sport, reviewing existing literature, and presenting a fresh perspective on the topic. The paper will conduct a bibliometric analysis (Donthu et al., 2021) to identify research trends and emerging themes by combining and summarizing existing theories.

METHODOLOGY

The domain-specific bibliometric review was conducted to examine the evolving scholarship of sport and destination marketing (An, 2024; Paul & Criado, 2020). MacInnis (2011) method of Envisioning, Explicating, Relating, and Debating guided examining how the relationships between destination marketing and sport were defined and operationalized (Envisioning phase), arranging findings (Explicating phase) and integrating perspectives (Relating phase), and assessing the evolving scholarship (Debating phase).

A bibliometric review is a quantitatively oriented systematic literature review with citation dynamics by quantifying backward-looking and forward-looking impacts across the disciplines (Donthu et al., 2021). Study design for data collection and data analysis and data analysis for assessing findings with data visualization and interpretation were guided by Zupic and Čater (2015) and Coombes (2023). One hundred and fifty studies were gathered by searching the keyword strings of ("destination marketing" and "sport") with the Web of Science database. The analyses were conducted using the Bibliometric package with the programming R and VOS viewer software to retrieve, review, and report the data (Paul & Rosado-Serrano, 2019).

Results

The results section provides an overview of research trends and emerging themes by providing impact analysis in chronological dynamics, citation count, and thematic analysis with keyword co-occurrence, co-citation, and bibliographic coupling analysis.

Impact Analysis: Publication Trend and Most Cited Papers

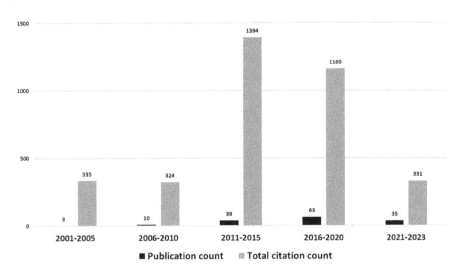

Figure 1 indicates the rising scholarly interests and impacts in the subject over two decades in terms of publication count and total citation count. The scholarship emerged in the early 2000s and continued to show the growth in the 2010s with their productivity and impact, generating robust trends in the first few years of the 2020s.

In the 2000s, scholarly attention emerged to investigate the intersection of mega sport event and destination marketing. Kim and Chalip (2004) examined the expectations for the upcoming FIFA World Cup with American soccer club members via a survey. Smith (2005) investigated the role of sports initiatives in destination marketing with three cases in the U.K.: Birmingham, Manchester, and Sheffield. The former addresses the demand side of destination marketing, but the latter focuses on the supply side of destination marketing.

Stakeholder theoretical perspectives were important to the scholarship in the 2010s. Scholars have examined the destination marketing effectiveness of the 2010 FIFA World Cup in the context of an emerging country (e.g., South Africa) via a qualitative method, highlighting the important roles of the destination's local residents and media coverage (Knott et al., 2015). Zehrer and Hallmann (2015) examined the success factors of destination marketing from the policy and planning perspective. Sato et al. (2018) investigated the drivers of sports destination satisfaction from travel decision-makers and non-decision-makers in active sport tourism (e.g., amateur sports participation during a vacation).

Destination loyalty was a popular topic in the scholarship in the 2020s. Newland and Yoo (2020) investigated active sport tourism and destination loyalty while considering attributes of destination and active sport. Mirzaalian and Halpenny (2021) analyzed user-generated content via social media in a national park to show how winter sports were consumed in a destination. Joo et al. (2023) examined the role of sporting event-induced emotional solidarity to destination loyalty as a precursor for destination marketing success.

Table 1. Most cited papers

Title	Author	Year	Total citations	Yearly citation
Residents' perceived risk, emotional solidarity, and support for tourism amidst the covid-19 pandemic	Joo et al.	2021	113	28.25
Visual destination images of peru: comparative content analysis of dmo and user-generated photography	Stepchenkova & Zhan	2013	269	22.42
Perceived value and flow experience: application in a nature-based tourism context	Kim & Thapa	2018	113	16.14
Virtual reality and tourism marketing: conceptualizing a framework on presence, emotion, and intention	Yung et al.	2021	55	13.75

continued on following page

Table 1. Continued

Title	Author	Year	Total citations	Yearly citation
Image and perceived risk: a study of uganda and its official tourism website	Lepp et al.	2011	175	12.50
Why travel to the fifa world cup? effects of motives, background, interest, and constraints	Kim & Chalip	2004	187	8.90
Identifying the spatial structure of the tourist attraction system in south korea using gis and network analysis: an application of anchor-point theory	Kang et al.	2018	60	8.57
Adventure tourism motivation and destination loyalty: a comparison of decision and non-decision makers	Sato et al.	2018	58	8.28
The nation branding opportunities provided by a sport mega-event: south africa and the 2010 fifa world cup	Knott et al.	2015	80	8.00
The influence of image on destination attractiveness	Kim & Perdue	2011	111	7.93

Source: Author's own creation

Table 1 indicates the most cited papers in the domain based on the yearly citation count. This analysis enhances our understanding of popular methods and empirical context in existing literature. 70% of highly cited papers based on yearly citations were published in the 2010s. Active tourism was popular in the scholarship (Kim & Perdue, 2011; Kim & Thapa, 2018; Sato et al., 2018) in addition to mega sports events (Kim & Chalip, 2004; Knott et al., 2015) and technology infusion (Stepchenkova & Zhan, 2013; Lepp et al., 2011; Kang et al., 2018; Yung et al., 2021).

Thematic Analysis: Keyword Co-occurrence, Co-citation, and Bibliographic Coupling Analysis

Themes of the research streams emerged from keyword co-occurrence analysis, backward-looking co-citation analysis, and forward-looking analysis impacts (Donthu et al., 2021).

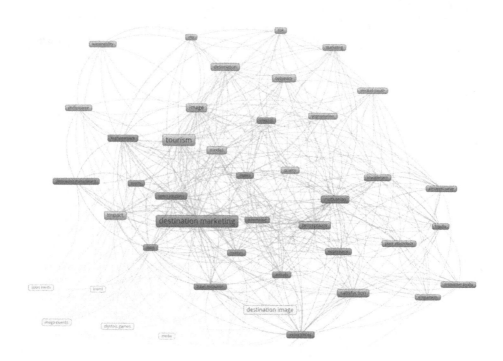

Co-occurrence of keywords analysis identified four clusters: destination image (green cluster), destination loyalty (blue cluster), destination marketing (red cluster), and sports events (yellow cluster) (Figure 2). The destination image cluster represents word-of-mouth behaviors and marketing segmentation strategy. The destination loyalty cluster focuses on perceived value, satisfaction, and loyalty to destinations as a function of destination marketing influencing their antecedents to the downstream outcomes. The destination marketing cluster includes travel motivations, experiences, and destination management. Sports events cluster involves mega sports events and their engagements with media and brands to create a destination image.

Co-citation analysis and bibliographic coupling analysis serve complementing roles for mapping the literature by providing a retrospective and prospective outlook, retrospectively. Implications for academics and practitioners will be given based on evidence by mapping the literature.

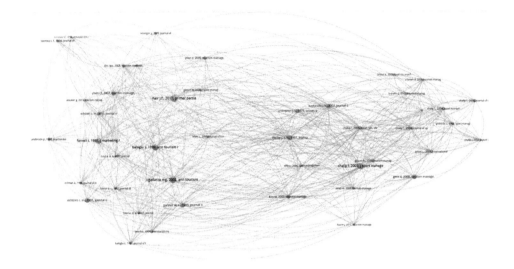

Co-citation analysis (Figure 3) revealed three clusters: sports events for destination marketing (red-colored) (Chalip et al., 2003; Ritchie & Smith, 1991), destination image formation and development with sport (blue-colored) (Gallarza et al., 2002; Baloglu & McClearly, 1999), and methods for sport and destination marketing (green-colored) (Fornell & Larcker, 1981; Hair et al., 2017).

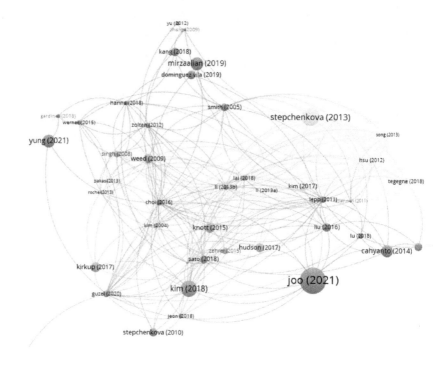

Bibliographic coupling analysis (Figure 4) uncovered five clusters: destination loyalty (red-colored) (Mirzaalian & Halpenny, 2021), destination associations and dynamics (yellow-colored) (Stepchenkova & Li, 2014), destination marketing strategy (violet-colored) (Joo et al., 2021), destination travel motivation (blue-colored) (Güzel et al., 2020), and sport destination tourism and consumer behavior (green-colored) (Weed, 2009).

Discussion

The results indicate the rising interest in active sport tourism and the need to investigate the intersection of sport and destination marketing, in addition to the established literature on mega sport events and destination marketing. The transition from professional-driven sports event tourism to amateur-driven active sports tourism helps practitioners and researchers explore opportunities for service innovation.

The growth of active sport tourism gives destination marketing practitioners opportunities to develop strategies to cater to amateur athletes at a vacation destination. This approach views active sports as leisure and focuses on short-term, intense participatory tourism through sports (Gibson, 1998). For service innovation, practitioners should be mindful of the rise of experiential marketing, which invites destinations as venues for entertainment, education, esthetics, and escapism (Oh et al., 2007; Pine & Gilmore, 1999).

Surfing, sport climbing, skateboarding, and break dancing epitomize this active tourism trend, which has recently broadened its footprint to professional sports, including Olympic sports (CNN, 2024). Blockchain-based metaverse can provide embodied self (e.g., avatar) and digital collectibles with non-fungible tokens (NFT). Immersive technology with digital twins may provide more accessibility and interactivity to experience a remote island for various activities in active sport tourism.

Tech-savvy innovation allows practitioners to leverage multi-modal data to cater to a more dynamic, real-time destination marketing experience beyond the conventional survey method. Practitioners and policymakers can make more informed decisions as the decision support system allows them to assess spatial spillover effects of sport tourism investments (e.g., spectator sport facilities, sporting goods manufacturers/wholesalers) with publicly available data through U.S. federal government agencies (e.g., U.S. Census Bureau, Center for Disease Control and Prevention) (Kim and Kim, 2023).

Big data analysis may help address the challenges from spectacles-driven, mega sports tourism for professional athletes, interacting throughout a consumer's journey for sport tourism. At the pre-tourism phase, search engine keyword streams associated with Geographic Information Systems (GIS) helped feature engineering for content marketing to personalized destination marketing campaigns. During sport tourism, the visitors' preferences are dynamically updated for deploying smart sport tourism, creating engagement with immersive technologies at a sport tourism destination. Geographically weighted regression can help simulate visitors' heterogeneous geographic preferences, which helps provide sport tourism choices (e.g., ticket price, restaurant attribute) for greater satisfaction and revenue possibilities (Chae et al., 2023).

For post-engagement of mega sports tourism, Vassiliadis et al. (2021) examine a delicate balance between resource allocation and feature management in sports-related destination marketing. Jung and Kim (2019) documented the difficulty in sustaining destination loyalty after the focal sport event in a competitive market, which can be detrimental to the host destinations due to the resource-intensive nature of mega-sport event demanding high-quality destination management and marketing. To address the challenges, generative artificial intelligence technology may generate creative content with preferred features by learning from the historical engagement data from first-time and repeat visitors. Immersive technology with a digital twin of the destination may create more engagement by creating continuous streams of excitement and user-generated content shareable on social media.

Table 2. Future research directions

UN SDG	Goal	Research questions	Article
1	No poverty	- How do active sport tourism and mega-sport tourism impact on economic stratification in a host destination?	Barreda et al. (2014)
2	Zero hunger	- How does the academic community foster the underexplored theme (e.g., zero hunger) in sport-based destination tourism?	Jung et al. (2024)
3	Good health and well-being	- What are the antecedents, decisions, and outcomes of active sport tourism on well-being?	Coghlan (2013)
4	Quality education	- How can education quality be enhanced with sustainable sport tourism practices?	Handler and Tan (2022)
5	Gender equality	- How can active tourism participation change gender equality?	Eime et al. (2021)
6	Clean water and sanitation	- How can design sport tourism destination development for water supply sustainability (e.g., island)?	Van Rheenen et al. (2024)
7	Affordable and clean energy	- How can engage with various stakeholders for decarbonization and sport tourism?	Ito and Higham (2023)
8	Decent work and economic growth	- How can assess the economic impact from diverse activitices in sport tourism on various stakeholders?	Drakakis et al. (2021)
9	Industry, innovation, and infrastructure	- How can creativity thrive with sport tourism (e.g., fandom-induced tourism)?	Ziakas and Tzanelli (2022)
10	Reduced inequalities	- How can sport tourism address inequalities of emerging and developed economy?	Coakley (2021)
11	Sustainable cities and communities	- How can sport tourism empower marginalized group (e.g., urban /rural community revitalization)?	Mousavi et al. (2022)
12	Responsible consumption and production	- How can foster sustabilabilty practices in sport tourism?	Homes et al. (2015)
13	Climate action	- How can address challenges of growing travel carbon footprints of nature-based individual sport activity in active sport tourism?	Wicker (2019)
14	Life below water	- How can form alliance to protect life below water (e.g., 11th hour racing)?	Savery and Ghezzi (2022)
15	Life on land	- How can environmentalist activism change sport tourism?	Power (2022)
16	Peace, justice, and strong institutions	- How can sport tourism foster peace, justice, and strong institutions in conflict-torn places?	Gelbman (2021)
17	Partnerships for the goals	- How can build the governance for sustainable sport tourism?	Sharma et al. (2024)

Source: Author's own creation

For future research directions, Table 2 summarizes research questions and notable research papers aligned with the United Nations Sustainable Development Goals (UN SDGs). Since research at the intersection of UN SDGs and sport tourism uses qualitative methods (e.g., interview, case study) from the cross-disciplinary perspective, the insights may complement the findings of this bibliometric research, which is a Western-centric, quantitative research. Future research may invite Transformative Service Research to examine how the transition from professional-driven sports event tourism to amateur-driven active sport tourism affects the well-being of various stakeholders.

CONCLUSION

The evolving scholarship on sport and destination marketing was examined. As Marques and Pimental Biscaia (2019) have noted the importance of service innovation, the synthesis of the scholarship has gained insights on how to move forward. For example, understanding micro-level (e.g., individuals' sport-induced destination travel motivation), meso-level (e.g., dynamics of competing destination management organizations), and macro-level (e.g., pandemic travel restrictions) is crucial to change value configuration and service innovation as it helps deploy contingent strategies on stakeholder management and emerging technologies (Witell et al., 2016; Snyder et al., 2016).

For an overview of the scholarship of sport and destination marketing, a bibliometric review was used to quantify the thematic evolution in addition to backward-looking and forward-looking impacts across the disciplines (Donthu et al., 2021). This systematic approach is helpful to instruct practitioners and academics to familiarize an emerging scholarship with the added value of high relevancy in a scalable and replicable manner. This augmented intelligence technique can operate with real-time search engine optimization and communication to be aligned with destination travelers for active sport tourism and mega sport events tourism. The synthesis of research progress and the suggested research agenda may facilitate the inclusion of emerging technologies to service innovation at the intersection of sport and destination marketing.

Questions and Answers

What is the overall problem presented in this case?

- The scholarship has not fully integrated the divide between amateur and professional sports in destination marketing

What are the factors affecting the problem(s) related to this case?
- Destination marketing community failed to capture the evolving landscape of the sport tourism trend from mega sports events to active sports tourism.

What are some of the emerging technologies that should be considered in solving the problem(s) related to the case?

- Artificial intelligence helps examine the dynamic relationship of destination marketing and sport for documented historical data from various stakeholders and personalized destination content from travel motivation to post-travel evaluation phase.

What is the final solution that can be recommended to the management of the organization described in the case? Provide your arguments in support of the recommended solution.

- Service innovation in destination marketing is possible by embracing emerging technologies, such as extended reality and blockchain, for more big data sources based on sensors and Geographic Information Systems (GIS) at a greater scale, scope, and speed.

What would be challenges for service innovation at the intersection of sport and destination marketing?

- Challenges may arise from the micro-level (e.g., individuals' sport-induced motivation for destination choice), meso-level (e.g., dynamics of competing destination management organizations), and macro-level (e.g., pandemic travel restrictions) for value configuration strategies.

Epilogue and Lessons Learned

- The insights for service innovation may be driven by examining the evolving scholarship of sport and destination marketing.
- The rise of active sport tourism is an opportunity for destination marketing with global audience.
- Destination marketing for mega sports event may need to revitalize their value configuration strategies.

REFERENCES

An, J. (2024). Maritime logistics and digital transformation with big data: Review and research trend. *Maritime Business Review*, 9(3), 229–242. DOI: 10.1108/MABR-10-2023-0069

Baloglu, S., & McCleary, K. W. (1999). A model of destination image formation. *Annals of Tourism Research*, 26(4), 868–897. DOI: 10.1016/S0160-7383(99)00030-4

Barreda, A. A., Zubieta, S., Chen, H., Cassilha, M., & Kageyama, Y. (2017). Evaluating the impact of mega-sporting events on hotel pricing strategies: The case of the 2014 FIFA World Cup. *Tourism Review*, 72(2), 184–208. DOI: 10.1108/TR-02-2017-0018

Chalip, L., Green, B. C., & Hill, B. (2003). Effects of sport event media on destination image and intention to visit. *Journal of Sport Management*, 17(3), 214–234. DOI: 10.1123/jsm.17.3.214

Choe, Y., Baek, J., & Kim, H. (2023). Heterogeneity in consumer preference toward mega-sport event travel packages: Implications for smart tourism marketing strategy. *Information Processing & Management*, 60(3), 103302. DOI: 10.1016/j.ipm.2023.103302

CNN. (2024). Break dancing makes its debut at the Paris Olympics. A timeline of when every Olympic sport was introduced. Available at: https://www.cnn.com/2024/08/04/sport/olympic-sports-timeline-history-dg/index.html (accessed September 30, 2024).

Coakley, J. (2021). The future of sports and society: a reflection and call to action. In *Research handbook on sports and society* (pp. 380–392). Edward Elgar Publishing. DOI: 10.4337/9781789903607.00038

Coghlan, A., & Filo, K. (2013). Using constant comparison method and qualitative data to understand participants' experiences at the nexus of tourism, sport, and charity events. *Tourism Management*, 35, 122–131. DOI: 10.1016/j.tourman.2012.06.007

Coombes, P. (2023). Systematic review research in marketing scholarship: Optimizing rigor. *International Journal of Market Research*, •••, 14707853231184729.

Donthu, N., Kumar, S., Mukherjee, D., Pandey, N., & Lim, W. M. (2021). How to conduct a bibliometric analysis: An overview and guidelines. *Journal of Business Research*, 133, 285–296. DOI: 10.1016/j.jbusres.2021.04.070

Drakakis, P., Papadaskalopoulos, A., & Lagos, D. (2021). Multipliers and impacts of active sport tourism in the Greek region of Messinia. *Tourism Economics*, 27(3), 527–547. DOI: 10.1177/1354816620902328

Eime, R., Charity, M., Harvey, J., & Westerbeek, H. (2021). Five-year changes in community-level sport participation, and the role of gender strategies. *Frontiers in Sports and Active Living*, 3, 710666. DOI: 10.3389/fspor.2021.710666 PMID: 34712951

Fornell, C., & Larcker, D. F. (1981). Evaluating structural equation models with unobservable variables and measurement error. *JMR, Journal of Marketing Research*, 18(1), 39–50. DOI: 10.1177/002224378101800104

Gallarza, M. G., Saura, I. G., & García, H. C. (2002). Destination image: Towards a conceptual framework. *Annals of Tourism Research*, 29(1), 56–78. DOI: 10.1016/S0160-7383(01)00031-7

Gelbman, A. (2021). Sport tourism and peace: Crossing the contested wall. In *Tourism places in Asia* (pp. 163–189). Routledge. DOI: 10.4324/9781003159711-9

Gibson, H. J. (1998). Active sport tourism: Who participates? *Leisure Studies*, 17(2), 155–170. DOI: 10.1080/026143698375213

Güzel, Ö., Sahin, I., & Ryan, C. (2020). Push-motivation-based emotional arousal: A research study in a coastal destination. *Journal of Destination Marketing & Management*, 16, 100428. DOI: 10.1016/j.jdmm.2020.100428

Hair, J. F., Matthews, L. M., Matthews, R. L., & Sarstedt, M. (2017). PLS-SEM or CB-SEM: Updated guidelines on which method to use. *International Journal of Multivariate Data Analysis*, 1(2), 107–123. DOI: 10.1504/IJMDA.2017.087624

Handler, I., & Tan, C. S. L. (2022). Are we teaching enough? A literature review on sustainable tourism events and the implications for Japanese Higher Education. *Journal of Hospitality & Tourism Education*, 34(3), 170–184. DOI: 10.1080/10963758.2021.1963744

Hao, A. W., Paul, J., Trott, S., Guo, C., & Wu, H. H. (2021). Two decades of research on nation branding: A review and future research agenda. *International Marketing Review*, 38(1), 46–69. DOI: 10.1108/IMR-01-2019-0028

Herstein, R., & Berger, R. (2013). Much more than sports: Sports events as stimuli for city re-branding. *The Journal of Business Strategy*, 34(2), 38–44. DOI: 10.1108/02756661311310440

Higham, J., & Hinch, T. (2018). *Sport Tourism Development* (Vol. 84). Channel View Publications.

Holmes, K., Hughes, M., Mair, J., & Carlsen, J. (2015). *Events and sustainability*. Routledge. DOI: 10.9774/gleaf.9781315813011

Hungenberg, E., Gray, D., Gould, J., & Stotlar, D. (2016). An examination of motives underlying active sport tourist behavior: A market segmentation approach. *Journal of Sport & Tourism*, 20(2), 81–101. DOI: 10.1080/14775085.2016.1189845

Ito, E., & Higham, J. (2023). An evidence-base for reducing the CO2 emissions of national mega sports events: Application of the three-hub model to the Japan 2019 Rugby World Cup. *Journal of Sustainable Tourism*, •••, 1–17. DOI: 10.1080/09669582.2023.2177301

Jeong, Y., & Kim, S. K. (2019). The key antecedent and consequences of destination image in a mega sporting event. *South African Journal of Business Management*, 50(1), 1–11. DOI: 10.4102/sajbm.v50i1.1480

Johann, M., Mishra, S., Malhotra, G., & Tiwari, S. R. (2022). Participation in active sport tourism: Impact assessment of destination involvement and perceived risk. *Journal of Sport & Tourism*, 26(2), 101–123. DOI: 10.1080/14775085.2021.2017326

Joo, D., Cho, H., & Woosnam, K. M. (2023). Anticipated emotional solidarity, emotional reasoning, and travel intention: A comparison of two destination image models. *Tourism Management Perspectives*, 46, 101075. DOI: 10.1016/j.tmp.2023.101075

Jung, S., Draper, J., Malek, K., Padron, T. C., & Olson, E. (2024). Bridging Theory and Practice: An Examination of How Event-Tourism Research Aligns With UN Sustainable Development Goals. *Journal of Travel Research*, 63(7), 00472875241231273. DOI: 10.1177/00472875241231273

Kang, S., Lee, G., Kim, J., & Park, D. (2018). Identifying the spatial structure of the tourist attraction system in South Korea using GIS and network analysis: An application of anchor-point theory. *Journal of Destination Marketing & Management*, 9, 358–370. DOI: 10.1016/j.jdmm.2018.04.001

Kim, C., & Kim, J. (2023). Spatial spillovers of sport industry clusters and community resilience: Bridging a spatial lens to building a smart tourism city. *Information Processing & Management*, 60(3), 103266. DOI: 10.1016/j.ipm.2023.103266

Kim, D., & Perdue, R. R. (2011). The influence of image on destination attractiveness. *Journal of Travel & Tourism Marketing*, 28(3), 225–239. DOI: 10.1080/10548408.2011.562850

Kim, M., & Thapa, B. (2018). Perceived value and flow experience: Application in a nature-based tourism context. *Journal of Destination Marketing & Management*, 8, 373–384. DOI: 10.1016/j.jdmm.2017.08.002

Kim, N. S., & Chalip, L. (2004). Why travel to the FIFA World Cup? Effects of motives, background, interest, and constraints. *Tourism Management*, 25(6), 695–707. DOI: 10.1016/j.tourman.2003.08.011

Knott, B., Fyall, A., & Jones, I. (2015). The nation branding opportunities provided by a sport mega-event: South Africa and the 2010 FIFA World Cup. *Journal of Destination Marketing & Management*, 4(1), 46–56. DOI: 10.1016/j.jdmm.2014.09.001

Lepp, A., Gibson, H., & Lane, C. (2011). Image and perceived risk: A study of Uganda and its official tourism website. *Tourism Management*, 32(3), 675–684. DOI: 10.1016/j.tourman.2010.05.024

MacInnis, D. J. (2011). A framework for conceptual contributions in marketing. *Journal of Marketing*, 75(4), 136–154. DOI: 10.1509/jmkg.75.4.136

Maiello, A., & Pasquinelli, C. (2015). Destruction or construction? A (counter) branding analysis of sport mega-events in Rio de Janeiro. *Cities (London, England)*, 48, 116–124. DOI: 10.1016/j.cities.2015.06.011

Marques, L., & Pimentel Biscaia, M. S. (2019). Leisure and innovation: Exploring boundaries. *World Leisure Journal*, 61(3), 162–169. DOI: 10.1080/16078055.2019.1639257

Mirzaalian, F., & Halpenny, E. (2021). Exploring destination loyalty: Application of social media analytics in a nature-based tourism setting. *Journal of Destination Marketing & Management*, 20, 100598. DOI: 10.1016/j.jdmm.2021.100598

Mousavi, R., Najafabadi, M. O., Mirdamadi, S. M., & Hosseini, S. J. F. (2022). Rural sports and local games: Missing link between sports tourism development and sustainability. *Journal of Sport & Tourism*, 26(3), 201–223. DOI: 10.1080/14775085.2022.2058069

Newland, B. L., & Yoo, J. J. E. (2021). Active sport event participants' behavioural intentions: Leveraging outcomes for future attendance and visitation. *Journal of Vacation Marketing*, 27(1), 32–44. DOI: 10.1177/1356766720948249

Oh, H., Fiore, A. M., & Jeoung, M. (2007). Measuring experience economy concepts: Tourism applications. *Journal of Travel Research*, 46(2), 119–132. DOI: 10.1177/0047287507304039

Paul, J., & Criado, A. R. (2020). The art of writing literature review: What do we know and what do we need to know? *International Business Review*, 29(4), 101717. DOI: 10.1016/j.ibusrev.2020.101717

Paul, J., & Rosado-Serrano, A. (2019). Gradual internationalization vs born-global/ international new venture models: A review and research agenda. *International Marketing Review*, 36(6), 830–858. DOI: 10.1108/IMR-10-2018-0280

Paul, J., & Rosado-Serrano, A. (2019). Gradual internationalization vs born-global/ international new venture models: A review and research agenda. *International Marketing Review*, 36(6), 830–858. DOI: 10.1108/IMR-10-2018-0280

Pine, B. J.II, & Gilmore, H. J. (1999). *The Experience Economy: Work isTheatre & Every Business a Stage*. Harvard Business School Press.

Power, S. (2022). Enjoying your beach and cleaning it too: A Grounded Theory Ethnography of enviro-leisure activism. *Journal of Sustainable Tourism*, 30(6), 1438–1457. DOI: 10.1080/09669582.2021.1953037

Ramshaw, G. (2020). *Heritage and sport: An introduction*. Channel View Publications.

Ritchie, J. B., & Smith, B. H. (1991). The impact of a mega-event on host region awareness: A longitudinal study. *Journal of Travel Research*, 30(1), 3–10. DOI: 10.1177/004728759103000102

Salgado-Barandela, J., Barajas, Á., & Sánchez-Fernández, P. (2021). Sport-event portfolios: An analysis of their ability to attract revenue from tourism. *Tourism Economics*, 27(3), 436–454. DOI: 10.1177/1354816619884448

Sato, S., Kim, H., Buning, R. J., & Harada, M. (2018). Adventure tourism motivation and destination loyalty: A comparison of decision and non-decision makers. *Journal of Destination Marketing & Management*, 8, 74–81. DOI: 10.1016/j.jdmm.2016.12.003

Savery, J., & Ghezzi, A. (2022). Applying Sustainable Development Goal 14. In *The Routledge Handbook of Sport and Sustainable Development* (pp. 364-367). Routledge.

Sharma, A., Lesjak, M., & Borovčanin, D. (2024). *Sport Tourism, Events and Sustainable Development Goals: An Emerging Foundation*. Taylor & Francis. DOI: 10.4324/9781003384786

Smith, A. (2005). Reimaging the city: The value of sport initiatives. *Annals of Tourism Research*, 32(1), 217–236. DOI: 10.1016/j.annals.2004.07.007

Snyder, H., Witell, L., Gustafsson, A., Fombelle, P., & Kristensson, P. (2016). Identifying categories of service innovation: A review and synthesis of the literature. *Journal of Business Research*, 69(7), 2401–2408. DOI: 10.1016/j.jbusres.2016.01.009

Stepchenkova, S., & Li, X. R. (2014). Destination image: Do top-of-mind associations say it all? *Annals of Tourism Research*, 45, 46–62. DOI: 10.1016/j.annals.2013.12.004

Stepchenkova, S., & Zhan, F. (2013). Visual destination images of Peru: Comparative content analysis of DMO and user-generated photography. *Tourism Management*, 36, 590–601. DOI: 10.1016/j.tourman.2012.08.006

Van Rheenen, D., Naria, O., Melo, R., & Sobry, C. (2024). *Sport Tourism, Island Territories and Sustainable Development*. Springer. DOI: 10.1007/978-3-031-51705-1

Vassiliadis, C. A., Mombeuil, C., & Fotiadis, A. K. (2021). Identifying service product features associated with visitor satisfaction and revisit intention: A focus on sports events. *Journal of Destination Marketing & Management*, 19, 100558. DOI: 10.1016/j.jdmm.2021.100558

Weed, M. (2009). Progress in sports tourism research? A meta-review and exploration of futures. *Tourism Management*, 30(5), 615–628. DOI: 10.1016/j.tourman.2009.02.002

Wicker, P. (2019). The carbon footprint of active sport participants. *Sport Management Review*, 22(4), 513–526. DOI: 10.1016/j.smr.2018.07.001

Witell, L., Snyder, H., Gustafsson, A., Fombelle, P., & Kristensson, P. (2016). Defining service innovation: A review and synthesis. *Journal of Business Research*, 69(8), 2863–2872. DOI: 10.1016/j.jbusres.2015.12.055

Yung, R., Khoo-Lattimore, C., & Potter, L. E. (2021). Virtual reality and tourism marketing: Conceptualizing a framework on presence, emotion, and intention. *Current Issues in Tourism*, 24(11), 1505–1525. DOI: 10.1080/13683500.2020.1820454

Zehrer, A., & Hallmann, K. (2015). A stakeholder perspective on policy indicators of destination competitiveness. *Journal of Destination Marketing & Management*, 4(2), 120–126. DOI: 10.1016/j.jdmm.2015.03.003

Ziakas, V., Tzanelli, R., & Lundberg, C. (2022). Interscopic fan travelscape: Hybridizing tourism through sport and art. *Tourist Studies*, 22(3), 290–307. DOI: 10.1177/14687976221092169

Zupic, I., & Čater, T. (2015). Bibliometric methods in management and organization. *Organizational Research Methods*, 18(3), 429–472. DOI: 10.1177/1094428114562629

ADDITIONAL READING

Gao, Y., Zhang, Q., Xu, X., Jia, F., & Lin, Z. (2022). Service design for the destination tourism service ecosystem: A review and extension. *Asia Pacific Journal of Tourism Research*, 27(3), 225–245. DOI: 10.1080/10941665.2022.2046119

Geffroy, V. (2017). 'Playing with space': A conceptual basis for investigating active sport tourism practices. *Journal of Sport & Tourism*, 21(2), 95–113. DOI: 10.1080/14775085.2016.1271349

Gibson, H. J., Lamont, M., Kennelly, M., & Buning, R. J. (2018). Introduction to the special issue active sport tourism. *Journal of Sport & Tourism*, 22(2), 83–91. DOI: 10.1080/14775085.2018.1466350

Hinch, T., & Holt, N. L. (2017). Sustaining places and participatory sport tourism events. *Journal of Sustainable Tourism*, 25(8), 1084–1099. DOI: 10.1080/09669582.2016.1253703

Tajeddini, K., Ratten, V., & Merkle, T. (Eds.). (2019). *Tourism, hospitality and digital transformation: strategic management aspects*. Routledge. DOI: 10.4324/9780429054396

Chapter 9
Summer Olympic Villages as Catalysts for Accessible and Inclusive Places:
Between Experiences and Reflections in the Places and Society of the Host Cities

Valerio della Sala

Department of Geography, Universitat Autonoma of Barcelona, Spain & Sport Research Institute IRE-UAB, Spain & Interdepartmental Research Centre for Urban and Mega-Events Studies (OMERO), Italy

EXECUTIVE SUMMARY

The aim of this chapter is to examine the different use of the Summer Olympic Village over the years. Initially, the article will observe the temporal evolution of the built Olympic villages, establishing significant patterns that have followed over time. The evolution of Olympic Village models implies a critical reflection on how host communities experiment with collaborative forms and practices aimed at decreasing the phenomena of social exclusion. The composition of new housing units in central areas of metropolises may foment the emergence of new forms of gentrification or segregation within host cities.

DOI: 10.4018/979-8-3693-1548-4.ch009

INTRODUCTION TO OLYMPIC CITIES

The Beijing Olympics in August 2008 marked a change in the global audience for mega-events, setting record revenues from the sale and marketing of audiovisual rights (Sands, 2008). According to the International Olympic Committee (IOC) 2021 report, London 2012 and Rio 2016 had an audience of almost 5 billion people globally. Meanwhile, the Sochi 2014 and PyeongChang 2018 Winter Olympics reached an audience of 2.5 billion total viewers (IOC, 2021). Therefore, the difference between audience and funding from the IOC and Olympic sponsors allows us to assume that the Winter Olympics are at a disadvantage. Consequently, the dependency relationship between the city and the Olympic Games only continues in the summer edition (della Sala, 2024). Therefore, considering the significant investment in infrastructure, it is crucial to emphasise the importance of developing a strategic plan in cooperation with all regional, national and international stakeholders (della Sala, 2023). The strategic plan makes it possible to leave a legacy to the community regarding venues, facilities, parks, and everything designed for the Olympic Games (Rose & Spiegel, 2009). In order to develop an excellent strategic plan, it is undoubtedly necessary to maintain long communication with all parties involved and to plan even for 10 to 20 years, as an essential factor that advances mixed management between public and private companies (PwC, 2010). This is the case, for example, of Barcelona, which in 1976 drew up the city's General Metropolitan Plan[1] In an agreement with the public administration to host the 1992 Olympic Games. The case of Barcelona has become a model to follow in the management and organisation of these 'mega-events', but unfortunately, not all states have the same capacities and human resources (World Economic Forum, 2010). In this sense, the theory that not all cities can host these events and achieve the same results is proven (della Sala, 2022). Cities such as Sydney, New York, Barcelona, Atlanta and Sochi have invested heavily in marketing before, during and after the event. There is no doubt that the most significant tangible value we can associate with a city's image is tourism (Preuss, 2000).

Furthermore, Michael Pane, who has worked with the International Olympic Committee for more than 20 years, agrees that the optimal management of this type of 'Mega-Event' should be entrusted to a joint venture with specialists in the economic sector (Payne, 2007). Therefore, the bid for the Games can represent an opportunity for the development of a change in the host city's operational philosophy (PwC, 2010). However, the planning of the facilities must integrate urban social policies, fostering the development of the city over time (della Sala, 2023). Integrating the event into a strategic plan for the entire region or nation can turn the event into a long-term dynamic process (della Sala, 2024). As stated by Gold (2008, 2016) and Roche (1992, 2000, 2002, 2003, 2006), mega-events, if successful in terms of organisation and promotion of the city's image, can contribute to the international projection of a new city image and identity (Viehoff, 2018).

Urban Transformation at the Summer Olympics

Over time, mega-events have induced major urban transformations in host cities. As we observe in the following section, the Summer Olympic Games were developed through a model of sports promotion that transformed into a model of metropolitan development. To analyse the different main stages of urban transformations in the host cities, we will examine the evolution through five phases (della Sala, 2022).

Phase I: Minimal Transformation (1896-1924)

The first phase of the Olympic Games began with the event's first edition until the first Olympic Village in Paris was constructed in 1924. Meanwhile, subsequent editions are characterised by private funding, an interest in promoting sport through host cities, and economic organisation. Therefore, Olympic cities in this first phase will only carry out minimal transformations, proposing a model of temporary accommodation in military areas or through public availability (della Sala, 2022)[2].

Phase II: Emerging Spatial Organisation (1932-1956)

Then, in the second phase, the Olympic cities will focus on the construction of sports facilities for the foundation of a new sports district in the peripheral areas of the cities [3].

The Olympic editions in the second phase catalysed the construction of new sports facilities and Olympic accommodations that, in the post-Olympic period, became new permanent neighbourhoods for the host cities. Thus, the second phase saw the emergence of spatial organisation and the creation of new practices for infrastructural transformations, which we will observe in the third phase. In this phase, the Berlin 1936 project will promote a new spatial solution for the future host cities of Helsinki and Melbourne (della Sala, 2022).

Phase III: Reconfiguration of Cities (1960-1988)

In the third phase, the Olympic cities will be deeply inspired by the design of the 1960 Rome Olympic Games. The Rome edition is recognised as the first to consider the Olympic event as an instrument of urban development and as an opportunity for reconfiguring the city (Essex & Chalkley, 1998).

The city of Rome will concentrate on working in different areas, developing a modern transport system, and constructing the airport. The 1964 Tokyo edition followed the same philosophy as the previous edition, using the Olympic event as an instrument of urban renewal. However, Tokyo took advantage of the event to promote a ten-year development plan that improved the infrastructure system, roads, harbour, housing, water supply and public health. The Tokyo edition was one of the Olympics's most extensive urban development projects (della Sala, 2022).

For the 1968 Mexico City edition, a spatial organisation was planned that included the development of new infrastructure and housing to expand a peripheral area of the metropolis. Meanwhile, the Munich 1972 edition proposed redeveloping a brownfield site to construct a sports park, including residences.[4]. The Munich plan foresaw the construction of a new self-sufficient community and other road improvements in the city. Various improvements such as the restoration and pedestrianisation of the old town, the expansion of public transport lines, the creation of underground car parks, the development of a new shopping centre and the construction of three new motorways were carried out. Subsequently, the Montreal 1976 and Moscow 1980 editions will propose new housing solutions and infrastructural works to reconfigure the cities. The Montreal edition is recognised as one of the moments of most significant concern for the increase in the size of the Olympic event. Therefore, the 1984 Los Angeles Games will be organised through private funding with existing or temporary structures.[5]. On the other hand, the 1988 edition in Seoul allowed the Olympic Games to resume their role as a vehicle for urban transformation. The Seoul project was based on a twenty-year plan introducing new programmes to ensure higher health and hygiene standards throughout the city. In addition, the project included measures for air pollution, rubbish control, and water quality, as well as a significant plan to decontaminate the Han River. Thanks to the Olympics, the city was able to develop three new underground lines to ease traffic congestion and 47 bus lines were extended. The airport was expanded, and new projects were developed to emphasise the cultural aspects of the Olympic event. The city was able to have a programme of renovation and reconstruction of historical monuments, such as palaces and shrines (della Sala, 2022).

Phase IV: Large-Scale Urban Transformations (1992-2004)

The fourth phase will begin with Barcelona 1992 (recognised as the best example of the role of the Olympic Games as a catalyst for change and urban renewal[6]), and will end with Athens 2004.

Barcelona 1992 proposed a new strategy for reconstructing and redefinition post-industrial cities. The transformation of a city in crisis will be the common element of all the Olympic cities in the next phase. The city of Barcelona has become an example of post-industrial reconversion by constructing a new image for the exploitation of tourism in the post-Olympic period. In this way, the Olympic Games became a means of ensuring a significant change in urban infrastructures through a mixed economy. From 1992 onwards, tourism became a fundamental element of the economy of the host cities in the post-Olympic phase (Hughes, 1993). Barcelona will present a new image and development strategy for the candidate cities (Moragas, 1996).

Following the same philosophy as Barcelona, Sydney 2000 proposed an ambitious project for reconfiguring abandoned areas by applying new sustainable practices. Sydney is recognised as the first Olympic city to introduce the theme of environmental sustainability into the development of the Olympic event (della Sala, 2022). The stadium and Olympic Village were included in the *Homebush Bay* area[7], located in a peripheral area of the city.

The area was neglected for many years, and thanks to the Olympia bid, the municipality strengthened and accelerated the renovation of the whole area, establishing a new structural plan for reconfiguring the area (della Sala, 2022). Subsequently, the Athens project in 2004 was included in a programme of transformation of the primary infrastructure of the Greek city[8]. The port's reconfiguration, the central areas' redevelopment, the construction of a new airport and the provision of the metro were the major infrastructural works that were advanced for the modernisation of Athens (Georgiadis, 2016).

Phase V: Metropolitan Development (2008-2028)

Finally, the fifth and final phase begins with the first Chinese edition of Beijing 2008 and ends with the last edition assigned to Los Angeles in 2028.

In this phase, the cities are characterised by metropolitan development that uses the central empty spaces to reconfigure the host cities. Thus, the Olympic Games will emphasise environmental protection and the sustainable development of the Olympic project (della Sala, 2022). The establishment of an environmental park[9] In Beijing (Jia, 2012), planning a water recycling system in London can be considered an innovative measure for environmental protection in the candidate cities. Furthermore, since London 2012, the tangible and intangible Olympic legacy has assumed great importance for post-Olympic planning (Imrie, 2008). As such, temporary facilities and innovative solutions will be used in the following editions.

Compared to previous phases, the Beijing and London projects have favoured the emergence of one-off infrastructure works such as airport reconfiguration and rail and metro expansion (Cook, 2012).

Subsequently, the 2016 edition of Rio de Janeiro will bring further changes in the allocation of host cities, which, for the first time, will be chosen without any competition. The allocation of the event through a proclamation process will involve the inclusion of temporary structures and the reuse of existing sports facilities in the candidate cities. Therefore, the IOC identified Paris and Los Angeles as cities that could represent the new evolution and organisation of the Olympic event. The following stages allow us to affirm that the Olympic Games throughout urban history were inspirational for the candidate cities and that the variables specific to each city have favoured legitimising the Olympic city as a distinct urban genre. Over time, urban planners have proposed different projects that have become development models for other cities. The following stages help us reflect on the history of the physical impact of the Games and how it has changed over two centuries (della Sala, 2022).

Table 1. Summary of the main urban transformations of the Summer Olympics (Source: Own implementation on Essex, 1998)

Phase I	1896-1924	Minimal transformation. Sports cities.	Prospects for the development of sport. Temporary accommodation. Private interests initiated the event, but the public sector jointly funded it.
Phase II	1932-1956	Emerging spatial organisation Emerging cities	Creation of a sports quarter in the peripheral areas of the cities Sports facilities The foundations for infrastructure development are laid.
Phase III	1960-1988	Urban development tools, especially transport, Olympic Villages and economic development opportunities Reconfiguration of cities	Infrastructure investment as part of modernisation Public sector financing Concern arises over the increasing size of the event

continued on following page

Table 1. Continued

Phase	Years		
Phase IV	1992-2004	Large-scale urban transformations. Post-industrial development tool Cities in crisis	The role of the Olympic Games as a means of securing a significant change in urban infrastructures Mixed economy due to new marketing revenues from the event The Olympic Games as a tool for promoting a new image of the candidate cities Tourism asserts itself as a critical element of the Olympic cities' economy.
Phase V [10]	2008-2028	Metropolitan development and legacy planning Global cities	Metropolitan development in empty spaces. Tool for the redefinition and reorganisation of the urban fabric. Greater emphasis on environmental protection and sustainable development. The Olympic legacy assumes great importance in the planning of the post-Olympic phase. Temporary installations and demountable solutions

Benchmarking Cases of Effective Olympic Village Management

Effective management is critical in ensuring the Olympic Games leave a positive and lasting legacy for the host cities. It involves careful planning and management of the infrastructure, urban development, branding, tourism and community engagement associated with hosting the Games. Effective destination management can transform the Olympics from a simple sporting event to a catalyst for sustainable growth, urban revitalisation and increased global recognition. This section explores several key cases of Olympic destination management, highlighting their strategies, challenges and successes and offering a comparative analysis of the different approaches implemented by host cities.

Barcelona 1992: A Model of Urban Regeneration

The 1992 Barcelona Olympics are often considered the gold standard for hosting the Games as a destination management tool. Before the Olympics, Barcelona was a relatively unknown city on the world stage, but the Games represented a unique opportunity to completely renew the city's infrastructure, urban landscape and international image. One of the most significant elements of Barcelona's destination management strategy was the transformation of its waterfront. The Olympic Village was built in this area, and the development has included the creation of beaches, parks and public spaces that have revitalised the city's coastline. This has improved residents' quality of life and helped position Barcelona as one of Europe's leading tourist destinations. Barcelona's long-term tourism strategy was linked to the post-Olympic use of venues such as the Palau Sant Jordi, which remains famous for concerts and sporting events. In addition, the Games were used to improve transport, including the expansion of the city's metro network and roads, which helped improve accessibility for residents and visitors. For instance, Barcelona's 1992 Summer Olympics is often a benchmark for leveraging the Games to bolster urban tourism. Before the Olympics, Barcelona was relatively unknown globally, attracting approximately 1.7 million international tourists annually. However, within a decade of the Games, tourism numbers surged to over 4.4 million annually, reaching approximately 7.9 million by 2019 (UNWTO, 2023). This growth underscores the Games' role as a catalyst for rebranding Barcelona as a cultural and leisure destination. Moreover, tourism receipts reflected a similar upward trajectory, with revenues supporting broader economic activities across hospitality, transport, and retail sectors. The 1992 Olympics led to a significant increase in tourism, and today, Barcelona continues to benefit from the global visibility achieved during the event.

Sydney 2000: A Focus on Sustainability

The Sydney 2000 Olympic Games are often celebrated for their strong focus on sustainability and environmental management. The Games were dubbed the 'Green Games' and this commitment to sustainability was evident in the destination management strategies adopted by the city. The Olympic Village was designed with green technology in mind, incorporating solar panels, rainwater harvesting systems and energy-efficient materials. In addition, Sydney sought to create an environmentally friendly transport system by improving public transport links and introducing sustainable transport options such as bicycle lanes and pedestrian streets. Another aspect of Sydney's destination management strategy has been legacy planning for the Olympic venues. Sydney Olympic Park, the site of the Games, was designed with post-Olympic use in mind and has since become a thriving residential and commercial centre. However, one of the challenges Sydney faced was ensuring the continued use of all Olympic venues. While the Sydney Olympic Park was successful, other facilities, such as the Superdome and the Aquatic Centre, struggled to remain financially viable in the years following the Games. Despite these challenges, Sydney's reputation as a global city was greatly enhanced by hosting the Olympics, and the city experienced long-term economic and tourism benefits.

London 2012: Community and Legacy Oriented Destination Management

The London 2012 Olympics utilised a destination management strategy with a strong focus on community development and long-term legacy planning. The Games were held in East London, a historically underdeveloped and economically disadvantaged area. The decision to build the Olympic Park in this region was intended to revitalise the area and create new opportunities for residents. A significant component of London's destination management strategy was the emphasis on legacy. The London Legacy Development Corporation (LLDC) was established to oversee the post-Olympic transformation of the Olympic Park into a vibrant mixed-use development. Today, the area is known as Queen Elizabeth Olympic Park and includes housing, commercial space, schools and recreational facilities. The 'legacy' approach to destination management has also extended to the design of Olympic venues. For example, the Olympic Stadium was built with the intention of being reused after the Games and has since become the home of West Ham United Football Club. London 2012 also leveraged its Olympic legacy to enhance its tourism profile. Before the Games, London welcomed 29 million visitors annually, generating approximately £16 billion in tourism revenues. Post-games data from the UNWTO and Visit Britain highlighted an increase to 31.2 million international arrivals by 2013, contributing over £18.5 billion to the economy. Key drivers included enhanced transport connectivity, the revitalization of East London, and international media exposure reinforcing London's global image. London's "Games Time" tourism campaigns and legacy-focused projects like the Queen Elizabeth Olympic Park ensured sustained tourism growth. In addition, London used the Games to promote itself as a world-leading cultural and business destination. The city implemented an aggressive marketing campaign that showcased its cultural diversity and world-class infrastructure, helping to attract millions of international tourists during and after the Games.

Rio de Janeiro (2016): Opportunities and Missed Challenges

The Rio 2016 Olympics, in contrast to the success stories of Barcelona, Sydney and London, present a case for destination management that faced several challenges and missed opportunities. Rio's destination management strategy aimed to use the Olympics to strengthen its global image and drive economic growth, but the reality was much more complex. Although the city has seen improvements in infrastructure, particularly with new public transport systems such as the BRT (Bus Rapid Transit) and the revitalisation of the port area through the 'Porto Maravilha' project, many of the Olympic venues have fallen into disrepair. For example, the Maracanã Stadium, which hosted the opening and closing ceremonies, was largely unused and its maintenance was costly. The Olympic Village, located in the Barra da Tijuca district, was intended to become a residential community after the Games, but much of it remains unoccupied, with some parts even abandoned. Rio has also been criticised for the forced evictions of residents of favelas (informal settlements) to make way for Olympic developments, which led to widespread social unrest and an overall negative perception of the city's handling of the Games. Rio de Janeiro's experience with the 2016 Games illustrates the complexities and pitfalls of mega-event tourism planning. While international arrivals temporarily increased during the Games, Rio needed help to maintain these gains. Post-Games, visitor numbers stagnated due to challenges in urban safety, deteriorating infrastructure, and inadequate follow-up marketing strategies. Furthermore, discrepancies in economic benefits were evident, with limited spillover effects to smaller businesses and peripheral regions. These outcomes emphasize the need for robust long-term strategies that align with sustainable tourism principles and equitable economic distribution. Although tourism in Rio increased during the Games, the long-term benefits were not as evident as in previous Olympic host cities. The Rio 2016 Games highlight the importance of robust legacy planning and community involvement in effective destination management.

Tokyo 2020/2021: A Pandemic Challenge

The Tokyo 2020 Olympics, postponed to 2021 due to the COVID-19 pandemic, faced unique challenges in destination management. Hosting an international mega-event during a global health crisis required significant adjustments, especially in terms of health and safety protocols. The pandemic forced Tokyo to rethink its destination management strategy, as international tourism was severely restricted, and spectators were largely absent from the Games. Despite these challenges, Tokyo used the Olympics to promote its image as a technologically advanced and resilient city. The Games showcased Japan's technological innovations, such as robot assistants, hydrogen buses and renewable energy sources. Although the absence of international spectators diminished the immediate tourism impact, Tokyo's long-term destination management strategy remains focused on exploiting the Games to enhance its brand and infrastructure globally. The Olympic Village has been converted into a large residential complex known as Harumi Flag, offering accommodation and commercial space in a desirable waterfront location. The Tokyo experience underlines the importance of flexibility and adaptability in destination management, especially in the face of unforeseen global challenges.

The Impact of the New Guidelines: Paris 2024 and Los Angeles 2028

The awarding of the Paris 2024 and Los Angeles 2028 Olympic Games introduced new guidelines aimed at creating more sustainable and inclusive events. These guidelines emphasise the use of existing infrastructure and the temporary transformation of venues, reducing the need for new construction projects. A new collaboration process, starting ten years before the event, allows for greater coordination between local authorities, planners, and communities to ensure that the Olympic Village contributes to long-term urban development goals.

For example, the Paris 2024 Olympic Village has been developed with a focus on accessibility and inclusiveness. The Village will be located in the Seine-Saint-Denis region, one of Paris's most economically disadvantaged areas, to provide long-term benefits to the local community (della Sala, 2024). After the Games, the Village will be transformed into a mixed-use neighbourhood focusing on affordable housing, green spaces and public services. This approach reflects a shift towards using the Olympics as a tool for social inclusion and urban regeneration.

Similarly, the Los Angeles 2028 Games will build on the city's previous experience in hosting the Olympics, utilising existing facilities and prioritising sustainability. The Los Angeles Olympic Village will be located at the University of Southern California, where student housing will be used to house the athletes, thus avoiding the need for new construction. This model reduces costs and ensures that the facilities have a clear use after the Games.

Olympic Villages and Social Inclusion: A Critical Reflection

Olympic urbanism often triggers gentrification, a phenomenon characterised by the displacement of low-income residents due to rising property values and redevelopment initiatives. Urban renewal projects associated with the Games may improve infrastructure and local economies but often increase social inequalities. While Olympic villages have the potential to act as catalysts for inclusive and accessible urban development, they also raise critical questions about gentrification and social segregation. The introduction of new housing units in the core areas of host cities can lead to the displacement of low-income residents as property values rise and new affluent residents move in. This phenomenon, known as Olympics-driven gentrification, has been observed in cities such as London and Rio de Janeiro, where the development of the Olympic Village has contributed to the displacement of long-established communities (della Sala, 2022).

For example, the London 2012 Olympic Village was initially praised for its focus on providing affordable housing. However, in the years following the Games, many affordable housing units were converted into luxury flats, displacing low-income residents. Similarly, in Rio de Janeiro, the development of the Olympic Village for the 2016 Games was accompanied by the forced eviction of thousands of residents from nearby favelas, exacerbating social inequalities in the city.

These examples highlight the need for careful planning and community involvement to ensure that Olympic Villages contribute to social inclusion rather than exclusion. To mitigate such impacts, urban planners and policymakers must adopt strategies emphasizing equitable development. Inclusive zoning laws, community land trusts, and robust social housing policies can help balance the benefits of gentrification while minimizing displacement. Furthermore, participatory planning processes, which involve local residents and stakeholders in decision-making, can ensure that redevelopment initiatives align with community needs. Host cities must prioritise the needs of residents and ensure that the Olympic Village's benefits are distributed fairly among the population. Introducing the new guidelines for Paris 2024 and Los Angeles 2028 is a step in the right direction, but continued vigilance is needed to prevent the negative social impacts of Olympic-driven urban development.

CONCLUSION

Throughout history, the Olympic Village has transformed from a temporary housing solution for athletes to a complex urban development project with long-term implications for host cities. As demonstrated in this chapter, Olympic Villages have the potential to act as catalysts for accessible and inclusive urban spaces, but they also raise critical questions about gentrification, social exclusion and urban inequality.

By studying the evolution of Olympic Villages over time and examining the impact of the new guidelines for Paris 2024 and Los Angeles 2028, we can better understand how these projects can contribute to more sustainable and inclusive cities. The challenge for future host cities will be to balance the demands of the Olympic Games with the needs of local communities, ensuring that the legacy of the Olympic Village is one of social inclusion and urban regeneration rather than exclusion and displacement.

Ultimately, the success of the Olympic Village as a catalyst for accessible and inclusive places will depend on the ability of host cities to engage with local communities, plan for the long term and prioritise the needs of all residents. In this way, the Olympic Games can leave a positive legacy far beyond the excitement of competition, creating more inclusive and equitable cities for future generations.

REFERENCES

Cook, I. G., & Miles, S. (2012). Beijing 2008: Chapter taken from Olympic Cities. *Routledge Online Studies on the Olympic and Paralympic Games*, 1(36), 340–358. DOI: 10.4324/9780203840740_chapter_17

Corporació Metropolitana de Barcelona (CMB). (1976). Plan general metropolitano de ordenación urbana, de la entidad municipal metropolitana de Barcelona.

Dansero, E., & De Leonardis, D. (2006). Torino 2006. La territorializzazione olimpica e la sfida dell'eredità. *Bollettino della Società Geografica Italiana*, XI, •••.

Dansero, E., & Mela, A. (2007). Olympic territorialisation. *Revue de Geographie Alpine*, •••, 95–3.

della Sala, V. (2022). The Olympic Village and the Olympic Urbanism: Perception and Expectations of Olympic Specialists. *Bollettino della Società Geografica Italiana serie 14*, 5(2), 51–64.

della Sala, V. (2022). *The Olympic Villages and Olympic urban planning. Analysis and evaluation of the impact on territorial and urban planning (XX-XXI centuries)*. Doctoral thesis. UAB. POLITO

della Sala, V. (2023). Olympic Games and expectations: The factor analysis model about Olympic Urbanism and Olympic Villages. *Sociologia e ricerca sociale: 132, 3, 2023*, 127-147.

della Sala, V. (2024). Le Village Olympique de Seine-Saint-Denis: analyse critique d'un projet d'aménagement urbain. *Dossier sur les JO de la revue Savoir/agir*, 115,126.

della Sala, V. (2024). Olympic Games: Between Expectations and Fears. Factor Analysis Model Applied to Olympic Urbanism and Olympic Villages. *Rivista Internazionale di Scienze Sociali*, 132(1), 55–86.

Essex, S., & Chalkley, B. (1998). Olympic games: Catalyst of urban change. *Leisure Studies*, 17(3), 187–206. DOI: 10.1080/026143698375123

Gold, J. M. M. G. (2016). *Olympic Cities: City Agendas, Planning, and the World's Games*, 1896 (3rd ed.). Routledge.

Gold, J. R., & Gold, M. M. (2008). Olympic Cities: Regeneration, City Rebranding and Changing Urban Agendas. *Geography Compass*, 2(1), 300–318. DOI: 10.1111/j.1749-8198.2007.00080.x

Hughes, H. (1993). Olympic tourism and urban regeneration; 1996 Summer Olympics. *Festival Management & Event Tourism*, 1(4), 137–184.

Imrie, R., Lees, L., & Raco, M. (2008). *Regenerating London: Governance, Sustainability and Community in a Global City*. Routledge Taylor & Francis Group.

IOC. (2021). *Marketing Fact*.

Jia, H., Lu, Y., Yu, S. L., & Chen, Y. (2012). Planning of LID-BMPs for urban runoff control: The case of Beijing Olympic Village. [). Elsevier.]. *Separation and Purification Technology*, 84, 112–119. DOI: 10.1016/j.seppur.2011.04.026

Moragas, M. (1996). *Olympic villages: a hundred years of urban planning and shared experiences: International Symposium on Olympic Villages*. In Centre d'Estudis Olímpics i de l'Esport Universitat Autònoma de Barcelona; Olympic Museum (Ed.), Olympic Villages Hundred Years of Urban Planning and Shared Experiences. Lausanne.

Muñoz, F. (1996). Historic evolution and urban planning typology of Olympic Village. Hundred years of urban planning and shared experiences, International Symposium on Olympic Villages. IOC

Payne, M. (2007). A Gold-Medal Partnership. *Strategy & Business*.

Preuss, H. (2000). *Economics of The Olympic Games: Hosting the Games 1972 – 2000. Walla Walla Press*. The University of Germany.

PwC. (2010). *Cities of Opportunity*.

PwC. (2010). *Public-Private Partnerships: The US Perspective*.

Roche, M. (1992). Mega-Events and Micro-Modernisation: On the Sociology of the New Urban Tourism. *The British Journal of Sociology*, 43(4), 563–600. DOI: 10.2307/591340

Roche, M. (2000). *Mega-events and Modernity: Olympics and Expos in the Growth of Global C*. Routledge.

Roche, M. (2002). Olympic and Sport Mega-Events as Media-Events: Reflections on the Globalisation paradigm. *Symposium A Quarterly Journal in Modern Foreign Literatures*, pp. 1–12.

Roche M. (2003). The Olympics and the Development of "Global Society", in M. De Moragas, C. Kennett, N. Puig (a cura di), *The Legacy of the Olympic Games*, Document of the Olympic Museum, International Olympic Committee, Losanna.

Roche, M. (2006). Mega-Events and Modernity Revisited: Globalization and the Case of the Olympics. *The Sociological Review*, 54(2, suppl), 27–40. DOI: 10.1111/j.1467-954X.2006.00651.x

Rose, A. K., & Mark, M. Spiegel (2009). The Olympic Effect. *National Bureau of Economic Research*, October 2009.

Sands Lee M. (2008). The 2008 Olympics' Impact on China, *The China Business Review*, July August 2008.

UNWTO. (2023). *Tourism Statistics Database*. Available at UNWTO.

Viehoff, V. G. P. (2018). *Mega-event Cities: Urban Legacies of Global Sports Events* (1st ed.). Routledge.

Visit Britain (2013). *Post-Games Tourism Performance Report*.

World Economic Forum. (2020). *Global Risks 2020: A Global Risk Network Report*.

ENDNOTES

[1] Plan general metropolitano de ordenación urbana, de la entidad municipal metropolitana de Barcelona, Economic Study (February 1976), Corporació Metropolitana de Barcelona (CMB), Barcelona, January 1976.

[2] In 1904, the Games were held in St. Louis over several months as an adjunct to the World's Fair, and the swimming events were held in an artificial pool at the fairgrounds (Gordon, 1983).

[3] The second phase started in Los Angeles in 1932 and continued until Melbourne in 1956.

[4] To improve orientation, they were coloured to match the separate areas or residential places to which they led and were also equipped with signs, notice boards or display boards (COJO, 1972, p.109).

[5] To avoid large capital expenditures, the organisers used existing sports facilities and accommodation over a wide geographical area, including the Olympic Stadium in 1932 and student residences at the Universities of California and Southern California (Essex, 1998).

[6] By the end of the Olympic event, 330 urban interventions were counted (Holsa, 1992).

7   The Olympic Stadium and Village will be in an area known as Homebush Bay, 14 km west of the city centre (Young, 1992; NSW Government, 1994; Brogan, 1996). The 760-hectare site has been marked for many decades by noxious land uses and areas of contaminated brownfield land used for dumping domestic and industrial waste, including State Brickworks, State Abattoir, and Royal Australian Armaments Depot (Sanders, 1995; Essex, 2008).

8   Beriators and Gospodini (2004, p. 197) described the Games master plan as a dispersed model that suggests a strategy to promote regeneration and multi-core urban development.

9   Beijing spent a total of $12.2 billion on protecting and improving the ecological environment at the end of 2008. The overall project foresees the construction of fourteen sewage treatment plants to treat water from 42% to 905 (COJO, 2008).

10 The next phase was implemented by researching the Olympic events held up to the date of the study.

APPENDIX

Teaching Note

The case study explores how different Olympic host cities have approached destination management and the various outcomes regarding urban development, community engagement, tourism and legacy planning. It focuses on five key examples: Barcelona 1992, Sydney 2000, London 2012, Rio de Janeiro 2016 and Tokyo 2020/2021. The case allows students to analyse the strategies implemented by each city, evaluate the successes and challenges faced and develop an understanding of how large-scale events such as the Olympics can be harnessed for long-term urban growth.

Learning Objective

At the end of this chapter, students will be able to:

1. Understand destination management. Explain the concept of destination management, especially in the context of mega-events such as the Olympic Games.
2. Analyse strategies. Assess the different approaches to destination management used by Olympic Games host cities and identify the key factors contributing to their success or failure.
3. Assess long-term impact Critically examine the Olympic Games' long-term impact on host cities, focusing on infrastructure, tourism, social inclusion, and legacy.
4. Identify best practices. Recognise effective strategies in destination management and apply these principles to other global events or urban development projects.

Teaching Plan

1. Introduction
   o   Begin the session by introducing the concept of destination management and its importance in the context of large-scale global events such as the Olympics. Explain that destination management encompasses all efforts a city or region makes to plan, implement and sustain the benefits of hosting the Games.
2. Overview of cases
   o   Provide an overview of the five key case studies: Barcelona 1992, Sydney 2000, London 2012, Rio de Janeiro 2016 and Tokyo 2020/2021.

Briefly discuss the unique contexts in which each city hosted the Games, including the economic, political and social factors that influenced destination management strategies.
- o Highlight the main challenges faced by each city, such as financial pressure, venue maintenance and community displacement, as well as successes, including urban regeneration, sustainable development and global branding.
3. Group discussion
    - o Divide the students into small groups and assign each one of the five cities to examine in depth. Ask them to identify the key elements of the city's destination management strategy, focusing on the planning process, the post-Games legacy, and any sustainability or community engagement efforts.
    - o Ask each group to present their findings, comparing the different approaches used by cities and discussing what worked well and what did not. Encourage students to consider local context, long-term vision and financial management.
4. Comparative analysis
    - o Use the comparative case study table to facilitate a class-wide discussion on the different outcomes of destination management in different cities. Ask students to evaluate which city they think has demonstrated the most effective approach to managing the Olympic Games as a destination and why.
    - o Discuss how these principles can be applied to other mega-events, such as the FIFA World Cup or Expo events, and explore the role of legacy planning in ensuring that large-scale investments lead to sustainable urban growth.
5. Conclusion and application
    - o Summarise critical lessons from the case study and emphasise the importance of strategic planning, community involvement and sustainability in destination management.
    - o Assign students a final question for reflection: 'How can future Olympic host cities avoid the pitfalls of Rio de Janeiro and capitalise on the successes of cities like Barcelona and London?

Assessment

To assess understanding, students can be asked to write a short reflection on the key components of effective destination management and propose a destination management strategy for a hypothetical future Olympic host city, considering factors such as budgetary constraints, community involvement and environmental sustainability.

Key Findings

The case study shows that although hosting the Olympics offers significant opportunities for urban transformation and global recognition, success depends on careful destination management prioritising long-term legacy, community needs and sustainability. By analysing several case studies, students can understand the complex challenges of mega-event management and the importance of planning a city's future beyond the Games.

Chapter 10
Addressing and Overcoming Destination Rejection From a Destination Management Perspective

Ali Inanir
https://orcid.org/0000-0001-8647-3375
Burdur Mehmet Akif Ersoy University, Turkey

Yusuf Karakuş
https://orcid.org/0000-0002-4878-3134
Recep Tayyip Erdoğan University, Turkey

EXECUTIVE SUMMARY

Factors such as the development of technological possibilities, the growth of economies, social changes and the disappearance of borders have led individuals to travel to more distant regions. Depending on this situation, individuals have had to choose among multiple destinations. As a matter of fact, some destinations may be rejected for different reasons. Effective plans and policies should be developed to reduce the rejection of destinations. However, plans and policies to be developed for destination preference will not work in case of destination rejection. Because the consumer will remain a tourism product that is not even involved in the purchase decision process. This book chapter makes some inferences to contribute to the destination management process to eliminate this negative situation.

DOI: 10.4018/979-8-3693-1548-4.ch010

INTRODUCTION

Destination rejection behaviour is the phenomenon of anti-consumption in tourism. This situation is expressed as the tourist directly removing a tourist destination from his/her preferences despite having factors such as money, time and motivation. In this context, the rejection of certain destinations by tourists reveals the situation that these destinations experience serious problems in the long term. This situation may negatively affect the marketing of the destination, tourist behaviour and the overall attractiveness of the destination. As a matter of fact, it may negatively affect tourists' satisfaction, tendency to visit again, loyalty, as well as the image and competitiveness of the destination. In this case, it may cause the destination to decline in the long term (Karakuş & Kalay, 2017).

ANTI-CONSUMPTION BEHAVIOR

Consumers' anti-purchase and anti-consumption behaviours have received increasing attention in consumer research (Karakuş & Kalay, 2017; Tjiptono & Yang, 2018; Renzi et al., 2018). Anti-consumption behaviour refers to the deliberate avoidance or rejection of certain products or brands for various reasons such as ethical concerns, environmental impact or political motivations (Sandıkçı & Ekici, 2009). This behaviour is a form of consumer resistance to overconsumption and can take both active and passive forms (Albinsson et al., 2010). The literature on anti-consumption behaviour emphasises the need for a better understanding of why consumers prefer to avoid consumption (Ozanne & Ballantine, 2010).

Consumers' anti-consumption behaviour is influenced by various factors such as attitudes, emotions and post-consumption experiences. Studies have focused on consumers' anti-consumer behaviour (Fazal-e-Hasan et al., 2020). In addition, the role of moral outrage and consumer retaliation, especially in the form of boycott behaviour, has been identified as a subcategory of anti-consumer behaviour (Omar et al., 2017). Furthermore, the influence of religiosity and its moderating role in shaping anti-consumption views has been explored, pointing to the complexity of factors contributing to this behaviour (Xie et al., 2022). The impact of anti-consumption behaviour extends to markets. Because consumers have the ability to influence change through their purchasing behaviour (Kozar & Connell, 2013). This behaviour can also be influenced by the perceived value of products, as shown by the impact of negative experiences on consumer purchases (Olbrich et al., 2015). Furthermore, the concept of politically motivated brand refusal has been introduced as an emerging form of anti-consumption behaviour, highlighting the intersection of consumer behaviour with political motivations (Sandıkçı & Ekici, 2009).

In the context of sustainable consumption, eco-labels and environmental advertisements have been examined to understand their impact on consumer purchase behaviour. Furthermore, the impact of logistics service quality on consumers' post-purchase behaviour in online shopping has been empirically examined, highlighting the role of service quality in shaping consumer behaviour (Yang et al., 2011). In general, consumers' purchase and anti-consumption behaviours are complex phenomena that are influenced by many factors such as emotions, attitudes, ethical concerns and environmental awareness. Understanding these behaviours is of great importance for developing sustainable consumption patterns and addressing the impacts of consumer preferences on the market and the environment.

TOURIST DESTINATION AS A PRODUCT

The touristic product, which plays an important role in the preference or rejection of a destination, has two levels as stated in Middleton's (1989) study. The first of these levels is the consideration of a specific product. For example, a day tour, a hotel room, or an aeroplane seat are touristic products on their own. On the other hand, when an integrated approach is taken, the touristic product refers to a single product that includes everything that the individual experiences, uses, etc. during the whole journey. From this point of view, it is possible to see tourist destinations as a product. Tourist destinations can be conceptualised as complex products that include various elements to attract and satisfy tourists. A tourist destination as a product consists of numerous components such as attractions, accessibility, convenience, intermediaries and ancillary services, organisation of tourist services and availability of ready-made tourist products (Zhandilla, 2023). These elements collectively contribute to the overall experience and satisfaction of tourists visiting the destination. Furthermore, a tourist destination is seen as a set of relational networks in which intermediaries are connected through collaborative links to facilitate the delivery of a tourist product or experience to visitors (Camprubí et al., 2008). This emphasises the interdependence of various stakeholders and service providers in delivering a coherent and attractive tourist experience. From a marketing perspective, tourist destination attributes are designed to appeal to tourists and marketed as solutions to meet tourists' needs and demands, thus increasing the competitiveness of a particular tourist destination (Marpaung and Tania, 2021). The image of a tourist destination plays a crucial role in influencing tourist behaviour and satisfaction. Moreover, the management of tourist destinations is crucial for attracting tourists, as it involves not only marketing but also ensuring the availability of quality services and experiences to meet tourists' needs and preferences (Chaniago, 2022). Destination image is among the tools to manage and promote a positive destination image by influencing tourists' destination choice, consumption of products and services, and repeat business (Bilynets et al., 2021). In addition, perceived change of the urban destination can influence destination loyalty, indicating that tourist perceptions and behaviours are dynamic in response to evolving destination characteristics (Mei et al., 2022).

Tourist satisfaction is a key aspect of the tourist destination product and is directly linked to destination choice, consumption of products and services and repeat business (Meng et al., 2008). All of the sub-product components within tourist destinations, which have an integrated structure, should be optimally designed. Because even if all other components are successful for a destination-level product, for example, a problem in accommodation will affect the quality perception of the whole product (Karakuş & Çoban, 2018). For this reason, managing destinations, which are a tourist product, is very difficult and vital for success.

WHAT IS DESTINATION REJECTION BEHAVOUR

Destination rejection behaviour is actually a reflection of anti-consumption behaviour in terms of tourism industry. In this chapter, anti-consumption behaviour is examined in terms of touristic consumers. It is noteworthy that the reasons why individuals who make up the touristic demand reject certain destinations while choosing among alternatives in the purchasing process and the need for awareness to manage this situation. In this sense, the anti-consumption behaviour exhibited by consumers can be defined as follows: It is the situation where individuals (those who have money, time, opportunity and desire) who form the tourist demand reject certain destinations during the destination selection phase (Karakuş & Kalay, 2017). In this sense, one of the critical points is that the individual provides the necessary conditions (time, economic power, willingness and opportunity) for a touristic visit. In scope, the concept of anti-consumption is the individual's rejection of one or some of the alternative destinations for certain reasons, and the basic situation is the difference between refusing to buy and not preferring. In a situation where the buyer does not prefer a destination, that destination is considered as an alternative but not purchased. It is possible for a situation to be a reason for refusal as well as a reason for non-preference. In order to be able to talk about an anti-consumption attitude or behaviour, it is necessary to reject the destination directly rather than preferring a better destination as a result of the comparison.

Consumer rejection of tourist destinations can cause vital problems for the tourism industry. Consumer rejection of a destination can affect various aspects of tourism, including destination marketing, tourist behaviour and the overall attractiveness of the destination. Consumer rejection of tourist destinations can affect destination marketing strategies. Persson-Fischer and Liu (2021) emphasise that sustainable tourist behaviour can facilitate residents' rejection of tourists, highlighting the importance of fostering a hospitable community to increase tourist satisfaction and the likelihood of repeat visits. This suggests that destination marketing efforts should focus on promoting sustainable and responsible tourism practices to reduce consumer rejection (Persson-Fischer & Liu, 2021). Moreover, consumer rejection of tourist destinations can affect tourist satisfaction and repeat visits. Kozak & Rimmington (2000) emphasise the importance of tourists' own experiences of the destination as a source of information. Consumers' rejection of a destination can lead to lower levels of satisfaction among tourists, affecting their likelihood of revisiting the destination and word-of-mouth recommendations (Kozak & Rimmington, 2000). In addition, consumer rejection of tourist destinations can affect destination loyalty and image. Consumer rejection of a destination can negatively affect the destination's image, affecting its competitiveness and attractiveness for potential tourists (Akroush et al., 2016).

From another perspective, consumers' rejection of tourist destinations can be influenced by various factors such as security concerns, political constraints and risk perceptions. Ma et al. (2020) and Nwankwo (2020) addressed the impact of security, risk and political constraints on tourist behaviour and destination rejection. Destinations perceived as risky or unsafe may be rejected by potential tourists, which requires efforts to address safety concerns and develop risk management strategies (Ma et al., 2020; Nwankwo, 2020). Furthermore, destination rejection behaviour can be influenced by the impact of external factors such as disasters and global events. Consumer rejection of destinations with a negative image may be exacerbated by global events and may require destinations to adapt and address concerns to reduce rejection (Zhou et al., 2022).

CONSUMER ANTI-PURCHASE BEHAVIOR IN TOURISM INDUSTRY

Consumer anti-purchase behaviour in the tourism and hospitality industry can have significant consequences for businesses and destinations. This behaviour, characterised by deliberate avoidance or rejection of certain tourism products or services, can affect various aspects of the industry. When the relevant literature is reviewed, it is possible to find some indications about the potential effects of consumer purchase aversion in the tourism and hospitality industry:

Such behaviours can be influenced by various factors such as perceived risk, overcrowding, adaptation and cultural dimensions (Karakuş & Kalay, 2017). Perceived risk has been identified as an important determinant of avoiding certain destinations (Cahyanto et al., 2016). Moreover, perceived destination adaptation negatively affects tourist satisfaction and can lead to reactive behaviours such as approach, avoidance and tolerance (Papadopoulou et al., 2022). Risk perception is also crucial for tourists' avoidance behaviour, especially in the context of health concerns, such as during the COVID-19 pandemic (Han et al., 2021).

Cultural dimensions such as individualism and uncertainty avoidance play an important role in influencing travel behaviour and destination rejection. For example, integrating individualism and uncertainty avoidance into a theoretical model contributes to a more comprehensive understanding of the impact of travel behaviour on emerging tourism marketing (Yang et al., 2022). Moreover, tourists from cultures with high levels of uncertainty avoidance are more likely to perceive higher security incidents, leading to a negative attitude towards visiting certain destinations (Wang, 2014). Similarly, tourists from cultures with high uncertainty avoidance tend to take more risk and uncertainty-reducing measures while travelling compared to those from cultures with low uncertainty avoidance (Manrai & Manrai, 2011).

The concept of rush-hour avoidance travel behaviour has been studied in the context of daily commuting, but there is a lack of research on holiday tourists (Zhu et al., 2019). However, understanding domestic tourists' post-pandemic emotional reactions and protective behaviours and their holiday intentions or avoidance behaviours is crucial in the current tourism environment (Çınar et al., 2022). Furthermore, the influence of tourists' national cultures on their behaviour in a destination has been highlighted, highlighting the impact of individualism/collectivism and uncertainty avoidance on social interaction and business transactions (Risitano et al., 2017). In addition to cultural factors, the phenomenon of overtourism has led to anti-tourism movements and protests in various destinations, causing concerns about sustainability and the welfare of local residents (Zaman et al., 2022). Especially in destinations exposed to overtourism and anti-tourism sentiments, the supportive behaviour of residents has been central to tourism development (Zaman et al., 2022). On the other hand, the impact of food tourism policy, authenticity of experiences, sustainability challenges and preservation of local cuisines can also influence destination avoidance behaviour (Taheri and Gannon, 2021).

Language barrier has been identified as an important constraint affecting tourist behaviour and destination choices (Cho et al., 2014)Chen and Hsu, 2000; Gu et al., 2019; Geipel et al., 2018; Kim et al., 2019; Okrainec et al., 2014; Arli et al., 2018; Godfrey et al., 2019). Research has consistently emphasised the impact of language barriers on various aspects of tourism, including safer destination choices, cultural adaptation, and perceptions of host communities. Furthermore, cultural and language barriers have been found to separate voluntourists from the host community (Godfrey et al., 2019). In addition, language barriers have been identified as an important constraint that affects the perceived image of overseas destinations among tourists

(Chen & Hsu, 2000). Therefore, individuals may exclude a destination from their purchasing alternatives when making a travel decision due to language barriers.

Historical hostility between countries has been found to significantly influence destination refusal behaviour among tourists (Campo & Alvarez, 2019; Alvarez et al., 2020; Abraham et al., 2020; Little et al., 2011; Josiassen et al., 2020; Stepchenkova et al., 2018; Loureiro et al., 2021; Li et al., 2012). Research has consistently highlighted the impact of hostility on consumer behaviour and purchase intentions, especially in the context of historical conflicts and political tensions between nations. For example, a study by Campo & Alvarez (2019) confirmed that consumer hostility towards a particular country is a multidimensional construct consisting of various reasons such as the country's perceived human rights violations, political system, people and culture, history, military interventions, and economic relations with other countries. Similarly, Alvarez et al. (2020) found that for millennials, hostility stems from conflicts and past historical events or political and social problems in the destination country, affecting their support for receiving tourists from the non-preferred country. Moreover, historical hostility has been associated with tourists' willingness to visit or avoid certain destinations. For example, Abraham & Poria (2020) suggested that hostility would prevent tourists from experiencing various stages of an important historical process or spending money on tax-free products that can be purchased at the border. Similarly, Kearney et al. (2018) investigated the extent to which promotional materials influence potential tourists' image perceptions, attitudes and behavioural intentions towards a country-vacation destination in a situation of political and economic conflict between two countries, and suggested that hostility may deter tourists from visiting certain destinations.

Rejection of a destination can be influenced by various factors such as overcrowding, high costs and perceived risks. Overtourism leading to overcrowding has been identified as an important factor contributing to the rejection of tourist destinations (Alonso-Almeida et al., 2019). Service quality decreases in overcrowded destinations, leading to dissatisfaction among tourists and rejection by locals. Moreover, the high costs associated with certain destinations can also lead to rejection behaviour. The economic rationality of tourists may lead them to reject a destination if they perceive that the costs outweigh the benefits, reducing the likelihood of returning to the same destination (Ferdinand, 2021). Furthermore, the perceived risks associated with a destination can significantly influence visitors' decisions to visit or reject a destination (Manci, 2022). In addition to these factors, the theory of planned behaviour has been used to understand tourists' intentions to visit a destination. Constructs of the theory of planned behaviour such as subjective norms, attitude and perceived behavioural control have been found to significantly influence the intention to visit a destination (Pahrudin et al., 2021). However, it is important to note that the relationship between attitude and behavioural intention may not play a significant role in influencing destination visit intention (Leung & Jiang, 2018).

The concept of destination loyalty and the influence of friends' opinions on the choice or rejection of destination alternatives were investigated. Loyalty can be measured by behavioural, attitudinal and composite approaches in the marketing context and the distance between acceptance and rejection is a key factor (Gilboa and Herstein, 2012). It has been found that the opinions of friends and thoughts from memory are effective in the selection or rejection of destination alternatives (Martin & Woodside, 2008). In addition, personality traits of individuals have been found to shape their travel behaviour. Some personality types may be more inclined to reject sustainable destinations and seek hedonic destinations without prohibitions and strict regulations (Terzić et al., 2022). Moreover, a sustainable tourist behaviour may make it easier for residents to reject tourists, while a hospitable community may increase tourist satisfaction and the likelihood of tourists returning to the destination (Persson-Fischer & Liu, 2021). Karakuş and Kalay (2017) identified 15 factors as reasons for rejecting destinations and ranked them according to the level of importance for their research. The most important factors are "Terrorist activities in or near the country" and "High crime rate in the destination". as the most important factor. Other important factors include health risks perceived by consumers. Other reasons can also be mentioned in relation to the concept of destination rejection. Some of them can be listed as follows:

Safety Concerns: Safety and security are critical factors affecting destination rejection. Tourists may avoid destinations perceived as risky or unsafe due to concerns about personal safety and well-being (Han et al. (2021).

Overcrowding: Overtourism and overcrowding can lead to destination rejection as it can cause a decline in service quality and the overall experience for tourists, leading to rejection by both tourists and locals (Alonso-Almeida et al., 2019).

Destination Image: The image of a tourist destination plays an important role in influencing tourists' perceptions and attitudes. Negative destination images due to cultural differences, perceived costs or other factors can lead to destination rejection (Chon, 1990).

Perceived Risk: Perceived risk elements, such as concerns about the desirability of a destination or the feasibility of visiting a destination, can lead to destination rejection by influencing tourists' decision-making intention (Pahrudin et al., 2021).

Cultural Differences: Cultural variances in norms, values, and practices can contribute to destination rejection, particularly when tourists perceive a lack of alignment with their own cultural preferences and expectations (Priyatmoko and Maulana, 2022).

Economic Factors: Economic impacts, such as rising housing rental prices and shifts in market trends, can lead to destination rejection, particularly in the context of over-tourism and economic dependence on tourism (Martín et al., 2018).

Psychological Distance: The psychological distance of a destination, encompassing cognitive and emotional perceptions, can influence tourists' judgments and perceptions of a destination, potentially leading to destination rejection (Wang et al., 2022).

Perceived Crowding: Tourists' tolerance levels for perceived crowding and over-tourism can influence their satisfaction and destination loyalty, potentially leading to destination rejection (Papadopoulou et al., 2022).

However, it is crucial to emphasize once again that such behavior is not merely a matter of non-preference. Each of these reasons may lead to a decision not to choose a destination, but they could also result in the direct rejection of a destination. Understanding these two distinct situations is essential because, from the perspective of consumers or tourists, addressing these different behaviors may require destination management to develop varied planning, policy-making, and strategic approaches.

ADDRESSING THE CONCEPT OF DESTINATION REJECTION IN TERMS OF DESTINATION MANAGEMENT

Understanding tourists' destination rejection behavior provides significant benefits for destination management, offering valuable insights and opportunities for strategic development and improvement. Destination management phonemon very important factor for destinations (İnanır, 2019). The comprehension of factors contributing to destination rejection can inform various aspects of destination management, including marketing strategies, enhancements to visitor experience, and sustainable tourism practices. One of the most crucial benefits of understanding destination rejection behavior is the ability to develop targeted marketing strategies for the destination. By identifying specific factors leading to destination rejection, destination management can tailor marketing efforts to address these concerns and promote a more positive image of the destination (Chen et al., 2020). This purposeful approach can help attract a more diverse visitor base and increase visitation, contributing to the economic growth of the destination. Additionally, knowledge about destination rejection behavior can facilitate the development of improvements in visitor experience. Destination managers can work to address and alleviate these concerns by understanding the reasons for rejection, enhancing service quality, reducing overcrowding, addressing perceived risks, and creating a more attractive destination for tourists (Akroush et al., 2016). Furthermore, understanding destination rejection behavior can contribute to the development of sustainable tourism practices. Destination management, by addressing factors leading to destination rejection, can make informed decisions regarding infrastructure development, environmental protection, and community involvement, thereby promoting responsible and sustainable tourism (Mei et al., 2022).

Knowing the reasons behind destination rejection can assist in identifying market segments and developing benefit segmentation frameworks. Destination managers, by recognizing specific benefits sought by different visitor segments and addressing factors contributing to rejection, can tailor their offerings to meet the diverse needs of visitors. Consequently, they can enhance the overall attractiveness of the destination and attract a broader range of tourists (Ullah et al., 2022). Moreover, awareness of these tourist behaviors can contribute to the creation of a more comprehensive and sustainable approach in destination management. By addressing factors leading to destination rejection, destination managers can work towards creating a more inclusive, environmentally friendly, and socially responsible destination, thus contributing to the overall well-being of the destination community and environment (Moraga et al., 2021). Additionally, information about destination rejection behavior can guide destination management organizations in planning and implementing effective tourism development programs. Considering the reasons for rejection, destination managers can make informed decisions regarding infrastructure development, enhancements to visitor experience, and sustainable tourism practices to address identified concerns and enhance the overall attractiveness of the destination (Franzoni and Bonera, 2019).

According to the study conducted by Karakuş and Kalay (2017), the benefits of understanding destination rejection behavior are listed as follows:

Understanding destination rejection behavior has a crucial benefit in developing marketing strategies for the destination. Destination management, by identifying specific factors leading to destination rejection, can tailor marketing efforts to address these concerns and promote a more positive image of the destination (Karakuş and Kalay, 2017). This targeted approach can help attract a more diverse visitor base and increase visitation, contributing to the economic growth of the destination.

Destination managers can work to address and alleviate these concerns by understanding the reasons for rejection. This may involve improving service quality, reducing overcrowding, addressing perceived risks, and thus creating a more attractive destination for tourists.

Destination management, by addressing factors leading to destination rejection, can make informed decisions regarding infrastructure development, environmental protection, and community involvement. This way, it can promote responsible and sustainable tourism.

Destination managers, by recognizing specific benefits sought by different visitor segments and addressing factors contributing to rejection, can tailor their offerings to meet the diverse needs of visitors. Consequently, they can enhance the overall attractiveness of the destination and attract a broader range of tourists.

Furthermore, understanding destination rejection behavior can contribute to the creation of a more comprehensive and sustainable approach in destination management. Destination managers, by addressing factors leading to destination rejection, can work towards creating a more inclusive, environmentally friendly, and socially responsible destination, thereby contributing to the overall well-being of the destination community and environment.

Knowing destination rejection behavior can guide destination management organizations in planning and implementing effective tourism development programs. Destination managers, considering the reasons for rejection, can make informed decisions regarding infrastructure development, enhancements to visitor experience, and sustainable tourism practices to address identified concerns and enhance the overall attractiveness of the destination.

A CASE IN TERMS OF DESTINATION REJECTION BEHAVIOUR

It has been mentioned that destination rejection behaviour can occur for many reasons. While these reasons may cause the destination not to be preferred as an alternative, they may also cause rejection. In this context, it is possible to mention a specific example in terms of Cappadocia destination for Japanese tourists. In 2013, there was a very sad incident in which a mentally unstable person killed one of the two young Japanese girls visiting the region with a knife and sexually abused the other one (milliyet.com.tr, 2013). The incident, which was an undesirable event, naturally caused a reaction in the public opinion with the influence of the media. The Cappadocia region is a very important destination that is unique in the world. It is also known that the region, which is a destination with intensive cultural tourism, is a very interesting place for Far Eastern tourists. While the number of Japanese tourists visiting the region was around 140 thousand in 2012 before this incident, after the incident, around 88 thousand in 2014, 32 thousand in 2015 and 5400 in 2016 (Ministry of Culture and Tourism Statistics, 2024). Although this tragic event is quite impressive, it is important to know that behind this dramatic drop in demand is a consumer behaviour developed by Japanese tourists. Because despite this incident, Turkey is in a safer position than even leading countries such as the USA, France and Canada according to world crime indices (numbeo.com, 2024). At this point, it should be noted that it is not the case that Japanese tourists do not prefer Turkey because it is a country with very low tourist safety. If this consumer behaviour was not rejection but non-preference, very different planning policies and strategies would have to be carried out to solve the problem in terms of destination management. However, here it can be said that there is a tourist behaviour such as the destination is not even seen as an alternative as a tourism destination. Of course, at this point, it will be necessary to understand the origin of destination rejection behaviour well and take different actions to overcome it. Especially the fact that mass communication channels have created the perception of the destination as an absolutely unsafe region by taking the event out of the scope will make efforts necessary to manage the destination position in the target market mind.

CONCLUSION

Purchase behavior is a decision-making process that involves individuals acquiring and using a product or service. Consumer purchase behavior is defined as individuals buying products or services for individual or household use (Pride and Ferrell, 2000). Consumers' purchase behavior is influenced by social factors such as culture, subculture, social class, reference groups, family; personal factors including motivation, personality perception, learning, as well as technological, economic, and political factors (Oktay, 2006; Durmaz and Bahar Oruç, 2011). The positive development of these elements from the consumer's perspective facilitates the purchase of a product, while their negative development leads to the rejection of the product.

In tourism, consumer purchase behavior is known as the sum of purchasing, consuming tourist services, and consumer behaviors, attitudes, and decisions. The factors influencing this situation emerge as personal, social, and situational factors (Acar, 2018). The negative development of purchasing behavior in tourism gives rise to the phenomenon of consumer purchase opposition in tourism. Indeed, this situation brings along several problems, especially triggering the rejection of destinations. Various economic, political, cultural, and psychological factors can play a role in the rejection of destinations. When the literature on destination rejection is examined, factors such as negative image, historical hostilities between countries, high costs, decreased satisfaction of tourists, security issues in destinations, overtourism, climate problems, disloyalty towards the destination, psychological distance, and health problems can play a role (Lawson and Thyne, 2001; Mohammed and Sookram, 2015).

Undoubtedly, effective destination management, carried out through destination management organizations established in destinations, plays a crucial role in mitigating these emerging negatives. In this context, stakeholder relationships based on the governance philosophy in the management process of destinations can eliminate adversities and facilitate the development of effective plans, policies, and strategies. Additionally, awareness among destination managers regarding the factors leading to destination management issues can contribute to the more sustainable management of destinations. Destinations managed sustainably may experience economic development due to an increased number of visitors. As economically growing destinations improve in areas such as infrastructure, superstructure, and the welfare of the local population, they are likely to face less rejection in the long term. This positive trajectory aligns with the sustainable growth of destinations, reducing the risk of rejection.

REFERENCES

Abraham, V., Bremser, K., Carreño, M., Crowley-Cyr, L., & Moreno, M. J. G. (2020). Exploring the Consequences of COVID-19 on Tourist Behaviors: Perceived Travel Risk, Animosity and Intentions to Travel. *Tourism Review*, ahead-of-print(ahead-of-print). Advance online publication. DOI: 10.1108/TR-07-2020-0344

Abraham, V., & Poria, Y. (2020). Perceptions of a Heritage Site and Animosity: The Case of the West Bank. *Tourism Review*, 75(5), 765–777. Advance online publication. DOI: 10.1108/TR-06-2019-0278

Acar, A. (2018). Turizmde Tüketici Davranışını Etkileyen Faktörler. *Uluslararası Turizm, İşletme. Ekonomi Dergisi.*, 2(2), 390–394.

Akroush, M. N., Jraisat, L., Kurdieh, D. J., AL-Faouri, R. N., & Qatu, L. T. (2016, April 18). AL-Faouri, R. N., & Qatu, L. T. (2016). Tourism Service Quality and Destination Loyalty – The Mediating Role of Destination Image From International Tourists' Perspectives. *Tourism Review*, 71(1), 18–44. Advance online publication. DOI: 10.1108/TR-11-2014-0057

Albinsson, P. A., Wolf, M., & Kopf, D. A. (2010). Anti-consumption in East Germany: Consumer Resistance to Hyperconsumption. *Journal of Consumer Behaviour*, 9(6), 412–425. Advance online publication. DOI: 10.1002/cb.333

Alonso-Almeida, M.-M., Borrajo-Millán, F., & Liu, Y. (2019). Are Social Media Data Pushing Overtourism? The Case of Barcelona and Chinese Tourists. *Sustainability (Basel)*, 11(12), 3356. Advance online publication. DOI: 10.3390/su11123356

Alvarez, M. D., Campo, S., & Fuchs, G. (2020). Tourism in Conflict Zones: Animosity and Risk Perceptions. *International Journal of Culture, Tourism and Hospitality Research*, 14(2), 189–204. Advance online publication. DOI: 10.1108/IJCTHR-08-2019-0136

Arli, D., Kim, J., Rundle-Thiele, S., & Tkaczynski, A. (2018). Australian Migrants' Social Cultural Adaptation and Consumption Behaviour Towards Food and Alcohol. *International Journal of Consumer Studies*. Advance online publication. DOI: 10.1111/ijcs.12439

Bilynets, I., Cvelbar, L. K., & Dolnicar, S. (2021). Can Publicly Visible Pro-Environmental Initiatives Improve the Organic Environmental Image of Destinations? *Journal of Sustainable Tourism*. Advance online publication. DOI: 10.1080/09669582.2021.1926469

Cahyanto, I., Wiblishauser, M., Pennington-Gray, L., & Schroeder, A. (2016). The Dynamics of Travel Avoidance: The Case of Ebola in the U.S. *Tourism Management Perspectives*, 20, 195–203. Advance online publication. DOI: 10.1016/j.tmp.2016.09.004 PMID: 32289007

Campo, S., & Alvarez, M. D. (2019). Animosity Toward a Country in the Context of Destinations as Tourism Products. *Journal of Hospitality & Tourism Research (Washington, D.C.)*, 43(7), 1002–1024. Advance online publication. DOI: 10.1177/1096348019840795

Camprubí, R., Guia, J., & Comas, J. (2008). Destination Networks and Induced Tourism Image. *Tourism Review*, 63(2), 47–58. Advance online publication. DOI: 10.1108/16605370810883941

Chaniago, A. (2022). *Digital Marketing and Destination Management Models in Shaping Tourist Behaviour*. DOI: 10.46254/EU05.20220609

Chen, J., & Hsu, C. (2000). Measurement of Korean Tourists' Perceived Images of Overseas Destinations. *Journal of Travel Research*, 38(4), 411–416. Advance online publication. DOI: 10.1177/004728750003800410

Chen, X., Cheng, Z., & Kim, G.-B. (2020). Make It Memorable: Tourism Experience, Fun, Recommendation and Revisit Intentions of Chinese Outbound Tourists. *Sustainability (Basel)*, 12(5), 1904. Advance online publication. DOI: 10.3390/su12051904

Cho, M., Bonn, M. A., & Brymer, R. A. (2014). A Constraint-Based Approach to Wine Tourism Market Segmentation. *Journal of Hospitality & Tourism Research (Washington, D.C.)*. Advance online publication. DOI: 10.1177/1096348014538049

Chon, K. (1990). The Role of Destination Image in Tourism: A Review and Discussion. *Tourism Review*, 45(2), 2–9. Advance online publication. DOI: 10.1108/eb058040

Çınar, K., Kavacık, S. Z., Bişkin, F., & Çinar, M. (2022). Understanding the Behavioral Intentions About Holidays in the Shadow of the COVID-19 Pandemic: Application of Protection Motivation Theory. *Health Care*, 10(9), 1623. Advance online publication. DOI: 10.3390/healthcare10091623 PMID: 36141234

Durmaz, Y. ve Bahar Oruç, R. (2011). Tüketicilerin Satın Alma Davranısları Üzerinde Sosyolojik Faktörlerin Etkisinin İncelenmesine Yönelik Bir Çalısma. *Elektironik Sosyal Bilimler Dergisi*, 10(37), 60–77.

Fazal-e-Hasan, S. M., Ahmadi, H., Mortimer, G., Sekhon, H., Kharouf, H., & Jebarajakirthy, C. (2020). The Interplay of Positive and Negative Emotions to Quit Unhealthy Consumption Behaviors: Insights for Social Marketers. *Australasian Marketing Journal (Amj)*. DOI: 10.1016/j.ausmj.2020.07.004

Franzoni, S., & Bonera, M. (2019). How DMO Can Measure the Experiences of a Large Territory. *Sustainability (Basel)*, 11(2), 492. Advance online publication. DOI: 10.3390/su11020492

Geipel, J., Hadjichristidis, C., & Klesse, A. K. (2018). Barriers to Sustainable Consumption Attenuated by Foreign Language Use. *Nature Sustainability*, 1(1), 31–33. Advance online publication. DOI: 10.1038/s41893-017-0005-9

Gilboa, S., & Herstein, R. (2012). Place Status, Place Loyalty and Well Being: An Exploratory Investigation of Israeli Residents. *Journal of Place Management and Development*. DOI: 10.1108/17538331211250035

Godfrey, J., Wearing, S., Schulenkorf, N., & Grabowski, S. (2019). The 'Volunteer Tourist Gaze': Commercial Volunteer Tourists' Interactions With, and Perceptions Of, the Host Community in Cusco, Peru. *Current Issues in Tourism*. Advance online publication. DOI: 10.1080/13683500.2019.1657811

Gu, Q., Zhang, H. Q., King, B., & Huang, S. (2019). Understanding the Wine Tourism Experience: The Roles of Facilitators, Constraints, and Involvement. *Journal of Vacation Marketing*. Advance online publication. DOI: 10.1177/1356766719880253

Han, H., Che, C., & Lee, S. (2021). Facilitators and Reducers of Korean Travelers' Avoidance/Hesitation Behaviors Toward China in the Case of COVID-19. *International Journal of Environmental Research and Public Health*, 18(23), 12345. Advance online publication. DOI: 10.3390/ijerph182312345 PMID: 34886067

Hwang, J.-A., Park, Y., & Kim, Y. (2016). Why Do Consumers Respond to Eco-Labels? The Case of Korea. *SpringerPlus*, 5(1), 1915. Advance online publication. DOI: 10.1186/s40064-016-3550-1 PMID: 27867822

İnanır, A. (2019). Turistik destinasyon yönetiminde paydaşlar arası ilişkiler: Göller Yöresi Örneği. *Türk Turizm Araştırmaları Dergisi*, 3(3), 517–541. DOI: 10.26677/TR1010.2019.176

Josiassen, A., Kock, F., & Norfelt, A. (2020). Tourism Affinity and Its Effects on Tourist and Resident Behavior. *Journal of Travel Research*. Advance online publication. DOI: 10.1177/0047287520979682

Karakuş, Y., & Çoban, S. (2018). Evaluation of Stakeholders' Expectations Towards Congress Tourism by Kano Model: Case of Nevşehir. *Anais Brasileiros De Estudos Turísticos*, 8(2), 8–20. DOI: 10.34019/2238-2925.2018.v8.3207

Karakuş, Y., & Kalay, N. (2017). A Study on the Concept and Causes of Destination Rejection. *International Journal of Management Economics and Business*. DOI: 10.17130/ijmeb.2017331320

Kearney, J. (2010). Food Consumption Trends and Drivers. *Philosophical Transactions of the Royal Society of London. Series B, Biological Sciences*, 365(1554), 2793–2807. Advance online publication. DOI: 10.1098/rstb.2010.0149 PMID: 20713385

Kim, H. J., Kehoe, P., Gibbs, L., & Lee, J. A. (2019). Caregiving Experience of Dementia Among Korean American Family Caregivers. *Issues in Mental Health Nursing*, 40(2), 158–165. Advance online publication. DOI: 10.1080/01612840.2018.1534909 PMID: 30620625

Kozak, M., & Rimmington, M. (2000). Tourist Satisfaction With Mallorca, Spain, as an Off-Season Holiday Destination. *Journal of Travel Research*, 38(3), 260–269. Advance online publication. DOI: 10.1177/004728750003800308

Kozar, J. M., & Connell, K. Y. H. (2013). Socially and Environmentally Responsible Apparel Consumption: Knowledge, Attitudes, and Behaviors. *Social Responsibility Journal*, 9(2), 315–324. Advance online publication. DOI: 10.1108/SRJ-09-2011-0076

Lawson, R., & Thyne, M. (2001). Destination Avoidance and Inept Destination Sets. *Journal of Vacation Marketing*, 7(3), 199–208. DOI: 10.1177/135676670100700301

Leung, X. Y., & Jiang, L. (2018). How Do Destination Facebook Pages Work? An Extended TPB Model of Fans' Visit Intention. *Journal of Hospitality and Tourism Technology*, 9(3), 397–416. Advance online publication. DOI: 10.1108/JHTT-09-2017-0088

Li, X., Yang, J., Wang, X., & Lei, D. (2012). The Impact of Country-of-Origin Image, Consumer Ethnocentrism and Animosity on Purchase Intention. *Journal of Software*, 7(10). Advance online publication. DOI: 10.4304/jsw.7.10.2263-2268

Little, J., Little, E. L., & Cox, K. C. (2011). *U.S. Consumer Animosity Towards Vietnam: A Comparison of Generations. Journal of Applied Business Research*. Jabr., DOI: 10.19030/jabr.v25i6.991

Loureiro, S. M. C., Guerreiro, J., & Han, H. (2021). Past, Present, and Future of Pro-Environmental Behavior in Tourism and Hospitality: A Text-Mining Approach. *Journal of Sustainable Tourism.* Advance online publication. DOI: 10.1080/09669582.2021.1875477

Ma, H., Chiu, Y., Tian, X., Zhang, J., & Guo, Q. (2020). Safety or Travel: Which Is More Important? The Impact of Disaster Events on Tourism. *Sustainability (Basel)*, 12(7), 3038. Advance online publication. DOI: 10.3390/su12073038

Manci, A. R. (2022). Determining Destination Risk Perceptions, Their Effects on Satisfaction, Revisit and Recommendation Intentions: Evidence From Sanliurfa/Turkey. *Journal of Multidisciplinary Academic Tourism.* DOI: 10.31822/jomat.2022-7-1-81

Manrai, L. A., & Manrai, A. K. (2011). *Hofstede's Cultural Dimensions and Tourist Behaviors: A Review and Conceptual Framework.* Cuadernos De Difusión., DOI: 10.46631/jefas.2011.v16n31.02

Marpaung, B. O. Y., & Tania, F. (2021). Visitor Satisfaction and Tourist Attraction Image. *International Journal of Psychological Studies*, 13(2), 33. Advance online publication. DOI: 10.5539/ijps.v13n2p33

Martin, D., & Woodside, A. G. (2008). Grounded Theory of International Tourism Behavior. *Journal of Travel & Tourism Marketing*, 24(4), 245–258. Advance online publication. DOI: 10.1080/10548400802156695

Martín, J. M. M., Martínez, J. M. G., & Fernández, J. A. S. (2018). An Analysis of the Factors Behind the Citizen's Attitude of Rejection Towards Tourism in a Context of Overtourism and Economic Dependence on This Activity. *Sustainability (Basel)*, 10(8), 2851. Advance online publication. DOI: 10.3390/su10082851

Mei, H., Yang, X.-J., Liu, D., & Fang, H. (2022). Effects of Perceived Change of Urban Destination on Destination Attachment. *Frontiers in Psychology*, 13, 1022421. Advance online publication. DOI: 10.3389/fpsyg.2022.1022421 PMID: 36483727

Middleton, V. T. (1989). Tourism Marketing and Managemet Handbook. In S. F. Witt & L. Moutinho (Eds.), *Tourist Product.* Hempel Hempstead: Prentice Hall.

Milliyet. (2013). *Japon turisti öldürüp kız istemeye gitmiş* - Son Dakika Milliyet. Retrieved May 29, 2024, from https://www.milliyet.com.tr/gundem/japon-turisti-oldurup-kiz-istemeye-gitmis-1763156

Ministry of Culture and Tourism Statistics. (2024). İstatistikler. Retrieved May 29, 2024, from https://www.ktb.gov.tr/TR-96695/istatistikler.html

Mohammed, A., & Sookram, S. (2015). The Impact of Crime on Tourist Arrivals A Comparative Analysis of Jamaica and Trinidad and Tobago. *Social and Economic Studies*, 64(2), 153–176.

Moraga, E. T., Rodríguez-Sánchez, C., & Esper, F. S. (2021). Understanding Tourist Citizenship Behavior at the Destination Level. *Journal of Hospitality and Tourism Management*, 49, 592–600. Advance online publication. DOI: 10.1016/j.jhtm.2021.11.009

numbeo.com. (2024). Crime Index by Country 2024. Retrieved May 28, 2024, from https://www.numbeo.com/crime/rankings_by_country.jsp

Nwankwo, E. A. (2020). *Exploring the Three-Way Destination Safety Solution to Crisis Management in Tourist Destinations in Rural Nigeria.* DOI: 10.5772/intechopen.89727

Okrainec, K., Booth, G. L., Hollands, S., & Bell, C. M. (2014). Impact of Language Barriers on Complications and Mortality Among Immigrants With Diabetes: A Population-Based Cohort Study. *Diabetes Care*. Advance online publication. DOI: 10.2337/dc14-0801 PMID: 25028526

Oktay, K. (2006). Kırgızistan'daki Tuketicilerin Giyim Tercihleri Uzerine Bir Arastırma. *Manas Universitesi Sosyal Bilimler Dergisi.*, 15, 197–211.

Olbrich, R., Jansen, H. C., & Teller, B. (2015). Quantifying Anti-Consumption of Private Labels and National Brands: Impacts of Poor Test Ratings on Consumer Purchases. *The Journal of Consumer Affairs*. Advance online publication. DOI: 10.1111/joca.12084

Omar, N. A., Nazri, M. A., Alam, S. S., & Ali, M. H. (2017). *Consumer Retaliation to Halal Violation Incidents: The Mediating Role of Trust Recovery*. Jurnal Pengurusan., DOI: 10.17576/pengurusan-2017-51-09

Ozanne, L. K., & Ballantine, P. W. (2010). Sharing as a Form of Anti-consumption? An Examination of Toy Library Users. *Journal of Consumer Behaviour*, 9(6), 485–498. Advance online publication. DOI: 10.1002/cb.334

Pahrudin, P., Chen, C.-T., & Liu, L. (2021). A Modified Theory of Planned Behavioral: A Case of Tourist Intention to Visit a Destination Post Pandemic Covid-19 in Indonesia. *Heliyon*, 7(10), e08230. Advance online publication. DOI: 10.1016/j.heliyon.2021.e08230 PMID: 34708160

Papadopoulou, N. M., Ribeiro, M. A., & Prayag, G. (2022). Psychological Determinants of Tourist Satisfaction and Destination Loyalty: The Influence of Perceived Overcrowding and Overtourism. *Journal of Travel Research*. Advance online publication. DOI: 10.1177/00472875221089049

Persson-Fischer, U., & Liu, S. (2021). What Is Interdisciplinarity in the Study of Sustainable Destination Development? *Sustainability (Basel)*, 13(7), 3639. Advance online publication. DOI: 10.3390/su13073639

Pride William, M. ve Ferrell, O. C. (2000). *Marketing Concepts and Strategies*, Houghton Mifflin Compony. U.S.A.

Priyatmoko, R., & Maulana, A. (2022). *Halal Tourism and Its Misconceptions: A Study on the Rejection of Indonesian Non-Muslim Destinations*. Dinar Jurnal Ekonomi Dan Keuangan Islam., DOI: 10.21107/dinar.v9i1.13976

Renzi, M. F., Loureiro, S., Toni, M., & Panchapakesan, P. (2018). Relationship between destination affect and intention to visit: the case of destination dislike. *In 47th International EMAC conference-People Make Marketing*.

Risitano, M., Tutore, I., Sorrentino, A., & Quintano, M. (2017). The Influence of Tourists' National Culture on Their Behaviors in a Sport Mega-Event. *International Journal of Culture, Tourism and Hospitality Research*, 11(2), 193–210. Advance online publication. DOI: 10.1108/IJCTHR-07-2015-0077

Sandıkçı, Ö., & Ekici, A. (2009). Politically Motivated Brand Rejection. *Journal of Business Research*, 62(2), 208–217. Advance online publication. DOI: 10.1016/j.jbusres.2008.01.028

Stepchenkova, S., Su, L., & Shichkova, E. (2018). Marketing to Tourists From Unfriendly Countries: Should We Even Try? *Journal of Travel Research*. Advance online publication. DOI: 10.1177/0047287517752883

Taheri, B., & Gannon, M. (2021). Contemporary Issues and Future Trends in Food Tourism. *International Journal of Tourism Research*, 23(2), 147–149. Advance online publication. DOI: 10.1002/jtr.2446

Terzić, A., Petrevska, B., & Bajrami, D. D. (2022). Personalities Shaping Travel Behaviors: Post-Covid Scenario. *Journal of Tourism Futures*. DOI: 10.1108/JTF-02-2022-0043

Tjiptono, F., & Yang, L. (2018). To go or not to go: a typology of Asian tourist destination avoidance. *Asian cultures and contemporary tourism*, 183-200.

Ullah, N., Khan, J., Saeed, I., Zada, S., Xin, S., Kang, Z., & Hu, Y. (2022). Gastronomic Tourism and Tourist Motivation: Exploring Northern Areas of Pakistan. *International Journal of Environmental Research and Public Health*, 19(13), 7734. Advance online publication. DOI: 10.3390/ijerph19137734 PMID: 35805393

Wang, F., Feng, Y., & Wang, Z. (2022). Inspiring Desirability or Ensuring Feasibility: Destination Image and Psychological Distance. *International Journal of Tourism Research*, 24(5), 667–676. Advance online publication. DOI: 10.1002/jtr.2529

Wang, P. (2014). *The Influence of Tourists' Safety Perception During Vacation Destination-Decision Process: An Integration of Elaboration Likelihood Model and Theory of Planned Behavior*. DOI: 10.1007/978-3-319-10211-5_23

Xie, L., Shahzad, M. F., Waheed, A., Ain, Q. U., Saleem, Z., & Ali, M. A. (2022). Do Meat Anti-Consumption Opinions Influence Consumers' Wellbeing?–The Moderating Role of Religiosity. *Frontiers in Psychology*, 13, 957970. Advance online publication. DOI: 10.3389/fpsyg.2022.957970 PMID: 36312138

Yang, Y., Nan, L., Meijian, L., & Li, S. (2011). Study on the Effects of Logistics Service Quality on Consumers' Post-Purchase Behavior of Online Shopping. *International Journal on Advances in Information Sciences and Service Sciences*. DOI: 10.4156/aiss.vol3.issue11.30

Zaman, U., Aktan, M., Agrusa, J., & Khwaja, M. G. (2022). Linking Regenerative Travel and Residents' Support for Tourism Development in Kaua'i Island (Hawaii): Moderating-Mediating Effects of Travel-Shaming and Foreign Tourist Attractiveness. *Journal of Travel Research*. Advance online publication. DOI: 10.1177/00472875221098934

Zhandilla, B. (2023). Conceptual Foundations of the Category of Tourist Destination. *Bulletin of the Karaganda University Economy Series*. DOI: 10.31489/2022ec4/135-143

Zhou, B., Liu, S., Wang, L., Wang, L., & Wang, Y. (2022). COVID-19 Risk Perception and Tourist Satisfaction: A Mixed-Method Study of the Roles of Destination Image and Self-Protection Behavior. *Frontiers in Psychology*, 13, 1001231. Advance online publication. DOI: 10.3389/fpsyg.2022.1001231 PMID: 37035511

Zhu, H., Guan, H., Han, Y., & Li, W. (2019). A Study of Tourists' Holiday Rush-Hour Avoidance Travel Behavior Considering Psychographic Segmentation. *Sustainability (Basel)*, 11(13), 3755. Advance online publication. DOI: 10.3390/su11133755

KEY TERMS AND DEFINITIONS

Destination: It can be defined as a multidimensional and perceptual geographical area consisting of tourist goods and services and the resulting tourist experiences.

Destination Management: All of the operational, managerial, marketing, etc. efforts necessary for the development of a sustainable tourism activity in the destination, including understanding tourist behavior and managing demand by taking proactive or active actions.

Destination Rejection: It involves addressing the phenomenon of consumer opposition in tourism. This situation is expressed as the tourist excluding a specific tourist destination from their preferences despite having factors such as money, time, and motivation.

Tourist behaviour: It is all of the reactions that tourists exhibit before, during and after travelling, influenced by various factors such as motivation, demographics, lifestyle, culture, destination perception, social interaction and travel experience, and varying in consumption stages.

Tourist purchase decision process: When a need arises to participate in tourism activities in some way, it is the process of choosing the tourism activities and therefore the tourist destination that will meet this need and these needs-based desires. In this process, it is essential to choose the most suitable alternative for the individual among the available alternatives. However, in terms of destination management, being or not being one of these alternatives will require very different efforts.

Chapter 11
Tourism and Destination Positioning Through Territorial Branding:
The Case of Brazil

Giovana Goretti Feijó de Almeida
https://orcid.org/0000-0003-0956-1341
CiTUR, Portugal

Sarah Minasi
https://orcid.org/0000-0002-1193-3274
University of Vale do Itajaí, Brazil

EXECUTIVE SUMMARY

Purpose The purpose is to examine how a territorial brand positions a tourism destination. Design/methodology/approach The strategy used a case study using a qualitative approach. Findings/Conclusion The results highlight the use of the territorial brand and scope-creating local events in urban areas. Studying the territorial brand in the context of cultural studies also extends to the study of tourism. Research limitations The study's shortcoming was that it was limited to cities in the interior. We propose broadening the study to include the realities of other small towns. Practical and Theoretical Implications The contributions address the complexity of the investigated themes, destination branding, place branding, and territorial brand. Originality There are certain places, such as Brazil, where the brand of the place is still embryonic. The territorial brand led from the feeling of local belonging. The reality of the city of Pelotas can reflect the existence of other territorial brands, and this study contributes to exposing this.

DOI: 10.4018/979-8-3693-1548-4.ch011

1. INTRODUCTION

Numerous cities worldwide have sought to enhance their identity and attractiveness through place branding strategies, creating a territorial brand for themselves. An example of this scenario is the case of Pelotas city, Brazil, which took an unusual initiative by creating a territorial brand through a municipal decree, ensuring its perpetuity even amidst changes in government. These territorial branding strategies have propelled Pelotas' transformation into a burgeoning tourist destination. Imagine flipping through the pages of a local newspaper and coming across enthusiastic headlines about Pelotas' rebirth, driven by its new territorial brand. This captivating narrative not only underscores the growing importance of territorial brands but also highlights their tangible impact on the economic and cultural revitalization of a community. This chapter delves into how territorial brands, such as Pelotas', have the potential not only to redefine a city's identity but also to inspire engagement and interest from visitors, thereby contributing to sustainable and inclusive tourism development.

Territorial brands have been adopted over the years and are recurrent in interdisciplinary literature (de Almeida, 2023). This brand serves as a tool for tourism marketing, government policies, and the travel and tourism marketing business. In this sense, nomenclatures such as place branding, city branding, destination branding, and territorial brand are frequent (Jin & Cheng, 2020).

Each concept has particularities and cannot be considered synonymous. The implications of destination marketing are also based on events of multiple types, recognizing the complexity of place branding, an area situated between the geography of tourism and marketing (Rinaldi & Beeton, 2015; Hall, 2008). Furthermore, territorial brands are associated with cultural, historical, environmental, or social factors, conveying a sense of excellence and authenticity (Lorenzini et al., 2011), evolving over time (Charters & Spielmann, 2014), and also acquiring new uses and functions (Almeida et al., 2023). Therefore, they are long-term strategies.

A broad understanding of place branding and destination branding may prejudice an understanding of these concepts (Kasapi & Cela, 2017). From the perspective of the commercialization of places, place branding is also multidisciplinary, focusing solely on the area's physical characteristics (Kotler & Gertner, 2002). Farhat (2018) also considers place branding a contested "cultural politics." The uses and appropriations of the territory, marketing, and branding concepts and their application within the territorial context are all misrepresented (Almeida, 2018; 2023). Increased brand value can lead to greater brand competitiveness (Wong, 2015) in addition to the competitiveness of a destination brand (Lodge, 2002).

The question problem highlighted two elements: how can a local tourist destination position itself as a brand? How does tourism contribute to territorial brand development, implementation, and dissemination? The research aims to analyze how a territorial brand positions a tourist destination, understanding the role of tourism in the production process of these brands. The study employs a case study of the territorial brand (*Sou + Pel*) of the city of Pelotas, Brazil, meticulously examining the key elements and the influence of tourism on its creation. Thus, the gap in the study centers on the lack of understanding of the addressed concepts and their interrelationships.

Research justifications indicate that destination branding has the main objective of helping the diversity of social actors (Kasapi & Cela, 2017) and in a multiplicity of measurable elements (Kaplanidou & Vogt, 2007). Tourism destination strategists use destination branding strategically (Gartner, 2014). The relation between the concepts is behind the production of destination images (Cardoso et al., 2019). Expanding local competitive advantages makes destinations offer diverse experiences (Bookman, 2013; Rather, 2019). These experiences are sensory, affective, intellectual, and behavioral (Kumar & Kaushik, 2020), to also move the local economy. Other forms of capital are generated, such as symbolic capital, because of the pressure of globalization (Bouchard, 2021). Anthropological, historical, sociological, or spatial dimensions and their Social, urban, and cultural processes are in tourism (Sampaio et al., 2021). Therefore, this is a case study that explores the complexities of the territorial brand and emphasizes its importance to tourism marketing, government policy, cultural studies, and the travel industry.

Thus, this chapter provides significant contributions to understanding how a territorial brand can position a tourist destination. By examining the case of Pelotas, Brazil, this study meticulously examines key elements and the influence of tourism on the creation of the "Sou + Pel" territorial brand. Moreover, by highlighting the gap in understanding the addressed concepts and their interrelationships, this research contributes to the literature by offering valuable insights into how tourism can shape the development, implementation, and dissemination of territorial brands. By addressing this issue, the chapter enhances our understanding of the role of tourism in shaping the identity and attractiveness of destinations, providing a solid foundation for future research and practice in territorial branding and tourism.

2. THEORETICAL FRAMEWORK

2.1. Place Branding: Creating Value and Identity in Space

Place branding is a strategic process that creates value in space by reinforcing and cohesively representing the assets of a place as a narrative image of the place itself (Grenni et al., 2020). Anholt (2007; 2008) suggests that places can apply trademark techniques to build their image and sustain local identity. In the age of globalization, adapting the perception of a place requires more than just graphic design, advertising, or public relations campaigns (Anholt, 2010). Anholt (2010) further acknowledges the conceptual confusion between the terms "brand" and "branding" within the context of place branding. This highlights the complexity of the concept and the importance of a clear understanding of its elements for successful implementation.

Almeida (2018) further extends the complexity of place branding by discussing the conceptual confusion between territory, region, and place within the relationship between regional development and place branding. These discussions emphasize the multifaceted nature of place branding and highlight the importance of considering the nuances and interconnectedness of these concepts. Abankina (2013) stresses the potential of cultural resources and the tourism sector in driving regional development. Events, local parties, farmers' markets, gastronomy, and wine tourism are all part of these resources, and they leverage place branding to enhance the reputation of a place (Mikulić et al., 2016; Garner & Ayala, 2018; Crespi-Vallbona & Mascarilla-Miró, 2020). Källström and Ekelund (2016) describe these resources as value propositions, offering economic and cultural benefits for municipalities, their residents, and tourists. This illustrates the intricate relationship between place branding and regional development, emphasizing their synergistic potential.

Place branding is closely tied to the relationship between place brand and place identity. Kavaratzis and Hatch (2013) argue that place branding practice and literature often adopt a static view of place identity, assuming it can be easily articulated and communicated for place branding purposes. However, this approach underestimates the complexity of place identity and the role and potential of place branding. The essence of place branding lies in the interaction and dialogue between stakeholders (Kavaratzis & Hatch, 2013).

Van Assche et al. (2020) emphasize the importance of place narratives in spatially transforming a place. Almeida (2018) adds that this transformation can also be symbolic, playing a role in maintaining or disputing local hegemonic identity, or being part of the urban imaginary. Grenni et al. (2020) highlight the significance of place narratives in planning and developing spatial strategies, demonstrating the interconnection between cultural narratives, local planning, and place branding in shaping perceived meanings and images of place. This dynamic and interconnected approach to place branding acknowledges the complexities of place identity and emphasizes the importance of stakeholder engagement and cultural narratives in shaping the image and reputation of a place.

Anholt (2008) introduces five new insights within place branding or competitive identity:

- Public policies' influence on place image: Governmental actions and policies can significantly impact how a place is perceived, both domestically and internationally.
- Place reputation's role in sustaining transactions: A positive place reputation is crucial for supporting interactions between the place brand and its stakeholders, including residents, tourists, and investors.
- Brand value as an asset: A strong place brand can contribute to the overall value of a place, attracting investment, promoting economic development, and enhancing quality of life for its inhabitants.

The idea of brand purpose is establishing a clear and compelling brand purpose can help create internal dynamics that drive the development and promotion of a place brand. The importance of sustained innovation: Consistent and innovative efforts in line with national activities can help maintain and improve a place's competitiveness in the global market. These insights align with Almeida's (2018) perspective on regional development, which emphasizes the importance of internal and external strategies in generating a reputation for the place. The territorial brand, as a cultural product, can benefit from these insights to foster a more effective and cohesive approach to place branding.

Anholt (2016) posits that places, to build their brands, should evoke three essential elements: identity, image, and reputation. These elements draw parallels to the branding tripod of marketing brands, which comprises brand identity, brand positioning, and brand communication (Almeida, 2015). While Anholt's (2016) studies focus on the reputation of places, Almeida (2018) incorporates the communication platform of product brands into the discussion.

When applying the branding tripod (Almeida, 2015) to places, there is a clear approximation of elements with Anholt's (2016) studies. The term "reputation" (Anholt, 2016) aligns with the elements of brand positioning (brand reputation) and communication (which builds brand image) in the branding tripod. Both authors emphasize the significance of brand identity in place branding, highlighting its importance as a foundational element.

This integrated perspective on place branding elements acknowledges the unique aspects of place reputation while incorporating relevant branding brand concepts. By understanding the interplay between identity, image, and reputation, places can develop more comprehensive and effective branding strategies that resonate with stakeholders and foster development.

2.2. Territorial Brand and Marketing of Places

Almeida (2018) posits that territorial brands play a significant role in territorial and regional development dynamics. This perspective considers the territory as a central protagonist, shaped by planned, summarized, and strategic discourse. In this study, we adopt Almeida's (2018) notion of a territorial brand, which represents a collection of symbols, cultures, and identities portrayed visually, discursively, or through mixed strategies. These strategies generate power relations within a territory, whether they are planned or develop organically.

Kotler and Gertner (2002) argue that the marketing of places follows an economic proposal centered around the traditional 4Ps of marketing: product, price, place, and promotion. This approach primarily focuses on the tangible characteristics of a place. However, brand positioning aligns more closely with the intangible elements of a brand, such as its values, culture, and identity (Kaplan, 2010; Kapferer, 2004). By incorporating both tangible and intangible aspects, place branding can create a comprehensive and compelling representation of a territory, fostering regional development and competitiveness.

To address these challenges, Kavaratzis (2012) proposes adopting a practice-based, collaboratively participative paradigm to better reflect on the performance and deployment of the local brand. This approach acknowledges the importance of local-global promotion in strengthening the competitiveness of countries, states, and cities. While urban rankings often focus on the physical elements of a place, it is essential to recognize that each territory is unique due to disparities in characteristics, cultures, historical trajectories, and power relations. As a result, direct comparisons between territories may not be appropriate (Cleave & Arku, 2020).

Branding has evolved beyond its primary purpose of creating a place's image, becoming increasingly influenced by local planning and urban development (Cleave & Arku, 2020). Although this scenario does not preclude other economies from adopting similar methods, it underscores the importance of tailoring place branding strategies to each territory's unique context and complexities. By acknowledging the distinct qualities of each place and engaging stakeholders in collaborative branding efforts, territories can build more effective and representative brands that support regional development and competitiveness.

In the context of product brand positioning, Kapferer (2004) identifies two crucial factors: 1) the identification of the product's category in contrast to the competition, and 2) the distinction of the brand itself from its competitors. When applying these factors to territorial brands, the category can be likened to the type of tourism destination (e.g., adventure, religious, or cultural). However, it is essential to recognize that a brand's positioning goes beyond a simple slogan (Ries & Trout, 1991). At its core, positioning is the promise of value to customers, highlighting the unique benefits and experiences offered by the brand.

Kapferer (2004) defines positioning as the distinguishing evidence between one brand and another in terms of competitiveness and target audience. Similarly, territorial brands require strategic positioning, which may include the city's name or other identifying features. By effectively positioning a territorial brand, destinations can differentiate themselves in the competitive tourism market, attract their desired target audience, and contribute to regional development.

2.3. Destination Branding

Destination branding is approached in various ways throughout the literature. The World Tourism Organization (WTO, 2009) defines a destination brand as "a dynamic interplay between the place's fundamental assets and how potential tourists perceive them." It is crucial to acknowledge the significance of visitor perception in destination branding (Beerli & Martín, 2004). Rather than focusing solely on a destination's authenticity, Lin (2020) underscores that the perception of authenticity varies depending on the visitor, time, and heritage place.

The positioning theory, as mentioned by Pike and Mason (2010), emphasizes the competitiveness among destinations. Destination branding can be understood as a theoretical model that combines several factors, such as physical and symbolic attributes of the destination, brand equity, brand personality, brand as a symbol, image, and loyalty, into a cohesive brand (Kaplanidou & Vogt, 2007). This approach aims to create an emotional connection with the customer while presenting an appealing and competitive market proposition (Lodge, 2002). In essence, destination branding serves as a projection tool to enhance public perceptions of a destination (Jerez, 2023).

Effective collaboration across institutions and organizations is vital for successful destination branding (Vela et al., 2017). All entities must work together to ensure that destination branding contributes positively to regional development (Saraniemi & Komppula, 2017; Cardoso et al., 2019). Interactions between social players can result in contradictory agreements or collaborations, revealing power dynamics between brands and destinations (Saraniemi & Komppula, 2017). Destination branding strategies can drive social change and economic capital (Gerosa & Tartari, 2021), further highlighting the importance of a coordinated approach in creating a strong and competitive destination brand.

3. METHODOLOGY RESEARCH

The case study method with a qualitative approach was applied (Yin, 2015). The research addresses the case of Pelotas, Brazil. Different reasons chose Pelotas city: it's a consolidated brand, is a city in the interior, and is a local destination seeking national or regional renown. These factors led us to other towns, but Pelotas attracted our attention since the city adopted a Municipal Law ensuring the brand's existence beyond the four-year term of the government that created it, which is uncommon in Brazil (Nachmias & Nachmias, 1987).

The study's research protocol employs qualitative techniques (Miles et al., 2020). The research protocol is structured around the constructs of territorial brand (Almeida, 2018) and destination brand, focusing on five key variables:

- Elaboration and voting process of the Pelotas brand: This involves identifying the various types of social actors involved in the creation and selection of the brand, including stakeholders from the public, private, and third sectors.
- Dissemination strategies for the chosen brand: This aspect entails analyzing the different types and names of strategies used to promote and disseminate the selected brand.
- Brand presence in the years 2019-2020: This variable assesses the brand's contemporaneity by examining the various forms in which the brand was present during this period.
- Social media networks of the Pelotas brand: This component explores the names and strategies associated with the brand's social media presence, such as Instagram and Facebook accounts.
- Brand positioning through the slogan Sou+Pel: Lastly, this variable investigates the name and types of brand positioning strategies employed, specifically focusing on the brand's slogan, "Sou+Pel.

By examining these variables, the research protocol aims to provide a comprehensive understanding of the Pelotas territorial brand and the role of tourism in its creation. The use of qualitative techniques will allow for a thorough and nuanced analysis of the data collected, ensuring a deep understanding of the case study and its implications for the broader field of territorial branding.

The study was carried out in four stages:

1) A review of the literature - We conducted a thorough review of the existing literature to establish a solid theoretical foundation and to identify gaps, trends, and relevant theories in the field. This stage allowed us to contextualize our research

within the broader scholarly discourse and to refine our research questions and objectives.

2) The development of the research protocol - Building upon insights gleaned from the literature review, we meticulously crafted a research protocol that outlined our methodological approach, including the selection of participants, data collection methods, and analytical techniques. This protocol served as a guiding framework throughout the study, ensuring consistency and rigor in our research procedures.

3) Data collection - With the research protocol in place, we proceeded to collect primary data through various methods, employing a multifaceted approach to gather primary data tailored to our research questions and objectives. This involved systematic data collection methods, including:

Observations: Conducted in various settings within the city of Pelotas, allowing for firsthand insights into local activities, events, and cultural aspects relevant to the territorial brand.

Social networks: Data were collected from official social media accounts associated with the city of Pelotas, including Instagram (@pelotasturismo) and Facebook (@pelotasturismo), through systematic monitoring of posts, interactions, and user-generated content.

Press releases: We accessed official press releases related to the Pelotas brand from reputable sources, including governmental agencies, tourism departments, and local media outlets.

Archival research: Relevant archival materials, such as historical documents, promotional materials, and official records, were consulted to provide historical context and insights into the evolution of the Pelotas brand over time.

Throughout the data collection process, we strictly adhered to established guidelines, including ethical considerations and data management protocols, to ensure the integrity and reliability of our findings. By leveraging these diverse data sources, we gained a comprehensive understanding of the Pelotas brand and its associated strategies, thereby enriching our analysis and insights into territorial branding dynamics.

4) Data analysis - The collected data was subjected to rigorous analysis using appropriate qualitative techniques, using comparative analysis. We employ systematic coding procedures, thematic analysis to derive meaningful insights, patterns and conclusions from the data.

Pelotas is a city located in the southern Brazilian state of Rio Grande do Sul (Figure 1).

Figure 1. Location of Pelotas

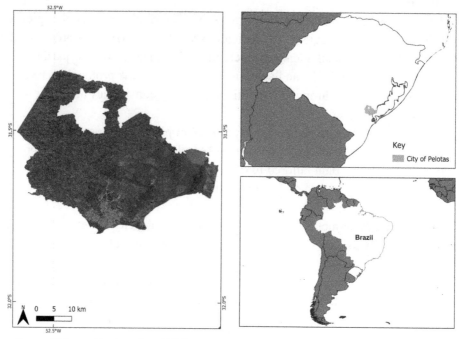

Source: Elaborated by the authors (2021).

The city is well-known for its annual municipal celebration and the Feira Nacional do Doce (Fenadoce), a festival named after the traditional Portuguese sweets sold during the event. Fenadoce brings together the ethnic groups responsible for the region's sweet culture and is currently in its 28th edition (Fenadoce, n.d.). The festival contributes to the city's unique identity and is an essential aspect of its territorial brand. By analyzing the data collected from the mentioned sources, the study aims to shed light on the role of tourism in the creation and promotion of the Pelotas brand, as well as the importance of events like Fenadoce in shaping the city's unique identity and appeal (Figure 2).

Figure 2. Feira Nacional do Doce (Fenadoce) in Pelotas city

Source: https://casaraoimoveis.com.br/blog/fenadoce-uma-doce-celebracao-em-pelotas/

In 2016/2017, the Municipal Tourism Plan led to the development of the brand proposal for Pelotas (Figure 3). The city's municipal public management for tourism decided to revive the slogan "Pelotas do Sal ao Açúcar" (Pelotas from Salt to Sugar), incorporating a brand proposal that symbolized the fusion of the two elements (salt and sugar).

Figure 3. Process brand Pelotas

Source: (RU, 2017).

The Pelotas Municipal Tourism Council organized a competition to design the new brand, which was later approved by the City Council. Two local universities, the Federal University of Pelotas (UFPel) and the Federal Institute of Rio Grande do Sul (IFSul), participated in the brand development process. Students from the Graphic Design and Digital Design (UFPel) and Visual Communication (IFSul) courses were involved in the activity. Six brand concepts were created by the participating universities. In the first stage, the Municipal Tourism Council selected two of the six proposed brands. Subsequently, the Council presented these two chosen brands to the public, allowing them to vote for the final selection (Figure 4).

Figure 4. Brand Pelotas

Source: *(UFPel, 2017a).*

The chosen brand was announced by the local government during the celebration of Pelotas' 205th anniversary.

4. RESULTS AND DISCUSSION

The process of selecting a brand for the municipality began based on the demand produced by the local government through the tourism management agency in Pelotas. This is the first initiative in developing a brand for the city. Creating a territorial brand linked to the Fenadoce festival was the strategy adopted. Due to this strategy, the slogan of the Pelotas brand emphasized the process of local historical formation. The article published on the website of Rádio Universidade da UFPel highlights, right from the first line, the purpose of the brand proposal "[...] to be used for commercial, institutional and tourist purposes, without being linked to governments, to identify the City" (UFPel, 2017a). The process of developing a brand was collaborative (RU, 2017). A press release issued by Radio UFPel, brought a collaborative approach, which declared that "[...] it was the form of creation, of collective construction among the group [...]. It was very enriching [...]" (UFPel, 2017a; 2017b). During the 205th anniversary festivities of Pelotas, the leading news release (DM, 2017) contains the headline [...] disclosure of the choice of the visual identity of the city". That text began with: "A brand to represent Pelotas and its people, regardless of government." With these comments, the Mayor announced the contest's outcome, sponsored by City Hall, and was open for voting (DM, 2017). The press release's presentation shows that the selected brand represents the "[...] concept of diversity and sharing, and the proposal seeks to look to the future without neglecting the past." The emphasis on the use of 'Pel' as a graphic "[...] element brings a close relationship with Pelotas, framing his daily life and embracing his facets. The brand does not have to tell stories, but to give an idea of that place" (UFPel, 2017a; 2017b).

In the text published by Caminhos da Zona Sul blog (2017), the *Sou + Pel* brand was reported as a new identification symbol of the city, next to the official anthem and coat of arms. The brand remains a unifying symbol of the city's identification. Also, the government or private initiative appropriates the brand, which is an institutional and a tourism brand (Caminhos da Zona Sul, 2017). This intention is corroborated at the end of the publication when the school uniforms will incorporate the brand and the recommendation to use in other articles, such as accessories, souvenirs, and signs.

Figure 5. Pelotas brand application in municipal schools.

In 2019, from the resources destined by the Ministry of Tourism, four porticos were created located in the accesses to the town (PMP, 2019) (Figure 6).

Figure 6. Porticos of Pelotas

Source: Revista News (2020)
https://revistanews.com.br/2020/01/07/pelotas-ganha-novo-portico-de-entrada-no-simoes-lopes/

These constructions highlighted the Pelotas brand. The location next to the city accesses aims to appeal to tourists (PMP, 2019). However, in the April 25, 2020, news, only a single gantry was installed among the four planned. The local government and the press attended the news opening. Among the speeches recorded is that of the government, reiterating this project's conclusion: They will brand the city's entrance and attract the attention of tourists (Revista News, 2020).

Regarding social networks, there are two profiles: Facebook - *Marca Cidade de Pelotas* and another one on Instagram – *Soumaispel* (Figure 7).

Figure 7. Facebook Sou+Pel

During the *Sou+Pel* brand contest, there were two social media profiles. Although their latest updates are still available, they date back to the day the contest closed in 2017. However, social media serves and has served the purpose of referencing and documenting parts of Sou+Pel's design, development, and applications. In the official social media profile of this brand, organized and maintained by the municipal tourism administration, there were brand elements in posts promoting local events and tourist attractions. It was also possible to note that the colors used harmonized with the proposal of the *Sou+Pel* brand.

4.1. Analysis Pelotas Brand Process

The demand generated by the tourism sector of the local government has led to the construction of a top-down brand merged minimally in a bottom-up process. Also, network socials noticed the involvement of expert actors (local universities with courses focused on design, publicity, and advertising) and civil society (internet voting). We realized that it was not the first time that a hybrid process was used in the construction of a territorial brand (top-down with bottom-up) in Brazil. In 2012-2013, the city of Porto Alegre, the capital of the State of Rio Grande did Sul, in Brazil, created a similar process (Almeida, 2018), using the same process of building a territorial brand. In a top-down approach, greater importance comes to how the local public authorities perceive and appropriate the territory and the interests involved. In the legitimacy of the bottom-up process, the opposite is accurate, and the company would be most interested in building this brand, including proposing its creation.

We observe that the social actors of the territorial brand come from hybrid processes in Pelotas and Porto Alegre. Without a specific vocabulary, this process was called territorial brand middle-up-down. It is, therefore, a hybrid process where territorial marks are present, involving, to different degrees, a set of social actors that goes beyond the issuing actor. Besides, three perspectives mentioned by Almeida (2018) are confirmed. The first is the presence of power relations interposed in the persuasive discourse of the territorial brand. The second is a specific ecosystem of social actors involved in territorial brand production. The third perspective is that it is a hybrid process (top-down and bottom-up). In this third perspective, the contribution of this proposed study complements Almeida's (2018) view of the brand's middle-up-down territorial nomenclature.

The brand Pelotas used the strategy of linking a local historical fact (salted flower) to the brand slogan. In doing so, the social actors who fostered the territorial brand productive process included two speeches. Therefore, one linked to local historical formation is unquestionable and justifies the brand's creation before civil society, highlighting aspects of the territory. And another discourse, which is hidden or subliminal, exposes the interests of the actors that emit the brand. In the article by Rádio UFPel (2017a), these speeches became evident when it appears that [...] it was the form of creation, of collective construction among the group [...]. It was very enriching [...]. The Pelotas brand was a technical creation of local universities that met a demand from the local government. The construction was collective in that sense. However, civil society was only in the last phase of creating the Pelotas brand, in which there was an internet vote for two brand options. It is also a strategy common to the marketing universe in which the consumer audience decides on something (Almeida, 2015). In the case of territorial brands, we observed that this strategy was adapted and inserted in its production process to corroborate with minimal civil society participation, justifying the brand's creation and acceptance by more social actors.

4.2. Analysis Disclosure of the Brand Pelotas

To confirm that society is present in a brand of a territorial nature, it usually uses a local event. It happened with the city of Porto Alegre, where the City Hall announced the creation of the brand during the festivities of the host cities chosen for the 2014 World Cup, a sporting event of global magnitude. However, Pelotas followed the same path at a local event while celebrating Pelotas' 205th anniversary. In the media release, the advertising and marketing appeal referred to the choice of the city's visual identity and a brand that would represent the city, the citizens, and the government. The speech promoted in 2017 culminated not yet with the demand to create a brand (which would justify a collective construction in a bottom-up process) but with the opening of the voting of one of the two brands previously chosen by the Municipality of Pelotas (top-down approach). At the height of this event, a new local government discourse emerged based on diversity and sharing. The proposal sought to look to the future without neglecting the past. The emphasis on the use of 'Pel' as a graphic element brings a close relationship with Pelotas, framing his daily life and welcoming these facets. The brand does not have to tell stories but give an idea of that place (UFPel, 2017a). Contradictory to the brand's concept linked to that place's narrative, the flower of salt. In the speech of the government, provided by the Mayor, one wonders what it would be like to give an idea of that place. In this sense, the concept refers to the positioning of a class or group of social actors, or it can even refer to a unique position.

The said speech by the Mayor of Pelotas also corroborates the presence of power relations in the territory; therefore, the territorial brand terminology is appropriate. We also confirm that it is an ecosystem of territorial branding from a specific production process anchored in persuasive discourses adapted from the universe of trademarks (Almeida, 2018). In this case, the social actors who created the Sou+Pel brand do not see the city as a place where proximity ties are evident, justifying Anholt's (2007) brand terminology. Power relations (established and under construction) define and delimit the city of Pelotas, as mentioned by Raffestin (1993).

Are contained past and present in the city of Pelotas brand positioning. *Sou+Pel*, the brand's slogan, sought to reinforce the identification of the people who live in that space to unify the town through the brand. The presence of the territorial brand was also confirmed, in Almeida's perspective (2018), as it encompassed other nomenclatures linked to the territory, such as place-brand, an institutional brand of the city, and the tourist brand of Pelotas. Creating a specific decree, making Sou+Pel a lifetime brand, without considering it a government brand but a brand of the local society, came from a top-down process. The Mayor revealed his intentional speech when he announced that the Pelotas brand would be on the school uniforms of all municipal schools and on the facade of public buildings.

4.3. Analysis of Recent Years 2019 - 2020

The brand created in 2017 showed an inevitable abandonment in its management (place branding) in the last two years (2019-2020), is even difficult to find news about the Pelotas brand. The scenario shows what Almeida (2018) had already seen in his studies that minting a territorial brand and managing a territorial brand are distinct processes. The management of a brand of this nature refers to a continuous process called place branding (Anholt, 2007), which corroborates that there are different terminologies: place branding, place-brand, and territorial brand. Place branding is not the same as running a government. The situation becomes evident in the case of the Porto Alegre brand in 2014 (Almeida, 2018) and similarly in the case of the Pelotas brand in 2017.

The disclosure that the Pelotas brand will be present in the city's access doors demonstrated the brand's minimal presence in 2019, referring to a weakened place branding process. At no point did the researchers find a survey that catered to the perception of this specific audience (tourists) and the relationship between Flor de Sal (which would be the one for those not from Pelotas) and *Sou+Pel*. According to Almeida (2018), when the idea of territorial branding focused on regional development is not understood, it is marketing or advertising actions linked, forcibly, to a particular space through a brand, referring to a logo and not to the brand itself.

When the Mayor of Pelotas announced that the city portico [...] would mark the entrance to the city and attract the attention of tourists (Revista News, 2020), the presence of power relations and persuasive discourses was again *in loco*. The lectures of a brand demand repetition over time; therefore, time is absorbed and naturalized by the target audience. When the Pelotas brand does not use this maxim of advertising and marketing, it reveals incomprehension about what a brand is and its management (place branding).

4.4. Analysis of Pelotas Brand Social Networks

Although the Pelotas brand exists on social networks (Facebook and Instagram), the latest updates date from 2017, confirming the brand's neglect by the same government that created it. The exposed situation signals that the social networks of the Pelotas city brand met three records (objectives): the registration of the brand contest, the registration of the brand's production process, and the roster that it is the first brand for the city. Meanwhile, the brand was on Pelotas' official tourism profile on Facebook through posts and visual identity with the Sou+Pel brand in 2019 and 2020. At the same time, there was no mention of the Pelotas brand concept or strategy (known and adopted in market brands) to establish the position of the city brand.

4.5. Analysis of Sou+Pel Brand Positioning

The investigation confirmed the existence of interposed power relations under construction in Pelotas. The tourism department proposed and developed a brand for the town, and the municipal management must approve its use. Although this exposes the top-down process, it is also a regular practice of marketing brands regarding the care of the correct application of the brand. Here, care was observed, even if technical, with the city brand, which revealed that the knowledge of the place branding and destination branding process is still minimal and cannot be just a technicality of the territorial brand. Also, an ecosystem of brands was found, revealing a specific set of actors who discussed, to different degrees, the city's brand, confirming Almeida's studies (2018). The brand includes local public authorities (municipal administration, tourism secretariat, city council, tourism council), universities, and civil society. Each actor was present in the discussion of the brand, however, at different times and equally with varying degrees of participation.

The practices led to a productive brand process in a middle-up-down format in which power relations. These relationships have a top-down structure not only in public management but also in the specialized actor who was part of creating the Pelotas brand, universities. The Pelotas brand contest involved only higher education courses from participating institutions, excluding possible undergraduate initiatives. Furthermore, in the brand voting stage, the choice of the means of disclosure prioritized online voting through the city hall website, with only a single digital totem available for in-person voting. Although the internet is a popular medium in contemporary times, it does not encompass the entire population of Pelotas or Brazil. The territorial brand situation has distanced the brand and community, making it difficult for those living there to take ownership.

Another point to note is that the Pelotas brand, and its creation and approval process, also considered the historical heritage of blacks in that space. The history of beef jerky and the sweet of Pelotas comes from a more privileged local elite. In this sense, the criticism is the presence of a less favorable class and classes more distant from the city center that possibly did not identify themselves so much with the *Sou+Pel* brand. Here it is interesting to debate and investigate how blacks living in the city feel represented in the Pelotas brand. The fact that the actors issuing the brand referred to the flower of salt (salt = white color) may indicate that in territorial brands, there may be, subliminally, ethnic distinctions.

Further reinforces the power relations contained in a brand of a territorial nature. Besides, involvement and experiences based on local cuisine can contribute to tourist loyalty to local products and the destination (Di-Clemente et al., 2019) and the maintenance of the territorial brand. In this sense, Fenadoce, the largest local popular party, plays an essential role in regional tourism, extending this role to the territorial brand.

Thus, there is a complexity of relationships and elements that make up the brand of Pelotas, establishing a certain status as a tourist destination in the State of Rio Grande do Sul, Brazil. One of the positions is maintaining the tourist value that promotes an elite culture. The *Sou+Pel* brand, although it includes historical-cultural cuts, does not cover the totality of identities present in that territory (excluding ethnicities and cultures). This scenario is in line with what Almeida (2018; 2020) mentioned: a brand will always demand choices and cuts regardless of whether it is market or territorial, which happens precisely because of the dynamics of the brands: simplified message, tangible and intangible selections, the definition of the target audience (which is distinct from consumer audience), presence of a persuasive speech, use of the media (means of communication) as a means of strategic branding. Even if it is a territorial brand, the primary or fundamental nature of the brand itself is maintained. What happens are adaptations to an already consolidated dynamic, leading to a management that is still not well understood in Brazil by those who create territorial brands or manage a brand through the place branding process.

5. CONCLUSION

Throughout this study, we investigated in depth how a territorial brand can position a tourist destination, focusing on the "Sou + Pel" territorial brand of the city of Pelotas, Brazil. Our research sought to answer the fundamental questions of how a local tourist destination can position itself as a brand and how tourism plays a crucial role in the formation, implementation, and dissemination of territorial brands. However, our findings go beyond the borders of Pelotas and have implications that transcend the city, contributing to a broader understanding of destination branding processes and their relationship with tourism.

The study proposal was met and allowed to examine how a territorial brand positions a tourism destination. Strategic marketing tools for tourism are in government programs and companies focusing on travel and tourism marketing.

Finding research emphasizes the role of tourism in territorial branding processes and creating the reputation and identities of cities and regions. In the process of selecting territorial brands in cities and towns are some technical repetitions: a top-down process mixed with a bottom-up approach; the use of local events to create the territorial brand; misunderstanding about the place branding process; and linking the territorial brand to the gastronomy of the tourism destination.

The theoretical contributions address the complexity of the investigated themes, destination branding, place branding, and territorial brand. The contributions of this study are multifaceted. Firstly, we highlight the complexity of the topics investigated, which include destination branding, place branding and territorial branding. In addition, we identified key elements in the process of selecting territorial brands, including an approach that combines top-down and bottom-up aspects, the use of local events to build the territorial brand and challenges in understanding the place branding process.

Destinations may also reinforce or build a positioning by using the territorial brand. Tourism is one of the social players involved in creating, developing, and promoting territorial brands, but it is not the only one. In the context of tourism, territorial brands adopt characteristics focused on the economic growth of destinations. The disclosure in the top-down format guarantees its maintenance and existence due to the Municipal Decree created.

Thus, there are certain places, such as Brazil, where the brand of the place is still embryonic, necessary to "force" the permanence of the brand in the local context. The territorial brand led from the feeling of local belonging. Still, due to the lack of understanding of destination branding, the government forces the brand to remain active in this reality. The reality of the city of Pelotas can reflect the existence of other territorial brands, and this study contributes to exposing this.

Our findings have significant theoretical, social and practical implications. Theoretically, our study broadens the understanding of how territorial brands are developed and how they relate to tourism. In addition, we highlight the importance of a more unified and precise approach to defining and applying the concepts of territorial branding, destination and place. On a social level, our findings highlight the relevance of tourism in the process of building the reputation and identity of cities and regions. We also underline the need for a deeper and more collaborative understanding between the different actors involved in creating and promoting territorial brands, including governments and tourism companies.

From a practical point of view, our findings have direct implications for tourism marketing strategies, emphasizing the importance of alignment with existing territorial brands. In addition, our research highlights the need for public policies that support the development and maintenance of territorial brands, especially in places where these brands are still in the early stages of formation, as is the case in many regions of Brazil. Therefore, our study offers valuable insights for academics, tourism professionals and policymakers who wish to better understand the role of tourism in the context of territorial brands.

The study's shortcoming was that it was limited to cities in the interior. We propose broadening the study to include the realities of other small towns. Additionally, it is recommended to explore the impact of the hotel industry on the development of Pelotas' territorial brand, aiming to better understand its influence within the context of destination branding.

Local events in cities and towns help to build the territorial brand and scope. This understanding supports the study's goal of evaluating how a territorial brand positions a tourism destination. The conclusion confirms the use of the territorial brand linked to cultural studies and regional development, with tourism also included in these fields of knowledge.

In addition, it is important to note that local events in cities and municipalities play a fundamental role in building the territorial brand and expanding its influence. This understanding further strengthens the aim of this study to assess how a territorial brand positions a tourist destination. By recognizing the interconnection between local events, territorial branding and tourism, our research offers a holistic view of destination promotion strategies. Therefore, we conclude that territorial branding, when integrated into the areas of cultural study and regional development, combined with tourism, proves to be a powerful resource for boosting the economic growth and cultural identity of tourist destinations, establishing itself as an invaluable tool for the sustainable development of communities and regions.

REFERENCES

Abankina, T. (2013). Regional development models using cultural heritage resources. *International Journal of Culture, Tourism and Hospitality Research*, 7(1), 3–10. DOI: 10.1108/17506181311301318

Almeida, G. G. F. (2015), "*A identidade territorial gaúcha no branding das marcas regionais: caso da marca da cerveja Polar.*" Master's thesis. University of Santa Cruz do Sul, Brazil.

Almeida, G. G. F. (2018), "*Marca territorial como produto cultural no âmbito do Desenvolvimento Regional: o caso de Porto Alegre, RS, Brasil.*" Doctoral's thesis. University of Santa Cruz do Sul, Brazil.

Almeida, G. G. F., Almeida, P., Cardoso, L., & Lima Santos, L. (2023). Uses and Functions of the Territorial Brand over Time: Interdisciplinary Cultural-Historical Mapping. *Sustainability (Basel)*, 15(8), 6448. DOI: 10.3390/su15086448

Anholt, S. (2007). *Competitive identity: the new Brand management for nations, cities, and regions*. Palgrave Macmillan. DOI: 10.1057/9780230627727

Anholt, S. (2008). Place branding: Is it marketing, or isn't it? *Place Branding and Public Diplomacy*, 4(1), 1–6. DOI: 10.1057/palgrave.pb.6000088

Beerli, A., & Martín, J. D. (2004). Factors influencing destination image. *Annals of Tourism Research*, 31(3), 657–681. DOI: 10.1016/j.annals.2004.01.010

Bookman, S. (2013). Brands and Urban Life: Specialty Coffee, Consumers, and the Co-creation of Urban Café Sociality. *Space and Culture*, 17(1), 85–99. DOI: 10.1177/1206331213493853

Bouchard, M. E. (2021). Popular Brazilian Portuguese through capoeira: From local to global. *Etnográfica (Lisboa)*, 25(1), 95–116. DOI: 10.4000/etnografica.8751

Caminhos da Zona Sul. *Marca de Pelotas promove a cidade*. (2017, July, 13). https://bit.ly/2H9bmkC

Cardoso, L., Dias, F., de Araújo, A. F., & Andrés Marques, M. I. (2019). A destination imagery processing model: Structural differences between dream and favorite destinations. *Annals of Tourism Research*, 74, 81–94. DOI: 10.1016/j.annals.2018.11.001

Charters, S., & Spielmann, N. (2014). Characteristics of strong territorial brands: The case of champagne. *Journal of Business Research*, 67(7), 1461–1467. DOI: 10.1016/j.jbusres.2013.07.020

Cleave, E., & Arku, G. (2020). Place branding and growth machines: Implications for spatial planning and urban development. *Journal of Urban Affairs*, •••, 1–18.

Crespi-Vallbona, M., & Mascarilla-Miró, O. (2020). Wine lovers: Their interests in tourist experiences. *International Journal of Culture, Tourism and Hospitality Research*, 14(2), 239–258. DOI: 10.1108/IJCTHR-05-2019-0095

De Almeida, G. G. F. (2023). Territorial Brand in Regional Development: Interdisciplinary Discussions. *Encyclopedia*, 3(3), 870–886. DOI: 10.3390/encyclopedia3030062

Di-Clemente, E., Hernández-Mogollón, J. M., & Campón-Cerro, A. M. (2019). Tourists' involvement and memorable food-based experiences as new determinants of behavioral intentions towards typical products. *Current Issues in Tourism*, •••, 1–14.

Farhat, R. R. (2018). What Brand Is This Place? Place-Making and the Cultural Politics of Downtown Revitalization. *Space and Culture*, 22(1), 34–49. DOI: 10.1177/1206331217751778

Fenadoce. (n.d). Retrieved April 5, 2022, from https://bit.ly/3celfZF

Garner, B., & Ayala, C. (2018). Regional tourism at the farmers' market: Consumers' preferences for local food products. *International Journal of Culture, Tourism and Hospitality Research*, 13(1), 37–54. DOI: 10.1108/IJCTHR-07-2018-0095

Gartner, W. C. (2014). Brand equity in a tourism destination. *Place Branding and Public Diplomacy*, 10(2), 1–9. DOI: 10.1057/pb.2014.6

Gerosa, A. and Tartari, M. (2021), "The Bottom-up Place Branding of a Neighborhood: Analyzing a Case of Selective Empowerment." *Space and Culture*, July.

Hall, C. M. (2008). Servicescapes, Designscapes, Branding, and The Creation of Place-Identity: South of Litchfield, Christchurch. *Journal of Travel & Tourism Marketing*, 25(3-4), 233–250. DOI: 10.1080/10548400802508101

Jerez, M. R. (2023). Tourism marketing of the Autonomous Communities of Spain to promote gastronomy as part of their destination branding. *International Journal of Gastronomy and Food Science*, 32, 1–11, 100727. DOI: 10.1016/j.ijgfs.2023.100727

Jin, X., & Cheng, M. (2020). Communicating mega events on Twitter: Implications for destination marketing. *Journal of Travel & Tourism Marketing*, 37(6), 739–755. DOI: 10.1080/10548408.2020.1812466

Jornal Diário da Manhã. *Pelotenses conhecem a nova marca da cidade*. (2017, July, 13). https://bit.ly/2Ef2WHm

Källström, L., & Ekelund, C. (2016). What can a municipality offer to its residents? Value propositions and interactions in a place context. *International Journal of Culture, Tourism and Hospitality Research*, 10(1), 24–37. DOI: 10.1108/IJCTHR-05-2015-0040

Kapferer, J.-N. (2004). Marcas: Capital de empresa. *The Bookman*.

Kaplan, M. D. (2010). Branding Places: Applying Brand Personality Concept to Cities. *European Journal of Marketing*, 44(9-10), 1286–1304. DOI: 10.1108/03090561011062844

Kaplanidou, K., & Vogt, C. (2007). The Interrelationship between Sports Events and Destination Image and Sport Tourists' Behaviours. *Journal of Sport & Tourism*, 12(3-4), 183–206. DOI: 10.1080/14775080701736932

Kasapi, I., & Cela, A. (2017). Destination branding: A review of the city branding literature. *Mediterranean Journal of Social Sciences*, 8(4), 129–142. DOI: 10.1515/mjss-2017-0012

Kavaratzis, M. (2012). From 'necessary evil' to necessity: Stakeholders' involvement in place branding. *Journal of Place Management and Development*, 5(1), 7–19. DOI: 10.1108/17538331211209013

Kavaratzis, M., & Hatch, M. J. (2013). The dynamics of place brands: An identity-based approach to place branding theory. *Marketing Theory*, 13(1), 69–86. DOI: 10.1177/1470593112467268

Kotler, P., & Gertner, D. (2002). Country as brand, product and beyond: A place marketing and brand management perspective. *Journal of Brand Management*, 9(4-5), 249–261. DOI: 10.1057/palgrave.bm.2540076

Kumar, V., & Kaushik, A. K. (2020). Does experience affect engagement? Role of destination brand engagement in developing brand advocacy and revisit intentions. *Journal of Travel & Tourism Marketing*, 37(3), 332–346. DOI: 10.1080/10548408.2020.1757562

Lin, Y. C. (2020). Measuring authenticity through spatial metaphors: How close are tourists to the back regions? *Current Issues in Tourism*, •••, 1–15.

Lodge, C. (2002). Success and failure: The brand stories of two countries. *Journal of Brand Management*, 9(4), 372–384. DOI: 10.1057/palgrave.bm.2540084

Lorenzini, E., Calzati, V., & Giudici, P. (2011). Territorial brands for tourism development: A statistical analysis on the Marche region. *Annals of Tourism Research*, 38(2), 540–560. DOI: 10.1016/j.annals.2010.10.008

Mikulić, J., Miličević, K., & Krešić, D. (2016). The relationship between brand strength and tourism intensity: Empirical evidence from the EU capital cities. *International Journal of Culture, Tourism and Hospitality Research*, 10(1), 14–23. DOI: 10.1108/IJCTHR-06-2015-0054

Miles, M. B., Huberman, A. M., & Saldana, J. (2020). *Qualitative Data Analysis - A Methods Sourcebook. 4.* Sage.

Nachimias, D., & Nachimias, C. F. (1987). *Research methods in the social sciences*. St. Martin's Press.

Pike, S., & Mason, R. (2010). Destination competitiveness through the lens of brand positioning: The case of Australia's Sunshine Coast. *Current Issues in Tourism*, 14(2), 169–182. DOI: 10.1080/13683501003797523

Prefeitura Municipal de Pelotas. "Ministério do Turismo garante verba para quatro pórticos em Pelotas" (2019, May, 9) https://bit.ly/2EcUM28

Rather, R. A. (2019). Customer experience and engagement in tourism destinations: The experiential marketing perspective. *Journal of Travel & Tourism Marketing*, 37(1), 15–32. DOI: 10.1080/10548408.2019.1686101

Revista News. "Pelotas ganha novo pórtico de entrada no Simões Lopes" (2020, April, 25) https://bit.ly/3kwpnY5

Ries, A., & Trout, J. (1991). *Posicionamento: a batalha pela mente*. Pioneira.

Rinaldi, C., & Beeton, S. (2015). Success in Place Branding: The Case of the Tourism Victoria Jigsaw Campaign. *Journal of Travel & Tourism Marketing*, 32(5), 622–638. DOI: 10.1080/10548408.2014.953288

Sampaio, S., Vidal, F., & Lourenço, I. (2021). Desafios do "turístico" na atualidade: Uma introdução surpreendida por uma pandemia. *Etnográfica (Lisboa)*, 25(1), 119–129. DOI: 10.4000/etnografica.9851

Saraniemi, S., & Komppula, R. (2017). The development of a destination brand identity: A story of stakeholder collaboration. *Current Issues in Tourism*, 31(17), 1116–1132.

Universidade Federal de Pelotas. "Concurso para a marca de Pelotas" (2017a, July, 7) https://bit.ly/3c8fHjx

Universidade Federal de Pelotas. "Votação para a marca de Pelotas" (2017b, July) https://bit.ly/3mtU7KN

Van Assche, K., Beunen, R., & Oliveira, E. (2020). Spatial planning and place branding: Rethinking relations and synergies. *European Planning Studies*, 28(7), 1274–1290. DOI: 10.1080/09654313.2019.1701289

Vela, E.. (2017). The visual landscape as a key element of the local brand. *Journal of Place Management and Development*, 10(1), 23–44. DOI: 10.1108/JPMD-09-2016-0060

Wong, P. P. W. (2015). Role of components of destination competitiveness in the relationship between customer-based brand equity and destination loyalty. *Current Issues in Tourism*, 21(5), 504–528. DOI: 10.1080/13683500.2015.1092949

WTO. World Tourism Organisation (2009), "Handbook on Tourism Destination Branding." Europe-World Tourism Organization.

Yin, R. K. (2015). Estudo de caso: Planejamento e métodos. *The Bookman*.

Chapter 12
Tourists' Expectations-Based Countryside Walking Tourism Management

Danka Milojković
 https://orcid.org/0000-0002-4434-9576
Singidunum University, Belgrade, Serbia

Snežana Štetić
 https://orcid.org/0000-0002-1137-4441
The College of Tourism, Belgrade, Serbia & Balkan Network of Tourism Experts, Belgrade, Serbia

Igor Trišić
 https://orcid.org/0000-0002-6497-9276
Faculty of Geography, University of Belgrade, Serbia

EXECUTIVE SUMMARY

Countryside walking tourism contributes to sustainable rural socio-economic development. The purpose of the research is to observe the possibility of managing countryside walking tourism in a village according to the expectations of tourists during their travel and vacation in rural destinations. The research methodology was based on a descriptive statistical analysis using the survey for gathering data from the rural tourism demand market, and the VICE model for sustainable tourism for getting conclusions. The key result indicated that countryside walking tourism management should consider the tourists' expectations related to the clean environment. It preserved nature as the most influencing factor in the choice of a walking tour in

DOI: 10.4018/979-8-3693-1548-4.ch012

rural destinations, and at the same time, it is more important to the female than to the male population. The authors recommend incorporating countryside walking tourism into walking strategies as a part of rural and tourism development policies.

INTRODUCTION

It is obvious that not every area is suitable for tourism that natural and anthropogenic resources are limited and that negative climate changes in the future may affect the further reduction of the land for tourism development. The question is whether there is enough ecologically quality space at all. The ecological component of the countryside is perhaps the key link in the chain of sustainable development. Mass tourism uses more and more space for its development, reducing the possibility of its protection. The question of possibilities for increasing the area suitable for tourism development is constantly present. That is why this paper studies a type of specific form of tourism, the development of which requires a healthy environment and a well-organized nature.

Tourism, as an initiator of sustainable development, contributes to each Sustainable Development Goal (SDG) (IISD, 2023; UNWTO, 2023a; Milojković et al., 2023a). The poverty reduction of tourism is led by government institutions according to government policies through stakeholders' networking focused on residents in less developed areas to participate in tourism activities (Gohori & van der Merwe, 2020; Butler et al., 2013; Moyo & Tichaawa, 2017; Lor et al., 2019; Azizpour & Fathizadeh, 2016), involving tourism to drive local socio-economic development, and creating employment opportunities (Milojković et al., 2023b; Njoya & Seetaram, 2018). To improve living standards, most countries develop cities forgetting rural areas (Milojković et al., 2023b; Liu & Li, 2017). Rural tourism arose as a response to the development of urban tourism to meet the needs of urban residents and tourists by using attractions such as rural and agricultural resources and providing recreation, health, and wellness services (Cawley & Gillmor, 2008; Royo, 2009; Gogonea & Zaharia, 2023). Rural tourism stimulates local economic development and growth, job creation, and overall social improvement, and becomes a crucial part of the rural economy (Milojković et al., 2023a; Su et al., 2022). The development of this form of tourism contributes to employment opportunities for the local community. This type of tourism creates economic, social, and ecological benefits, preserving the natural and cultural resources of rural settlements and influencing their sustainable development. In addition, it supports the synergy between urban and rural development due to rural revitalization (Sharpley & Vass, 2006; Huang et al., 2014).

Tourism can be developed based on the diversity of the area, the sedative and stimulating effects of the climate, the specificity of monuments, the authenticity of folklore, the uniqueness of gastronomy, as well as the existence of relics and endemics, etc. Activities, such as walking, horse riding, traditional food preparation, winemaking, and tasting, depending on the characteristics of the destination. These leisure activities contribute at the same time to both the creation of a special experience and the generation of an important economic impact (Belliggiano et al., 2021, Cioban, 2022). In small and medium-sized cities, a key role of walking is to represent environmentally friendly travel, which is feasible by adapting the characteristics of walking tours and environments and increasing awareness of walking (Zhang et al., 2022). Walking promotes socio-economic development, and as a low-carbon way of travel contributes to environmental protection, and public health (Zhang et al., 2023). Walking provides physical, mental, social, and health benefits for people of almost all ages and capacities (Buehler & Pucher, 2023a; Buehler et al., 2011b; Buehler et al., 2020c). During the past three decades, it has recorded great progress and its key role in urban areas is to promote sustainable transport systems, liveable cities, and healthy people (Buehler & Pucher, 2023a). For the realization of walking as a tourist-recreational activity, obstacles such as insecurity and poor infrastructure should be removed (Gehl, 2013, pp. 91-104; Hass-Klau, 2014, pp. 281-284; Tranter & Tolley, 2020, pp. 121-134; Speck, 2012, pp. 93-12; Buehler & Pucher, 2023d).

Since space is the basis of tourist movements, and modern tourists increasingly desire preserved nature and authentic countryside as a whole, tourism should be the driving force or guardian of such potentials. People visit a destination consider satisfies their needs (Chhetri et al., 2004). The new type of multi-motivational tourist expects to consume different tourism services and infrastructures in the tourism resort forcing local governments and businesses to develop new tourist products (Tsartas et al., 2015). According to UNWTO (2023b) in the future development of tourism, one of the tourism products is sustainable rural tourism due to its great potential for stimulating local economic growth. Countryside walking tourism, as a form of rural tourism, due to low-costs investment and high benefits in improving peoples' physical and mental well-being, contributes to strategic recovery and development of rural tourism (Milojković et al., 2023a). The management of countryside walking tourism based on researching tourists' expectations is one of the significant directions for achieving sustainable rural tourism development. The purpose of this research is to observe the possibility of managing countryside walking tourism in a village according to the expectations of tourists during their travel and vacation in rural destinations. The success of village tourism is the synergy between environmental activities and tourism (Gjedrem & Log, 2020). Revival of historic landscapes and the cultivation of indigenous races and varieties are valuable for sustainable food production, functional biodiversity, and countryside tourism development is a source of income important for supporting ongoing village restoration initiatives (Gjedrem & Log, 2020). The tourist's expectation is related to the tourism service that encounters the needs of tourists' visits. Based on research that the expectation is significantly correlated with satisfaction and revisiting intention (Kung, 2018), by meeting expectations, tourist satisfaction and a higher degree of revisiting intention will be gained. By researching the expectations of tourists, the countryside walking tourism management can design the tourism products to more fully meet or exceed the expectations of tourists (Boonpart & Suvachart, 2014), and satisfy them to achieve a competitive advantage.

Tourism can be developed based on the diversity of the area, the specificity of monuments, the authenticity of folklore, the uniqueness of gastronomy, the climate characteristics, as well as the existence of relics and endemics, etc. The goal of tourist destination management is to improve protection and develop tourism in a way that does not damage nature (Trišić et al., 2023b). This means that tourism must be developed on a sustainable basis. Considering that tourism has, sometimes, negative sociocultural impacts, the implementation of tourism development strategies (Trišić et al., 2023c; Ahmed, 2023) and policies based on sustainability that promote both respect for environmental resources and increase local awareness of the ethical role of rural tourism (Belliggiano et al., 2021) are important. Because of that, the concept of tourism carrying capacity and sustainable development should be included in the planning for tourism initiated by governments (O'Reilly, 1986; Mirea & Nistoreanu, 2021).

LITERATURE REVIEW

The benefits of walking nature are aesthetic impressions, stress relief, and healthy movement (Riis et al., 2020; Hartig & Staats, 2006). Sports activities, running, swimming in the river and lakes, orientation, and beautiful scenery are a special enjoyment for tourists. In addition to walking in the forest, among the activities important for health are picking forest fruits, medicinal herbs, and mushrooms (Donis & Straupe, 2011; Janeczko et al., 2019; Slusariuc, 2020; Thiele et al., 2020; Wood et al., 2022). Tourists' readiness to walk includes different age groups from teenagers to elders and heterogeneous gender groups. According to the research on customer behaviour by Tomić et al. (2019), differences in the age of tourists are statistically significant concerning their activity preferences in a tourist destination. Elderly travellers generally expressed greater post-satisfaction judgments compared to their younger counterparts (Oh et al., 2002). The research on the influence of marital status on customer-centric measures of Haverila et al. (2023) showed that single individuals exhibited the least favourable scores in customer-centric measures, while those in partnerships with children displayed the highest scores. This pattern also extended to perceptions of value for money (Haverila et al., 2023). In addition, it must be taken into account that the use of different landscapes for recreational purposes often leads to the overloading of some popular destinations, while other destinations have low exploitation (Mao et al., 2021). In this research, the behaviour of tourists is investigated according to the choice of destination, departure time, and mobility (Mao et al., 2021; Trišić et al., 2023a). Walking is not a sport; it is a recreational activity (Chhetri et al., 2004). According to research, walkers usually easily walk for 2 to 3 hours before returning to the point of departure (LEADER II, 2001). According to the same research, the main trends in walking are related to the presence of women, who make up 50% of walkers in Germany, and significantly more in France. Also, an important part is family walks, as well as walking for people over 50 years old. This includes hikers and mountaineers with medium and higher income levels (LEADER II, 2002). Exploring different influences on the type, time, and length of the walk, different reasons appear. Men walk more on weekends, when there are no work responsibilities, while the female population depends on household duties, taking care of children and their role in the family (married, single, widowed, etc. (Han et al., 2023). For students, walking represents physical activity maintaining healthy body weight, supporting community belonging, stimulating getting better grades, timely studies and graduation, lower stress, and less depression (King et al., 2020; Prial et al., 2023; Hajrasouliha, 2019). State-supported countryside walking tourism contributes to the promotion of safety, tourists' needs for outdoor activities, environmental protection, and sustainable development. It is particularly significant due to the inclusion of the local population and the provision of authentic gastronomy services and traditional products (Milojković et al., 2023a). All this is important for the well-being of the rural population and their connection with tourists, as well as the direct involvement of the local community in the sustainable development of the destination. Tourists prefer an authentic local house and cuisine, and the services of a local tour guide, looking at a village as the epicentre of countryside walking tourism (Štetić & Šimičević, 2017, p.63). According to previous research, the age group from 26 to 35 years, prefers globally recognized destinations, and planned family trips and children's stays in the countryside and nature, while divorced people the possibility of consuming authentic gastronomy, wine, souvenirs, and textile items footwear are favourable (Milojković et al., 2023a). Families with four or more children rather choose the safer stay, better content, and more affordable prices for their countryside holiday (Milojković et al., 2023a). Based on tourists' needs for indoor and outdoor activities research, "the management of walking tourism should take into account the differences that exist concerning indoor and outdoor activities between tourists of gender, age, marital status, number of children, education, work status, and annual personal investment for tourist travel and vacation" (Milojković et al., 2023b, p.1).

From the tourist's point of view, the expectation and experience differ from individual to individual, but on the other side, the common thing is that the experience stays in a long-time memorable and remarkable (Larsen, 2007). In the tourism economy' aspect, the creation of the experience contributes to the creation of value from the collaboration between different actors and resources like local food products (Jensen & Prebensen, 2015; UNWTO, 2023c; Zhang et al., 2019). „Tourist resources represent the possibility, the potential for tourism development and the achievement of complementarity with other elements of a tourist destination" (Štetić & Trišić, 2018).

The widely accepted model, the VICE model, for sustainable tourism focuses on the environment as a central component of the model correlates with other components such as the local community, visitors, and the tourism industry presented in Figure 1 (Abdul-Rauf Abdul-Mugod, 2016; Szabó, 2015). Tourism destination stakeholders shifted focus from marketing and promotion to a strategic approach to destination management, and besides the influence of other elements of the VICE model, took into consideration tourists' expectations, perceptions, and needs as an influential factor outside the tourism industry's control (PATA, 2023; Niekerk & Coetzee, 2011).

Figure 1. The VICE model.

Source: The authors' editing is based on Abdul-Rauf Abdul-Mugod (2016) and Szabó (2015)

In this research, the main hypothesis was placed:

(H1) - A clean environment and healthy nature are the most influencing factors in the choice of a walking tour in rural destinations.

The following working hypotheses were set:

(H2) – A clean environment and healthy nature as a factor influencing the choice of a walking tour in rural destinations is more important for females than for males;
(H3) - There are differences in factors influencing the choice of a walking tour in rural destinations according to age, marital status, number of children, education, work status, and annual personal investment for tourist travel and vacation;
(H4) - Tourists are interested in learning how to prepare traditional food, trying old crafts during their vacation in the rural destination, and trying to grow plants or keep domestic animals on the property of an authentic household;

(H5) - Camping, and gathering fruits, mushrooms, or medicinal herbs in untouched nature are tourists' expectations during their travel and vacation;
(H6) - Visiting places famous for myths and legends, waterfalls, shales, caves, and cultural monuments are tourists' expectations during their travel and vacation;
(H7) - Using a carriage, bicycle, or horseback riding along with walking, and trying paragliding, caving, cliff climbing, skiing, Norwegian walking, and running, are tourists' expectations during their travel and vacation;
(H8) - Tourists prefer to make rather than buy authentic souvenirs on a tourist trip.

METHODS

The research intentions to study the quality of rural areas for the possibility of managing countryside walking tourism according to the expectations of tourists during their travel and vacations in rural destinations. The quantitative empirical research, supplemented by qualitative analysis, was conducted by content analysis, hypothetical-deductive, and statistical methods (Vuković & Štrbac, 2019, pp. 32-41). The authors developed a bilingual, English, and Serbian language, structured questionnaire with closed-ended multiple-choice questions. The case of the 'Va' Sentiero' project (Simeoni & De Crescenzo, 2019) was a model for the development of the questionnaire. The survey was online conducted focusing on academic and social networks. The questionnaire consisted of 40 questions divided into four sections:

1. Personal data of the respondent,
2. Information on the respondent's indoor and outdoor activities,
3. Information on the respondent's expectations during their travel and vacation,
4. Information on the funding of country walking tourism development.

This research was initiated by the author's previous work (Milojković et al., 2023a), and the factors that impact the interest of tourists in state-supported countryside walking tourism were examined. In that research, the most influential factors that affect the interests of tourists are safety, price, destination, and content (Milojković et al., 2023a), Among the mentioned factors, slightly more important factors for women were authentic food and beverages as well as traditional handmade products purchasing, interacting with the local population, and urban residents' well-being (Milojković et al., 2023a). In the second research paper (Milojković et al., 2023b), the data related to the questions from the first and third sections of the questionnaire were analysed to manage the sustainable development of the countryside and walking tourism, taking into consideration the indoor and outdoor needs of tourists during their travel and vacation.

The 467 electronic questionnaires, 420 in Serbian language and 47 in the English language were collected on the probabilistic sample from March 20, 2022, to May 2, 2022. A simple random was used for the research. This means that all members of the population have an equal chance of being selected. One of the advantages of a simple random sample is precisely that it does not require any knowledge of the population, while one of the disadvantages is that the sample does not have to be representative of all properties (sample size, population homogeneity, etc.), especially if it is not too large. Representative samples are difficult to obtain because they request surveys at the national or regional level. The sample was suitable and used for research purposes to gain insight into the current state or region of mind, and accordingly, the research results are significant. All gathered questionnaires were used for the research. The data were processed by SPSS software. The t-test and the Kruskal-Wallis H test were used for the precise indication of statistically significant differences according to demographic and socioeconomic variables. The collected data were matched through the VICE model which enables destination management through the interaction of tourists, the tourism industry, the local community, and the environment focusing on the profiles, demands, and expectations of the visitors (Hassan, 2020; Popesku, 2016), then processed to get conclusions and create modelling (Figure 2). The obtained data on the importance of the environment are essential for planning the countryside for the needs of tourism.

Figure 2. The linear sequential method of research development.

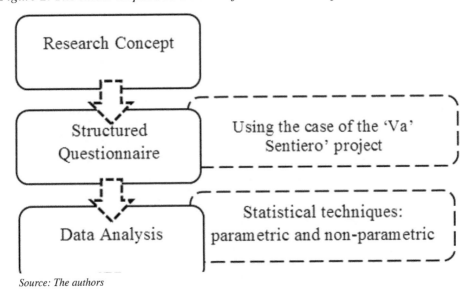

Source: The authors

The linear sequential method was used to manage the data whereby a sequential approach to research development begins at a systematic level and progresses through modelling, discussion, inference, and recommendations.

FINDINGS AND DISCUSSION

Walking tourism should develop activities based on natural values, the environment, rural landscapes, and marked roads and walking trails. On this occasion, the characteristics of potential users of walking tours must be taken into account and observed. To observe the possibility of managing countryside walking tourism in a village according to the expectations of tourists during their travel and vacation in rural destinations, 467 questionnaires were gathered by the random sampling method.

In addition to demographic and socio-economic characteristics, the structure of respondents is presented in Table 1.

Table 1. The structure of the respondents

Gender	Frequency	Percent
female	310	66.4
male	157	33.6
Total	467	100.0
Age	**Frequency**	**Percent**
<=25	82	17.6
26-35	54	11.6
36-45	119	25.5
46-55	128	27.4
>=56	84	18.0
Total	467	100.0
Marital status	**Frequency**	**Percent**
single	125	26.8
cohabitation	61	13.1
married	238	51.0
divorced	29	6.2
widow/widower	14	3.0
Total	467	100.0
Number of children	**Frequency**	**Percent**
0	182	39.0

continued on following page

Table 1. Continued

1	100	21.4
2	142	30.4
3	41	8.8
>=4	2	.4
Total	467	100.0

In the structure of respondents according to work status and education, the most numerous are the employed 280 (60.0%) and university-educated 310 (66.4%) respectively. Regarding work status, follow students 71 (15.2%), self-employed 46 (9.9%), unemployed and retired each group per 30 (6.4%), and other 10 (2.1%), and regarding education, follow respondents with secondary education 92 (19.7%), college 60 (12.8%), primary education 3 (0.6%), and without formal education 2 (0.4%). Based on the readiness of respondents to annually invest in tourist trips and vacations, the numerous respondents 180 (38.5%) were in the group who invested less than 500 euros, followed by 159 (34.0%) respondents who invested from 500 to 1,000 euros, and 128 (27.4%) respondents who invested more than 1,000 euros.

The research results decisively influence the choice of walking tours in rural destinations presented in Figure 3.

Figure 3. An overview of the factors influencing the choice of a walking tour in rural destinations.

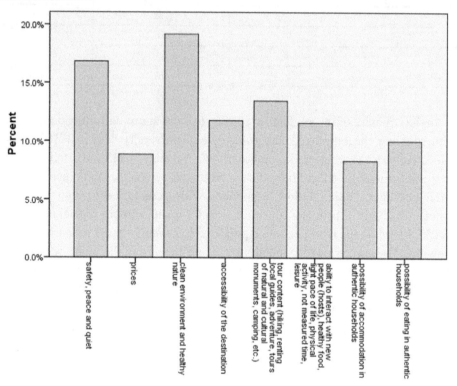

Source: The authors' calculations

The most frequent factor was "clean environment and healthy nature" (F3) supported by 296 (63.2%) respondents followed by activities: "safety, peace, and quiet" (F1) and "tour content (walking, renting local guides, adventure, tours of natural and cultural monuments, camping, etc." (F5) supported by 259 (55.5%) and 207 (44.3%) respondents respectively. In addition, the following activities were chosen by the respondents: "accessibility of the destination" (F4) 181 (38.8%), "ability to interact with new people (hosts), healthy food, the light pace of life, physical activity, not measured time, leisure" (F6) 178 (38.1%), "possibility of eating in authentic households" (F8) 154 (33.0%), "prices" (F2) 136 (29.1%), "possibility of accommodation in authentic households" (F7) 128 (27.4%). Asking the question about a clean environment and healthy nature, the authors want to see the level of awareness of tourists about the importance of a preserved environment. The results of descriptive statistics confirmed hypothesis H1 that the most influencing factor on the choice of a walking tour in rural destinations is a clean environment and healthy nature. This result also indicates a high level of awareness of nature conservation among walking tourism participants.

The research determined whether there are differences in the factors influencing the choice of a walking tour in rural destinations (Table 2).

Table 2. T-test and statistically significant differences by gender.

Factors influencing the choice of a walking tour in rural destinations	t-test for Equality of Means						
	t	df	Sig. (2-tailed)	Mean Difference	Std. Error Difference	95% Confidence Interval of the Difference	
						Lower	Upper
F1	2.37	308.38	0.018	0.12	0.05	0.02	0.21
F2	1.26	329.94	0.210	0.05	0.04	-0.03	0.14
F3	0.64	465.00	0.520	0.03	0.05	-0.06	0.12
F4	0.57	465.00	0.568	0.03	0.05	-0.07	0.12
F5	-0.28	465.00	0.782	-0.01	0.05	-0.11	0.08
F6	1.19	321.69	0.235	0.06	0.05	-0.04	0.15
F7	0.45	465.00	0.656	0.02	0.04	-0.07	0.11
F8	0.16	465.00	0.872	0.01	0.05	-0.08	0.10

Results of the t-test and Cohen's criteria for interpreting differences (Cohen, 1988) indicated small statistically significant differences for the factor F1 between females (M=0.59, SD=0.49) and males (M=0.48, SD=0.50), t(308.38)=2.37, p=0.02, Mean difference 0.12, 95% CI: 0.02 to 0.21, eta square=0.012, meaning that the gender difference explains only 1.2% of the variance of the factor F1; The results of the parametric technique t-test indicated existing small statistically significant differences in the opinion of female and male populations regarding the factor F1 that influence the choice of a walking tour in rural destinations, confirming the hypothesis H2. Factor F1 "safety, peace, and quiet" is more important for females than males. T-test did not indicate statistically significant differences in the opinion of female and male populations for other factors.

The research activities showed significant differences in the choice of a walking tour in rural destinations by the following grouping variables: age, marital status, number of children, education, work status, and annual personal investment for tourist travel and vacation (Table 3).

Table 3. Kruskal – Wallis test results.

	F1	F2	F3	F4	F5	F6	F7	F8
Factors influencing the choice of a walking tour in rural destinations: age								
Chi-Square	9,146	16,015	3,369	9,957	12,005	5,583	12,085	3,877
df	4	4	4	4	4	4	4	4
Asymp. Sig.	,058	,003	,498	,041	,017	,232	,017	,423
Factors influencing the choice of a walking tour in rural destinations: marital status								
Chi-Square	6,852	1,395	1,200	7,467	3,766	3,154	8,990	6,560
df	4	4	4	4	4	4	4	4
Asymp. Sig.	,144	,845	,878	,113	,439	,532	,061	,161
Factors influencing the choice of a walking tour in rural destinations: number of children								
Chi-Square	2,444	9,897	4,115	11,340	3,865	8,607	6,446	7,650
df	4	4	4	4	4	4	4	4
Asymp. Sig.	,655	,042	,391	,023	,425	,072	,168	,105
Factors influencing the choice of a walking tour in rural destinations: education								
Chi-Square	5,916	8,632	7,179	9,926	7,486	3,085	2,895	1,752
df	4	4	4	4	4	4	4	4
Asymp. Sig.	,205	,071	,127	,042	,112	,544	,576	,781
Factors influencing the choice of a walking tour in rural destinations: work status								
Chi-Square	3,872	9,003	1,893	7,457	2,343	3,961	8,580	6,951
df	5	5	5	5	5	5	5	5
Asymp. Sig.	,568	,109	,864	,189	,800	,555	,127	,224
Factors influencing the choice of a walking tour in rural destinations: annual personal investment for tourist travel and vacation								
Chi-Square	.636	9.917	3.068	4.772	8.016	4.704	.649	1.194
df	2	2	2	2	2	2	2	2
Asymp. Sig.	.727	.007	.216	.092	.018	.095	.723	.550

Using the Kruskal-Wallis H Test, there were statistically significant differences concerning the following factors:

- F1 between the *age groups* (≤25, n=82, 26-35 n=54, 36-45 n=119, 46-55 n=128, ≥56 n=84), c^2 (2, n=467) =16.01, p=0.003, Md=0;
- F4 between the *age groups* (≤25, n=82, 26-35 n=54, 36-45 n=119, 46-55 n=128, ≥56 n=84), c^2 (2, n=467) =9.957, p=0.041, Md=0.
- Regarding the mean values of group ranks, F1 and F4 were at the highest level in the 26-35 *age group*, and at the lowest level in the ≥56 *age group*.

- F5 between the *age groups* (≤25, n=82, 26-35 n=54, 36-45 n=119, 46-55 n=128, ≥56 n=84), c^2 (2, n=467) =12.005, p=0.017, Md=0; regarding the mean values of group ranks, F5 was at the highest level in the 26-35 *age group*, and at the lowest level in the 36-45 *age group*;
- F7 between the *age groups* (≤25, n=82, 26-35 n=54, 36-45 n=119, 46-55 n=128, ≥56 n=84), c^2 (2, n=467) =12.085, p=0.017, Md=0; regarding the mean values of group ranks, F7 was at the highest level in the 46-55 *age group*, and the lowest level in the ≤25 *age group*.

The analysis indicated that the young group (26-35 age) choice of a walking tour in rural destinations is most influenced by safety, peace, and quiet, as well as the accessibility of the destination, and tour content (walking, renting local guides, adventure, tours of natural and cultural monuments, camping, etc.). The factors such as safety, peace, and quiet, and the accessibility of the destination are least influential for the elderly group (56+ age group), and the tour content is least influential for the middle-aged group (36-45 age group). For the older middle-aged group (46-55 age group), the possibility of accommodation in authentic households is the most influential factor in the choice of a walking tour in rural destinations, but at the same time least influential factor for the young age group (equal and less than 25 years old).

- F2 between the *number of children groups* (0, n=182; 1, n=100; 2, n=142; 3, n=41; ≥4, n=2), c^2 (2, n=467) =9.897, p=0.042; 0-3 number of children groups had the equal median (Md=0), ≥4 number of children group had Md=1;
- F4 between the *number of children groups* (0, n=182; 1, n=100; 2, n=142; 3, n=41; ≥4, n=2), c^2 (2, n=467) =11.340, p=0.023; 0-3 number of children groups had the equal median (Md=0), ≥4 number of children group had Md=0.5.

Regarding the mean values of group ranks, F2 and F4 were at the highest level in the ≥4 *number of children group*, and at the lowest level in the 2 *number of children group*.

For people with four or more children, factors such as prices and accessibility of the destination are the most important in choosing a walking tour in rural destinations. The mentioned factors are the least significant for people with two children.

- F4 between the *education groups* (without formal education, n=2; primary education, n=3; secondary education, n=92; college, n=60; university, n=310), c^2 (2, n=467)=9.926, p=0.042; Md=0; regarding the mean values

of group ranks, F4 was at the highest level in the *university group,* and at the lowest level in the *without formal education* and *primary education groups.*
- For people with a university education, the accessibility of the destination is the highly influential factor in choosing a walking tour in rural destinations on one side, and on the other side least influential factor for low-level educated people.
- F2 between the *annual personal investment for tourist travel and vacation groups* (<500 EUR, n=180; 500-1000 EUR, n=159; >1000 EUR, n=128), c^2 (2, n=467) =9.917, p=0.007, Md=0; regarding the mean values of group ranks, F2 was at the highest level in the *<500 EUR group,* and at the lowest level in the *>1000 EUR group;*
- F5 between the *annual personal investment for tourist travel and vacation groups* (<500 EUR, n=180; 500-1000 EUR, n=159; >1000 EUR, n=128), c^2 (2, n=467) =8.016, p=0.018, for the first two groups Md=0 and the last group Md=1; regarding the mean values of group ranks, F5 was at the highest level in the *>1000 EUR group,* and at the lowest level in the *<500 EUR group.*

The price is at the highest importance level for people who are ready to invest less than EUR 500 in their tourist travel and vacation annually and at the lowest important level for people who invested over EUR 1,000. The tour content is the most significant for people who invested more than EUR 1,000 for their tourist travel and vacation annually, but the least significant for people who invested up to EUR 500.

There were statistically significant differences by *age, number of children, education, and annual personal investment for tourist travel and vacation* regarding the factors influencing the choice of a walking tour in rural destinations. There was no statistically significant difference between *marital status* and *work status groups.* Hypothesis H3 was not confirmed.

The survey on respondent's expectations during their travel and vacation in rural destinations indicated (Table 4):

- Most respondents are interested in learning how to prepare traditional food, and learning the old craft during their vacation in a rural destination (76.4.4%), or trying to grow plants or keep domestic animals on the property of an authentic household (58.7%) which confirmed hypothesis H4;
- More than half of respondents (69.4%) expressed that camping, gathering fruits, mushrooms, or medicinal herbs in untouched nature are their expectations during their travel and vacation which confirmed hypothesis H5;

- Most common need during their travel and vacation is visiting places famous for myths and legends (90.8%), waterfalls, shales, caves (96.6%), and cultural monuments (92.3%) which confirmed hypothesis H6;
- Tourists mainly use a carriage, bicycle, or horseback riding along with walking (71.7%) and try paragliding, caving, cliff climbing, skiing, Norwegian walking, and running (52.2%). Hypothesis H7 was confirmed.
- Tourists generally prefer to buy (81.4%) rather than to make (48.4%) authentic souvenirs on a tourist trip. Hypothesis H8 was not confirmed.

Table 4. Tourists' expectations during their travel and vacation in rural destinations

Value label	Frequency	Percent
Would you like to learn how to prepare traditional food on vacation or learn the old craft of the area where you are on vacation?		
No	44	9.4
Yes	357	76.4
Indifferent	66	14.1
Total	467	100.0
Would you try to grow plants or keep domestic animals on the property of an authentic household?		
No	108	23.1
Yes	274	58.7
Indifferent	85	18.2
Total	467	100.0
Would you camp, and gather fruits, mushrooms, or medicinal herbs in untouched nature?		
No	94	20.1
Yes	324	69.4
Indifferent	49	10.5
Total	467	100.0
Would you visit places famous for myths and legends?		
No	16	3.4
Yes	424	90.8
Indifferent	27	5.8
Total	467	100.0
Would you visit waterfalls, shales, and caves?		
No	4	0.9
Yes	451	96.6

continued on following page

Table 4. Continued

Value label	Frequency	Percent
Indifferent	12	2.6
Total	467	100.0
Would you visit cultural monuments in the area?		
No	5	1.1
Yes	431	92.3
Indifferent	31	6.6
Total	467	100.0
Would you visit religious monuments in the area?		
No	21	4.5
Yes	402	86.1
Indifferent	44	9.4
Total	467	100.0
Would you use a carriage, bicycle, or horseback riding along with walking?		
No	72	15.4
Yes	335	71.7
Indifferent	60	12.8
Total	467	100.0
Would you try paragliding, caving, cliff climbing, skiing, Norwegian walking, running, etc.?		
No	175	37.5
Yes	244	52.2
Indifferent	48	10.3
Total	467	100.0
What kind of souvenirs do you buy on a tourist trip?		
Nothing	31	6.6
Something commercial	25	5.4
Something authentic	380	81.4
Indifferent	31	6.6
Total	467	100.0
Would you make authentic souvenirs of the area where you are resting?		
No	145	31.0
Yes	226	48.4
Indifferent	96	20.6
Total	467	100.0

Focusing on one of the VICE model components, the authors developed the visitors' component of the VICE model to countryside walking tourism, as a sustainable form of rural tourism to enhance tourists', industries', local communities', and environment' relationships (Table 5.).

Table 5.

Visitor's expectations during their travel and vacation to the countryside	Actions of stakeholders (*local authorities, countryside management organisations, associations, and individuals*) for countryside walking tourism development
- clean environment and healthy nature - safety, peace, and quiet - tour content such as walking, renting local guides, adventure, tours of natural and cultural monuments, camping, etc. - accessibility of the destination - interact with new people (hosts), healthy food, the light pace of life, physical activity, not measured time, leisure - eat in authentic households - get tourist products at affordable prices - accommodate authentic households - learn how to prepare traditional food - learn the old craft - try to grow plants or keep domestic animals on the property of an authentic household - camp, gather fruits, mushrooms, or medicinal herbs in untouched nature - visit places famous for myths and legends - visit waterfalls, shales, caves - visit cultural monuments - use a carriage, bicycle, or horseback riding along with walking - try paragliding, caving, cliff climbing, skiing, Norwegian walking, running - buy authentic souvenirs	- establishing the legal framework for countryside walking tourism development (*planning and development work by public bodies, and detailed analysis by countryside management organization*); - developing the countryside walking tourism programmes (*targeting the customer base, analysing the accessibility, nature, and heritage capacities, and selecting countryside walking routes*). - implementing the countryside walking programmes (*improvement work and facilities on the path, marking trails and footpaths, the maintenance of the tourist infrastructure, walking culture building training for walking-related jobs and walkers-related service providers*) - improving the preservation of tourism resources through the support of local and regional projects (*increasing the local population's consciousness of the value of their nature and heritage, energy efficiency, recycling, organic food production, etc.*); - accommodation as a countryside walking holiday product (*rooms adapted to the needs of walkers, healthy food that includes traditional food, information on walking routes, the region, and its heritage, meeting walkers' specific needs such as picnic packages, etc.*) - guided countryside walking tours (*guide training for getting satisfied tourists/walkers*) - information and promotion (*topographical guide as a promotional instrument, a showcase of what the village has to offer related to walking, websites, social networks, advertising in special journals, the regional press, spreading information via local and region's tourist information centres, organization of walking festivals, etc.*); - marketing countryside walking tourism (*marketing channels include producers for direct sale, generalised and specialised tour operators, and retailers*) - price calculation (*product's cost price embeds numerous elements such as accommodation, food, guide's services, transport, promotional and marketing expenses, and infrastructure expenses; selling price determination based on season, a customer with or without children, reservation conditions, etc.*).

Source: the authors

CONCLUSION

Tourism can be developed based on the diversity of the area, the quality of the countryside, the sedative and stimulating effects of the climate, the specificity of monuments, the authenticity of folklore, the uniqueness of gastronomy, as well as the existence of relics and endemics, etc. Therefore, it is extremely important to know all the qualities of areas that are potential for the growth of tourism, because the reasons for some failures in the evolution of tourist destinations or specific forms of tourism are precisely the lack of knowledge of the area. This deficiency can be overcome by the joint work of experts dealing with spatial planning and tourism development.

A strategic approach to managing the development of countryside walking tourism should take into account the difference between the female and male populations, as well as the influence of the following factors: age, the number of children, education, and annual personal investment during their travel and vacation. The most influencing factors in the choice of a walking tour in rural destinations are a clean environment and a healthy nature. This data, often neglected by economists, confirms the importance of land for the creation and development of tourism. The obtained results also indicate the awareness of people who are involved in special forms of tourism. Although mass tourism prevails, specific forms of tourism are the future of the development of this economic activity. Safety, peace, and quiet are more important for females than males in the countryside destination. While young adults aged 26-35 take care of safety, peace, quiet, the accessibility of the destination, and tour content during their choice of a walking tour in rural destinations, for older people 56+ years mentioned factors are least significant. For middle-aged adults aged 36-55, the tour content is least important and the possibility of accommodation in authentic households is the most influential factor in the choice of a walking tour in rural destinations, but at the same time least significant for adolescents (0-25 years). For families with 4+ children, prices and accessibility of the destination are the most important to choose a walking tour in rural destinations, but the least significant for families with 2 children. While university-educated people are highly influenced by the accessibility of the destination in choosing a walking tour in rural destinations, low-level educated people are least influenced. For people who are ready to invest less than EUR 500 in their tourist travel and vacation annually, the price is at the highest importance level and the tour content is at the lowest. For people who are ready to invest over EUR 1,000 in their tourist travel and vacation annually, the tour content is at the highest importance level and the price is at the lowest.

The statistical analysis of the research indicates that a strategic approach to the management of village development should focus on activities that allow tourists to get involved in the everyday life, work, customs, traditions, and culture of the local community. In this way, tourists establish direct contact with the local population. The exchange of knowledge and involvement in the life of the local community is an important factor in the sustainable development of the village. Tourists understand the importance of an authentic household and the benefits it provides to tourists through the preparation of traditional food, learning old crafts, growing plants, or getting to know domestic animals on the farm. An active vacation in the rural environment is made possible through camping, gathering fruit, mushrooms, or medicinal herbs in untouched nature, visiting natural and anthropogenic resources, exploring places known for myths and legends, as well as using carriages, bicycles, paragliding, as well as through various other forms activities.

The basis of proper development of rural areas is the involvement of various stakeholders. Following tourists' expectations in countryside destinations, and the results obtained from the research, the authors recommend the following activities for the improvement and development of walking tourism in the countryside:

- Preservation and protection of natural and anthropogenic resources
- Improving the preservation of tourism resources through the support of local and regional projects;
- Training the local population for inclusion in tourism
- Establishing the legal framework for countryside walking tourism development;
- Developing and implementing countryside walking tourism programmes;
- Adapting accommodation capacities;
- Guided countryside walking tours;
- Information and promotion;
- Marketing countryside walking tourism; and
- Pricing.

A distinction should be made between hikers and countryside walkers, as well as who the countryside walkers are and what kind of walk, they choose. Despite the large number of walkers, information about them is missing. The contribution of this research reflects the connection between tourism activities and the importance of the countryside, as well as a good understanding of the overall market of rural tourism development. The paper points out the need to create a base of customers who gravitate toward rural areas and the expectations of these tourists staying in a natural environment. An additional contribution is putting the focus of the authors on a strategic approach to rural destination management by taking into consideration tourists' expectations as an influential factor outside the tourism industry's control.

The influence on the development of sustainable tourism in rural areas and the involvement of the local community in education about the sustainable development of tourism is extremely important. Special attention should be paid to the fact that the local population plays a special role through direct contact with tourists. Transferring the knowledge, culture, customs, and hospitality of the host to the tourist is an experience that cannot be repeated or paid for. That is why it is very important that in the management process, the role of the host and his contribution to the sustainable development of tourism should be pointed out.

The authors recommend incorporating countryside walking tourism into walking strategies as a part of rural and tourism development politics. Government policies that would increase countryside walking rates while improving safety should include:

- Networks of safe and convenient countryside walking infrastructure;
- Facilities designed for the needs of countryside walkers;
- Land-use regulations;
- Guided countryside tours focused on better environmental protection;
- Support to local supply;
- Traffic laws that give priority to countryside walkers;
- Improved the countryside walking culture-based education;
- Tax surcharges on vehicles; etc.

LIMITATIONS AND FUTURE RESEARCH

The authors acknowledge that this research has three limitations that are related to the survey and model. The first limitation is that the sample size is relatively small, which limits the generalization of research results. Additionally, the emergence of expectation-oriented tourism requires a deeper understanding of tourists' countryside choice behaviour. Also, the authors did not consider correlations for all components of the VICE model, and accordingly, they just considered implications on the visitors' component. The future research work will focus on enlarging the sample size, deeper understanding of tourists' countryside choice behaviour, the influence of the area on the planning of the expansion of specific forms of tourism, and modelling the complete VICE model. Knowing all these limitations, the authors continued their research through all the possibilities that will affect the comprehensive understanding of this issue.

REFERENCES

Abdul-Rauf Abdul-Mugod, A. (2016). Sustainable tourism planning by using the VICE model (applied on Minia Governorate). *MJTHR*, 1, 98–113.

Ahmed, N. (2023). Residents support towards cultural heritage tourism: The relevance of heritage proximity and tourism perceived impacts. *Journal of Tourism*, 32, 1–16. http://revistadeturism.ro/rdt/article/view/606

Azizpour, F., & Fathizadeh, F. (2016). Barriers to collaboration among tourism industry stakeholders. Case study: Mashhad Metropolis. *Alma Tourism J., 7,* 48–65. https://doi.org/DOI: 10.6092/issn.2036-5195/5991

Belliggiano, A., Bindi, L., & Ievoli, C. (2021). Walking along the sheeptrack…Rural tourism, ecomuseums, and bio-cultural heritage. *Sustainability (Basel)*, 13(16), 8870. DOI: 10.3390/su13168870

Boonpart, O., & Suvachart, N. (2014). Tourist expectation and tourist experience in cultural tourism. *JTHM*, 2, 124–132.

Buehler, R., & Pucher, J. (Eds.). (2021d). *Cycling for sustainable cities* (pp. 21–25). MIT Press. DOI: 10.7551/mitpress/11963.001.0001

Buehler, R., & Pucher, J. (2023a). Overview of walking rates, walking safety, and government policies to encourage more and safer walking in Europe and North America. *Sustainability (Basel)*, 15(7), 5719. DOI: 10.3390/su15075719

Buehler, R., Pucher, J., & Bauman, A. (2020c). Physical activity from walking and cycling for daily travel in the United States, 2001–2017: Demographic, socioeconomic, and geographic variation. *Journal of Transport & Health*, 16, 100811. DOI: 10.1016/j.jth.2019.100811

Buehler, R., Pucher, J., Merom, D., & Bauman, A. (2011b). Active travel in Germany and the U.S.: Contributions of daily walking and cycling to physical activity. *American Journal of Preventive Medicine*, 41(3), 241–250. DOI: 10.1016/j.amepre.2011.04.012 PMID: 21855737

Butler, R., Curran, R., & O'Gorman, K. D. (2013). Pro-poor tourism in a first world urban setting: Case study of Glasgow. *International Journal of Tourism Research*, 15(5), 443–457. DOI: 10.1002/jtr.1888

Cawley, M., & Gillmor, D. A. (2008). Integrated rural tourism: Concepts and practice. *Annals of Tourism Research*, 35(2), 316–337. DOI: 10.1016/j.annals.2007.07.011

Chhetri, P., Arrowsmith, C., & Jackson, M. (2004). Determining hiking experiences in nature-based tourist destinations. *Tourism Management*, 25(1), 31–43. DOI: 10.1016/S0261-5177(03)00057-8

Cioban, G.-L. (2022). Tourist destination – Bucovina. *Journal of Tourism*, 34, 1–6. http://revistadeturism.ro/rdt/article/view/596

Cohen, J. (1988). *Statistical power analysis for the behavioural sciences* (2nd ed.). Lawrence Erlbaum Associates.

Donis, J., & Straupe, I. *The Assessment of Contribution of Forest Plant Non-Wood Products in Latvia's National Economy*. In Proceedings of the Annual 17th International Scientific Conference "Research for Rural Development 2011", Jelgava, Latvia, 18-20 May 2011.

Gehl, J. (2013). *Cities for people*. Island Press.

Gjedrem, A. M., & Log, T. (2020). Study of heathland succession, prescribed burning, and future perspectives at Kringsjå, Norway. *Land (Basel)*, 9(12), 485. DOI: 10.3390/land9120485

Gogonea, R.-M., & Zaharia, M. (2023). Agro-tourism South-West Oltenia in the post-pandemic period. Are there trends returning? *Journal of Tourism*, 35, 1–9. http://revistadeturism.ro/rdt/article/view/611/354

Gohori, O., & van der Merwe, P. (2020). Towards a tourism and community-development framework: An African perspective. *Sustainability (Basel)*, 12(13), 5305. DOI: 10.3390/su12135305

Hajrasouliha, A. (2019). Connecting the dots: Campus form, student perceptions, and academic performance. *Focus (San Francisco, Calif.)*, 15, 38–48.

Han, B., Yang, J., Liu, G., & Sun, Z. (2023). Exploring gender differences through the lens of spatiotemporal behavior patterns in a cultural market: A case study of Panjiayuan market in Beijing, China. *Land (Basel)*, 12(4), 889. DOI: 10.3390/land12040889

Hartig, T., & Staats, H. (2006). The need for psychological restoration as a determinant of environmental preferences. *Journal of Environmental Psychology*, 26(3), 215–226. DOI: 10.1016/j.jenvp.2006.07.007

Hass-Klau, C. (2014). *The pedestrian and the city*. Routledge. DOI: 10.4324/9780203067390

Hassan, A. (2020). In Walia, S. K. (Ed.), *Sustainable initiatives for community-based tourism development. In the Routledge handbook of community-based tourism management: concepts, issues and implications* (1st ed., pp. 130–137). Routledge.

Haverila, M., Haverila, K.C. & Twyford, J.C. (2023). The influence of marital status on customer-centric measures in the context of a ski resort using the importance-performance map analysis (IPMA) framework, *European Journal of Management Studies, 28*(1), 49-68, https://doi.org/DOI: 10.1108/EJMS-05-2021-0034

Huang, C. M., Tuan, C. L., & Wongchai, A. (2014). Development analysis of leisure agriculture–a case study of Longjing Tea Garden, Hangzhou, China. *APCBEE Procedia, 8*, 210–215. DOI: 10.1016/j.apcbee.2014.03.029

IISD. (2023). *UNWTO Report Links Sustainable Tourism to 17 SDGs.* Available online: https://sdg.iisd.org/news/unwto-report-links-sustainable-tourism-to-17-sdgs/ (accessed on 5 June 2023).

Janeczko, E., Fialova, J., Tomusiak, R., Woźnicka, M., & Prochazkova, P. (2019). Running as a form of recreation in the Polish and Czech forests-advantages and disadvantages. *Sylwan, 163*, 522–528.

Jensen, Ø., & Prebensen, K. N. (2015). Innovation and value creation in experience-based tourism. *Scandinavian Journal of Hospitality and Tourism, 15*(sup1), 1–8. DOI: 10.1080/15022250.2015.1066093

King, S. B., Kaczynski, A. T., Knight Wilt, J., & Stowe, E. W. (2020). Walkability 101: A multi-method assessment of the walkability at a University Campus. *SAGE Open, 10*(2), 1–9. DOI: 10.1177/2158244020917954

Kung, R. (2018). A Study of the tourists expectation, satisfaction and revisiting intention in the Neiwan, Hsinchu. *IJNDES, 2*, 43–49.

Larsen, S. (2007). Aspects of a psychology of the tourist experience. *Scandinavian Journal of Hospitality and Tourism, 7*(1), 7–18. DOI: 10.1080/15022250701226014

LEADER II. (2001). *Developing Walking Holidays in Rural Areas. Guide on How to Design and Implement a Walking Holiday Project.* Available online: https://ec.europa.eu/enrd/sites/default/files/leaderii_dossiers_tourism_walking-holidays.pdf (accessed on 10 Jun 2023).

Liu, Y., & Li, Y. (2017). Revitalize the world's countryside. *Nature, 548*(7667), 275–277. DOI: 10.1038/548275a PMID: 28816262

Lor, J. J., Kwa, S., & Donaldson, J. A. (2019). Making ethnic tourism good for the poor. *Annals of Tourism Research, 76*, 140–152. DOI: 10.1016/j.annals.2019.03.008

Mao, Y., Ren, X., Yin, L., Sun, Q., Song, K., & Wang, D. (2021). Investigating Tourists' Willingness to Walk (WTW) to Attractions within Scenic Areas: A Case Study of Tongli Ancient Town, China. *Sustainability (Basel)*, 13(23), 12990. DOI: 10.3390/su132312990

Milojković, D., Nikolić, M. & Milojković, H. (2023b). Walking tourism management based on tourists' needs for indoor and outdoor activities in the function of sustainable local economic development. *RSEP*, 8, 1-18, p.1. https://doi.org/DOI: 10.19275/RSEP152

Milojković, D., Nikolić, M., & Milojković, K. (2023a). The development of countryside walking tourism in the time of the post-covid crisis. *Ekonomika Poljoprivrede*, 70(1), 131–144. DOI: 10.59267/ekoPolj2301131M

Mirea, C.-N., & Nistoreanu, P. (2021). Research methodologies on keywords: Tourism, Danube, sustainable development. *Journal of Tourism*, 32, 1–6. http://revistadeturism.ro/rdt/article/view/541

Moyo, S., & Tichaawa, T. M. (2017). Community involvement and participation in tourism development: A Zimbabwe study. *AJHTL*, 6, 1–15.

Niekerk, M., & Coetzee, W. (2011). Utilizing the VICE model for the sustainable development of the Innibos arts festival. *Journal of Hospitality Marketing & Management*, 20(3-4), 347–365. DOI: 10.1080/19368623.2011.562422

Njoya, E. T., & Seetaram, N. (2018). Tourism contribution to poverty alleviation in Kenya: A dynamic computable general equilibrium analysis. *Journal of Travel Research*, 57(4), 513–524. DOI: 10.1177/0047287517700317 PMID: 29595836

O'Reilly, A. M. (1986). Tourism carrying capacity: Concept and issues. *Tourism Management*, 7(4), 254–258. DOI: 10.1016/0261-5177(86)90035-X

Oh, H., Parks, S. C., & Demicco, F. J. (2002). Age- and Gender-Based Market Segmentation. *International Journal of Hospitality & Tourism Administration*, 3(1), 1–20. DOI: 10.1300/J149v03n01_01

PATA. (2023). *Sustainable Tourism Online: Destinations and Communities*. Available online: https://www.pata.org/blog/sustainable-tourism-online-destinations-and-communities (accessed on 20 March 2023).

Popesku, J. (2016). *Menadžment turističke destinacije* (5. Izdanje). Univerzitet Singidunum, Beograd, Srbija, str. 98-104. (In Serbian)

Prial, A., Zhu, X., Bol, L., & Williams, M. R. (2023). The impact of moderate physical activity and student interaction on retention at a community college. *Journal of American College Health*, 71(1), 154–161. DOI: 10.1080/07448481.2021.1881103 PMID: 33734951

Riis, T., Kelly-Quinn, M., Aguiar, F. C., Manolaki, P., Bruno, D., Bejarano, M. D., Clerici, N., Fernandes, M. R., Franco, J. C., Pettit, N., Portela, A. P., Tammeorg, O., Tammeorg, P., Rodríguez-González, P. M., & Dufour, S. (2020). Global overview of ecosystem services provided by riparian vegetation. *Bioscience*, 70(6), 501–514. DOI: 10.1093/biosci/biaa041

Royo, V. M. (2009). Rural-cultural excursion conceptualization: A local tourism marketing management model based on tourist destination image measurement. *Tourism Management*, 30(3), 419–428. DOI: 10.1016/j.tourman.2008.07.013

Sharpley, R., & Vass, A. (2006). Tourism, farming and diversification: An attitudinal study. *Tourism Management*, 27(5), 1040–1052. DOI: 10.1016/j.tourman.2005.10.025

Simeoni, F., & De Crescenzo, V. *Walking tourism: opportunities and threats for sustainable development.The case of the 'Va' Sentiero' project*. In Proceedings of the XXII International conference excellence in services, Thessaloniki, Greece, 29-30 August 2019.

Slusariuc, G. (2020). Health tourism – evolutions and perspectives. *Journal of Tourism*, 29, 1–4. http://revistadeturism.ro/rdt/article/view/471

Speck, J. (2012). *Walkable city: how downtown can save America, one step at a time*. Macmillan Publishers.

Štetić, S. & Šimičević, D. (2017). *Menadžment turističke destinacije*. Visoka turistička škola strukovnih studija, Beograd, Srbija. (In Serbian).

Štetić, S., & Trišić, I. (2018). *Strengthening the tourism offer–case study Braničevo District. In Modern Management Tools and Economy of Tourism Sector in Present Era*, (3rd Ed.). Bevanda, V. & Štetić, S., Eds. Association of Economists and Managers of the Balkans, Belgrade, Serbia, Volume 3, 637-650.

Su, Y., Mei, J., Zhu, J., Xia, P., Li, T., Wang, C., Zhi, J., & You, S. (2022). A global scientometric visualization analysis of rural tourism from 2000 to 2021. *Sustainability (Basel)*, 14(22), 14854. DOI: 10.3390/su142214854

Szabó, D. R. (2015). *Sustainable tourism destination management strategies: using the EVIDENCES model for evaluating TDM tenders*. In some current issues in economics; Karlovitz, J. T., Ed.; International research institute sro., Komárno, Slovakia, 249-258.

Thiele, J., Albert, C., Hermes, J., & von Haaren, C. (2020). Assessing and quantifying offered cultural ecosystem services of German river landscapes. *Ecosystem Services*, 42, 101080. DOI: 10.1016/j.ecoser.2020.101080

Tomić, S., Leković, K., & Tadić, J. (2019). Consumer behaviour: The influence of age and family structure on the choice of activities in a tourist destination. *Ekonomska Istrazivanja*, 32(1), 755–771. DOI: 10.1080/1331677X.2019.1579663

Tranter, P., & Tolley, R. (2020). *Slow cities: conquering our speed addiction for health and sustainability* (1st ed.). Elsevier.

Trišić, I., Milojković, D., Ristić, V., Nechita, F., Maksin, M., Štetić, S., & Candrea, A. N. (2023a). Sustainable tourism of Important Plant Areas (IPAs)—A case of three protected areas of Vojvodina Province. *Land (Basel)*, 12(7), 1278. DOI: 10.3390/land12071278

Trišić, I., Nechita, F., Milojković, D., & Štetić, S. (2023b). Sustainable tourism in protected areas—Application of the Prism of sustainability model. *Sustainability (Basel)*, 15(6), 5148. DOI: 10.3390/su15065148

Trišić, I., Privitera, D., Ristić, V., Štetić, S., Milojković, D., & Maksin, M. (2023c). Protected areas in the function of sustainable tourism development—A case of Deliblato sands special nature reserve, Vojvodina Province. *Land (Basel)*, 12(2), 487. DOI: 10.3390/land12020487

Tsartas, P., Despotaki, G., & Sarantakou, E. (2015). New trends for tourism products: the issue of tourism resources. 10. 194-204. https://www.researchgate.net/publication/322055295_New_trends_for_tourism_products_The_Issue_of_tourism_resources

UNWTO. (2023a). *Tourism and the Sustainable Development Goals – Journey to 2030.* Available online: https://www.e-unwto.org/doi/book/10.18111/9789284419401 (accessed on 7 June 2023).

UNWTO. (2023b). *Product Development.* Available online: https://www.unwto.org/tourism-development-products (accessed on 10 June 2023).

UNWTO. (2023c). *Indicators of Sustainable Development for Tourism Destinations.* Available online: https://www.e-unwto.org/doi/epdf/10.18111/9789284407262?role=tab (accessed on 3 June 2023).

Vuković, M. & Štrbac, N. (2019). *Metodologija naučnih istraživanja*. Tehnički fakultet u Boru Univerziteta u Beogradu, Bor, Srbija, str. 32-41. (In Serbian)

Wood, L. E., Vimercati, G., Ferrini, S., & Shackleton, R. T. (2022). Perceptions of ecosystem services and disservices associated with open water swimming. *Journal of Outdoor Recreation and Tourism*, 37, 100491. DOI: 10.1016/j.jort.2022.100491

Zhang, T., Chen, J., & Hu, B. (2019). Authenticity, quality, and loyalty: Local food and sustainable tourism experience. *Sustainability (Basel)*, 11(12), 3437. DOI: 10.3390/su11123437

Zhang, Y., Zou, Y., Zhu, Z., Guo, X., & Feng, X. (2022). Evaluating pedestrian environment using DeepLab models based on street walkability in small and medium-sized cities: Case study in Gaoping, China. *Sustainability (Basel)*, 14(22), 15472. DOI: 10.3390/su142215472

Zhang, Z., Fisher, T., & Wang, H. (2023). Walk score, environmental quality and walking in a campus setting. *Land (Basel)*, 12(4), 732. DOI: 10.3390/land12040732

Chapter 13
Heritage-Led Destination Management:
Strategies for Competitive Advantage

Aditi Nag
https://orcid.org/0000-0002-0604-6945
Birla Institute of Technology, Mesra, India

Smriti Mishra
https://orcid.org/0000-0001-7594-4960
Birla Institute of Technology, Mesra, India

EXECUTIVE SUMMARY

Heritage-led destination management is crucial for gaining a competitive edge in the global tourism industry. This paper explores the link between heritage assets and destination competitiveness, emphasizing their role in attracting visitors, generating economic benefits, and distinguishing a destination. It delves into factors enabling differentiation, including heritage preservation, effective interpretation, infrastructure, cultural events, and community collaboration. Case studies illustrate how these strategies boost visitor numbers, revenue, and destination image. Challenges like balancing conservation and tourism, over-tourism, and community involvement are discussed. The paper advocates sustainable heritage-led tourism to ensure long-term success and heritage preservation. It serves as a guide for destinations aiming to leverage their heritage for competitive advantage.

DOI: 10.4018/979-8-3693-1548-4.ch013

1 INTRODUCTION

Heritage-led destination management is a holistic and strategic approach that places the preservation, interpretation, and sustainable utilisation of a destination's cultural, historical, and natural heritage at its core (Wang & Gu, 2020; Dubini & Di Biase, 2008). It encompasses a range of activities aimed at safeguarding the heritage assets of a location while simultaneously leveraging them to enhance the overall tourism experience and promote economic growth (Koutsi, Lagarias, & Stratigea, 2022). At its essence, heritage-led destination management involves careful planning and integration of heritage resources into the destination's development strategy (Derakhshan, 2019). This includes preserving historical sites, artefacts, and traditions, often through meticulous restoration and conservation efforts (Dubini & Di Biase, 2008). It also entails interpreting the significance of these heritage assets and creating engaging narratives that help visitors understand the historical, cultural, and social context. This interpretation enhances the visitor experience, fostering a deeper connection between tourists and the destination's heritage (Wang & Gu, 2020). Additionally, heritage-led destination management emphasises community engagement (Derakhshan, 2019). Local residents, artisans, and businesses are active participants, offering authentic experiences that showcase the destination's unique heritage. This involvement generates economic opportunities and instils a sense of pride and ownership in the community, leading to the sustainable preservation of traditions and customs (Smith & General, 2008). Strategic marketing and promotion are integral components of heritage-led destination management (Koutsi, Lagarias, & Stratigea, 2022). Effective campaigns highlight the destination's authentic experiences, attracting tourists interested in immersive cultural encounters. Creating differentiated tourism products centred around heritage allows destinations to stand out in the competitive tourism market, drawing visitors who seek genuine and meaningful interactions (Smith & General, 2008). Furthermore, sustainability lies at the heart of heritage-led destination management. It involves balancing economic growth with environmental and cultural preservation (Koutsi & Stratigea, 2019). Sustainable practices ensure that tourism activities do not harm the natural environment and that the cultural integrity of the destination is respected (Colavitti & Usai, 2019; Derakhshan, 2019; Dubini & Di Biase, 2008). This approach benefits the destination in the long term and aligns with the global trend toward responsible and eco-conscious travel. Heritage-led destination management is a nuanced and integrated strategy that cherishes a destination's historical and cultural roots while harnessing them for economic and social development (Lopez & Pérez, 2020). Table 1 in Appendix-I serves as a comprehensive reference, encapsulating key terminologies and their nuanced definitions within the context of this study. Providing clear definitions enhances the readers' understanding, ensuring a solid foundation for the subsequent exploration and analysis presented in this research.

1.1 Heritage-Led Destination Management Evolution

The evolution of heritage-led destination management spans several decades, reflecting a gradual shift in global perspectives towards cultural preservation and tourism. In the post-World War II era, the widespread devastation prompted international organisations like UNESCO to emphasise the crucial need for preserving cultural heritage (Sölvell, 2015). This early recognition laid the groundwork for global efforts in safeguarding historical and architectural treasures, marking the initial steps toward heritage conservation. As the preservation movement gained momentum in the 1960s and 1970s, legislation was enacted in many countries to protect cultural heritage sites. Although the primary focus was preservation, the 1980s witnessed a significant transformation in tourism preferences. Travellers began seeking more genuine and immersive experiences, prompting tourism boards to recognise the potential of heritage sites as unique attractions (Petr, 2002). During this period, the idea of utilising preserved sites for tourism began to take shape, emphasising the fusion of historical preservation and tourism development. The momentum continued into the 2000s and beyond, with the emergence of sustainable tourism practices (Colavitti & Usai, 2019). As awareness grew about the economic advantages of heritage-led tourism, destinations started incorporating heritage assets into their tourism strategies. This evolution marked a pivotal shift from mere preservation to proactive management and interpretation (Wang & Gu, 2020). Best practices emerged, emphasising community involvement, sustainable development, and tailored marketing strategies highlighting each destination's unique heritage. Academic research and publications further shaped heritage-led destination management theories and practices. The interconnectedness of preservation, community engagement, and tourism became evident, forming the foundation for a comprehensive approach. Heritage-led destination management is a well-established concept intertwining cultural preservation with tourism experiences (Nag & Mishra, 2024; Nag, 2024; Nag & Mishra, 2023; Gilmore, Carson, & Ascenção, 2007). It represents the careful preservation of historical and cultural assets and their strategic and sustainable utilisation to enhance the visitor experience and foster economic growth (Wang & Gu, 2020; Dubini & Di Biase, 2008). This interconnected journey illustrates the symbiotic relationship between heritage conservation and tourism, shaping how cultural and historical sites are managed and appreciated worldwide.

1.2 Significance of Heritage in Tourism

Heritage holds a multifaceted significance in tourism, creating a tapestry of benefits that intertwine culture, economics, and community development (Gombault & Petr, 2007). At its core, heritage tourism provides a profound avenue for cultural understanding and preservation. Heritage sites serve as portals to the past, offering visitors insights into the intricacies of historical, social, and artistic legacies (Colavitti & Usai, 2019; Porter, 2011). This exploration fosters a deep appreciation for diverse cultures, encouraging tolerance and respect among people from different backgrounds (Smith & General, 2008). Economically, heritage tourism is a robust driver for local economies. Tourists visiting these sites inject capital into the community through expenditures on accommodations, local cuisine, guided tours, and souvenirs (Porter, 2011). This financial influx not only supports existing businesses but also encourages the growth of new enterprises, creating employment opportunities and bolstering the overall economic landscape of the region (Boniface & Fowler, 2002). However, the significance of heritage tourism goes beyond economic factors. It plays a pivotal role in community empowerment by providing avenues for local involvement (Huang, Tsaur, & Yang, 2012). Residents often participate actively in tourism-related activities, such as guiding tours, showcasing traditional crafts, or performing cultural rituals (Koutsi, Lagarias, & Stratigea, 2022). This engagement generates income and nurtures a sense of pride within the community, strengthening their connection to their heritage and traditions (Dubini & Di Biase, 2008). Moreover, heritage tourism contributes significantly to sustainable development. It promotes responsible tourism practices by highlighting the importance of preserving natural and cultural heritage (Koutsi & Stratigea, 2019). This emphasis on sustainability ensures that delicate ecosystems are conserved, and historical sites are protected for future generations. It encourages eco-friendly initiatives, fostering a harmonious coexistence between tourism and the environment. In addition, heritage tourism serves as a platform for educational endeavours and research initiatives (Jimura, 2011; Boniface & Fowler, 2002). Schools, universities, and researchers often utilise these sites as practical learning environments, enriching academic pursuits. This educational aspect not only enhances the knowledge base of the visitors but also contributes to the broader understanding of history, archaeology, and cultural anthropology (Yang, Lin, & Han, 2010; Smith & General, 2008). Lastly, heritage tourism is vital for the preservation of traditions and skills. Tourists' demand for traditional crafts and artisanal products provides economic incentives for local craftsmen (Derakhshan, 2019). This sustains these age-old skills, ensuring the survival of cultural practices and enriching the heritage tapestry (Wang & Gu, 2020; Dubini & Di Biase, 2008). Heritage tourism weaves a vibrant fabric of cultural appreciation, economic growth, community engagement, environmental consciousness, and educational enrichment (Laing et al.,

2014). Its significance resonates deeply, connecting individuals and communities across the globe through the threads of shared heritage and understanding.

1.3 Objectives of the Research

Objectives are vital in research as they provide clear focus, guiding researchers and readers about the study's specific goals and intended outcomes. They ensure the research stays on track, influence the choice of methods, and structure the content and organisation of the study. Objectives also direct the literature review, making it targeted and relevant. Ultimately, they lead to practical applications, shaping the study's real-world impact and offering valuable insights for future research endeavours.

These objectives collectively aim to provide a comprehensive understanding of heritage-led destination management, offer practical insights for stakeholders, and contribute valuable knowledge to the academic and professional community.

1. Explore Concepts: The paper aims to deeply understand the fundamental concepts related to heritage-led destination management. This includes clarifying the nuances of heritage preservation, sustainable tourism practices, and crafting meaningful tourism experiences.
2. Highlight Significance: The paper underscores the importance of integrating heritage into tourism strategies by emphasising the multifaceted significance of heritage in tourism. It showcases heritage as a historical artefact and a dynamic, living element that can fuel economic growth, cultural exchange, and environmental preservation.
3. Offer Guidance: One of the primary objectives is to provide practical guidance. This includes insights into successful heritage-led destination management strategies, case studies demonstrating effective implementation, and recommendations for policymakers and destination managers. By offering actionable advice, the paper equips stakeholders with the knowledge necessary to make informed decisions and create sustainable, culturally rich tourism destinations.

1.4 Methodology

This section outlines the specific methods employed and the steps taken during the research process, ensuring the validity and reliability of the findings. The study involved multiple authors, both from architecture and urban planning backgrounds, who contributed distinct expertise to various stages of the research.

The research adopted a qualitative approach to comprehensively explore the link between heritage assets and destination competitiveness. Data collection involved an extensive literature review, where existing literature on heritage-led tourism, destination competitiveness, and sustainable tourism practices was reviewed to identify key themes, trends, and gaps. Multiple heritage destinations were selected as case studies to illustrate the practical application of heritage-led tourism strategies. The criteria for selecting these case studies included their diversity in geographic location, heritage significance, and tourism impact.

For the case studies, data was gathered primarily from publicly available reports, articles, and publications about the selected heritage sites. This included government reports, tourism board publications, and site management plans, providing insights into policies and strategies related to heritage preservation, tourism development, and community involvement. The data triangulation involved comparing findings from different sources to ensure consistency and reliability.

For data analysis, qualitative methods were employed. Document analysis was conducted to extract relevant information related to heritage preservation efforts, tourism infrastructure, community engagement initiatives, and economic impacts. Data from case studies and document analysis were coded and analyzed to identify recurring themes and patterns. Thematic analysis was used to explore the relationship between heritage assets and destination competitiveness.

The first author, who specializes in heritage planning and tourism management, led the literature review and analyzed qualitative data from case studies, particularly those related to heritage preservation and sustainable tourism practices. The first author also conducted the thematic analysis of data and wrote the main findings. The second author, specializing in stakeholder collaboration, supervised the research process, provided guidance and feedback on the research design, data collection, and analysis, and reviewed the manuscript.

To ensure the validity and reliability of the research, triangulation was used by utilizing multiple data sources and methods (literature review, case studies, and document analysis) to cross-verify findings and enhance validity. Qualitative insights from various sources were compared to ensure consistency and reliability. Peer review sessions were conducted where both authors critically evaluated each other's contributions and interpretations. Feedback from external experts in heritage tourism, architecture, and urban planning was sought to validate the research methodology and findings.

Ethical considerations were adhered to by ensuring the ethical use of data collected from secondary sources and following ethical guidelines in conducting research and reporting findings. By employing these methods, the study ensured a rigorous and comprehensive exploration of heritage-led tourism and its impact on destination competitiveness. The collaborative efforts of authors from architecture and urban planning backgrounds enriched the research, providing a holistic understanding of the subject matter.

2 THE ROLE OF HERITAGE IN TOURISM

The role of heritage in tourism is pivotal, encompassing a myriad of cultural, historical, and economic dimensions that significantly influence travellers' choices (Koutsi, Lagarias, & Stratigea, 2022; Derakhshan, 2019). Heritage attractions, as integral components of this phenomenon, embody a destination's cultural richness and historical narratives. They act as magnets, drawing tourists with the promise of unique experiences that intertwine the past's allure with the present's authenticity (Calver & Page, 2013). These attractions are not merely static monuments but living testaments to a community's traditions, architecture, and artistry. Travellers journey through time by exploring these heritage sites, immersing themselves in the customs and stories that have shaped societies. The appeal of heritage attractions lies not just in their aesthetic charm but also in their ability to evoke a sense of wonder, curiosity, and connection to the world's diverse heritage. Understanding this appeal is fundamental, as it underpins the essence of heritage tourism, creating a symbiotic relationship between travellers and the cultural treasures they explore. In the forthcoming section, we delve deeper into the aspects that make heritage attractions so captivating, shedding light on the intricacies of their appeal and their significant role in shaping the global tourism landscape.

2.1 Understanding the Appeal of Heritage Attractions

Understanding the appeal of heritage attractions is essential in the realm of tourism (refer to Figure 1). Heritage attractions hold a unique allure for travellers due to their historical, cultural, and emotional significance. Tourists are drawn to these sites because they offer a tangible connection to the past, immersing visitors in the rich tapestry of history and tradition (Kolar & Zabkar, 2010). The appeal of heritage attractions often lies in the authenticity they provide. Unlike modern, commercialised sites, heritage attractions offer a genuine glimpse into the heritage and roots of a community or civilisation. This authenticity creates a profound cultural immersion, allowing visitors to experience traditions, architecture, art, and rituals that have stood the test of time (Sölvell, 2015). Moreover, heritage attractions evoke a sense of nostalgia and curiosity. Travellers are often intrigued by the stories and legends associated with historical sites, sparking a desire to explore and understand the events that unfolded within those ancient walls or on those hallowed grounds (Porter, 2011). This sense of mystery and the opportunity to unravel the past contribute significantly to the appeal of heritage attractions (Wang & Gu, 2020). Additionally, heritage attractions often serve as symbols of national or regional pride. They showcase a community's achievements, cultural heritage, and resilience, instilling a sense of identity among locals and visitors (Gilmore, Carson, &

Ascenção, 2007). Tourists are naturally drawn to these sites, seeking to understand the cultural fabric that defines a particular region or country. Furthermore, heritage attractions frequently serve as educational hubs (Jimura, 2011). Schools, universities, and researchers use these sites as practical learning environments, enriching academic pursuits and deepening historical understanding. This educational aspect attracts intellectually curious travellers, historians, and students eager to explore the intricate narratives woven into the heritage attractions (Chen, & Chen, 2010). In summary, the appeal of heritage attractions stems from their authenticity, the sense of mystery and curiosity they evoke, their role in preserving cultural identity, and their educational value. For tourists, these sites offer a unique opportunity to step back in time, connect with history, and gain a profound understanding of the cultural heritage that shapes the world we live in today.

Figure 1. Heritage attraction appeal themes

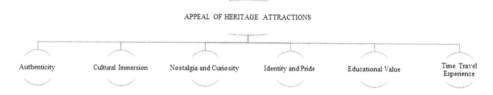

2.2 Heritage as a Driver of Tourism Demand

Heritage, encompassing historical sites, cultural artefacts, traditional practices, and local narratives, is a powerful magnet for tourists worldwide. Its historical and cultural richness forms a cornerstone of tourism, attracting travellers seeking authentic and immersive experiences. The appeal lies in the opportunity to step back in time, witness the echoes of ancient civilisations, and engage with traditions that have withstood the test of time (Bourgeon-Renault et al., 2006). Heritage tourism's ability to offer travellers an authentic cultural immersion distinguishes it. Visitors are not merely spectators; they actively engage in traditional rituals, savour local delicacies, and partake in customs passed down through generations (Smith & General, 2008). This immersive experience provides a genuine connection to the heritage, allowing travellers to become a part of the living tapestry of the community they visit (Wang & Gu, 2020; Dubini & Di Biase, 2008). For both tourists and locals, heritage sites serve as anchors of identity and sources of pride. These sites represent the essence of a community's history and cultural heritage (Koutsi & Stratigea, 2019). As visitors explore these places, they forge emotional connections, gaining a deeper understanding of the community's roots. Simultaneously, heritage sites symbolise the local population's identity, fostering a sense of belonging and reinforcing cultural pride (Su & Lin, 2014; Porter, 2011). The influx of tourists often leads to increased resources for preserving heritage sites. Revenue generated from tourism activities funds conservation efforts, ensuring these sites are protected for future generations (Choi et al., 2010). Furthermore, heritage tourism encourages sustainable practices. Communities recognise the delicate balance between welcoming visitors and preserving their heritage. As a result, responsible tourism initiatives emerge, promoting sustainable coexistence between tourism and cultural preservation (Petr, 2002). Beyond their visual appeal, heritage sites serve as immersive classrooms, offering a wealth of knowledge. Scholars, students, and enthusiasts flock to these sites, eager to learn about art, architecture, archaeology, and history. Additionally, heritage tourism fosters cultural exchange (Derakhshan, 2019). Travelers engage in meaningful dialogues as cultural ambassadors, bridging gaps between diverse communities. These interactions promote mutual understanding, respect, and appreciation, nurturing a sense of global unity (Calver & Page, 2013; Chen & Chen, 2010). Heritage tourism is not merely a journey through time but a profound exploration of cultures, traditions, and human histories. The interconnected aspects of historical allure, cultural immersion, identity, preservation, education, and cultural exchange create a rich tapestry that defines heritage as a driving force behind tourism demand (refer to Figure 2).

Figure 2. Dynamics of Heritage Tourism Appeal

2.3 Economic and Socio-Cultural Impacts of Heritage Tourism

The economic and socio-cultural impacts of heritage tourism are multifaceted, shaping communities and economies in various ways. Heritage tourism brings in substantial revenue to local economies. Tourists spend on accommodations, food, transportation, guided tours, and locally-made crafts, injecting capital directly into the community (Ramsey & Everitt, 2008). This financial influx supports local businesses, from small handicraft shops to hotels and restaurants, fostering entrepreneurship and economic diversity (Dubini & Di Biase, 2008). The tourism sector, particularly heritage tourism, creates many employment opportunities. Locals find work as tour guides, hotel staff, artisans, and in various service sectors. This employment not only reduces unemployment rates but also enhances the overall standard of living for the community (Calver & Page, 2013; Yang, Lin, & Han, 2010; Gombault & Petr, 2007). The revenue generated from heritage tourism often contributes to local infrastructure development. Roads, bridges, airports, and public spaces are improved to accommodate the influx of tourists. Better infrastructure benefits tourists and enhances the quality of life for the local population. Heritage tourism encourages cultural entrepreneurship (Petr, 2015). Locals often showcase traditional arts, crafts, music, and dance, creating a market for their cultural heritage. This preserves traditional skills and provides economic incentives for artisans to continue their crafts (Chen & Chen, 2010; Boniface & Fowler, 2002).

Socio-culturally, heritage tourism plays a vital role in preserving traditions and cultural practices. Communities often maintain or revive traditional practices, arts, and rituals to appeal to tourists (Caton & Santos, 2007). This preservation effort ensures that these cultural elements are not lost to modernisation, fostering a sense of identity and pride among the local population. Heritage tourism promotes cultural exchange between tourists and local communities (Gilmore, Carson, & Ascenção, 2007). Visitors learn about local traditions, beliefs, and ways of life, while locals gain exposure to diverse cultures. This mutual learning enhances tolerance, understanding, and respect among people from different backgrounds (Koutsi, Lagarias, & Stratigea, 2022; Huang, Tsaur, & Yang, 2012; Dubini & Di Biase, 2008). Tourism often encourages communities to take pride in their heritage. Residents become active participants, serving as guides, storytellers, or artisans, and are eager to share their heritage with visitors (Poria, Butler, & Airey, 2004). This active involvement generates income and instils a sense of ownership and pride in the community's cultural heritage. Heritage tourism provides funding for conserving and restoring historical sites and artefacts. This ensures that these valuable cultural heritage elements are preserved for future generations, contributing to a collective sense of history and heritage (Koutsi, Lagarias, & Stratigea, 2022; Colavitti & Usai, 2019; Laing et al., 2014; Poria, Reichel, & Biran, 2006).

The economic and socio-cultural impacts of heritage tourism are intertwined. Economic benefits support cultural preservation efforts, while socio-cultural interactions foster mutual understanding and appreciation. Heritage tourism can sustainably bring about significant positive economic and cultural changes, enriching local communities' lives and enhancing travellers' experiences.

3 COMPETITIVE ADVANTAGE IN DESTINATION MANAGEMENT

Competitive advantage in tourism is the cornerstone of a destination or tourism-related business's success. It refers to the unique qualities, resources, or strategies that distinguish one entity from its competitors, making it more appealing to tourists (Yang, Lin, & Han, 2010). In a globalised and competitive tourism industry, having a competitive advantage is crucial for attracting visitors, sustaining growth, and ensuring economic prosperity. At its core lies the Unique Selling Proposition (USP), a defining characteristic that sets a destination apart. This could range from cultural heritage to natural wonders or innovative, sustainable practices (Boniface & Fowler, 2002). A compelling USP forms the foundation, creating an unmistakable identity that resonates with travellers seeking unique experiences. Integral to this advantage is consistently delivering high-quality services and memorable experiences (Sölvell, 2015; Porter, 2011). Exceptional hospitality, expert-guided tours, and seamless logistical arrangements significantly enhance visitor satisfaction. Positive encounters translate into glowing recommendations and enthusiastic word-of-mouth referrals, amplifying the destination's allure and competitiveness (Laing et al., 2014). Destinations steeped in cultural and historical significance enjoy a natural advantage. Museums, historical landmarks, indigenous crafts, and traditional festivals offer immersive journeys into the past, appealing to travellers intrigued by heritage exploration (Su & Lin, 2014). These sites enrich the visitor experience and contribute to the destination's unique appeal. Embracing innovation and sustainable practices amplifies a destination's competitive edge. Adapting to emerging trends, integrating technology into tours, and promoting eco-friendly initiatives are pivotal (Lopez & Pérez, 2020). Sustainability and responsible tourism practices are ethically crucial and a significant draw for the modern, eco-conscious traveller. Such initiatives reflect a destination's commitment to the environment and local communities, enhancing its desirability (Wang & Gu, 2020). Effective marketing and branding strategies play a pivotal role (Huang, Tsaur, & Yang, 2012). Consistent branding across various platforms, compelling storytelling, and targeted campaigns create emotional connections with potential visitors (Ryan & Higgins, 2006). Furthermore, collaborative efforts between stakeholders—hotels, local businesses, and governmental bodies—further enrich the visitor experience (Chandler, 2004). By offering comprehensive packages encompassing accommodation, dining, and local excursions, destinations can cater to travellers seeking convenience and diverse experiences. In essence, competitive advantage in tourism weaves a tapestry of unique offerings, exceptional services, sustainable practices, and strategic collaborations. Interconnected, these elements form a powerful allure, ensuring a destination's enduring appeal and prominence in the competitive global tourism landscape.

Several factors influence a destination's competitiveness in the global tourism industry, shaping its attractiveness to travellers. These factors are pivotal in determining a destination's appeal and ability to stand out amidst many travel options (refer to Table 2).

Table 1. Factors and their influence on destination's appeal

Factors	Influence	References
Natural and Cultural Attractions	The presence of scenic landscapes, diverse ecosystems, historical landmarks, archaeological sites, cultural festivals, and traditions significantly enhance a destination's appeal. Unique natural and cultural attractions provide a compelling reason for tourists to visit.	Huang, Tsaur, & Yang, 2012; Bourgeon-Renault et al., 2006; Boniface & Fowler, 2002
Infrastructure and Accessibility	Well-developed infrastructure, including transportation networks, roads, airports, and public facilities, ensures easy accessibility and convenience for travellers. Destinations with efficient transportation and accessibility options are more likely to attract tourists.	Choi et al., 2010; Bourgeon-Renault et al., 2006
Quality of Services	High-quality services, including accommodations, hospitality, guided tours, recreational activities, and dining options, play a crucial role. Exceptional customer service and memorable experiences create positive impressions, encouraging tourists to return and recommend the destination to others.	Porter, 2011; Jimura, 2011; Poria, Reichel, & Biran, 2006; Ryan & Higgins, 2006
Political Stability and Safety	Political stability and a safe environment are fundamental. Travellers are more likely to choose destinations where they feel secure. Destinations with stable political conditions and low crime rates are perceived as safer and more appealing.	Lopez & Pérez, 2020; Chandler, 2004
Marketing and Promotion	Effective marketing and promotional efforts create awareness and shape the destination's image. Strategic marketing campaigns, digital presence, and engaging content influence travellers' perceptions and decision-making processes.	Sölvell, 2015; Gombault & Petr, 2007; Boniface & Fowler, 2002
Price Competitiveness	The affordability of accommodations, activities, and overall travel expenses is a significant factor. Destinations offering competitive prices and value for money are attractive to budget-conscious travellers.	Lopez & Pérez, 2020; Ramsey & Everitt, 2008; Bourgeon-Renault et al., 2006
Sustainability and Responsible Tourism	Increasingly, travellers are concerned about environmental conservation and responsible tourism practices. Environmentally conscious tourists prefer destinations promoting sustainability, eco-friendly initiatives, and community engagement.	Sölvell, 2015; Porter, 2011; Gombault & Petr, 2007; Boniface & Fowler, 2002

continued on following page

Table 1. Continued

Factors	Influence	References
Local Culture and Community Engagement	Preservation of local culture and traditions, along with community involvement in tourism activities, creates authentic experiences. Tourists are drawn to destinations where they can interact with locals, participate in cultural events, and support local businesses.	Wang & Gu, 2020; Dubini & Di Biase, 2008; Smith & General, 2008; Poria, Reichel, & Biran, 2006
Accessibility to Information	The availability of information through online platforms, travel websites, and mobile apps significantly influences tourists' decision-making. Destinations providing comprehensive and easily accessible information have an advantage.	Cuccia & Cellini, 2007; Huh & Uysal, 2004; Kerstetter, Confer, & Graefe, 2001
Reviews and Recommendations	Positive reviews, recommendations from previous travellers, and word-of-mouth play a vital role. Travellers often rely on the experiences of others when choosing a destination, making online reviews and social media presence essential.	Colavitti & Usai, 2019; Gombault & Petr, 2007; Gilmore, Carson, & Ascenção, 2007

The interplay of natural attractions, infrastructure, quality of services, safety, marketing strategies, pricing, sustainability efforts, local culture, accessibility to information, and positive reviews collectively shape a destination's competitiveness in the dynamic tourism landscape. Successful destinations strategically leverage these factors to create a unique and appealing travel experience for visitors.

In a crowded marketplace, differentiation grabs the attention of potential tourists. It makes a destination or a tourism-related business stand out amidst numerous options, ensuring that travellers notice and consider it. Differentiation allows destinations to offer unique and memorable experiences to tourists (Flowers & Easterling, 2006). A destination can create lasting impressions on visitors by highlighting distinctive cultural, natural, or experiential features (Quinn, 2006), enhancing their satisfaction and the likelihood of return visits. Differentiation contributes significantly to building a strong brand identity (Jimura, 2011; Du Cros et al., 2005). It helps define what a destination stands for, what it offers, and why it is special. A well-differentiated brand becomes synonymous with certain qualities, making it recognisable and desirable to potential tourists (HuangTsaur, & Yang, 2012; Boniface & Fowler, 2002). Differentiation enables destinations to tailor their offerings to specific market segments. Destinations can attract the right audience and meet their specific needs and preferences by identifying unique selling points that resonate with certain types of travellers, such as adventure seekers, cultural enthusiasts, or eco-conscious tourists (Colbert, 2003). When tourists have unique and satisfying experiences, they are likelier to become loyal customers (Dubini & Di Biase, 2008; Buckley, 2004). Differentiation fosters customer loyalty by creating emotional connections and positive memories, encouraging repeat visits and positive word-of-mouth recommendations

(Gilmore, Carson, & Ascenção, 2007). Differentiation adds value to a destination or a tourism business in the eyes of the consumer. Unique offerings and experiences justify pricing, enhancing the perceived value for money (Huang, Tsaur, & Yang, 2012; Chen & Chen, 2010). Travellers are willing to pay a premium for experiences they perceive as exceptional and exclusive. The pursuit of differentiation often drives innovation. Destinations and businesses continually strive to introduce new services, experiences, or sustainable practices to stand out (Timothy & Boyd, 2003). This innovation attracts tourists and contributes to the tourism industry's growth and evolution (Koutsi, Lagarias, & Stratigea, 2022). Differentiation is essential for long-term growth and sustainability. A destination that differentiates itself effectively can maintain its appeal over time, adapting to changing trends and consumer preferences (Smith & General, 2008). This adaptability ensures continued relevance and attractiveness in the tourism market.

4 STRATEGIES FOR HERITAGE-LED DESTINATION MANAGEMENT

In the intricate tapestry of global tourism, heritage-led destination management stands as a beacon of cultural preservation and sustainable economic growth. Preserving historical and cultural treasures while enticing travellers requires a delicate balance of strategies that weave together tradition, innovation, and community engagement. This intricate process demands meticulous planning, collaborative efforts, and a deep understanding of the intersection between heritage conservation and the demands of modern tourism (Boyd, 2002). In this context, the following discussion delves into a comprehensive exploration of the strategies essential for effective heritage-led destination management. From community empowerment to sustainable practices and innovative marketing, these strategies converge to create a roadmap for destinations seeking to showcase their cultural legacies while ensuring responsible and enriching visitor experiences.

In heritage-led destination management, a holistic approach encompasses interconnected strategies. Central to this approach is the meticulous preservation and conservation of historical assets, safeguarding them from the impact of tourism (Hughes, 2013). Actively engaging local communities becomes paramount, empowering them to participate in tourism endeavours and benefit economically. Education is crucial for tourists and locals, fostering a deep understanding of the heritage's significance (Holmes et al., 2006). This knowledge dissemination occurs through educational programs and interactive tours. Culturally enriching experiences are curated through events such as festivals and workshops, allowing tourists to authenticate with local traditions. Sustainability underpins these strategies, promoting eco-friendly initiatives and responsible tourism practices (Petr, 2009; Gombault & Petr, 2007). Concurrently, strategic infrastructure development aligns with the destination's heritage, ensuring seamless experiences while minimising environmental impact. Effective branding and marketing campaigns emphasise the unique cultural offerings, reaching a broader audience through digital platforms (Koutsi, Lagarias, & Stratigea, 2022; Jimura, 2011). Regulatory measures, including visitor quotas and codes of conduct, are implemented to protect heritage sites from overcrowding and degradation. Public-private partnerships are nurtured, fostering innovation and resource-sharing (OCDE, 2014). Continuous monitoring and evaluation drive adaptive management, ensuring heritage preservation while promoting sustainable economic growth (Hughes, 2013; Chen & Chen, 2010). These integrated strategies form a cohesive framework, ensuring the harmonious coexistence of cultural preservation and thriving heritage-led tourism.

4.1 Heritage Preservation and Conservation

At the heart of cultural stewardship lies heritage preservation, a meticulous endeavour focused on maintaining the existing state of historical and cultural assets. Through meticulous documentation and structural stabilisation, preservation aims to prevent further deterioration, ensuring that artefacts, monuments, and historical sites remain intact. This process not only safeguards tangible heritage but also extends to preserving intangible cultural elements like languages, customs, and traditional knowledge (OCDE, 2014). Preservation efforts act as a bridge, connecting present and future generations to their rich cultural legacy. Conservation, a dynamic facet of heritage management, delves deeper into restoration and repair (Sölvell, 2015). This intricate process involves extensive research, scientific analysis, and skilled craftsmanship to revive heritage assets to their former glory (Timothy, 2011). Conservationists employ their expertise to repair damages caused by various factors while preserving the authentic historical characteristics of the artefact or site (Huh & Uysal, 2004). It is a delicate balance between revitalising the past and preserving the genuine essence of the heritage, ensuring that the story embedded within it continues to resonate (Huh & Uysal, 2004; Stamboulis & Skayannis, 2003).

Heritage preservation encompasses both cultural and natural realms. On the cultural front, it involves safeguarding intangible aspects such as languages, traditions, and rituals. Cultural preservation efforts extend to oral history projects and educational initiatives, preserving the unique identity of communities (Koutsi & Stratigea, 2019; Dubini & Di Biase, 2008). In natural heritage, the focus shifts to maintaining biodiversity, wildlife habitats, and landscapes of exceptional beauty (Richards & Wilson, 2006). These efforts involve sustainable resource management and climate change mitigation, ensuring these areas' ecological balance and natural allure remain unspoiled. Beyond the tangible and intangible assets, heritage preservation holds immense cultural, social, and environmental significance (Lopez & Pérez, 2020; Colavitti & Usai, 2019). It fosters a profound sense of community identity and pride, grounding them in their cultural roots (Richards, 2001). Moreover, heritage sites serve as educational hubs, attracting scholars, researchers, and tourists, fostering cultural exchange, and enriching global understanding (Sölvell, 2015). Equally important, preservation encourages sustainable practices, promoting eco-friendly initiatives and the responsible use of resources (Wang & Gu, 2020; Dubini & Di Biase, 2008; Smith & General, 2008). Through these interconnected efforts, heritage preservation safeguards the past and paves the way for a culturally vibrant and environmentally conscious future.

4.2 Interpretation and Storytelling

Interpretation in the context of heritage and tourism refers to explaining, analysing, and presenting historical, cultural, and natural heritage to visitors. It involves translating complex information about heritage sites into engaging narratives and interactive experiences (Huh & Uysal, 2004). Skilled interpreters, often guides or educators, bridge the gap between the heritage site and the visitor, helping the audience understand the significance, context, and stories associated with the place (Laing et al., 2014; Jimura, 2011). Interpretation aims to create meaningful connections, evoke emotions, and enhance the visitor's understanding and appreciation of the presented heritage (Richards, 2001).

Storytelling is a powerful tool for interpretation. It involves weaving narratives around historical events, cultural practices, or natural phenomena associated with a heritage site. Stories add depth, context, and a human touch to the interpretation process (Quinn, 2006; Kerstetter, Confer, & Graefe, 2001). Through storytelling, heritage sites come to life, capturing the imagination of visitors and immersing them in the rich tapestry of the past (Petr, 2002). Effective storytelling engages emotions, fosters empathy, and creates memorable experiences (Gilmore, Carson, & Ascenção, 2007; Holmes et al., 2006). It transforms dry facts into compelling narratives, making the heritage more relatable and relevant to the audience.

Interpretation and storytelling are interconnected elements essential in heritage tourism. Interpretation provides the factual foundation, explaining a heritage site's historical, cultural, and environmental significance (Timothy, 2011; Richards, 2001). It contextualises the information, making it accessible to a diverse audience. Storytelling, on the other hand, adds a layer of emotion and relatability (Colavitti & Usai, 2019; Porter, 2011; Chen & Chen, 2010; Caton & Santos, 2007). By framing historical facts within a narrative structure, storytelling makes the information more engaging and memorable. Interpretation and storytelling create immersive experiences, enabling visitors to connect with the heritage site personally and emotionally. In essence, interpretation and storytelling are the vehicles through which heritage sites communicate with visitors. They transform static artefacts and historical facts into dynamic, living experiences. Heritage sites preserve and share their stories through these techniques, ensuring cultural and historical significance resonates with present and future generations.

4.3 Infrastructure Development

Infrastructure development encompasses planning, designing, constructing, and maintaining essential physical and organisational structures, facilities, and systems that support and enhance the functioning of societies and industries (UNWTO, 2010; OECD, 2009). In various sectors, including transportation, energy, communication, and tourism, robust infrastructure drives economic growth, ensures social well-being, and fosters sustainable development (refer to Tables 3 and 4).

Table 2. Key aspects of infrastructure development and their influence

Key Aspects of Infrastructure Development	Influence	References
Transportation Networks	Well-developed transportation infrastructure, including roads, bridges, railways, ports, and airports, facilitates the seamless movement of goods, services, and people. Efficient transportation systems reduce travel times, enhance connectivity, and stimulate economic activities in urban and rural areas.	UNWTO, 2010; Holmes et al., 2006; Boniface, & Fowler, 2002
Energy Supply and Distribution	Reliable energy infrastructure, encompassing power plants, grids, and renewable energy sources, is essential for powering industries, homes, and businesses. Access to uninterrupted and affordable energy drives economic productivity and innovation while promoting environmental sustainability.	Choi et al., 2010; Shore, 2010; Bourgeon-Renault et al., 2006
Communication and Information Technology	Advanced communication infrastructure, such as high-speed internet, mobile networks, and data centres, connects people globally and fosters digital transformation. Information and communication technology infrastructure support e-commerce, education, healthcare, and efficient government services.	Laing et al., 2014; Porter, 2011; Holmes et al., 2006; Boniface, & Fowler, 2002
Tourism and Hospitality Facilities	Within the tourism sector, infrastructure development involves creating accommodations, recreational facilities, attractions, and visitor services. Well-designed hotels, resorts, heritage sites, and entertainment venues enhance the tourist experience, attracting visitors and contributing to the local economy.	Lopez & Pérez, 2020; Shore, 2010; Petr, 2009; Quinn, 2006

continued on following page

Table 2. Continued

Key Aspects of Infrastructure Development	Influence	References
Water and Sanitation Systems	Adequate water supply and sanitation infrastructure ensure access to clean water, sanitation facilities, and wastewater management. Proper water infrastructure safeguards public health, promotes hygiene and supports agriculture and industries reliant on water resources.	Harzing & Giroud, 2014; Smit, 2010
Urban and Rural Development	Infrastructure development in urban areas includes smart city initiatives, public spaces, public transportation, and waste management systems. In rural areas, it involves improving road connectivity, electrification, healthcare centres, and educational institutions, bridging the urban-rural divide.	Lopez & Pérez, 2020; Lak, Gheitasi, & Timothy, 2020; Bourgeon-Renault et al., 2006; Poria, Butler, & Airey, 2004

Table 3. Importance of infrastructure development and their influence

Importance of Infrastructure Development	Influence	References
Economic Growth	Well-planned infrastructure stimulates economic activities, attracts investments, and creates job opportunities, fostering overall economic growth and prosperity.	Koutsi, Lagarias, & Stratigea, 2022; Wang & Gu, 2020; Huang, Tsaur, & Yang, 2012; Porter, 2011; Quinn, 2006
Enhanced Quality of Life	Adequate infrastructure leads to improved living standards and access to healthcare, education, and recreational facilities, enhancing the quality of life for residents.	Laing et al., 2014; Porter, 2011; Dubini & Di Biase, 2008; Holmes et al., 2006; Boniface & Fowler, 2002
Global Competitiveness	Countries with robust infrastructure are more competitive globally, attracting businesses, skilled professionals, and tourists, thus bolstering their international standing.	Lopez & Pérez, 2020; Shore, 2010; Petr, 2009; Quinn, 2006
Environmental Sustainability	Sustainable infrastructure practices, such as green energy and efficient public transportation, contribute to environmental conservation and climate change mitigation.	Harzing & Giroud, 2014; Jimura, 2011; Smit, 2010; Ramsey & Everitt, 2008; Du Cros et al., 2005
Resilience and Disaster Preparedness	Well-constructed infrastructure can withstand natural disasters and aids in disaster recovery, ensuring communities are resilient in the face of emergencies.	Lak, Gheitasi, & Timothy, 2020; Lopez & Pérez, 2020; Bourgeon-Renault et al., 2006; Poria, Butler, & Airey, 2004

Infrastructure development is the backbone of societal progress, underpinning economic vitality, social well-being, and environmental sustainability. Strategic planning and investment in diverse infrastructure sectors are essential for fostering sustainable development and creating resilient, connected, prosperous communities.

4.4 Cultural Events and Festivals

Festivals and cultural events are colourful manifestations of a community's history, customs, and creative spirit. They provide tourists with a singular chance to fully immerse themselves in the diversity of regional customs and celebrations, acting as windows into the cultural soul of a community (Škrabić Perić et al., 2021). These activities, which range from religious ceremonies to traditional performances and art exhibits, are essential to preserving cultural heritage, community involvement, and enhanced tourism (Huh & Uysal, 2004). Festivals and cultural events serve as stewards of customs, transferring rituals, music, dance, and crafts from generation to generation (Koutsi & Stratigea, 2021). Communities preserve their cultural legacy by honouring these traditions in public areas (Colbert, 2003). These gatherings transform into living museums that capture the spirit of a community's history and identity through customary rituals, storytelling, and artisan demonstrations (Dionisia & Stratigea, 2020). A sense of pride and belonging is fostered within communities through participation in cultural events (Boniface & Fowler, 2002). Intergenerational knowledge is preserved, and social ties are reinforced by the active participation of locals in event planning and performance. Community members who are actively involved ensure that traditions are carried on by educating younger generations and celebrating their heritage (Beal et al., 2019).

Festivals and other cultural events draw tourists from various backgrounds who want to experience a place's true spirit (Buckley, 2004). The vibrant exhibits, customary performances, and delectable food enthral visitors for an unforgettable and engaging travel experience. The increase in visitors creates job opportunities for local companies, craftspeople, and the hospitality sector, which boosts the local economy (Kerstetter, Confer, & Graefe, 2001). These gatherings offer forums for cross-cultural communication where locals and tourists can mingle, swap tales, and celebrate diversity. International artists, performers, and craftspeople are frequently featured at cultural events, which promotes appreciation and understanding of different cultures (Smit, 2010). Communities welcome the outside world through this interchange, fostering respect, tolerance, and peace. Festivals and cultural events voice intangible cultural heritage, like folklore, oral traditions, and traditional skills (UNWTO, 2010). These intangible qualities are celebrated and exhibited through folk music, dance, storytelling, and craft shows. These activities greatly enhance a community's overall cultural legacy by protecting intangible heritage (UNWTO, 2010; OECD, 2009).

Cultural events and festivals are vibrant tapestries that weave together heritage preservation, community vitality, tourism enrichment, and cultural exchange. They create a harmonious blend of tradition and celebration, inviting locals and tourists to partake in the colourful mosaic of a community's cultural heritage. Through these events, the past comes alive, and the future is infused with the richness of tradition, ensuring that cultural heritage remains a living, evolving entity.

4.5 Collaboration with Local Communities

Sustainable tourism practises and heritage preservation is predicated on collaboration with local communities (Koutsi, Lagarias, & Stratigea, 2022; Smit, 2010). Through meaningful engagement and creating a sense of ownership over cultural heritage, this collaborative approach empowers communities (Mu, 2022). Local communities significantly influence how their heritage is portrayed and preserved and how visitors are enhanced by active participation in tourism-related decision-making and initiatives (Sölvell, 2015). Providing local communities with opportunities to participate in tourism-related activities actively is key to empowering them. This can be anything from delivering expertly guided tours conducted by locals to showcasing traditional crafts and culinary talents (Egusquiza et al., 2021). Active tourism promotes economic independence for communities, supports small businesses and creates jobs, all of which contribute to self-sustainability development. Collaboration with local groups ensures that tourism developments respect and uphold the authenticity of the local culture (Chen & Chen, 2010; Du Cros et al., 2005). The planning and execution of tourism initiatives involve community members, striking a careful balance between heritage preservation and economic growth (Timothy, 2011). By working together, we can stop the commercialisation of culture and ensure that customs and traditions are upheld and carried on for subsequent generations (Brümmer & Karusseit, 2020). Local communities are frequently tasked with protecting the environment and cultural heritage (Richards & Wilson, 2006). Collaborative projects emphasise responsible tourism practises, urging visitors and locals to be mindful of the environment and cultural customs (Beal et al., 2019). Communities and visitors alike learn more about the significance of sustainable practises, like waste reduction, conservation, and moral interactions, through educational programmes and awareness campaigns (Shore, 2010; Richards, 2001). Visitors and locals can engage in genuine cultural exchanges when local communities work together (Smit, 2010). Guests are made to feel at home in the community and are free to participate in customs, celebrations, and daily activities (D'Auria, 2009). Visitors can have immersive and enriching experiences that foster appreciation and understanding of different cultures through these exchanges (Jimura, 2011; Ramsey & Everitt, 2008; Richards & Wilson, 2006; Du Cros et al.,

2005). Similarly, exposure to various viewpoints and cultures promotes tolerance and respect among community members.

Working together with local communities, intangible heritage—such as oral traditions, folklore, and traditional knowledge—is protected (D'Auria, 2009). These intangible heritage elements are shared and preserved with tourists through the involvement of local storytellers, artists, and performers in tourism activities. This collaborative approach guarantees the celebration and value of the distinct narratives and skills passed down through the generations (Dogruyol, Aziz, & Arayici, 2018). Working together to promote heritage-led tourism benefits both the locals and tourists in a mutually beneficial way. Collaborative efforts generate a sustainable tourism model through empowering communities, protecting intangible heritage, encouraging responsible tourism, maintaining cultural authenticity, and stimulating cultural interaction. Heritage places come to life through these partnerships, transforming into thriving centres where economic development and cultural preservation coexist peacefully.

5 CASE STUDIES

Heritage preservation is a landmark for sustainable tourism, steering destinations toward a careful balance between protecting the past and promoting economic development. The case studies here tell fascinating stories of tourism destinations that have effectively used their rich history to produce lively, immersive cultural experiences. These accounts provide insight into the strategic measures these destinations take and their significant effects on local communities, the economy, and the preservation of cultural heritage. We set off on a trip to investigate the various tactics used by locations and towns worldwide through these case studies. Travellers looking for genuine experiences are drawn to these destinations because of their legacy, which ranges from impressive old archaeological sites to well-preserved mediaeval neighbourhoods. We embarked on a journey to explore the many strategies employed by places and communities via these case studies. Due to its history, which includes anything from stunning old archaeological sites to well-preserved mediaeval villages, travellers seeking authentic experiences are drawn to these destinations. By examining these case studies (refer to Table 5), we learn a lot about the creative methods, neighbourhood partnerships, and environmentally friendly practices that have elevated these destinations to the forefront of heritage-led tourism. Every case study demonstrates how careful work can turn historical locations into living narratives and is a tribute to the transformational power of heritage preservation. Investigating these tales reveals the complex tactics, depth of culture, and dynamism of the economy that characterise effective heritage-led destination management. These narratives highlight the significance of heritage as a catalyst for sustainable tourism and a link between the past and the future, inspiring and educating for future endeavours.

Table 4. Case studies - Heritage leverage strategy, outcomes and site's recent economic data

Case Study	Heritage Leverage Strategy	Outcomes	Recent Economic Data
Kyoto, Japan	Kyoto, renowned for its well-preserved historical sites and traditional culture, strategically leveraged its heritage to attract tourists. The city focused on preserving ancient temples, shrines, and traditional tea houses while encouraging local artisans to continue traditional crafts. Collaborations between the government and local communities ensured the preservation of cultural authenticity.	Kyoto's heritage-led approach transformed it into a premier cultural destination. Tourists flock to experience traditional tea ceremonies, visit ancient temples, and witness geisha performances. The city's economy thrived, benefiting from tourism revenues. The local community actively participated, leading to sustainable economic growth and cultural preservation.	Kyoto's tourism sector generated over $15 billion in 2022, with a significant portion attributed to heritage tourism.
Dubrovnik, Croatia	Dubrovnik, a UNESCO World Heritage Site, strategically utilised its well-preserved medieval architecture and historic sites to boost tourism. The city implemented strict conservation measures to maintain the integrity of its buildings. Additionally, Dubrovnik diversified its offerings, combining heritage tourism with cultural events and festivals, creating a unique visitor experience.	Dubrovnik's heritage-led tourism approach attracted a surge in international visitors. The city's economy flourished due to increased tourism revenue, supporting local businesses. By combining heritage with cultural events, Dubrovnik created a year-round tourist destination, mitigating the impact of seasonality. The city also successfully balanced the tourism influx while preserving its historic charm.	Dubrovnik's tourism sector contributed approximately €1.2 billion to the local economy in 2021, highlighting the success of its heritage tourism strategy.
Machu Picchu, Peru	Machu Picchu, one of the world's most iconic heritage sites, implemented a sustainable tourism model. The Peruvian government regulated visitor numbers, introduced guided tours, and restricted access to sensitive areas. Additionally, local communities were involved, offering guided tours and authentic cultural experiences, ensuring responsible tourism practices.	Machu Picchu's careful management preserved the site's integrity while offering enriching experiences to visitors. The local communities became active stakeholders, benefiting economically from tourism. Sustainable practices protected the delicate ecosystem, ensuring the site's preservation for future generations. The site became a beacon for responsible heritage tourism, setting an example globally.	In 2022, Machu Picchu generated over $5 billion in tourism revenue, with a substantial portion supporting local communities.

continued on following page

Table 4. Continued

Case Study	Heritage Leverage Strategy	Outcomes	Recent Economic Data
Bhaktapur, Nepal	Bhaktapur, a medieval city in Nepal, strategically leveraged its rich heritage by preserving its ancient architecture, intricate woodwork, and traditional pottery. The city implemented strict conservation policies to maintain the authenticity of its heritage sites, and local craftsmen were encouraged to continue traditional arts, such as pottery and Thangka painting. Bhaktapur also actively involved local communities in tourism initiatives, enabling them to showcase their skills and culture.	Bhaktapur's heritage-led approach transformed the city into a cultural oasis. Tourists are attracted to its well-preserved medieval charm, participating in pottery workshops, exploring ancient temples, and witnessing traditional craft demonstrations. The local economy has flourished, with artisans and businesses benefiting from tourism revenues. Additionally, the sense of pride among the locals in preserving their heritage has strengthened community bonds and cultural identity.	Bhaktapur's tourism sector contributed significantly to the local economy, with annual revenues exceeding $50 million.
Cartagena, Colombia	Cartagena, a colonial city in Colombia, strategically utilised its well-preserved historic district, colourful colonial buildings, and cobblestone streets to attract tourists. The city implemented restoration programs to maintain the integrity of its heritage sites, transforming old mansions into boutique hotels and restaurants. Cartagena also diversified its offerings by hosting cultural events, such as music festivals and art exhibitions, within its historic quarters, creating a vibrant visitor atmosphere.	Cartagena's heritage-led tourism approach turned the city into a cultural hub. Tourists are captivated by its colonial architecture, exploring museums, art galleries, and historic forts. The city's economy has thrived due to increased tourism, supporting local businesses and artists. By integrating cultural events, Cartagena has become a dynamic destination throughout the year, ensuring a steady influx of tourists and preserving its historical charm.	Cartagena's tourism sector generated approximately $1 billion in 2022, underscoring its economic impact.
Petra, Jordan	Petra, an ancient city carved into rose-red cliffs, strategically leveraged its archaeological wonders and UNESCO World Heritage Site status. The Jordanian government implemented preservation efforts, including site restoration and visitor regulations, to protect Petra's architectural marvels. Additionally, the local Bedouin communities, with a historical connection with Petra, were engaged in tourism activities, offering guided tours and cultural experiences.	Petra's heritage-led approach turned it into a world-renowned archaeological site. Tourists are fascinated by its rock-cut architecture, exploring the Treasury, Monastery, and other ancient structures. The local Bedouin communities have become active stakeholders, benefiting economically from tourism. Sustainable practices and visitor regulations have ensured the site's preservation, making Petra a symbol of responsible heritage tourism.	In 2022, Petra's tourism revenue surpassed $2 billion, contributing significantly to Jordan's economy.

continued on following page

Table 4. Continued

Case Study	Heritage Leverage Strategy	Outcomes	Recent Economic Data
Bath, England	Bath strategically leveraged its well-preserved Roman baths, Georgian architecture, and UNESCO World Heritage Site status. The city focused on restoring historic buildings, transforming them into museums and visitor centres. Bath also implemented themed tours, allowing tourists to explore the city's historical and architectural heritage, and encouraged local artisans to create heritage-inspired crafts and products.	Bath's heritage-led tourism approach has turned it into a premier cultural destination. Tourists are captivated by the Roman baths, Georgian crescents, and medieval abbey. The city's economy has thrived, with tourism contributing significantly to local businesses and cultural institutions. Bath's successful heritage preservation efforts have transformed it into a living museum where visitors can experience the elegance and grandeur of the past.	Bath's tourism sector generated over £500 million in 2022, reflecting its economic significance.
Gyeongju, South Korea	Gyeongju, often called "the museum without walls," strategically utilised its ancient temples, burial mounds, and historical relics to attract tourists. The city implemented interpretative signage, interactive exhibits, and multimedia presentations to enhance visitor experiences. Gyeongju also organised cultural festivals, traditional music performances, and temple stay programs to immerse visitors in the region's rich heritage.	Gyeongju's heritage-led approach has made it a cultural treasure trove. Tourists are drawn to its ancient sites, including Bulguksa Temple and Seokguram Grotto, exploring the city's Silla Dynasty heritage. The local economy has prospered, benefitting from tourism revenues and the sale of traditional crafts and souvenirs. Gyeongju's commitment to preserving its historical legacy has made it a UNESCO World Heritage Site, ensuring the city's enduring appeal to history enthusiasts and cultural explorers.	Gyeongju's tourism revenue was estimated to exceed $1 billion in 2022, highlighting its success as a heritage tourism destination.

The case studies demonstrate a well-balanced interplay of tactics, highlighting the importance of community participation, diverse offers, stringent conservation measures, and sustainable practices. These shared values emphasise the all-encompassing, cooperative strategy that these destinations have chosen. By carefully maintaining cultural authenticity, involving local communities, and balancing tourism and conservation, these destinations have drawn tourists and sown the seeds of cultural preservation and economic prosperity. We witness a rich tapestry of strategies within this array of case studies. Strict preservation measures, community involvement, and the diversification of offerings emerge as common denominators, illustrating the multifaceted nature of heritage-led tourism. Integrating cultural events, thematic tours, and artisanal crafts enriches the visitor experience, adding depth to heritage exploration. Moreover, as seen in Bath and Gyeongju, the emphasis on interpretative tools and immersive programs enhances visitor understanding, forging profound connections with the heritage sites. The successful outcomes of these efforts demonstrate the beneficial relationship between sustainable tourism and cultural preservation. These tourism destinations have fostered strong local economies and drawn many visitors. These techniques have revitalised towns and encouraged pride and ownership by providing sustainable economic possibilities for companies and craftspeople. The secret is striking a balance between sharing these riches with the community and protecting their historical and cultural relevance.

These case studies are beacons of inspiration, illuminating the path for other heritage destinations worldwide. They underscore the transformative impact of creativity, community involvement, and immersive experiences. Through these narratives, we are invited to witness the seamless integration of heritage preservation, economic prosperity, and cultural enrichment. These destinations serve as success stories and guiding lights, emphasising the enduring value of heritage-led tourism in fostering cultural richness and financial well-being.

6 CHALLENGES AND CONSIDERATIONS

Preserving cultural riches and historical sites presents a distinct set of challenges that must be acknowledged as the world embraces the transformational potential of heritage-led tourism. The complex web of factors that destinations must take into account as they attempt to balance the demands of contemporary tourism with the rich fabric of their legacy is covered in this section. Among the numerous challenges that heritage-led tourism ventures confront include balancing development and conservation, handling the complications of over-tourism, encouraging community engagement, and promoting sustainable practices. There are chances for creative thinking and teamwork within these problems. Destinations may successfully negotiate these challenges by recognising the delicate interaction between promoting responsible tourism, encouraging community engagement, and maintaining the concrete and intangible parts of history. This investigation dives into the core of these challenges and provides insights into the deliberate approaches and factors required for heritage-led tourism to prosper sustainably. Heritage destinations may set the path for a future in which the past serves as a guide for the sustainable development of cultural resources, guaranteeing their survival for future generations by embracing the lessons acquired from these difficulties.

One of the foremost challenges in heritage-led tourism is striking a delicate balance between preserving a site's cultural and historical integrity while accommodating tourism development needs (Burnham, 2022). The challenge lies in implementing sustainable practices that protect heritage sites from wear and tear, ensuring that the influx of tourists does not compromise the authenticity of these invaluable treasures. Careful planning, conservation efforts, and responsible tourism practices are pivotal in maintaining this equilibrium (Boniface & Fowler, 2002). The rise in tourism, while beneficial for local economies, often leads to over-tourism, where heritage sites are inundated with an overwhelming number of visitors (Smit, 2010). This influx can strain infrastructure, erode cultural authenticity, and disturb the natural environment (El Faouri & Sibley, 2022). Critical considerations include managing visitor numbers, implementing crowd control measures, and regulating access (Colbert, 2003). Sustainable tourism strategies are essential to mitigate the adverse effects of over-tourism, ensuring that the sites remain enjoyable while preserving their historical significance. Incorporating local communities into the tourism narrative is critical to the success of heritage-led initiatives (Cuccia & Cellini, 2007). However, managing the delicate balance between community involvement and commercial interests is challenging. Residents and indigenous communities should actively participate in decision-making processes, ensuring their cultural heritage is respected and they receive equitable benefits (Calver & Page, 2013; Kolar & Zabkar, 2010). Effective stakeholder management fosters partnerships between governments, businesses, and communities, creating a collaborative environment where all stakeholders contribute to the sustainable development of heritage sites. Sustainable development principles are paramount in heritage-led tourism. The responsible management of resources, waste reduction, energy efficiency, and promoting eco-friendly practices are integral aspects (Laing et al., 2014; Gombault & Petr, 2007). Additionally, raising awareness among tourists about cultural sensitivity, environmental conservation, and respecting local traditions is crucial. Encouraging responsible behaviour among visitors through education and guidelines ensures that the sites are cherished and preserved for future generations (Porter, 2011). While physical heritage sites are tangible treasures, preserving intangible heritage, such as traditional practices, languages, and folklore, poses a unique challenge (Panagiotopoulou, Somarakis, & Stratigea, 2020). These aspects of cultural heritage are equally valuable and must be safeguarded. Efforts to document, promote, and transmit intangible heritage to younger generations are essential for its continuity. Balancing the preservation of tangible and intangible heritage enriches the overall heritage experience for tourists and communities (Wang & Gu, 2020; Dubini & Di Biase, 2008).

Heritage-led tourist destinations must take a comprehensive strategy incorporating sustainable practices, community involvement, and responsible tourism to navigate these issues effectively. Heritage sites may flourish as economic and cultural assets and be preserved for the benefit and enjoyment of future generations if these issues are carefully addressed.

7 SUSTAINABLE HERITAGE-LED TOURISM

Amidst growing concerns about how tourism affects cultural and natural heritage, sustainable heritage-led tourism has surfaced as a ray of hope, steering destinations toward a more conscientious and responsible approach. The fundamental ideas of sustainable tourism strongly emphasise striking a careful balance between socioeconomic growth, cultural preservation, and environmental conservation. Destinations may build an ecology where past treasures can be appreciated and treasured without jeopardising their integrity for coming generations by following these guidelines. Conscientious management of resources is essential to sustainable tourism. Destinations may reduce their influence on natural ecosystems by supporting trash reduction and recycling efforts, saving energy, and minimising their ecological imprint. Furthermore, maintaining cultural authenticity is critical. This entails preserving traditional customs, dialects, crafts, and historical sites. Respect and understanding between tourists and local populations are equally important goals of responsible tourism practices. Sustainable tourism principles guarantee that the tourist experience benefits both guests and hosts by promoting cultural awareness, promoting ethical relationships, and sustaining local customs.

Strategic approaches for responsible heritage tourism encompass a spectrum of initiatives to nurture heritage sites while ensuring positive outcomes for local communities. Engaging residents as active participants in heritage preservation transforms them into custodians of their culture. Empowering them to share their knowledge and traditions enhances the visitor experience and instils a sense of pride and ownership. To combat the adverse effects of overtourism, careful planning and management are vital. Implementing visitor guidelines, regulating visitor numbers, and introducing reservation systems can prevent overcrowding and preserve the site's integrity. An essential component of ethical historical tourism is education. Including instructional elements in tourist experiences—like seminars, guided tours, and interpretive signage—improves visitor comprehension. Incorporating visitors into the historical and cultural significance of the location fosters tremendous respect and appreciation for the legacy. In addition, establishing cooperative alliances among governmental bodies, nearby enterprises, and local populations guarantees the long-term viability of heritage-focused projects. These collaborations generate an atmosphere in which the preservation of cultural heritage and economic development go hand in hand by accelerating economic growth, opening up job possibilities, and promoting cultural interaction. The overarching objective of sustainable heritage-led tourism is to leave a legacy that honours the past, enriches the present, and safeguards the future. It transcends beyond merely preserving historical artefacts or attracting large numbers of tourists. Destinations can turn heritage sites into living, breathing entities by implementing responsible heritage tourism strategies and embracing sustainable tourism principles. This will ensure that the wonders of our shared heritage are preserved for future generations and will also support the local communities who call these locations home.

8 CONCLUSION

Heritage-led destination management is a thread in the global tourist tapestry that shines a route where future dreams resonate with past riches. This investigation delved through the complex subtleties of heritage-led tourism, revealing the guiding ideas, effective tactics, and obstacles faced by locations trying to balance contemporary tourism's needs and the preservation of cultural legacies. As we close our investigation, several vital themes come to light, highlighting the enormous potential and transformational strength of heritage-led destination management. Throughout our research, we explored the core of heritage-led tourism, stressing the value of stringent conservation regulations, community engagement, various offers, and sustainable practices. Responsible tourism is built on these values ingrained in the fabric of prosperous heritage-led projects. Involving local communities, protecting intangible cultural assets, and promoting cross-cultural interchange became essential elements, underscoring the comprehensive strategy required for the peaceful coexistence of tourist development and heritage preservation. The analysis and case studies emphasised that heritage-led destination management drives sustainable growth, cultural enrichment, and economic vibrancy rather than just a preservation project. Destinations may create immersive experiences for tourists and support local communities by adopting the heritage-led strategy, which turns historical places into lively cultural centres. In addition to protecting the past, preserving physical and intangible heritage enhances the present and gives communities a strong feeling of pride and identity.

Prospects for historic tourism are bright, with cutting-edge trends and changing tourist expectations. Immersive technology, including virtual and augmented reality, is anticipated to transform tourist experiences by providing interactive tours of historical periods. Sustainable practises will remain a fundamental component that propels environmentally conscious projects and efforts towards responsible tourism. In addition, incorporating storytelling, cultural festivals, and gastronomic experiences would improve legacy tourism's authenticity and provide guests with various historical interactions. Finally, heritage-led destination management proves the enduring value of our shared cultural legacy and the countless opportunities it presents. Heritage-led tourism may help to create a future in which the riches of antiquity coexist peacefully with the energy of the contemporary world by accepting the lessons learnt from the past, respecting the customs of the communities where it operates, and encouraging a culture of shared responsibility. Let's celebrate the richness of our heritage as we set out on this trip and work to ensure that it leaves a legacy that inspires and enriches the lives of everyone drawn to its enduring attraction.

9 LIMITATIONS

Several potential limitations were identified during the research process that could impact the academic rigor and reliability of the manuscript. Challenges in data collection arose due to the availability and accessibility of comprehensive data on heritage-led tourism and destination competitiveness. Time constraints limited the ability to conduct extensive fieldwork or primary data collection methods such as interviews or surveys, relying primarily on existing literature and document analysis. Access restrictions to confidential documents constrained the exploration of critical aspects of heritage preservation and community engagement strategies. Variations in methodologies across different data sources may have introduced biases or inconsistencies in the analysis. Lastly, while the case studies provided diverse insights, the findings may not be universally applicable due to local contextual factors influencing each heritage destination differently. Addressing these limitations transparently provides clarity on the research scope and boundaries, enhancing the manuscript's academic rigor. These insights underscore the importance of future research efforts in overcoming these challenges.

10 FUTURE RESEARCH DIRECTIONS

To build upon this study and address the identified limitations, future research should focus on enhancing data collection methodologies. This includes exploring innovative approaches to gather real-time data on visitor behaviors and community perceptions through surveys and interviews. Collaborations with local authorities and stakeholders can facilitate access to confidential documents and proprietary information, providing deeper insights into heritage preservation strategies and tourism management practices. Additionally, comparative studies across diverse heritage destinations can broaden the generalizability of findings, offering insights into the unique challenges and opportunities faced by different cultural contexts. By addressing these avenues, future research can contribute robustly to the field of heritage-led tourism and destination competitiveness.

11 RECOMMENDATIONS

Heritage-led tourism offers a unique opportunity to celebrate and preserve cultural and historical assets while fostering economic and community development. However, achieving this balance requires a strategic approach that addresses the inherent challenges of heritage preservation, sustainable tourism practices, and community engagement. To guide decision-makers in developing effective action plans, the following recommendations provide a comprehensive framework to ensure that heritage sites can thrive as both cultural treasures and economic assets, benefiting current and future generations.

Table 5. Recommendations for Addressing Challenges in Heritage-Led Tourism Development

Challenge	Recommendations
Balanced Development and Conservation	1. Implement a regulatory framework that enforces strict conservation practices while allowing for responsible tourism development. 2. Develop comprehensive management plans that include guidelines for visitor capacity, site maintenance, and periodic impact assessments to monitor the effects of tourism on heritage sites.
Over-Tourism Management	1. Introduce visitor management systems that include reservation systems, timed entry, and visitor caps to prevent overcrowding. 2. Enhance infrastructure to support sustainable tourism, such as improved public transport, waste management systems, and eco-friendly facilities.
Community Engagement and Empowerment	1. Foster active participation of local communities in decision-making processes to ensure their voices are heard and their needs are addressed. 2. Develop community-led tourism initiatives that empower residents to share their knowledge and cultural practices, thereby enhancing the visitor experience and promoting a sense of ownership and pride among locals.
Sustainable Practices and Environmental Conservation	1. Promote sustainable tourism practices such as waste reduction, energy conservation, and the use of renewable resources. 2. Raise awareness among tourists about the importance of cultural sensitivity and environmental conservation through educational programs and clear guidelines.
Preservation of Intangible Heritage	1. Invest in documentation and promotion of intangible cultural heritage, such as traditional practices, languages, and folklore, to ensure their continuity. 2. Encourage intergenerational transmission of intangible heritage through community programs and educational initiatives.
Collaboration and Partnerships	1. Establish collaborative partnerships between governments, businesses, and local communities to create a supportive environment for sustainable heritage tourism. 2. Develop joint marketing and promotional strategies that highlight the unique cultural and historical aspects of heritage sites.

continued on following page

Table 5. Continued

Challenge	Recommendations
Innovative Technologies and Experiences	1. Integrate immersive technologies such as virtual and augmented reality to enhance the visitor experience and provide interactive tours of historical periods. 2. Promote cultural festivals, storytelling sessions, and gastronomic experiences to enrich the authenticity of heritage tourism and offer diverse interactions for visitors.
Continuous Monitoring and Evaluation	1. Implement ongoing monitoring and evaluation mechanisms to assess the effectiveness of heritage-led tourism initiatives. 2. Use data-driven insights to refine and adapt strategies, ensuring that tourism development remains sustainable and culturally sensitive.

By adopting these recommendations, heritage-led tourism destinations can navigate the challenges they face, enhance the visitor experience, and ensure the preservation of cultural and historical assets for future generations. These strategies will support the sustainable development of heritage sites, benefiting local communities and promoting a balanced approach to tourism growth.

FUNDING

The Department of Science and Technology-Inspire [Grant number IF210191, 2022], Ministry of Science and Technology, Government of India, provided funding for this work.

REFERENCES

Beal, L., Séraphin, H., Modica, G., Pilato, M., & Platania, M. (2019). Analysing the mediating effect of heritage between locals and visitors: An exploratory study using mission patrimoine as a case study. *Sustainability (Basel)*, 11(11), 3015. DOI: 10.3390/su11113015

Boniface, P., & Fowler, P. (2002). *Heritage and tourism in the global village*. Routledge. DOI: 10.4324/9780203033685

Bourgeon-Renault, D., Urbain, C., Petr, C., Le Gall-Ely, M., & Gombault, A. (2006). An experiential approach to the consumption value of arts and culture: The case of museums and monuments. *International Journal of Arts Management*, •••, 35–47. https://www.jstor.org/stable/41064896

Boyd, S. (2002). Cultural and heritage tourism in Canada: Opportunities, principles and challenges. *Tourism and Hospitality Research*, 3(3), 211–233. DOI: 10.1177/146735840200300303

Brümmer, L., & Karusseit, C. (2020). Conserving the NZASM: Latent opportunities through heritage-led regeneration. *South African Journal of Art History*, 35(1), 30–51.

Buckley, R. (2004). The effects of World Heritage listing on tourism to Australian national parks. *Journal of Sustainable Tourism*, 12(1), 70–84. DOI: 10.1080/09669580408667225

Burnham, B. (2022). A Blended Finance Framework for Heritage-Led Urban Regeneration. *Land (Basel)*, 11(8), 1154. DOI: 10.3390/land11081154

Calver, S. J., & Page, S. J. (2013). Enlightened hedonism: Exploring the relationship of service value, visitor knowledge and interest, to visitor enjoyment at heritage attractions. *Tourism Management*, 39, 23–36. DOI: 10.1016/j.tourman.2013.03.008

Caton, K., & Santos, C. A. (2007). Heritage tourism on Route 66: Deconstructing nostalgia. *Journal of Travel Research*, 45(4), 371–386. DOI: 10.1177/0047287507299572

Chandler, J. A. (2004). Comparing visitor profiles at heritage tourism destinations in Eastern North Carolina. *Journal of Travel & Tourism Marketing*, 16(1), 53–63. DOI: 10.1300/J073v16n01_06

Chen, C. F., & Chen, F. S. (2010). Experience quality, perceived value, satisfaction and behavioral intentions for heritage tourists. *Tourism Management*, 31(1), 29–35. DOI: 10.1016/j.tourman.2009.02.008

Choi, A. S., Ritchie, B. W., Papandrea, F., & Bennett, J. (2010). Economic valuation of cultural heritage sites: A choice modeling approach. *Tourism Management*, 31(2), 213–220. DOI: 10.1016/j.tourman.2009.02.014

Colavitti, A. N. N. A., & Usai, A. (2019). Place branding as a tool to improve heritage led-development strategies for a sustainable tourism in the Sulcis Iglesiente Region. In Planning Nature and Ecosystem Services (pp. 928-942). 2019 FedOA Press-Federico II Open Access University Press.

Colbert, F. (2003). Company profile: the Sydney opera house: an Australian icon. *International Journal of Arts Management*, ●●●, 69–77. DOI: 10.1080/09669580408667225

Cuccia, T., & Cellini, R. (2007). Is cultural heritage really important for tourists? A contingent rating study. *Applied Economics*, 39(2), 261–271. DOI: 10.1080/00036840500427981

D'Auria, A. (2009). Urban cultural tourism: Creative approaches for heritage-based sustainable development. *International Journal of Sustainable Development*, 12(2-4), 275–289. DOI: 10.1504/IJSD.2009.032782

Derakhshan, S. (2019). Designing a GIS-based people flow analytics tool for cultural event management in heritage-led cities. *PDEng thesis, Technische Universiteit Eindhoven, Eindhoven.*

Dionisia, K., & Stratigea, A. (2020). Leveraging underwater cultural heritage (UCH) potential for smart and sustainable development in Mediterranean islands. In *Computational Science and Its Applications–ICCSA 2020:20th International Conference, Cagliari, Italy, July 1–4, 2020, Proceedings, Part VII 20*, 237-252. Springer International Publishing. https://doi.org/DOI: 10.1007/978-3-030-58820-5_19

Dogruyol, K., Aziz, Z., & Arayici, Y. (2018). Eye of sustainable planning: A conceptual heritage-led urban regeneration planning framework. *Sustainability (Basel)*, 10(5), 1343. DOI: 10.3390/su10051343

Du Cros, H., Bauer, T., Lo, C., & Rui, S. (2005). Cultural heritage assets in China as sustainable tourism products: Case studies of the Hutongs and the Huanghua section of the Great Wall. *Journal of Sustainable Tourism*, 13(2), 171–194. DOI: 10.1080/09669580508668484

Dubini, P., & Di Biase, E. (2008). Heritage-led positioning and growth for Italian cities and towns. In *24th EGOS Colloquium-European Group for Organizational Studies*.

Egusquiza, A., Zubiaga, M., Gandini, A., de Luca, C., & Tondelli, S. (2021). Systemic Innovation Areas for heritage-led rural regeneration: A multilevel repository of best practices. *Sustainability (Basel)*, 13(9), 5069. DOI: 10.3390/su13095069

El Faouri, B. F., & Sibley, M. (2022). Heritage-led urban regeneration in the context of WH listing: Lessons and opportunities for the newly inscribed city of As-Salt in Jordan. *Sustainability (Basel)*, 14(8), 4557. DOI: 10.3390/su14084557

Flowers, J., & Easterling, K. (2006). Growing South Carolina's tourism cluster. *Business and Economic Review*, 52(3), 15–20.

Gilmore, A., Carson, D., & Ascenção, M. (2007). Sustainable tourism marketing at a World Heritage site. *Journal of Strategic Marketing*, 15(2-3), 253–264. DOI: 10.1080/09652540701318930

. Gombault, A., & Petr, C. (2007). *La réputation des musées et des monuments superstars* (No. halshs-00260154).

Grant, R. M. (1991). Porter's 'competitive advantage of nations': An assessment. *Strategic Management Journal*, 12(7), 535–548. DOI: 10.1002/smj.4250120706

Harzing, A. W., & Giroud, A. (2014). The competitive advantage of nations: An application to academia. *Journal of Informetrics*, 8(1), 29–42. DOI: 10.1016/j.joi.2013.10.007

Holmes, K., Jones, P., Lockwood, A., Miller, G., Scarles, C., Szivas, E., & Tribe, J. (2006). An eclectic agenda for Tourism and Hospitality Research. *Tourism and Hospitality Research*, 7(1), 76–82. DOI: 10.1057/palgrave.thr.6050035

Huang, C. H., Tsaur, J. R., & Yang, C. H. (2012). Does world heritage list really induce more tourists? Evidence from Macau. *Tourism Management*, 33(6), 1450–1457. DOI: 10.1016/j.tourman.2012.01.014 PMID: 32287738

Hughes, H. (2013). *Arts, entertainment and tourism*. Taylor & Francis. DOI: 10.4324/9780080499468

Huh, J., & Uysal, M. (2004). Satisfaction with cultural/heritage sites: Virginia historic triangle. *Journal of Quality Assurance in Hospitality & Tourism*, 4(3-4), 177–194. DOI: 10.1300/J162v04n03_12

Jimura, T. (2011). The impact of world heritage site designation on local communities–A case study of Ogimachi, Shirakawa-mura, Japan. *Tourism Management*, 32(2), 288–296. DOI: 10.1016/j.tourman.2010.02.005

Kerstetter, D. L., Confer, J. J., & Graefe, A. R. (2001). An exploration of the specialization concept within the context of heritage tourism. *Journal of Travel Research*, 39(3), 267–274. DOI: 10.1177/004728750103900304

Kolar, T., & Zabkar, V. (2010). A consumer-based model of authenticity: An oxymoron or the foundation of cultural heritage marketing? *Tourism Management*, 31(5), 652–664. DOI: 10.1016/j.tourman.2009.07.010

Koutsi, D., Lagarias, A., & Stratigea, A. (2022). Evidence-Based Exploration as the Ground for Heritage-Led Pathways in Insular Territories: Case Study Greek Islands. *Heritage*, 5(3), 2746–2772. DOI: 10.3390/heritage5030143

Koutsi, D., & Stratigea, A. (2019). Unburying hidden land and maritime cultural potential of small islands in the Mediterranean for tracking heritage-led local development paths. *Heritage*, 2(1), 938–966. DOI: 10.3390/heritage2010062

. Koutsi, D., & Stratigea, A. (2021). Releasing cultural tourism potential of less-privileged island communities in the Mediterranean: An ICT-enabled, strategic, and integrated participatory planning approach. *The impact of tourist activities on low-density territories: Evaluation frameworks, lessons, and policy recommendations*, 63-93. https://doi.org/DOI: 10.1007/978-3-030-65524-2_4

Laing, J., Wheeler, F., Reeves, K., & Frost, W. (2014). Assessing the experiential value of heritage assets: A case study of a Chinese heritage precinct, Bendigo, Australia. *Tourism Management*, 40, 180–192. DOI: 10.1016/j.tourman.2013.06.004

Lak, A., Gheitasi, M., & Timothy, D. J. (2020). Urban regeneration through heritage tourism: Cultural policies and strategic management. *Journal of Tourism and Cultural Change*, 18(4), 386–403. DOI: 10.1080/14766825.2019.1668002

Lopez, L., & Pérez, Y. (2020). Cultural Tourism and Heritage Education in the Portuguese Way of St. James. In *INTERNATIONAL SYMPOSIUM: New Metropolitan Perspectives, 178, 1897-1906*. Springer International Publishing., DOI: 10.1007/978-3-030-48279-4_179

Mu, Q. (2022). Understanding Heritage-Led Development of the Historic Villages of China: A Multi-case Study Analysis of Tongren. *The Historic Environment*, 13(2), 216–241. DOI: 10.1080/17567505.2021.1940575

OCDE. O. (2014). *OECD Tourism trends and policies 2014*. OECD Publishing.

OECD. (2009). *The Impact of Culture on Tourism*. OECD Publishing.

Panagiotopoulou, M., Somarakis, G., & Stratigea, A. (2020). Smartening up participatory cultural tourism planning in historical city centers. *Journal of Urban Technology*, 27(4), 3–26. DOI: 10.1080/10630732.2018.1528540

Petr, C. (2002). Tourist apprehension of heritage: A semiotic approach to behaviour patterns. *International Journal of Arts Management*, •••, 25–38. https://www.jstor.org/stable/41064753

Petr, C. (2009). Fame is not always a positive asset for heritage equity! Some clues from buying intentions of national tourists. *Journal of Travel & Tourism Marketing*, 26(1), 1–18. DOI: 10.1080/10548400802656694

Petr, C. (2015). How heritage site tourists may become monument visitors. *Tourism Management*, 51, 247–262. DOI: 10.1016/j.tourman.2015.05.018

Poria, Y., Butler, R., & Airey, D. (2004). Links between tourists, heritage, and reasons for visiting heritage sites. *Journal of Travel Research*, 43(1), 19–28. DOI: 10.1177/0047287504265508

Poria, Y., Reichel, A., & Biran, A. (2006). Heritage site perceptions and motivations to visit. *Journal of Travel Research*, 44(3), 318–326. DOI: 10.1177/0047287505279004

. Porter, M.E. (2011). *Competitive advantage of nations: creating and sustaining superior performance*. simon and schuster.

Quinn, B. (2006). Problematising 'festival tourism': Arts festivals and sustainable development in Ireland. *Journal of Sustainable Tourism*, 14(3), 288–306. DOI: 10.1080/09669580608669060

Ramsey, D., & Everitt, J. (2008). If you dig it, they will come!: Archaeology heritage sites and tourism development in Belize, Central America. *Tourism Management*, 29(5), 909–916. DOI: 10.1016/j.tourman.2007.11.002

Richards, G. (2001). The experience industry and the creation of attractions. In *Cultural attractions and European tourism* (pp. 55–69). Cabi Publishing., DOI: 10.1079/9780851994406.0055

Richards, G., & Wilson, J. (2006). Developing creativity in tourist experiences: A solution to the serial reproduction of culture? *Tourism Management*, 27(6), 1209–1223. DOI: 10.1016/j.tourman.2005.06.002

Ryan, C., & Higgins, O. (2006). Experiencing cultural tourism: Visitors at the Maori arts and crafts institute, New Zealand. *Journal of Travel Research*, 44(3), 308–317. DOI: 10.1177/0047287505279002

Shore, S. (2010). Cultural and heritage tourism-international. *Travel & Tourism Analyst*, •••, 8.

Škrabić Perić, B., Šimundić, B., Muštra, V., & Vugdelija, M. (2021). The role of unesco cultural heritage and cultural sector in tourism development: The case of EU countries. *Sustainability (Basel)*, 13(10), 5473. DOI: 10.3390/su13105473

Smit, A. J. (2010). The competitive advantage of nations: Is Porter's Diamond Framework a new theory that explains the international competitiveness of countries? *Southern African Business Review*, 14(1).

Smith, B., & General, S. (2008). Towards a 'City Model' for Heritage-Led Regeneration and Tourism Development. *Epoch*.

Sölvell, Ö. (2015). The Competitive Advantage of Nations 25 years–opening up new perspectives on competitiveness. *Competitiveness Review*, 25(5), 471–481. DOI: 10.1108/CR-07-2015-0068

Stamboulis, Y., & Skayannis, P. (2003). Innovation strategies and technology for experience-based tourism. *Tourism Management*, 24(1), 35–43. DOI: 10.1016/S0261-5177(02)00047-X

Su, Y. W., & Lin, H. L. (2014). Analysis of international tourist arrivals worldwide: The role of world heritage sites. *Tourism Management*, 40, 46–58. DOI: 10.1016/j.tourman.2013.04.005

Timothy, D. J. (2011). *Cultural heritage and tourism: An introduction* (Vol. 4). Channel View Publications. DOI: 10.21832/9781845411787

Timothy, D. J., & Boyd, S. W. (2003). *Heritage tourism*. Pearson Education.

UNWTO. (2010). *World Tourism Barometer January 2010*. UNWTO.

Wang, S., & Gu, K. (2020). Pingyao: The historic urban landscape and planning for heritage-led urban changes. *Cities (London, England)*, 97, 102489. DOI: 10.1016/j.cities.2019.102489

Yang, C. H., Lin, H. L., & Han, C. C. (2010). Analysis of international tourist arrivals in China: The role of World Heritage Sites. *Tourism Management*, 31(6), 827–837. DOI: 10.1016/j.tourman.2009.08.008 PMID: 32287732

Nag, A., & Mishra, S. (2023). Destination Competitiveness and Sustainability: Heritage Planning From the Perspective of the Tourism Industry Stakeholders. In *Cases on Traveler Preferences, Attitudes, and Behaviors: Impact in the Hospitality Industry* (pp. 1-32). IGI Global.

Nag, A. (2024). Local Development and Tourism Competitiveness: Analyzing the Economic Impact of Heritage Tourism Initiatives. In *Gastronomic Sustainability Solutions for Community and Tourism Resilience* (pp. 160-190). IGI Global.

Nag, A., & Mishra, S. (2024). Sustainable competitive advantage in heritage tourism: Leveraging cultural legacy in a data-driven world. In *Review of Technologies and Disruptive Business Strategies* (Vol. 3, pp. 137-162). Emerald Publishing Limited.

ADDITIONAL READING

Ashworth, G. J. (2000). Heritage, tourism and places: A review. *Tourism Recreation Research*, 25(1), 19–29. DOI: 10.1080/02508281.2000.11014897

Boyd, B., Cotter, M., O'Connor, W., & Sattler, D. (1996). Cognitive ownership of heritage places: Social construction and cultural heritage management. *TEMPUS-ST LUCIA QUEENSLAND*, 6, 123–140.

Caffyn, A., & Lutz, J. (1999). Developing the heritage tourism product in multi-ethnic cities. *Tourism Management*, 20(2), 213–221. DOI: 10.1016/S0261-5177(98)00075-2

Davies, A., & Prentice, R. (1995). Conceptualizing the latent visitor to heritage attractions. *Tourism Management*, 16(7), 491–500. DOI: 10.1016/0261-5177(95)00066-W

Garrod, B., & Fyall, A. (2000). Managing heritage tourism. *Annals of Tourism Research*, 27(3), 682–708. DOI: 10.1016/S0160-7383(99)00094-8

Go, F. M., & Govers, R. (2000). Integrated quality management for tourist destinations: A European perspective on achieving competitiveness. *Tourism Management*, 21(1), 79–88. DOI: 10.1016/S0261-5177(99)00098-9

Hassan, S. S. (2000). Determinants of market competitiveness in an environmentally sustainable tourism industry. *Journal of Travel Research*, 38(3), 239–245. DOI: 10.1177/004728750003800305

Healey, P. (1998). Building institutional capacity through collaborative approaches to urban planning. *Environment & Planning A*, 30(9), 1531–1546. DOI: 10.1068/a301531

Hubbard, P., & Lilley, K. (2000). Selling the past: Heritage-tourism and place identity in Stratford-upon-Avon. *Geography (Sheffield, England)*, 85(3), 221–232. DOI: 10.1080/20436564.2000.12219753

Smith, K. A. (1999). *The management of volunteers at heritage attractions: Literary heritage properties in the UK*. Nottingham Trent University.

APPENDIX

Table 6. Terminologies and their definitions

Terminology	Definition	References
Heritage	Cultural, historical, and natural assets that hold significance and value for a community. Heritage can include tangible elements like monuments, artefacts, and landscapes and intangible aspects such as traditions, languages, and customs.	Wang & Gu, 2020; Dubini & Di Biase, 2008; Smith & General, 2008
Destination	A specific place or location that is the focus of tourism activities. Destinations can range from cities and regions to specific cultural or natural sites.	Koutsi, Lagarias, & Stratigea, 2022; Lopez & Pérez, 2020; Derakhshan, 2019; Smith & General, 2008
Management	The process of planning, organising, and controlling resources and activities to achieve specific goals. In the context of heritage-led destination management, this includes overseeing the preservation, interpretation, and presentation of heritage assets.	Wang & Gu, 2020; Derakhshan, 2019; Smith & General, 2008; Dubini & Di Biase, 2008
Sustainability	Ensuring that tourism activities do not compromise the ability of future generations to enjoy the same natural, cultural, and economic resources. Sustainable heritage-led destination management involves practices that maintain the integrity of heritage assets over time.	Lopez & Pérez, 2020; Colavitti & Usai, 2019; Porter, 2011
Preservation	Protecting and conserving heritage assets to maintain their original form and significance. Preservation efforts can include restoration, documentation, and preventive measures to ensure the longevity of heritage sites.	Derakhshan, 2019; Smith & General, 2008
Interpretation	The communication of the significance and stories associated with heritage assets to visitors. Interpretation methods can include guided tours, signage, exhibits, and multimedia presentations, enhancing visitors' understanding and appreciation of the heritage.	Porter, 2011; Grant, 1991
Community Engagement	Involving local residents, businesses, and organisations in the decision-making processes related to tourism development. Community engagement ensures that the benefits of tourism are shared locally and that the cultural integrity of the community is respected.	Lopez & Pérez, 2020; Porter, 2011; Smith & General, 2008
Tourism Development	The planning and implementation of strategies to attract and accommodate tourists. In heritage-led destination management, tourism development focuses on creating experiences that showcase the destination's heritage assets.	Smith & General, 2008; Dubini & Di Biase, 2008
Authenticity	The genuine representation of the destination's heritage, culture, and traditions in tourism activities. Authentic experiences give visitors a real and immersive understanding of the destination's unique identity.	Wang & Gu, 2020; Dubini & Di Biase, 2008; Smith & General, 2008

Compilation of References

Aaker, J., & Smith, A. (2010). *The dragonfly effect: Quick, effective, and powerful ways to use social media to drive social change*. John Wiley & Sons.

Abankina, T. (2013). Regional development models using cultural heritage resources. *International Journal of Culture, Tourism and Hospitality Research*, 7(1), 3–10. DOI: 10.1108/17506181311301318

Abdul-Rauf Abdul-Mugod, A. (2016). Sustainable tourism planning by using the VICE model (applied on Minia Governorate). *MJTHR*, 1, 98–113.

Abraham, V., Bremser, K., Carreño, M., Crowley-Cyr, L., & Moreno, M. J. G. (2020). Exploring the Consequences of COVID-19 on Tourist Behaviors: Perceived Travel Risk, Animosity and Intentions to Travel. *Tourism Review*, ahead-of-print(ahead-of-print). Advance online publication. DOI: 10.1108/TR-07-2020-0344

Abraham, V., & Poria, Y. (2020). Perceptions of a Heritage Site and Animosity: The Case of the West Bank. *Tourism Review*, 75(5), 765–777. Advance online publication. DOI: 10.1108/TR-06-2019-0278

Abreu-Novais, M., Ruhanen, L., & Arcodia, C. (2016, May 11). Destination competitiveness: What we know, what we know but shouldn't and what we don't know but should. *Current Issues in Tourism*, 19(6), 492–512. DOI: 10.1080/13683500.2015.1091443

Acar, A. (2018). Turizmde Tüketici Davranışını Etkileyen Faktörler. *Uluslararası Turizm, İşletme. Ekonomi Dergisi.*, 2(2), 390–394.

Adamus-Matuszyńska, A., Dzik, P., Michnik, J., & Polok, G. (2021). Visual component of destination brands as a tool for communicating sustainable tourism offers. Retrieved from https://dx.doi.org/DOI: 10.3390/su13020731

Affatati, A., Scaini, C., & Scaini, A. (2024). The role of operators in sustainable whale-watching tourism: Proposing a continuous training framework. *PLoS One*, 19(1), e0296241. DOI: 10.1371/journal.pone.0296241 PMID: 38166106

Ahmed, N. (2023). Residents support towards cultural heritage tourism: The relevance of heritage proximity and tourism perceived impacts. *Journal of Tourism*, 32, 1–16. http://revistadeturism.ro/rdt/article/view/606

Akgün, A. E., Keskin, H., Ayar, H., & Erdogan, E. (2015). The influence of storytelling approach in travel writings on readers' empathy and travel intentions. *Procedia: Social and Behavioral Sciences*, 207, 577–586. DOI: 10.1016/j.sbspro.2015.10.129

Akroush, M. N., Jraisat, L., Kurdieh, D. J., AL-Faouri, R. N., & Qatu, L. T. (2016, April 18). AL-Faouri, R. N., & Qatu, L. T. (2016). Tourism Service Quality and Destination Loyalty – The Mediating Role of Destination Image From International Tourists' Perspectives. *Tourism Review*, 71(1), 18–44. Advance online publication. DOI: 10.1108/TR-11-2014-0057

Alaimo, S. P., & Carman, J. G. (2022). Decisions, decisions, decisions: Community foundations and community well-being. *International Journal of Community Wellbeing*, 5(2), 213–239. DOI: 10.1007/s42413-021-00125-7

Alberti, F., & Giusti, J. (2012). Cultural heritage, tourism and regional competitiveness: The Motor Valley cluster. *City Culture and Society*, 3(4), 261–273. DOI: 10.1016/j.ccs.2012.11.003

Albinsson, P. A., Wolf, M., & Kopf, D. A. (2010). Anti-consumption in East Germany: Consumer Resistance to Hyperconsumption. *Journal of Consumer Behaviour*, 9(6), 412–425. Advance online publication. DOI: 10.1002/cb.333

Aleksandrova, M. (2019). Importance of the slogans as a brand communication tool of tourist destinations. Retrieved from https://dx.doi.org/DOI: 10.36997/IJUSV-ESS/2019.8.3.154

Alieva, D., & Usmonova, G. (2021). Sustainability perceptions of community based tourism by stakeholders in Central Asia. *Local Development & Society*, 2(2), 244–254. DOI: 10.1080/26883597.2021.1953944

Aliperti, G., Sandholz, S., Hagenlocher, M., Rizzi, F., Frey, M., & Garschagen, M. (2019). Tourism, crisis, disaster: An interdisciplinary approach. *Annals of Tourism Research*, 79, 102808. DOI: 10.1016/j.annals.2019.102808

Alkier, R., Milojica, V., & Roblek, V. (2017). Challenges of the social innovation in tourism. *Tourism in Southern and Eastern Europe.*, 4, 1–13. DOI: 10.20867/tosee.04.24

Almeida, G. G. F. (2015), *"A identidade territorial gaúcha no branding das marcas regionais: caso da marca da cerveja Polar."* Master's thesis. University of Santa Cruz do Sul, Brazil.

Almeida, G. G. F. (2018), *"Marca territorial como produto cultural no âmbito do Desenvolvimento Regional: o caso de Porto Alegre, RS, Brasil."* Doctoral's thesis. University of Santa Cruz do Sul, Brazil.

Almeida, G. G. F., Almeida, P., Cardoso, L., & Lima Santos, L. (2023). Uses and Functions of the Territorial Brand over Time: Interdisciplinary Cultural-Historical Mapping. *Sustainability (Basel)*, 15(8), 6448. DOI: 10.3390/su15086448

Alonso-Almeida, M.-M., Borrajo-Millán, F., & Liu, Y. (2019). Are Social Media Data Pushing Overtourism? The Case of Barcelona and Chinese Tourists. *Sustainability (Basel)*, 11(12), 3356. Advance online publication. DOI: 10.3390/su11123356

Alvarez, M. D., Campo, S., & Fuchs, G. (2020). Tourism in Conflict Zones: Animosity and Risk Perceptions. *International Journal of Culture, Tourism and Hospitality Research*, 14(2), 189–204. Advance online publication. DOI: 10.1108/IJCTHR-08-2019-0136

Ancarani, F. (2001). *Marketing Places. A Resource-Based Approach And Empirical Evidence From The European Experience*. SDA Bocconi, Research Division Working Paper No. 01/55.

Andreopolou, Z., Leandros, N., Quaranta, G., & Salvia, R. (2016). *Tourism and New Media* (Zacharoula Andreopoulou, N. L., Ed.). Vol. 2). FrancoAngeli.

Anholt, S. (2007). *Competitive Identity. The New Brand Management for Nations, Cities and Regions*. Palgrave Macmillan.

Anholt, S. (2007). *Competitive identity: the new Brand management for nations, cities, and regions*. Palgrave Macmillan. DOI: 10.1057/9780230627727

Anholt, S. (2008). *Place Branding: Is Marketing or Isn't? Place Branding and Public Diplomacy*, 4(1), 1–6. DOI: 10.1057/palgrave.pb.6000088

An, J. (2024). Maritime logistics and digital transformation with big data: Review and research trend. *Maritime Business Review*, 9(3), 229–242. DOI: 10.1108/MABR-10-2023-0069

Arber, A. (2006). Reflexivity: A challenge for the researcher as practitioner? *Journal of Research in Nursing*, 11(2), 147–157. DOI: 10.1177/1744987106056956

Aref, F., Redzuan, M. R., Gill, S. S., & Aref, A. (2010). Community Capacity Building in Tourism Development in Local Communities. *Journal of Sustainable Development*, 3(1), 81–90. DOI: 10.5539/jsd.v3n1p81

Arli, D., Kim, J., Rundle-Thiele, S., & Tkaczynski, A. (2018). Australian Migrants' Social Cultural Adaptation and Consumption Behaviour Towards Food and Alcohol. *International Journal of Consumer Studies*. Advance online publication. DOI: 10.1111/ijcs.12439

Armenski, T., Gomezelj, D., Djurdjev, B., Djeri, L., & Dragin, A. (2011). Destination competitiveness: a challenging process for Serbia. Human Geographies -Journal of studies and research in Human Geography, 19-33.

Ashworth, G. J., & Larkham, P. J. (1994). Building a new heritage: tourism, culture, and identity in the new Europe. London; New York: Routledge.

Avraham, E. (2004). *Media strategies for improving an unfavorable city image.* Elsevier Ltd, 21(6), 471–479.

Azevedo, A., Magalhães, D., & Pereira, J. (2011): City Marketing. Gestão estratégica e Marketing de cidades. Editor Vida Económica. ISBN: 9789727883738.

Azevedo, A., Magalhães, D., & Pereira, J. (2011). *City Marketing: Myplace in XXI.* Vida Económica – Editorial SA.

Azizpour, F., & Fathizadeh, F. (2016). Barriers to collaboration among tourism industry stakeholders. Case study: Mashhad Metropolis. *Alma Tourism J., 7,* 48–65. https://doi.org/DOI: 10.6092/issn.2036-5195/5991

Babbie, E. (2007). The practice of social research (éd. 11). Belmont: Thompson Wadsworth.

Bagchi, S. (2021). Exploring the impact of covid-19 on tourism industry of Bangladesh: an empirical study. *International Journal of Study -Granthaalayah, 9*(8), 42–58. DOI: 10.29121/granthaalayah.v9.i8.2021.4141

Baloglu, S., & McCleary, K. W. (1999). A model of destination image formation. *Annals of Tourism Research*, 26(4), 868–897. DOI: 10.1016/S0160-7383(99)00030-4

Bardin, L. (1977). *Análise de Conteúdo*. Edições 70. Lisboa. 9- 14, 31, 38- 45, 95-141. *Research*, 26(2), 312–328.

Barke, M. (1999). City Marketing as a Planning Tool. In Pacionae, M. (Ed.), *Applied Geography: Principles and Practice*. Routledge.

Barreda, A. A., Zubieta, S., Chen, H., Cassilha, M., & Kageyama, Y. (2017). Evaluating the impact of mega-sporting events on hotel pricing strategies: The case of the 2014 FIFA World Cup. *Tourism Review*, 72(2), 184–208. DOI: 10.1108/TR-02-2017-0018

Bassano, C., Barile, S., Piciocchi, P., Spohrer, J. C., Iandolo, F., & Fisk, R. (2019). Storytelling about places: Tourism marketing in the digital age. *Cities (London, England)*, 87, 10–20. DOI: 10.1016/j.cities.2018.12.025

BBC. (2019, January 25). https://www.bbc.com/news/world-europe-46971182. Consulté le 2020, sur www.bbc.com

Beal, L., Séraphin, H., Modica, G., Pilato, M., & Platania, M. (2019). Analysing the mediating effect of heritage between locals and visitors: An exploratory study using mission patrimoine as a case study. *Sustainability (Basel)*, 11(11), 3015. DOI: 10.3390/su11113015

Beerli, A., & Martín, J. D. (2004). Factors influencing destination image. *Annals of Tourism Research*, 31(3), 657–681. DOI: 10.1016/j.annals.2004.01.010

Belliggiano, A., Bindi, L., & Ievoli, C. (2021). Walking along the sheeptrack...Rural tourism, ecomuseums, and bio-cultural heritage. *Sustainability (Basel)*, 13(16), 8870. DOI: 10.3390/su13168870

Bennett, D. (1995). *Dictionary of marketing terms*. American Marketing Association.

Bhuiyan, M. A., Zhang, Q., Xuan, W., Rahman, M. K., & Khare, V. (2023). Does good governance promote sustainable tourism? A systematic review of PESTEL analysis. *SN Business & Economics*, 3(33), 33. Advance online publication. DOI: 10.1007/s43546-022-00408-x PMID: 36684689

Bilynets, I., Cvelbar, L. K., & Dolnicar, S. (2021). Can Publicly Visible Pro-Environmental Initiatives Improve the Organic Environmental Image of Destinations? *Journal of Sustainable Tourism*. Advance online publication. DOI: 10.1080/09669582.2021.1926469

Blonski, K. (1998). *Krakow 2000: European City of Culture*. Voivodship.

Bolan, P., & Williams, L. (2008). The role of image in service promotion: Focusing on the influence of film on consumer choice within tourism. *International Journal of Consumer Studies*, 32(4), 382–390. DOI: 10.1111/j.1470-6431.2008.00672.x

Bondarenko, V. A., K., O., & Pisareva, E. (2018). *Marketing management of the territory in the aspect of the regional brand formation*. European Research Studies Journal, Volume XXI, Special Issue 2, 72-78.

Boniface, P., & Fowler, P. (2002). *Heritage and tourism in the global village*. Routledge. DOI: 10.4324/9780203033685

Bookman, S. (2013). Brands and Urban Life: Specialty Coffee, Consumers, and the Co-creation of Urban Café Sociality. *Space and Culture*, 17(1), 85–99. DOI: 10.1177/1206331213493853

Boonpart, O., & Suvachart, N. (2014). Tourist expectation and tourist experience in cultural tourism. *JTHM*, 2, 124–132.

Bornhorst, T., Ritchie, J. B., & Sheehan, L. (2010). Determinants of tourism success for DMOs & destinations: An empirical examination of stakeholders' perspectives. *Tourism Management*, 31(5), 572–589. DOI: 10.1016/j.tourman.2009.06.008

Bouchard, M. E. (2021). Popular Brazilian Portuguese through capoeira: From local to global. *Etnográfica (Lisboa)*, 25(1), 95–116. DOI: 10.4000/etnografica.8751

Boulaire, C., & Hervet, G. (2012). New Itinerancy: The Potential of Geocaching for Tourism. *International Journal of Management Cases*, 14(4), 210–218. DOI: 10.5848/APBJ.2012.00099

Bourgeon-Renault, D., Urbain, C., Petr, C., Le Gall-Ely, M., & Gombault, A. (2006). An experiential approach to the consumption value of arts and culture: The case of museums and monuments. *International Journal of Arts Management*, •••, 35–47. https://www.jstor.org/stable/41064896

Boyd, S. (2002). Cultural and heritage tourism in Canada: Opportunities, principles and challenges. *Tourism and Hospitality Research*, 3(3), 211–233. DOI: 10.1177/146735840200300303

Boys, K. A., DuBreuil White, K., & Groover, G. (2017). Fostering rural and agricultural tourism: Exploring the potential of geocaching. *Journal of Sustainable Tourism*, 25(10), 1474–1493. DOI: 10.1080/09669582.2017.1291646

Braun, E., & Zenker, S. (2010). *Towards an Integrated Approach for Place Brand Management. In 50th Congress of the European Regional Science Association: "Sustainable Regional Growth and Development in the Creative Knowledge Economy"*, Jönköping, Sweden: Towards an Integrated Approach for Place Brand Management. 36 (pp. 1–12)

Brochado, A., Stoleriu, O., & Lupu, C. (2021). Wine tourism: A multisensory experience. *Current Issues in Tourism*, 24(5), 597–615. DOI: 10.1080/13683500.2019.1649373

Brümmer, L., & Karusseit, C. (2020). Conserving the NZASM: Latent opportunities through heritage-led regeneration. *South African Journal of Art History*, 35(1), 30–51.

Buckley, R. (2004). The effects of World Heritage listing on tourism to Australian national parks. *Journal of Sustainable Tourism*, 12(1), 70–84. DOI: 10.1080/09669580408667225

Buehler, R., & Pucher, J. (2023a). Overview of walking rates, walking safety, and government policies to encourage more and safer walking in Europe and North America. *Sustainability (Basel)*, 15(7), 5719. DOI: 10.3390/su15075719

Buehler, R., & Pucher, J. (Eds.). (2021d). *Cycling for sustainable cities* (pp. 21–25). MIT Press. DOI: 10.7551/mitpress/11963.001.0001

Buehler, R., Pucher, J., & Bauman, A. (2020c). Physical activity from walking and cycling for daily travel in the United States, 2001–2017: Demographic, socioeconomic, and geographic variation. *Journal of Transport & Health*, 16, 100811. DOI: 10.1016/j.jth.2019.100811

Buehler, R., Pucher, J., Merom, D., & Bauman, A. (2011b). Active travel in Germany and the U.S.: Contributions of daily walking and cycling to physical activity. *American Journal of Preventive Medicine*, 41(3), 241–250. DOI: 10.1016/j.amepre.2011.04.012 PMID: 21855737

Burnham, B. (2022). A Blended Finance Framework for Heritage-Led Urban Regeneration. *Land (Basel)*, 11(8), 1154. DOI: 10.3390/land11081154

Butler, R., Curran, R., & O'Gorman, K. D. (2013). Pro-poor tourism in a first world urban setting: Case study of Glasgow. *International Journal of Tourism Research*, 15(5), 443–457. DOI: 10.1002/jtr.1888

Cabral, J., & Marques, T. (1996). - "*Do planeamento estratégico ao desenvolvimento sustentável: experiência em Portugal*", in Inforgeo, n°11. Lisboa.

Cahyanto, I., Wiblishauser, M., Pennington-Gray, L., & Schroeder, A. (2016). The Dynamics of Travel Avoidance: The Case of Ebola in the U.S. *Tourism Management Perspectives*, 20, 195–203. Advance online publication. DOI: 10.1016/j.tmp.2016.09.004 PMID: 32289007

Caldwell, N., & Freire, J. R. (2004). The differences between branding a country, a region and a city: Applying the Brand box model. *Journal of Brand Management*, 12(1), 50–61. DOI: 10.1057/palgrave.bm.2540201

Calver, S. J., & Page, S. J. (2013). Enlightened hedonism: Exploring the relationship of service value, visitor knowledge and interest, to visitor enjoyment at heritage attractions. *Tourism Management*, 39, 23–36. DOI: 10.1016/j.tourman.2013.03.008

Caminhos da Zona Sul. *Marca de Pelotas promove a cidade*. (2017, July, 13). https://bit.ly/2H9bmkC

Campo, S., & Alvarez, M. D. (2019). Animosity Toward a Country in the Context of Destinations as Tourism Products. *Journal of Hospitality & Tourism Research (Washington, D.C.)*, 43(7), 1002–1024. Advance online publication. DOI: 10.1177/1096348019840795

Camprubí, R., Guia, J., & Comas, J. (2008). Destination Networks and Induced Tourism Image. *Tourism Review*, 63(2), 47–58. Advance online publication. DOI: 10.1108/16605370810883941

Cardoso, L., Dias, F., de Araújo, A. F., & Andrés Marques, M. I. (2019). A destination imagery processing model: Structural differences between dream and favorite destinations. *Annals of Tourism Research*, 74, 81–94. DOI: 10.1016/j.annals.2018.11.001

Cardoso, L., Lopes, E., Almeida, G. G. F. D., Lima Santos, L., Sousa, B., Simões, J., & Perna, F. (2023). Features of Nautical Tourism in Portugal—Projected Destination Image with a Sustainability Marketing Approach. *Sustainability (Basel)*, 15(11), 8805. DOI: 10.3390/su15118805

Caton, K., & Santos, C. A. (2007). Heritage tourism on Route 66: Deconstructing nostalgia. *Journal of Travel Research*, 45(4), 371–386. DOI: 10.1177/0047287507299572

Cawley, M., & Gillmor, D. A. (2008). Integrated rural tourism: Concepts and practice. *Annals of Tourism Research*, 35(2), 316–337. DOI: 10.1016/j.annals.2007.07.011

Chalip, L., Green, B. C., & Hill, B. (2003). Effects of sport event media on destination image and intention to visit. *Journal of Sport Management*, 17(3), 214–234. DOI: 10.1123/jsm.17.3.214

Chan, J. K. L. (2023). Sustainable Rural Tourism Practices From the Local Tourism Stakeholders' Perspectives. *Global business finance review*, 28(3), 136–149. DOI: 10.17549/gbfr.2023.28.3.136

Chan, C.-S., Chang, T. C., & Liu, Y. (2022). Investigating Creative Experiences and Environmental Perception of Creative Tourism: The Case of PMQ (Police Married Quarters) in Hong Kong. *Journal of China Tourism Research*, 18(2), 223–244. DOI: 10.1080/19388160.2020.1812459

Chandler, J. A. (2004). Comparing visitor profiles at heritage tourism destinations in Eastern North Carolina. *Journal of Travel & Tourism Marketing*, 16(1), 53–63. DOI: 10.1300/J073v16n01_06

Chaniago, A. (2022). *Digital Marketing and Destination Management Models in Shaping Tourist Behaviour*. DOI: 10.46254/EU05.20220609

Charters, S., & Spielmann, N. (2014). Characteristics of strong territorial brands: The case of champagne. *Journal of Business Research*, 67(7), 1461–1467. DOI: 10.1016/j.jbusres.2013.07.020

Chen, C. F., & Chen, F. S. (2010). Experience quality, perceived value, satisfaction and behavioral intentions for heritage tourists. *Tourism Management*, 31(1), 29–35. DOI: 10.1016/j.tourman.2009.02.008

Chen, J., & Hsu, C. (2000). Measurement of Korean Tourists' Perceived Images of Overseas Destinations. *Journal of Travel Research*, 38(4), 411–416. Advance online publication. DOI: 10.1177/004728750003800410

Chen, J., Huang, Y., Wu, E. Q., Ip, R., & Wang, K. (2023). How does rural tourism experience affect green consumption in terms of memorable rural-based tourism experiences, connectedness to nature and environmental awareness? *Journal of Hospitality and Tourism Management*, 54, 166–177. DOI: 10.1016/j.jhtm.2022.12.006

Chen, X., Cheng, Z., & Kim, G.-B. (2020). Make It Memorable: Tourism Experience, Fun, Recommendation and Revisit Intentions of Chinese Outbound Tourists. *Sustainability (Basel)*, 12(5), 1904. Advance online publication. DOI: 10.3390/su12051904

Chhetri, P., Arrowsmith, C., & Jackson, M. (2004). Determining hiking experiences in nature-based tourist destinations. *Tourism Management*, 25(1), 31–43. DOI: 10.1016/S0261-5177(03)00057-8

Chirikure, S., Manyanga, M., Ndoro, W., & Pwiti, G. (2010). Unfulfilled promises? Heritage management and community participation at some of Africa's cultural heritage sites. *International Journal of Heritage Studies*, 16(1-2), 30–44. DOI: 10.1080/13527250903441739

Choe, Y., Baek, J., & Kim, H. (2023). Heterogeneity in consumer preference toward mega-sport event travel packages: Implications for smart tourism marketing strategy. *Information Processing & Management*, 60(3), 103302. DOI: 10.1016/j.ipm.2023.103302

Choi, A. S., Ritchie, B. W., Papandrea, F., & Bennett, J. (2010). Economic valuation of cultural heritage sites: A choice modeling approach. *Tourism Management*, 31(2), 213–220. DOI: 10.1016/j.tourman.2009.02.014

Choi, J., & Lim, S. (2024). Establishing a Marine Protected Area in the Waters Surrounding Dokdo: Necessity and Legality. *Sustainability (Basel)*, 16(2), 611. DOI: 10.3390/su16020611

Choi, S. S. (2016). A study on effect of tourism storytelling of tourism destination brand value and tourist behavioral intentions. *Indian Journal of Science and Technology*, 9(46). https://sciresol.s3.us-east-2.amazonaws.com/IJST/Articles/2016/Issue-46/Article89.pdf

Cho, M., Bonn, M. A., & Brymer, R. A. (2014). A Constraint-Based Approach to Wine Tourism Market Segmentation. *Journal of Hospitality & Tourism Research (Washington, D.C.)*. Advance online publication. DOI: 10.1177/1096348014538049

Chon, K. (1990). The Role of Destination Image in Tourism: A Review and Discussion. *Tourism Review*, 45(2), 2–9. Advance online publication. DOI: 10.1108/eb058040

Cidrais, Á. (1998), *O marketing territorial aplicado às cidades médias portuguesas: os casos de Évora e Portalegre*, Dissertação de mestrado apresentada à Faculdade de Letras da Universidade de Lisboa. 121 p.

Çınar, K., Kavacık, S. Z., Bişkin, F., & Çinar, M. (2022). Understanding the Behavioral Intentions About Holidays in the Shadow of the COVID-19 Pandemic: Application of Protection Motivation Theory. *Health Care*, 10(9), 1623. Advance online publication. DOI: 10.3390/healthcare10091623 PMID: 36141234

Cioban, G.-L. (2022). Tourist destination – Bucovina. *Journal of Tourism*, 34, 1–6. http://revistadeturism.ro/rdt/article/view/596

Clara, S., & Barbosa, B. (2021). People make places, what do stories do? Applying digital storytelling strategies to communicate the identity of cities and regions. In Handbook of Research on Contemporary Storytelling Methods Across New Media and Disciplines. DOI: DOI: 10.4018/978-1-7998-6605-3.ch005

Cleave, E., & Arku, G. (2020). Place branding and growth machines: Implications for spatial planning and urban development. *Journal of Urban Affairs*, •••, 1–18.

CNN. (2024). Break dancing makes its debut at the Paris Olympics. A timeline of when every Olympic sport was introduced. Available at: https://www.cnn.com/2024/08/04/sport/olympic-sports-timeline-history-dg/index.html (accessed September 30, 2024).

Coakley, J. (2021). The future of sports and society: a reflection and call to action. In *Research handbook on sports and society* (pp. 380–392). Edward Elgar Publishing. DOI: 10.4337/9781789903607.00038

Coghlan, A., & Filo, K. (2013). Using constant comparison method and qualitative data to understand participants' experiences at the nexus of tourism, sport, and charity events. *Tourism Management*, 35, 122–131. DOI: 10.1016/j.tourman.2012.06.007

Cohen, J. (1988). *Statistical power analysis for the behavioural sciences* (2nd ed.). Lawrence Erlbaum Associates.

Colavitti, A. N. N. A., & Usai, A. (2019). Place branding as a tool to improve heritage led-development strategies for a sustainable tourism in the Sulcis Iglesiente Region. In Planning Nature and Ecosystem Services (pp. 928-942). 2019 FedOA Press-Federico II Open Access University Press.

Cook, I. G., & Miles, S. (2012). Beijing 2008: Chapter taken from Olympic Cities. *Routledge Online Studies on the Olympic and Paralympic Games*, 1(36), 340–358. DOI: 10.4324/9780203840740_chapter_17

Coombes, P. (2023). Systematic review research in marketing scholarship: Optimizing rigor. *International Journal of Market Research*, •••, 14707853231184729.

Cooper, M., & Buckley, R. (2021). Tourist mental health drives destination choice, marketing, and matching. Retrieved from https://dx.doi.org/DOI: 10.1177/00472875211011548

Corporació Metropolitana de Barcelona (CMB). (1976). Plan general metropolitano de ordenación urbana, de la entidad municipal metropolitana de Barcelona.

Costa, A. (2013). *Destination Branding: o papel dos stakeholders na gestão de uma marca-destino – o caso da marca Douro* (Dissertação de mestrado). Universidade do Minho, Braga, Portugal.

Crespi-Vallbona, M., & Mascarilla-Miró, O. (2020). Wine lovers: Their interests in tourist experiences. *International Journal of Culture, Tourism and Hospitality Research*, 14(2), 239–258. DOI: 10.1108/IJCTHR-05-2019-0095

Creswell, J. W., & Creswell, J. D. (2018). *Research design: Qualitative, quantitative, and mixed methods approach* (5th ed.). Sage Publications.

Crouch, G. (2010). Destination Competitiveness: An Analysis of Determinant Attributes. *Journal of Travel Research*.

Croy, G., & Heitmann, S. (2011). Tourism and film. Research themes for tourism, 188-204.

Cuccia, T., & Cellini, R. (2007). Is cultural heritage really important for tourists? A contingent rating study. *Applied Economics*, 39(2), 261–271. DOI: 10.1080/00036840500427981

Cvelbar, L., Dwyer, L., Koman, M., & Mihalic, T. (2016). Drivers of destination competitiveness in tourism: A global investigation. *Journal of Travel Research*, 55(8), 1041–1050. DOI: 10.1177/0047287515617299

D'Auria, A. (2009). Urban cultural tourism: Creative approaches for heritage-based sustainable development. *International Journal of Sustainable Development*, 12(2-4), 275–289. DOI: 10.1504/IJSD.2009.032782

Dada, Z. A., Batool, N., & Shah, S. A. (2022). GIS-based analysis of green space in urban Himalayas and modelling the effects on destination business performance. *International Journal of Tourism Cities*, 8(4), 1102–1126. DOI: 10.1108/IJTC-06-2021-0121

Daines, A., & Veitch, C. (2012). 22 VisitBritain: Leading the World to Britain. *Best Practice in Accessible Tourism: Inclusion, Disability. Ageing Population and Tourism*, 53, 322.

Dalgic, T., & Leeuw, M. (1994). Niche marketing revisited: Concept, applications and some European cases. *European Journal of Marketing*, 28(4), 39–55. DOI: 10.1108/03090569410061178

Dansero, E., & De Leonardis, D. (2006). Torino 2006. La territorializzazione olimpica e la sfida dell'eredità. *Bollettino della Società Geografica Italiana*, XI, •••.

Dansero, E., & Mela, A. (2007). Olympic territorialisation. *Revue de Geographie Alpine*, •••, 95–3.

Das, I. R., Talukder, M. B., & Kumar, S. (2024). Implication of Artificial Intelligence in Hospitality Marketing. *Utilizing Smart Technology and AI in Hybrid Tourism and Hospitality*. IGI Global, USA. DOI: 10.4018/979-8-3693-1978-9.ch014

De Almeida, G. G. F. (2023). Territorial Brand in Regional Development: Interdisciplinary Discussions. *Encyclopedia*, 3(3), 870–886. DOI: 10.3390/encyclopedia3030062

De Zoysa, M. (2022). Ecotourism Development and Biodiversity Conservation in Sri Lanka: Objectives, Conflicts and Resolutions. *Open Journal of Ecology*, 12(10), 638–666. DOI: 10.4236/oje.2022.1210037 della Sala, V. (2022). *The Olympic Villages and Olympic urban planning. Analysis and evaluation of the impact on territorial and urban planning (XX-XXI centuries)*. Doctoral thesis. UAB. POLITO

della Sala, V. (2023). Olympic Games and expectations: The factor analysis model about Olympic Urbanism and Olympic Villages. *Sociologia e ricerca sociale: 132, 3, 2023*, 127-147.

della Sala, V. (2024). Le Village Olympique de Seine-Saint-Denis: analyse critique d'un projet d'aménagement urbain. *Dossier sur les JO de la revue Savoir/agir,* 115,126.

della Sala, V. (2022). The Olympic Village and the Olympic Urbanism: Perception and Expectations of Olympic Specialists. *Bollettino della Società Geografica Italiana serie 14*, 5(2), 51–64.

della Sala, V. (2024). Olympic Games: Between Expectations and Fears. Factor Analysis Model Applied to Olympic Urbanism and Olympic Villages. *Rivista Internazionale di Scienze Sociali*, 132(1), 55–86.

Denscombe, M. (2008). Communities of Practice: A Research Paradigm for the Mixed Methods Approach. *Journal of Mixed Methods Research*, 2(3), 270–283. DOI: 10.1177/1558689808316807

Denzin, N., & Lincoln, Y. (2011). *The SAGE Handbook of Qualitative Research*. SAGE Publisher.

Derakhshan, S. (2019). Designing a GIS-based people flow analytics tool for cultural event management in heritage-led cities. *PDEng thesis, Technische Universiteit Eindhoven, Eindhoven*.

Di-Clemente, E., Hernández-Mogollón, J. M., & Campón-Cerro, A. M. (2019). Tourists' involvement and memorable food-based experiences as new determinants of behavioral intentions towards typical products. *Current Issues in Tourism*, •••, 1–14.

Dionisia, K., & Stratigea, A. (2020). Leveraging underwater cultural heritage (UCH) potential for smart and sustainable development in Mediterranean islands. In *Computational Science and Its Applications–ICCSA 2020:20th International Conference, Cagliari, Italy, July 1–4, 2020, Proceedings, Part VII 20*, 237-252. Springer International Publishing. https://doi.org/DOI: 10.1007/978-3-030-58820-5_19

Dodds, R., Ali, A., & Galaski, K. (2018). Mobilizing knowledge: Determining key elements for success and pitfalls in developing community-based tourism. *Current Issues in Tourism*, 21(13), 1547–1568. DOI: 10.1080/13683500.2016.1150257

Dogra, N., Adil, M., Dhamija, A., Kumar, M., & Nasir, M. (2022). What makes a community sustainably developed? A review of 25 years of sustainable community tourism literature. *Community Development (Columbus, Ohio)*, 53(5), 585–606. DOI: 10.1080/15575330.2021.2015606

Dogruyol, K., Aziz, Z., & Arayici, Y. (2018). Eye of sustainable planning: A conceptual heritage-led urban regeneration planning framework. *Sustainability (Basel)*, 10(5), 1343. DOI: 10.3390/su10051343

Donaire, J. A., & Galí, N. (2012). Eslóganes turísticos: Un análisis de los eslóganes de los destinos catalanes. *Boletín de la Asociación de Geógrafos Españoles*, 60, 521–533.

Donis, J., & Straupe, I. *The Assessment of Contribution of Forest Plant Non-Wood Products in Latvia's National Economy*. In Proceedings of the Annual 17th International Scientific Conference "Research for Rural Development 2011", Jelgava, Latvia, 18-20 May 2011.

Donthu, N., Kumar, S., Mukherjee, D., Pandey, N., & Lim, W. M. (2021). How to conduct a bibliometric analysis: An overview and guidelines. *Journal of Business Research*, 133, 285–296. DOI: 10.1016/j.jbusres.2021.04.070

dos Anjos, F. A., & Kennell, J. (2019). Tourism, governance and sustainable development. *Sustainability (Basel)*, 11(16), 4257. DOI: 10.3390/su11164257

Drakakis, P., Papadaskalopoulos, A., & Lagos, D. (2021). Multipliers and impacts of active sport tourism in the Greek region of Messinia. *Tourism Economics*, 27(3), 527–547. DOI: 10.1177/1354816620902328

Du Cros, H., Bauer, T., Lo, C., & Rui, S. (2005). Cultural heritage assets in China as sustainable tourism products: Case studies of the Hutongs and the Huanghua section of the Great Wall. *Journal of Sustainable Tourism*, 13(2), 171–194. DOI: 10.1080/09669580508668484

Duarte, B. F., Vareiro, L. C., Sousa, B. B., & Figueira, V. (2021). The Influence of Tourist Characteristics on the Perceived Quality of Hostels in Portugal: An Exploratory Study. In *Rebuilding and Restructuring the Tourism Industry: Infusion of Happiness and Quality of Life* (pp. 221–240). IGI Global. DOI: 10.4018/978-1-7998-7239-9.ch011

Dubini, P., & Di Biase, E. (2008). Heritage-led positioning and growth for Italian cities and towns. In *24th EGOS Colloquium-European Group for Organizational Studies*.

Durmaz, Y. ve Bahar Oruç, R. (2011). Tüketicilerin Satın Alma Davranısları Üzerinde Sosyolojik Faktörlerin Etkisinin İncelenmesine Yönelik Bir Çalısma. *Elektironik Sosyal Bilimler Dergisi*, 10(37), 60–77.

Dziedzic, E. (2019). Storytelling as a tool of the place identity formation. *Przedsiębiorczość i Zarządzanie*, 2(1), 109–119.

Edgerton, G. (1986). The film bureau phenomenon in America and its relationship to independent filmmaking. *Journal of Film and Video*, •••, 40–48.

Egusquiza, A., Zubiaga, M., Gandini, A., de Luca, C., & Tondelli, S. (2021). Systemic Innovation Areas for heritage-led rural regeneration: A multilevel repository of best practices. *Sustainability (Basel)*, 13(9), 5069. DOI: 10.3390/su13095069

Eime, R., Charity, M., Harvey, J., & Westerbeek, H. (2021). Five-year changes in community-level sport participation, and the role of gender strategies. *Frontiers in Sports and Active Living*, 3, 710666. DOI: 10.3389/fspor.2021.710666 PMID: 34712951

El Faouri, B. F., & Sibley, M. (2022). Heritage-led urban regeneration in the context of WH listing: Lessons and opportunities for the newly inscribed city of As-Salt in Jordan. *Sustainability (Basel)*, 14(8), 4557. DOI: 10.3390/su14084557

Emden, M. S. (1998). Qualitative metasynthesis: Issues and techniques. *Research in Nursing & Health*.

Engeset, M. G., & Elvekrok, I. (2015). Authentic Concepts: Effects on Tourist Satisfaction. *Journal of Travel Research*, 54(4), 456–466. DOI: 10.1177/0047287514522876

Eriksson, P., & Kovalainen, A. (2016). *Qualitative methods in business research* (2nd ed.). SAGE Publications.

Essex, S., & Chalkley, B. (1998). Olympic games: Catalyst of urban change. *Leisure Studies*, 17(3), 187–206. DOI: 10.1080/026143698375123

Eusébio, C., Vieira, A. L., & Lima, S. (2018). Place attachment, host–tourist interactions, and residents' attitudes towards tourism development: The case of Boa Vista Island in Cape Verde. *Journal of Sustainable Tourism*, 26(6), 890–909. DOI: 10.1080/09669582.2018.1425695

Evans, N., Campbell, D., & Stonehouse, G. (2003). *Strategic Management for Travel and Tourism*. Butterworth-Heinemann.

Fallery, B. R. (2007). *Quatre approches pour l'analyse de données textuelles: lexicale, linguistique, cognitive, thématique*. Conference: Actes de la XVIème Conférence Internationale de l'Association Internationale de Management Stratégique. AIMS.

Farhat, R. R. (2018). What Brand Is This Place? Place-Making and the Cultural Politics of Downtown Revitalization. *Space and Culture*, 22(1), 34–49. DOI: 10.1177/1206331217751778

Farsari, I. (2023). Exploring the nexus between sustainable tourism governance, resilience and complexity research. *Tourism Recreation Research*, 48(3), 352–367. DOI: 10.1080/02508281.2021.1922828

Fazal-e-Hasan, S. M., Ahmadi, H., Mortimer, G., Sekhon, H., Kharouf, H., & Jebarajakirthy, C. (2020). The Interplay of Positive and Negative Emotions to Quit Unhealthy Consumption Behaviors: Insights for Social Marketers. *Australasian Marketing Journal (Amj)*. DOI: 10.1016/j.ausmj.2020.07.004

Fenadoce. (n.d). Retrieved April 5, 2022, from https://bit.ly/3celfZF

Fernandes, J. L. (2012). Tecnologia, georreferenciação e novas territorialidades: o caso do geocaching. Cadernos de Geografia, 30/31 (2011/12), 171-180. Coimbra: Faculdade de Letras da Universidade de Coimbra. Disponível em http://hdl.handle.net/10316/23635

Fernando, I. (2015). What competitive strategies way forward the regional competitiveness, A comparative economic approach to Sri Lankan tourism. *International Journal of Business and Management*, 10(4), 178–186. DOI: 10.5539/ijbm.v10n4p178

Fernando, I. L. (2012). New Conceptual Model on Cluster Competitiveness: A New Paradigm for Tourism? *International Journal of Biometrics*.

Ferreira, A. (2005). Gestão *estratégica de cidades e regiões*. Fundação Calouste Gulbenkian, 2ª edição, Lisboa.

Ferreira, A. (2022). Literary routes as a successful tourist offer in Porto. *International Conference on Tourism Research*, 15(1), 126–134. https://doi.org/DOI: 10.34190/ictr.15.1.279

Figueira, A. P., Figueira, V., & Monteiro, S. (2015). Turismo e cinema: A importância de uma film commission na promoção do destino Alentejo. *Int. J. Sci. Manag. Tour*, 1, 29–37.

Figueroa, R. B.Jr. (2023). Immersive capability and spatial presence in virtual reality photo-based tours: Implications for distance education. *Asian Association of Open Universities Journal*, 18(3), 201–217. DOI: 10.1108/AAOUJ-12-2022-0171

Flowers, J., & Easterling, K. (2006). Growing South Carolina's tourism cluster. *Business and Economic Review*, 52(3), 15–20.

Fonseca, F., & Ramos, R. (2006) *O planeamento estratégico em busca de potenciar o território – o caso de Almeida*. In II Congresso Luso-Brasileiro 107 de Planeamento Urbano Regional Integrado Sustentável, 27 a 29 de Setembro, Universidade do Minho, Braga.

Fornell, C., & Larcker, D. F. (1981). Evaluating structural equation models with unobservable variables and measurement error. *JMR, Journal of Marketing Research*, 18(1), 39–50. DOI: 10.1177/002224378101800104

Franch, M., Martini, U., Buffa, F., & Parisi, G. (2008). 4L tourism (landscape, leisure, learning and limit): Responding to new motivations and expectations of tourists to improve the competitiveness of Alpine destinations in a sustainable way. *Tourism Review*, 63(1), 4–14. DOI: 10.1108/16605370810861008

Franzoni, S., & Bonera, M. (2019). How DMO Can Measure the Experiences of a Large Territory. *Sustainability (Basel)*, 11(2), 492. Advance online publication. DOI: 10.3390/su11020492

G.I., C. (2007). Modelling destination competitiveness, A survey and analysis of the impacts of competitiveness attributes. Sustainable tourism cooperative Research centre report.

Gaetjens, A., Corsi, A. M., & Plewa, C. (2023). Customer engagement in domestic wine tourism: The role of motivations. *Journal of Destination Marketing & Management*, 27, 100761. DOI: 10.1016/j.jdmm.2022.100761

Galí, N., Camprubí, R., & Donaire, J. A. (2017). Analysing tourism slogans in top tourism destinations. *Journal of Destination Marketing & Management*, 3(6), 243–251. DOI: 10.1016/j.jdmm.2016.04.004

Gallarza, M. G., Saura, I. G., & García, H. C. (2002). Destination image: Towards a conceptual framework. *Annals of Tourism Research*, 29(1), 56–78. DOI: 10.1016/S0160-7383(01)00031-7

Gani, A. (2022). Leveraging the community development approach to examine the natural capital effect on sustainable development goal 3-target 2. *Community Development (Columbus, Ohio)*, 53(5), 607–623. DOI: 10.1080/15575330.2021.2023601

Gannon, M., Rasoolmanesh, S. M., & Taheri, B. (2021). Assessing the mediating role of residents' perceptions toward tourism development. *Journal of Travel Research*, 60(1), 149–171. DOI: 10.1177/0047287519890926

García-Villaverde, P. M., Elche, D., & Martinez-Perez, A. (2020). Understanding Pioneering Orientation in Tourism Clusters: Market Dynamism and Social Capital. *Tourism Management*, 76, 103966. https://Doi.Org/Https://Doi.Org/10.1016/J.Tourman.2019.103966. DOI: 10.1016/j.tourman.2019.103966

Garner, B., & Ayala, C. (2018). Regional tourism at the farmers' market: Consumers' preferences for local food products. *International Journal of Culture, Tourism and Hospitality Research*, 13(1), 37–54. DOI: 10.1108/IJCTHR-07-2018-0095

Garrido, M. (2005). La publicidad turística en Andalucía (2002–2005): Andalucía sólo hay una, la tuya vs. Andalucía te quiere. *Questiones publicitarias, 1*(10), 77–97.

Garrido, M., & Ramos, M. (2006). *La evolución del eslogan en la publicidad gráfica española. III Simposium de profesores universitarios de creatividad publicitaria.* Universidad Ramón Llull. Barcelona: Trípodos.

Gartner, W. C. (2014). Brand equity in a tourism destination. *Place Branding and Public Diplomacy*, 10(2), 1–9. DOI: 10.1057/pb.2014.6

Gehl, J. (2013). *Cities for people.* Island Press.

Geipel, J., Hadjichristidis, C., & Klesse, A. K. (2018). Barriers to Sustainable Consumption Attenuated by Foreign Language Use. *Nature Sustainability*, 1(1), 31–33. Advance online publication. DOI: 10.1038/s41893-017-0005-9

Gelbman, A. (2021). Sport tourism and peace: Crossing the contested wall. In *Tourism places in Asia* (pp. 163–189). Routledge. DOI: 10.4324/9781003159711-9

Geopt. (2016, fevereiro). Benefícios de praticar Geocaching. Geopt. Consultado em dezembro 26, 2023 em: https://www.geopt.org/index.php/artigos/outros-artigos/geocaching/item/3390-beneficios-de-praticar-geocaching

Georgiev, G., & Vasileva, M. (2012). Tangible and intangible cultural heritage in the Western Balkan countries and tourism development. Tourism and Hospitality Management Conference proceedings, (pp. 501-506).

Gerhardt, T. E, R. & Silveira, D. T. (2009). *Metodos de Pesquisa. Universidade Aberta Do Brasil- UAB/UFRGS E Pelo Curso de Graduação Tecnológica – Planejamento e Gestão para o Desenvolvimento Rural da SEAD/UFEGS*,1º, 1-120.

Gerosa, A. and Tartari, M. (2021), "The Bottom-up Place Branding of a Neighborhood: Analyzing a Case of Selective Empowerment." *Space and Culture*, July.

Gibson, H. J. (1998). Active sport tourism: Who participates? *Leisure Studies*, 17(2), 155–170. DOI: 10.1080/026143698375213

Gilboa, S., & Herstein, R. (2012). Place Status, Place Loyalty and Well Being: An Exploratory Investigation of Israeli Residents. *Journal of Place Management and Development*. DOI: 10.1108/17538331211250035

Gilmore, A., Carson, D., & Ascenção, M. (2007). Sustainable tourism marketing at a World Heritage site. *Journal of Strategic Marketing*, 15(2-3), 253–264. DOI: 10.1080/09652540701318930

Gjedrem, A. M., & Log, T. (2020). Study of heathland succession, prescribed burning, and future perspectives at Kringsjå, Norway. *Land (Basel)*, 9(12), 485. DOI: 10.3390/land9120485

Godfrey, J., Wearing, S., Schulenkorf, N., & Grabowski, S. (2019). The 'Volunteer Tourist Gaze': Commercial Volunteer Tourists' Interactions With, and Perceptions Of, the Host Community in Cusco, Peru. *Current Issues in Tourism*. Advance online publication. DOI: 10.1080/13683500.2019.1657811

Goffi, G. (2013, November). A Model of Tourism Destination Competitiveness: The case of the Italian Destinations of Excellence. *Anuario Turismo y Sociedad*, 14, 121–147.

Goffi, G., & Cucculelli, M. (2014, December). Components of Destination Competitiveness. The case of Small Tourism Destinations in Italy. *International Journal of Tourism Policy*, 5(4), 296–326. DOI: 10.1504/IJTP.2014.068035

Gogonea, R.-M., & Zaharia, M. (2023). Agro-tourism South-West Oltenia in the post-pandemic period. Are there trends returning? *Journal of Tourism*, 35, 1–9. http://revistadeturism.ro/rdt/article/view/611/354

Gohori, O., & van der Merwe, P. (2020). Towards a tourism and community-development framework: An African perspective. *Sustainability (Basel)*, 12(13), 5305. DOI: 10.3390/su12135305

Gold, J. M. M. G. (2016). *Olympic Cities: City Agendas, Planning, and the World's Games*, 1896 (3rd ed.). Routledge.

Gold, J. R., & Gold, M. M. (2008). Olympic Cities: Regeneration, City Rebranding and Changing Urban Agendas. *Geography Compass*, 2(1), 300–318. DOI: 10.1111/j.1749-8198.2007.00080.x

González, X. (Dir.) (2001). *Planeamento Estratégico e Mecanotecnia Territorial*. EixoAtlântico do Noroeste Peninsular.

Gram-Hansen, L. B. (2009), "Geocaching in a persuasive perspective", Conference: Persuasive Technology, Fourth International Conference, Persuasive 2009, California: Claremont, No. 34, pp. 1-8. https://doi.org/DOI: 10.1145/1541948.1541993

Grant, R. M. (1991). Porter's 'competitive advantage of nations': An assessment. *Strategic Management Journal*, 12(7), 535–548. DOI: 10.1002/smj.4250120706

Gu, Q., Zhang, H. Q., King, B., & Huang, S. (2019). Understanding the Wine Tourism Experience: The Roles of Facilitators, Constraints, and Involvement. *Journal of Vacation Marketing*. Advance online publication. DOI: 10.1177/1356766719880253

Gurunathan, A., & Lakshmi, K. S. (2023). Exploring the Perceptions of Generations X, Y and Z about Online Platforms and Digital Marketing Activities – A Focus-Group Discussion Based Study. *International Journal of Professional Business Review*, 8(5), e02122. DOI: 10.26668/businessreview/2023.v8i5.2122

Guthrie, C. (2011). VisitBritain: satisfying the online market dynamics. In *eTourism case studies* (pp. 181-189). Routledge.

Güzel, Ö., Sahin, I., & Ryan, C. (2020). Push-motivation-based emotional arousal: A research study in a coastal destination. *Journal of Destination Marketing & Management*, 16, 100428. DOI: 10.1016/j.jdmm.2020.100428

Gyan, C. (2021). Community development participation scale: A development and validation study. *Community Development (Columbus, Ohio)*, 52(4), 459–472. DOI: 10.1080/15575330.2021.1885049

Hair, J. F., Matthews, L. M., Matthews, R. L., & Sarstedt, M. (2017). PLS-SEM or CB-SEM: Updated guidelines on which method to use. *International Journal of Multivariate Data Analysis*, 1(2), 107–123. DOI: 10.1504/IJMDA.2017.087624

Hajeer, A., & Toptsi, J. (2022). Piloting a semi-structured interview schedule: The influence of MOOC descriptions on potential students. *Journal of Adult Learning. Knowledge and Innovation*, 5(1), 36–45. DOI: 10.1556/2059.2021.00043

Hajrasouliha, A. (2019). Connecting the dots: Campus form, student perceptions, and academic performance. *Focus (San Francisco, Calif.)*, 15, 38–48.

Hakim, C. (2000). *Research Design: Successful Designs for Social and Economic Research*. Psychology Press.

Hall, C. M. (2008). Servicescapes, Designscapes, Branding, and The Creation of Place-Identity: South of Litchfield, Christchurch. *Journal of Travel & Tourism Marketing*, 25(3-4), 233–250. DOI: 10.1080/10548400802508101

Ham, P. (2008). Place Branding: State of Art. *The Annals of the American Academy of Political and Social Science*, 616(1), 126–149. DOI: 10.1177/0002716207312274

Han, B., Yang, J., Liu, G., & Sun, Z. (2023). Exploring gender differences through the lens of spatiotemporal behavior patterns in a cultural market: A case study of Panjiayuan market in Beijing, China. *Land (Basel)*, 12(4), 889. DOI: 10.3390/land12040889

Handler, I., & Tan, C. S. L. (2022). Are we teaching enough? A literature review on sustainable tourism events and the implications for Japanese Higher Education. *Journal of Hospitality & Tourism Education*, 34(3), 170–184. DOI: 10.1080/10963758.2021.1963744

Han, H., Che, C., & Lee, S. (2021). Facilitators and Reducers of Korean Travelers' Avoidance/Hesitation Behaviors Toward China in the Case of COVID-19. *International Journal of Environmental Research and Public Health*, 18(23), 12345. Advance online publication. DOI: 10.3390/ijerph182312345 PMID: 34886067

Hao, A. W., Paul, J., Trott, S., Guo, C., & Wu, H. H. (2021). Two decades of research on nation branding: A review and future research agenda. *International Marketing Review*, 38(1), 46–69. DOI: 10.1108/IMR-01-2019-0028

Hao, X., Jiang, E., & Chen, Y. (2024). The sign Avatar and tourists' practice at Pandora: A semiological perspective on a film related destination. *Tourism Management*, 101, 104856. DOI: 10.1016/j.tourman.2023.104856

Hao, X., & Ryan, C. (2013). Interpretation, film language and tourist destinations: A case study of Hibiscus Town, China. *Annals of Tourism Research*, 42, 334–358. DOI: 10.1016/j.annals.2013.02.016

Hartig, T., & Staats, H. (2006). The need for psychological restoration as a determinant of environmental preferences. *Journal of Environmental Psychology*, 26(3), 215–226. DOI: 10.1016/j.jenvp.2006.07.007

Harzing, A. W., & Giroud, A. (2014). The competitive advantage of nations: An application to academia. *Journal of Informetrics*, 8(1), 29–42. DOI: 10.1016/j.joi.2013.10.007

Hassan, A. (2020). In Walia, S. K. (Ed.), *Sustainable initiatives for community-based tourism development. In the Routledge handbook of community-based tourism management: concepts, issues and implications* (1st ed., pp. 130–137). Routledge.

Hass-Klau, C. (2014). *The pedestrian and the city*. Routledge. DOI: 10.4324/9780203067390

Haverila, M., Haverila, K.C. & Twyford, J.C. (2023). The influence of marital status on customer-centric measures in the context of a ski resort using the importance-performance map analysis (IPMA) framework, *European Journal of Management Studies, 28*(1), 49-68, https://doi.org/DOI: 10.1108/EJMS-05-2021-0034

Healey, M. (2009). *Mi az a branding? (What is Branding?)*. Scolar Kiadó.

Hellenic Statistical Authority. (2023). *Census 2021*. https://elstat-outsourcers.statistics.gr/Census2022_GR.pdf

Henriques, C., & Custódio, M. J. (2010). *Turismo e Gastronomia: A valorização do património gastronómico na região do Algarve*. Revista Encontros Científicos - Tourism & Management Studies, (6), 69-81. *HSM Management*, 3(44), 61–72.

Herstein, R., & Berger, R. (2013). Much more than sports: Sports events as stimuli for city re-branding. *The Journal of Business Strategy*, 34(2), 38–44. DOI: 10.1108/02756661311310440

Heslinga, J., Groote, P., & Vanclay, F. (2019). Strengthening governance processes to improve benefit-sharing from tourism in protected areas by using stakeholder analysis. *Journal of Sustainable Tourism*, 27(6), 773–787. DOI: 10.1080/09669582.2017.1408635

Higham, J., & Hinch, T. (2018). *Sport Tourism Development* (Vol. 84). Channel View Publications.

Holland, K. K., Larson, L. R., Powell, R. B., Holland, W. H., Allen, L., Nabaala, M., Tome, S., Seno, S., & Nampushi, J. (2022). Impacts of tourism on support for conservation, local livelihoods, and community resilience around Maasai Mara National Reserve, Kenya. *Journal of Sustainable Tourism*, 30(11), 2526–2548. DOI: 10.1080/09669582.2021.1932927

Holmes, K., Hughes, M., Mair, J., & Carlsen, J. (2015). *Events and sustainability*. Routledge. DOI: 10.9774/gleaf.9781315813011

Holmes, K., Jones, P., Lockwood, A., Miller, G., Scarles, C., Szivas, E., & Tribe, J. (2006). An eclectic agenda for Tourism and Hospitality Research. *Tourism and Hospitality Research*, 7(1), 76–82. DOI: 10.1057/palgrave.thr.6050035

Hribar, M. B. (2017). Participatory research in community development: A case study of creating cultural tourism products. (U. Karlova, Éd.) Acta Universitatis Carolinae. Geographica, 52(2), 1-12. DOI: 10.14712/23361980.2017.13

Hsieh, A. T., & Chang, J. (2006). Shopping and tourist night markets in Taiwan. *Tourism Management*, 27(1), 138–145. DOI: 10.1016/j.tourman.2004.06.017

Hsieh, H.-F., & Shannon, S. E. (2005). Three approaches to qualitative content analysis. *Qualitative Health Research*, 15(9), 1277–1288. DOI: 10.1177/1049732305276687 PMID: 16204405

https://ec.europa.eu/regional_policy/en/atlas/programmes/2007-2013/crossborder/greece-the-former-yugoslav-republic-of-macedonia-ipa-cross-border-co-operation-programme-2007-2013. (2020, October 1). Récupéré sur https://ec.europa.eu: https://ec.europa.eu/regional_policy/en/atlas/programmes/2007-2013/crossborder/greece-the-former-yugoslav-republic-of-macedonia-ipa-cross-border-co-operation-programme-2007-2013

Huang, C. H., Tsaur, J. R., & Yang, C. H. (2012). Does world heritage list really induce more tourists? Evidence from Macau. *Tourism Management*, 33(6), 1450–1457. DOI: 10.1016/j.tourman.2012.01.014 PMID: 32287738

Huang, C. M., Tuan, C. L., & Wongchai, A. (2014). Development analysis of leisure agriculture–a case study of Longjing Tea Garden, Hangzhou, China. *APCBEE Procedia*, 8, 210–215. DOI: 10.1016/j.apcbee.2014.03.029

Hudson, S., & Ritchie, J. B. (2006). Promoting destinations via film tourism: An empirical identification of supporting marketing initiatives. *Journal of Travel Research*, 44(4), 387–396. DOI: 10.1177/0047287506286720

Hughes, H. (1993). Olympic tourism and urban regeneration; 1996 Summer Olympics. *Festival Management & Event Tourism*, 1(4), 137–184.

Hughes, H. (2013). *Arts, entertainment and tourism*. Taylor & Francis. DOI: 10.4324/9780080499468

Huh, J., & Uysal, M. (2004). Satisfaction with cultural/heritage sites: Virginia historic triangle. *Journal of Quality Assurance in Hospitality & Tourism*, 4(3-4), 177–194. DOI: 10.1300/J162v04n03_12

Hungenberg, E., Gray, D., Gould, J., & Stotlar, D. (2016). An examination of motives underlying active sport tourist behavior: A market segmentation approach. *Journal of Sport & Tourism*, 20(2), 81–101. DOI: 10.1080/14775085.2016.1189845

Huong, L. T., Hang, N. T., Huy, D. T., Tinh, D. T., & Huyen, D. T. (2021). Educating Students in History and Geography Subjects through Visiting Historical Sites to Develop Local Economy and Community Tourism Services in Thai Nguyen and Ha Giang Provinces, Vietnam. *Revista Gestão Inovação e Tecnologias.*, 11(3), 1–12. DOI: 10.47059/revistageintec.v11i3.1911

Hwang, J.-A., Park, Y., & Kim, Y. (2016). Why Do Consumers Respond to Eco-Labels? The Case of Korea. *SpringerPlus*, 5(1), 1915. Advance online publication. DOI: 10.1186/s40064-016-3550-1 PMID: 27867822

Iazzi, A., Rosato, P., & Gravili, S. (2015). Competitive processes in tourism destinations: The role of intangible assets. *International Journal of Management*.

Ihamäki, P. (2012). Geocachers: The creative tourism experience. *Journal of Hospitality and Tourism Technology*, 3(3), 152–175. DOI: 10.1108/17579881211264468

IISD. (2023). *UNWTO Report Links Sustainable Tourism to 17 SDGs*. Available online: https://sdg.iisd.org/news/unwto-report-links-sustainable-tourism-to-17-sdgs/ (accessed on 5 June 2023).

Imamović, I., Azevedo, A. J., & Sousa, B. M. (2022). The Urban Sensescapes and Sensory Destination Branding. In Valeri, M. (Ed.), *New Governance and Management in Touristic Destinations* (pp. 276–293). IGI Global., DOI: 10.4018/978-1-6684-3889-3.ch017

Imrie, R., Lees, L., & Raco, M. (2008). *Regenerating London: Governance, Sustainability and Community in a Global City*. Routledge Taylor & Francis Group.

İnanır, A. (2019). Turistik destinasyon yönetiminde paydaşlar arası ilişkiler: Göller Yöresi Örneği. *Türk Turizm Araştırmaları Dergisi*, 3(3), 517–541. DOI: 10.26677/TR1010.2019.176

IOC. (2021). *Marketing Fact*.

Ito, E., & Higham, J. (2023). An evidence-base for reducing the CO2 emissions of national mega sports events: Application of the three-hub model to the Japan 2019 Rugby World Cup. *Journal of Sustainable Tourism*, •••, 1–17. DOI: 10.1080/09669582.2023.2177301

Ivanovic, S., Milenkovski, A., & Milojica, V. (2015). Croatian tourism and hospitality industry: Current state and future development perspectives. *UTMS Journal of Economics (Skopje)*, 6(2), 293–305.

Jamal, T., & Stronza, A. (2009). Collaboration theory and tourism practice in protected areas: Stakeholders, structuring and sustainability. *Journal of Sustainable Tourism*, 17(2), 169–190. DOI: 10.1080/09669580802495741

Janeczko, E., Fialova, J., Tomusiak, R., Woźnicka, M., & Prochazkova, P. (2019). Running as a form of recreation in the Polish and Czech forests-advantages and disadvantages. *Sylwan*, 163, 522–528.

Jankowicz, A. (2005). *Business Research Projects*. Thomson Learning.

Jeelani, P., Shah, S. A., Dar, S. N., & Rashid, H. (2022). Sustainability constructs of mountain tourism development: The evaluation of stakeholders' perception using SUS-TAS. *Environment, Development and Sustainability*, 25(8), 8299–8317. DOI: 10.1007/s10668-022-02401-8 PMID: 35915719

Jensen, Ø., & Prebensen, K. N. (2015). Innovation and value creation in experience-based tourism. *Scandinavian Journal of Hospitality and Tourism*, 15(sup1), 1–8. DOI: 10.1080/15022250.2015.1066093

Jeong, Y., & Kim, S. K. (2019). The key antecedent and consequences of destination image in a mega sporting event. *South African Journal of Business Management*, 50(1), 1–11. DOI: 10.4102/sajbm.v50i1.1480

Jerez, M. R. (2023). Tourism marketing of the Autonomous Communities of Spain to promote gastronomy as part of their destination branding. *International Journal of Gastronomy and Food Science*, 32, 1–11, 100727. DOI: 10.1016/j.ijgfs.2023.100727

Jewell, B., & McKinnon, S. (2008). Movie tourism—A new form of cultural landscape? *Journal of Travel & Tourism Marketing*, 24(2-3), 153–162. DOI: 10.1080/10548400802092650

Jia, H., Lu, Y., Yu, S. L., & Chen, Y. (2012). Planning of LID-BMPs for urban runoff control: The case of Beijing Olympic Village. []. Elsevier.]. *Separation and Purification Technology*, 84, 112–119. DOI: 10.1016/j.seppur.2011.04.026

Jimura, T. (2011). The impact of world heritage site designation on local communities–A case study of Ogimachi, Shirakawa-mura, Japan. *Tourism Management*, 32(2), 288–296. DOI: 10.1016/j.tourman.2010.02.005

Jin, X., & Cheng, M. (2020). Communicating mega events on Twitter: Implications for destination marketing. *Journal of Travel & Tourism Marketing*, 37(6), 739–755. DOI: 10.1080/10548408.2020.1812466

Johann, M., Mishra, S., Malhotra, G., & Tiwari, S. R. (2022). Participation in active sport tourism: Impact assessment of destination involvement and perceived risk. *Journal of Sport & Tourism*, 26(2), 101–123. DOI: 10.1080/14775085.2021.2017326

Johnson, C. (2018). The 10 functions of storytelling. Retrieved January 9, 2022, from https://www.carlajohnson.co/the-10-functions-of-storytelling/

Joo, D., Cho, H., & Woosnam, K. M. (2023). Anticipated emotional solidarity, emotional reasoning, and travel intention: A comparison of two destination image models. *Tourism Management Perspectives*, 46, 101075. DOI: 10.1016/j.tmp.2023.101075

Jornal Diário da Manhã. *Pelotenses conhecem a nova marca da cidade*. (2017, July, 13). https://bit.ly/2Ef2WHm

Josiassen, A., Kock, F., & Norfelt, A. (2020). Tourism Affinity and Its Effects on Tourist and Resident Behavior. *Journal of Travel Research*. Advance online publication. DOI: 10.1177/0047287520979682

Jung, S., Draper, J., Malek, K., Padron, T. C., & Olson, E. (2024). Bridging Theory and Practice: An Examination of How Event-Tourism Research Aligns With UN Sustainable Development Goals. *Journal of Travel Research*, 63(7), 00472875241231273. DOI: 10.1177/00472875241231273

Juškelytė, D. (2016). Film induced tourism: Destination image formation and development. *Regional Formation and Development Studies*, 19(2), 54–67. DOI: 10.15181/rfds.v19i2.1283

Källström, L., & Ekelund, C. (2016). What can a municipality offer to its residents? Value propositions and interactions in a place context. *International Journal of Culture, Tourism and Hospitality Research*, 10(1), 24–37. DOI: 10.1108/IJCTHR-05-2015-0040

Kang, S., Lee, G., Kim, J., & Park, D. (2018). Identifying the spatial structure of the tourist attraction system in South Korea using GIS and network analysis: An application of anchor-point theory. *Journal of Destination Marketing & Management*, 9, 358–370. DOI: 10.1016/j.jdmm.2018.04.001

Kanwal, S., Rasheed, M. I., Pitafi, A. H., Pitafi, A., & Ren, M. (2020). Road and transport infrastructure development and community support for tourism: The role of perceived benefits, and community satisfaction. *Tourism Management*, 77, 104014. DOI: 10.1016/j.tourman.2019.104014

Kapferer, J. N. (1994). *Strategic brand management, new approaches to creating and evaluating brand equity*. The Free Press.

Kapferer, J.-N. (2004). Marcas: Capital de empresa. *The Bookman*.

Kaplanidou, K., & Vogt, C. (2007). The Interrelationship between Sports Events and Destination Image and Sport Tourists' Behaviours. *Journal of Sport & Tourism*, 12(3-4), 183–206. DOI: 10.1080/14775080701736932

Kaplan, M. D. (2010). Branding Places: Applying Brand Personality Concept to Cities. *European Journal of Marketing*, 44(9-10), 1286–1304. DOI: 10.1108/03090561011062844

Karadjoski, M. (2013). *Cross-border Cooperation between Macedonia and Greece as an Instrument for Good Neighbourhood Relations*. The Balkans Dialogue Conference 2013. Institute for Cultural Relations Policy.

Karakuş, Y., & Kalay, N. (2017). A Study on the Concept and Causes of Destination Rejection. *International Journal of Management Economics and Business*. DOI: 10.17130/ijmeb.2017331320

Karakuş, Y., & Çoban, S. (2018). Evaluation of Stakeholders' Expectations Towards Congress Tourism by Kano Model: Case of Nevşehir. *Anais Brasileiros De Estudos Turísticos*, 8(2), 8–20. DOI: 10.34019/2238-2925.2018.v8.3207

Kasapi, I., & Cela, A. (2017). Destination branding: A review of the city branding literature. *Mediterranean Journal of Social Sciences*, 8(4), 129–142. DOI: 10.1515/mjss-2017-0012

Kavaratzis, M. (2004). From city marketing to city branding: Towards a theoretical framework for developing city brands. *Place Branding and Public Diplomacy*, 1(1), 58–73. DOI: 10.1057/palgrave.pb.5990005

Kavaratzis, M. (2012). From 'necessary evil' to necessity: Stakeholders' involvement in place branding. *Journal of Place Management and Development*, 5(1), 7–19. DOI: 10.1108/17538331211209013

Kavaratzis, M., & Ashworth, G. J. (2005). City Branding: An effective assertion of identity or a transitory marketing trick? *Tijdschrift voor Economische en Sociale Geografie*, 96(5), 506–514. DOI: 10.1111/j.1467-9663.2005.00482.x

Kavaratzis, M., & Hatch, M. J. (2013). The dynamics of place brands: An identity-based approach to place branding theory. *Marketing Theory*, 13(1), 69–86. DOI: 10.1177/1470593112467268

Kc, B., & Leung, X. Y.KC. (2022). Geocaching in Texas state parks: A technology readiness analysis. *Journal of Hospitality and Tourism Technology*, 13(1), 182–194. DOI: 10.1108/JHTT-09-2020-0240

Kearney, J. (2010). Food Consumption Trends and Drivers. *Philosophical Transactions of the Royal Society of London. Series B, Biological Sciences*, 365(1554), 2793–2807. Advance online publication. DOI: 10.1098/rstb.2010.0149 PMID: 20713385

Kerstetter, D. L., Confer, J. J., & Graefe, A. R. (2001). An exploration of the specialization concept within the context of heritage tourism. *Journal of Travel Research*, 39(3), 267–274. DOI: 10.1177/004728750103900304

Keskin, H., Akgun, A. E., Zehir, C., & Ayar, H. (2016). Tales of cities: City branding through storytelling. *Journal of Global Strategic Management, 1*(10), 2016 June, 31–41. https://www.researchgate.net/profile/Hayat-Ayar-Sentuerk/publication/309465697_TALES_OF_CITIES_CITY_BRANDING_THROUGH_STORYTELLING/links/581b0c0d08ae3c82664d5098/TALES-OF-CITIES-CITY-BRANDING-THROUGH-STORYTELLING.pdf

Kietzmann, J. H., Hermkens, K., McCarthy, I. P., & Silvestre, B. S. (2011). Social media? Get serious! Understanding the functional building blocks of social media. *Business Horizons*, 54(3), 241–251. DOI: 10.1016/j.bushor.2011.01.005

Kim, C., & Kim, J. (2023). Spatial spillovers of sport industry clusters and community resilience: Bridging a spatial lens to building a smart tourism city. *Information Processing & Management*, 60(3), 103266. DOI: 10.1016/j.ipm.2023.103266

Kim, D., & Perdue, R. R. (2011). The influence of image on destination attractiveness. *Journal of Travel & Tourism Marketing*, 28(3), 225–239. DOI: 10.1080/10548408.2011.562850

Kim, H. J., Kehoe, P., Gibbs, L., & Lee, J. A. (2019). Caregiving Experience of Dementia Among Korean American Family Caregivers. *Issues in Mental Health Nursing*, 40(2), 158–165. Advance online publication. DOI: 10.1080/01612840.2018.1534909 PMID: 30620625

Kim, H., & Kim, C. W. (2024). Limitations and Problems Associated with Marine Healing Tourism: An Examination of the Chungcheongnam-Do Marine Healing Pilot Program. *Journal of Coastal Research*, 116(sp1). Advance online publication. DOI: 10.2112/JCR-SI116-087.1

Kim, H., & Richardson, S. L. (2003). Motion picture impacts on destination images. *Annals of Tourism Research*, 30(1), 216–237. DOI: 10.1016/S0160-7383(02)00062-2

Kim, M., & Thapa, B. (2018). Perceived value and flow experience: Application in a nature-based tourism context. *Journal of Destination Marketing & Management*, 8, 373–384. DOI: 10.1016/j.jdmm.2017.08.002

Kim, N. S., & Chalip, L. (2004). Why travel to the FIFA World Cup? Effects of motives, background, interest, and constraints. *Tourism Management*, 25(6), 695–707. DOI: 10.1016/j.tourman.2003.08.011

King, S. B., Kaczynski, A. T., Knight Wilt, J., & Stowe, E. W. (2020). Walkability 101: A multi-method assessment of the walkability at a University Campus. *SAGE Open*, 10(2), 1–9. DOI: 10.1177/2158244020917954

Klenosky, D. B., & Gitelson, R. E. (1997). Characteristics of effective tourism promotion slogans. *Annals of Tourism Research*, 24(1), 235–238. DOI: 10.1016/S0160-7383(96)00038-2

Knott, B., Fyall, A., & Jones, I. (2015). The nation branding opportunities provided by a sport mega-event: South Africa and the 2010 FIFA World Cup. *Journal of Destination Marketing & Management*, 4(1), 46–56. DOI: 10.1016/j.jdmm.2014.09.001

Kohli, C., Leuthesser, L., & Suri, R. (2007). Got slogan? Guidelines for creating effective slogans. *Business Horizons*, 50(5), 415–422. DOI: 10.1016/j.bushor.2007.05.002

Kolar, T., & Zabkar, V. (2010). A consumer-based model of authenticity: An oxymoron or the foundation of cultural heritage marketing? *Tourism Management*, 31(5), 652–664. DOI: 10.1016/j.tourman.2009.07.010

Kolehmainen, J., Irvine, J., Stewart, L., Karacsonyi, Z., Szabo, T., Alarinta, J., & Norberg, A. (2015). Quadruple Helix, Innovation and the Knowledge-Based Development: Lessons from Remote, Rural and Less-Favoured Regions. *Journal of the Knowledge Economy*.

Kosmaczewska, J. (2022). Should I stay or should I go out? Leisure and tourism consumption of geocachers under the existence of COVID restrictions and economic uncertainty in Poland. *Annals of Leisure Research*, •••, 1–19.

Kotler, P., & Gertner, D. (2002, April). Country as brand, product, and beyond: A place marketing and brand management perspective. *Journal of Brand Management*, 9(4-5), 249–261. DOI: 10.1057/palgrave.bm.2540076

Kotler, P., Haider, D. H., & Rein, I. (1993). *Marketing Places*. The Free Press.

Kotler, P., & Keller, K. L. (2006). *Marketing Management*. Akadémiai Kiadó.

Koutsi, D., Lagarias, A., & Stratigea, A. (2022). Evidence-Based Exploration as the Ground for Heritage-Led Pathways in Insular Territories: Case Study Greek Islands. *Heritage*, 5(3), 2746–2772. DOI: 10.3390/heritage5030143

Koutsi, D., & Stratigea, A. (2019). Unburying hidden land and maritime cultural potential of small islands in the Mediterranean for tracking heritage-led local development paths. *Heritage*, 2(1), 938–966. DOI: 10.3390/heritage2010062

Kozak, M., & Rimmington, M. (2000). Tourist Satisfaction With Mallorca, Spain, as an Off-Season Holiday Destination. *Journal of Travel Research*, 38(3), 260–269. Advance online publication. DOI: 10.1177/004728750003800308

Kozar, J. M., & Connell, K. Y. H. (2013). Socially and Environmentally Responsible Apparel Consumption: Knowledge, Attitudes, and Behaviors. *Social Responsibility Journal*, 9(2), 315–324. Advance online publication. DOI: 10.1108/SRJ-09-2011-0076

Krstic, B., Jovanovic, S., & Stanisic, T. (2015). Central and East European countries' tourism competitiveness as a factor of their national competitiveness level. Journal of tourism studies and research in tourism, 18, 61-68.

Kruger, M., & Viljoen, A. (2021). Terroir wine festival visitors: Uncorking the origin of behavioural intentions. *Current Issues in Tourism*, 24(5), 616–636. DOI: 10.1080/13683500.2019.1667310

Kudinova, I., & Terzi, S. (2023). Cultural heritage - the tourism brand of ukraine. *Journal of Lviv Polytechnic National University.Series of Economics and Management Issues*, 7(2), 27–40. DOI: 10.23939/semi2023.02.027

Kumar, S., Talukder, M. B., & Kaiser, F. (2024). Artificial Intelligence in Business: Negative Social Impacts. In *Demystifying the Dark Side of AI in Business* (pp. 81-97). IGI Global. https://doi.org/ DOI: 10.4018/979-8-3693-0724-3.ch005

Kumar, S., Talukder, M. B., Kabir, F., & Kaiser, F. (2024). Challenges and Sustainability of Green Finance in the Tourism Industry: Evidence from Bangladesh. In Taneja, S., Kumar, P., Grima, S., Ozen, E., & Sood, K. (Eds.), (pp. 97–111). Advances in Finance, Accounting, and Economics. IGI Global., DOI: 10.4018/979-8-3693-1388-6.ch006

Kumar, S., Talukder, M. B., & Pego, A. (Eds.). (2024). *Utilizing Smart Technology and AI in Hybrid Tourism and Hospitality*. IGI Global., DOI: 10.4018/979-8-3693-1978-9

Kumar, S., & Valeri, M. (2022). Understanding the relationship among factors influencing rural tourism: A hierarchical approach. *Journal of Organizational Change Management*, 35(2), 385–407.

Kumar, V., & Kaushik, A. K. (2020). Does experience affect engagement? Role of destination brand engagement in developing brand advocacy and revisit intentions. *Journal of Travel & Tourism Marketing*, 37(3), 332–346. DOI: 10.1080/10548408.2020.1757562

Kung, R. (2018). A Study of the tourists expectation, satisfaction and revisiting intention in the Neiwan, Hsinchu. *IJNDES*, 2, 43–49.

Kvítková, Z., & Petrů, Z. (2021). Approaches to storytelling and narrative structures in destination marketing. Retrieved from https://dx.doi.org/DOI: 10.20867/tosee.06.28

Kwong, Y. M. C. (2024). Engaging children's voices for tourism and marine futures through drawing in Gili Trawangan, Indonesia. *Frontiers in Sustainable Tourism*, 2, 1291142. DOI: 10.3389/frsut.2023.1291142

Lages, R. (2017). *O posicionamento e a imagem em contextos de marketing territorial: Estudo de caso aplicado à cidade de Braga*. Escola de Economia e Gestão da Universidade do Minho.

Laing, J., Wheeler, F., Reeves, K., & Frost, W. (2014). Assessing the experiential value of heritage assets: A case study of a Chinese heritage precinct, Bendigo, Australia. *Tourism Management*, 40, 180–192. DOI: 10.1016/j.tourman.2013.06.004

Lak, A., Gheitasi, M., & Timothy, D. J. (2020). Urban regeneration through heritage tourism: Cultural policies and strategic management. *Journal of Tourism and Cultural Change*, 18(4), 386–403. DOI: 10.1080/14766825.2019.1668002

Lamichhane, B. P. (2021). Good governance in Nepal: Legal provisions and judicial praxis. *Journal of Political Science*, 21, 19–30. DOI: 10.3126/jps.v21i0.35260

Larsen, S. (2007). Aspects of a psychology of the tourist experience. *Scandinavian Journal of Hospitality and Tourism*, 7(1), 7–18. DOI: 10.1080/15022250701226014

Lawson, R., & Thyne, M. (2001). Destination Avoidance and Inept Destination Sets. *Journal of Vacation Marketing*, 7(3), 199–208. DOI: 10.1177/135676670100700301

LEADER II. (2001). *Developing Walking Holidays in Rural Areas. Guide on How to Design and Implement a Walking Holiday Project*. Available online: https://ec.europa.eu/enrd/sites/default/files/leaderii_dossiers_tourism_walking-holidays.pdf (accessed on 10 Jun 2023).

Lebre, A. de F. da S. F. dos S. (2017). O Geocaching como estratégia competitiva para o Enoturismo da Bairrada. Dissertação de mestrado, Escola Superior de Educação – Instituto Politécnico de Coimbra, Coimbra, Portugal.

Lee, S., & Park, D. (2019). Community attachment formation and its influence on sustainable participation in a digitalized community: Focusing on content and social capital of an online community. *Sustainability (Basel)*, 11(10), 2935. DOI: 10.3390/su11102935

Lehto, X., Davari, D., & Park, S. (2020). Transforming the guest-host relationship: A convivial tourism approach. *International Journal of Tourism Cities*, 6(4), 1069–1088. DOI: 10.1108/IJTC-06-2020-0121

Lehto, X., Lee, G., & Ismail, J. (2014). Measuring congruence of affective images of destinations and their slogans. *International Journal of Tourism Research*, 16(3), 250–260. DOI: 10.1002/jtr.1923

Leong, A. M. W., Yeh, S. S., Zhou, Y., Hung, C. W., & Huan, T. C. (2024). Exploring the influence of historical storytelling on cultural heritage tourists' value co-creation using tour guide interaction and authentic place as mediators. *Tourism Management Perspectives*, 50, 101198. DOI: 10.1016/j.tmp.2023.101198

Lepp, A., Gibson, H., & Lane, C. (2011). Image and perceived risk: A study of Uganda and its official tourism website. *Tourism Management*, 32(3), 675–684. DOI: 10.1016/j.tourman.2010.05.024

Leung, X. Y., & Jiang, L. (2018). How Do Destination Facebook Pages Work? An Extended TPB Model of Fans' Visit Intention. *Journal of Hospitality and Tourism Technology*, 9(3), 397–416. Advance online publication. DOI: 10.1108/JHTT-09-2017-0088

Lewis, J. R. (2006). Qualitative Research Practice: A Guide for Social Science Students and Researchers (éd. 2). SAGE Publications.

Liberato, P. (2020). Movie Tourism and Attracting New Tourists in the Post-pandemic Period: A Niche Marketing Perspective. *Advances in Tourism, Technology and Systems: Selected Papers from ICOTTS20, Volume 1*, 208, 373.

Liberato, P., Alén, E., & Liberato, D. (2018). Smart tourism destination triggers consumer experience: The case of Porto. *European Journal of Management and Business Economics*, 27(1), 6–25. DOI: 10.1108/EJMBE-11-2017-0051

Light, D. (2007). Dracula tourism in Romania: Cultural identity and the state. *Annals of Tourism Research*, 34(3), 746–765. DOI: 10.1016/j.annals.2007.03.004

Lin, Y. C. (2020). Measuring authenticity through spatial metaphors: How close are tourists to the back regions? *Current Issues in Tourism*, •••, 1–15.

Li, S., Li, H., Song, H., Lundberg, C., & Shen, S. (2017). The economic impact of on-screen tourism: The case of Lord of the Rings and the Hobbit. *Tourism Management*, 60, 177–187. DOI: 10.1016/j.tourman.2016.11.023

Little, J., Little, E. L., & Cox, K. C. (2011). *U.S. Consumer Animosity Towards Vietnam: A Comparison of Generations. Journal of Applied Business Research*. Jabr., DOI: 10.19030/jabr.v25i6.991

Liu, C., Dou, X., Li, J., & Cai, L. A. (2020). Analyzing government role in rural tourism development: An empirical investigation from China. *Journal of Rural Studies*, 79, 177–188. DOI: 10.1016/j.jrurstud.2020.08.046

Liu, J., Wang, C., & Zhang, T. C. (2024). Exploring social media affordances in tourist destination image formation: A study on China's rural tourism destination. *Tourism Management*, 101, 104843. DOI: 10.1016/j.tourman.2023.104843

Liu, Y., & Li, Y. (2017). Revitalize the world's countryside. *Nature*, 548(7667), 275–277. DOI: 10.1038/548275a PMID: 28816262

Li, X., Yang, J., Wang, X., & Lei, D. (2012). The Impact of Country-of-Origin Image, Consumer Ethnocentrism and Animosity on Purchase Intention. *Journal of Software*, 7(10). Advance online publication. DOI: 10.4304/jsw.7.10.2263-2268

Lodge, C. (2002). Success and failure: The brand stories of two countries. *Journal of Brand Management*, 9(4), 372–384. DOI: 10.1057/palgrave.bm.2540084

Lopez, L., & Pérez, Y. (2020). Cultural Tourism and Heritage Education in the Portuguese Way of St. James. In *INTERNATIONAL SYMPOSIUM: New Metropolitan Perspectives, 178*, 1897-1906. Springer International Publishing., DOI: 10.1007/978-3-030-48279-4_179

Lorenzini, E., Calzati, V., & Giudici, P. (2011). Territorial brands for tourism development: A statistical analysis on the Marche region. *Annals of Tourism Research*, 38(2), 540–560. DOI: 10.1016/j.annals.2010.10.008

Lor, J. J., Kwa, S., & Donaldson, J. A. (2019). Making ethnic tourism good for the poor. *Annals of Tourism Research*, 76, 140–152. DOI: 10.1016/j.annals.2019.03.008

Loulanski, T. (2006, May). Revising the Concept for Cultural Heritage: The Argument for a Functional Approach. *International Journal of Cultural Property*, 13(2). Advance online publication. DOI: 10.1017/S0940739106060085

Loulanski, V. L., & Loulanski, V. (2011). The sustainable integration of cultural heritage and tourism: A meta-study. *Journal of Sustainable Tourism*, 19(7), 837–862. DOI: 10.1080/09669582.2011.553286

Loureiro, S. M. C., Guerreiro, J., & Han, H. (2021). Past, Present, and Future of Pro-Environmental Behavior in Tourism and Hospitality: A Text-Mining Approach. *Journal of Sustainable Tourism*. Advance online publication. DOI: 10.1080/09669582.2021.1875477

Lusa (2015, agosto). "Geocaching", a caça ao tesouro "evoluída": o que é e os cuidados a ter. *Jornal Expresso*. Consultado em dezembro 23, 2023 em: https://expresso.pt/sociedade/2015-08-03-Geocaching-a-caca-ao-tesouro-evoluida-o-que-e-e-os-cuidados-a-ter

Ma, H.-Y., Kao, J.-C., Kao, R.-H., Chiang, N.-T., & Cho, C.-C. (2024). A study on transboundary governance of marine plastic debris—The case of an adjacent waters between China and Taiwan. *Environmental Science and Pollution Study*. DOI: 10.1007/s11356-024-31876-3

MacBride-Stewart, S., Parsons, C., & Carati, I. (2021). *Playfulness and game play: Using geocaching to engage young people's wellbeing in a National Park. Gamification in tourism. Aspects of Tourism Series*. Channel View Publications. DOI: 10.2307/jj.22730549.15

Machado, J. T. M., & De Andrés, M. (2023). Implications of offshore wind energy developments in coastal and maritime tourism and recreation areas: An analytical overview. *Environmental Impact Assessment Review*, 99, 106999. DOI: 10.1016/j.eiar.2022.106999

MacInnis, D. J. (2011). A framework for conceptual contributions in marketing. *Journal of Marketing*, 75(4), 136–154. DOI: 10.1509/jmkg.75.4.136

Macionis, N. (2004). Understanding the film-induced tourist. In *International tourism and media conference proceedings* (Vol. 24, pp. 86-97). Tourism Research Unit, Monash University: Melbourne, Australia

Ma, H., Chiu, Y., Tian, X., Zhang, J., & Guo, Q. (2020). Safety or Travel: Which Is More Important? The Impact of Disaster Events on Tourism. *Sustainability (Basel)*, 12(7), 3038. Advance online publication. DOI: 10.3390/su12073038

Maiello, A., & Pasquinelli, C. (2015). Destruction or construction? A (counter) branding analysis of sport mega-events in Rio de Janeiro. *Cities (London, England)*, 48, 116–124. DOI: 10.1016/j.cities.2015.06.011

Mak, B. K. L., Cheung, L. T. O., and Hui, D. L. H. (2017). Community Participation in the Decision-Making Process for Sustainable Tourism Development in Rural Areas of Hong Kong, China. *Sustainability, 9*(10),1695, 1-13, DOI: 10.3390/su9101695

Malterud, K., Siersma, V. D., & Guassora, A. D. (2016). Sample size in qualitative interview studies: Guided by information power. *Qualitative Health Research*, 26(13), 1753–1760. DOI: 10.1177/1049732315617444 PMID: 26613970

Manci, A. R. (2022). Determining Destination Risk Perceptions, Their Effects on Satisfaction, Revisit and Recommendation Intentions: Evidence From Sanliurfa/Turkey. *Journal of Multidisciplinary Academic Tourism.* DOI: 10.31822/jomat.2022-7-1-81

Manrai, L. A., & Manrai, A. K. (2011). *Hofstede's Cultural Dimensions and Tourist Behaviors: A Review and Conceptual Framework.* Cuadernos De Difusión., DOI: 10.46631/jefas.2011.v16n31.02

Mao, Y., Ren, X., Yin, L., Sun, Q., Song, K., & Wang, D. (2021). Investigating Tourists' Willingness to Walk (WTW) to Attractions within Scenic Areas: A Case Study of Tongli Ancient Town, China. *Sustainability (Basel)*, 13(23), 12990. DOI: 10.3390/su132312990

Marpaung, B. O. Y., & Tania, F. (2021). Visitor Satisfaction and Tourist Attraction Image. *International Journal of Psychological Studies*, 13(2), 33. Advance online publication. DOI: 10.5539/ijps.v13n2p33

Marques, L., & Pimentel Biscaia, M. S. (2019). Leisure and innovation: Exploring boundaries. *World Leisure Journal*, 61(3), 162–169. DOI: 10.1080/16078055.2019.1639257

Martin, D., & Woodside, A. G. (2008). Grounded Theory of International Tourism Behavior. *Journal of Travel & Tourism Marketing*, 24(4), 245–258. Advance online publication. DOI: 10.1080/10548400802156695

Martin, D., & Woodside, A. G. (2011). Storytelling research on international visitors: Interpreting own experiences in Tokyo. *Qualitative Market Research*, 14(1), 27–54. DOI: 10.1108/13522751111099319

Martín, J. M. M., Martínez, J. M. G., & Fernández, J. A. S. (2018). An Analysis of the Factors Behind the Citizen's Attitude of Rejection Towards Tourism in a Context of Overtourism and Economic Dependence on This Activity. *Sustainability (Basel)*, 10(8), 2851. Advance online publication. DOI: 10.3390/su10082851

Martins, G. F. M. (2014). Caracterização da atividade de Geocaching no Parque Natural da Arrábida. Dissertação de mestrado, Universidade de Lisboa, Lisboa, Portugal.

Martins, J., Gonçalves, R., Branco, F., Barbosa, L., Melo, M., & Bessa, M. (2017). A multisensory virtual experience model for thematic tourism: A Port wine tourism application proposal. *Journal of Destination Marketing & Management*, 6(2), 103–109. DOI: 10.1016/j.jdmm.2017.02.002

Masengu, R., Bigirimana, S., Chiwaridzo, O. T., Bensson, R., & Blossom, C. (Eds.). (2023). *Sustainable Marketing, Branding, and Reputation Management: Strategies for a Greener Future*. IGI Global., DOI: 10.4018/979-8-3693-0019-0

Mason, J. (1996). *Qualitative Researching*. SAGE Publications.

Matarrita-Cascante, D., Lee, J. H., & Nam, J. W. (2020). What elements should be present in any community development initiative? Distinguishing community development from local development. *Local Development & Society*, 1(2), 95–115. DOI: 10.1080/26883597.2020.1829986

Matherson, L., Wright, V. H., Inman, C. T., & Wilson, E. K. (2008). Get up, Get out with Geocaching: Engaging Technology for the Social Studies Classroom. *Social Studies Research & Practice*, 3(3), 80–85. DOI: 10.1108/SSRP-03-2008-B0006

Mathews, R., & Wacker, W. (2007). *What's your story? Storytelling to move markets, audiences, people and brands*. Pearson Education.

Ma, X., & Su, W. (2024). Local government intervention in tourism-driven rural gentrification: Types and interpretative framework. *Tourism Management*, 100, 104828. DOI: 10.1016/j.tourman.2023.104828

McCunn, L. J., & Gifford, R. (2012). Do green offices affect employee engagement and environmental motivation? *Architectural Science Review*, 55(2), 128–134. DOI: 10.1080/00038628.2012.667939

McDonagh, P., & Prothero, A. (2014). Sustainability marketing research: Past, present and future. Journal of Marketing Management, 30(11 - 12), 1186 - 1219.

McKee, R. (2003). Storytelling that moves people. A conversation with screenwriting coach Robert McKee. *Harvard Business Review*, 81(6), 51–55, 136. PMID: 12800716

McKee, R., & Gerace, T. (2018). *Storynomics: story-driven marketing in the post-advertising world*. Methuen.

Mckercher, B., Ho, P., & du Cros, H. (2004, April). Attributes of popular cultural attractions in Hong Kong. *Annals of Tourism Research*, 31(2), 393–407. DOI: 10.1016/j.annals.2003.12.008

McKercher, B., Ho, P., & du Cross, H. (2005, August). Relationship between tourism and cultural heritage management: Evidence from Hong Kong. *Tourism Management*, 26(4), 539–548. DOI: 10.1016/j.tourman.2004.02.018

Megri, Z., & Bencherif, F. (2014). The Effect of Territorial Marketing on City Image Valuation: An Exploratory Study in Algeria. *International Journal of Marketing Studies*, 6(4), 145–156. DOI: 10.5539/ijms.v6n4p145

Mei, H., Yang, X.-J., Liu, D., & Fang, H. (2022). Effects of Perceived Change of Urban Destination on Destination Attachment. *Frontiers in Psychology*, 13, 1022421. Advance online publication. DOI: 10.3389/fpsyg.2022.1022421 PMID: 36483727

Metodijeski, D., & Temelkov, Z. (2014). Tourism policy of Balkan countries: Review of national tourism development strategies. *UTMS Journal of Economics (Skopje)*, 5(2), 231–239.

Michopoulou, E., Siurnicka, A., & Moisa, D. G. (2022). Experiencing the Story: The Role of Destination Image in Film-Induced Tourism. In *Global Perspectives on Literary Tourism and Film-Induced Tourism* (pp. 240-256). IGI Global.

Micic, V. (2010). Klasteri-Faktor unapredjenja konkurentnosti industrije Srbije. *Ekonomski Horizont*, 12(2), 57–74.

Middleton, V. T. (1989). Tourism Marketing and Managemet Handbook. In S. F. Witt & L. Moutinho (Eds.), *Tourist Product*. Hempel Hempstead: Prentice Hall.

Mihalic, T., & Aramberri, J. (2015, November 13-16). Myths of top tourism countries, tourism contribution and competitiveness. *Tourism Review*, 70(4), 276–288. DOI: 10.1108/TR-08-2014-0048

Mikulić, J., Miličević, K., & Krešić, D. (2016). The relationship between brand strength and tourism intensity: Empirical evidence from the EU capital cities. *International Journal of Culture, Tourism and Hospitality Research*, 10(1), 14–23. DOI: 10.1108/IJCTHR-06-2015-0054

Miles, M. B., Huberman, A. M., & Saldana, J. (2020). *Qualitative Data Analysis - A Methods Sourcebook. 4*. Sage.

Milliyet. (2013). *Japon turisti öldürüp kız istemeye gitmiş* - Son Dakika Milliyet. Retrieved May 29, 2024, from https://www.milliyet.com.tr/gundem/japon-turisti-oldurup-kiz-istemeye-gitmis-1763156

Milojković, D., Nikolić, M. & Milojković, H. (2023b). Walking tourism management based on tourists' needs for indoor and outdoor activities in the function of sustainable local economic development. *RSEP*, 8, 1-18, p.1. https://doi.org/DOI: 10.19275/RSEP152

Milojković, D., Nikolić, M., & Milojković, K. (2023a). The development of countryside walking tourism in the time of the post-covid crisis. *Ekonomika Poljoprivrede*, 70(1), 131–144. DOI: 10.59267/ekoPolj2301131M

Minciotti, S., & Silva, E. (2011). Marketing de Localidades: Uma abordagem ampliada sobre o desenvolvimento da cidade ou região. *Revista Turismo Visão e Ação*, 13(3), 329–346.

Ministry of Culture and Tourism Statistics. (2024). İstatistikler. Retrieved May 29, 2024, from https://www.ktb.gov.tr/TR-96695/istatistikler.html

Mirea, C.-N., & Nistoreanu, P. (2021). Research methodologies on keywords: Tourism, Danube, sustainable development. *Journal of Tourism*, 32, 1–6. http://revistadeturism.ro/rdt/article/view/541

Mirzaalian, F., & Halpenny, E. (2021). Exploring destination loyalty: Application of social media analytics in a nature-based tourism setting. *Journal of Destination Marketing & Management*, 20, 100598. DOI: 10.1016/j.jdmm.2021.100598

Moghavvemi, S., Woosnam, K. M., Hamzah, A., & Hassani, A. (2021). Considering Residents' Personality and Community Factors in Explaining Satisfaction with Tourism and Support for Tourism Development. *Tourism Planning & Development*, 18(3), 267–293. DOI: 10.1080/21568316.2020.1768140

Mohammad Badruddoza Talukder, Firoj Kabir, K. M., & Das, I. R. (2023). Emerging Concepts of Artificial Intelligence in the Hotel Industry: A Conceptual Paper. *International Journal of Study Publication and Reviews, Vol 4, no*, pp 1765-1769. https://doi.org/DOI: 10.55248/gengpi.4.923.92451

Mohammad Badruddoza Talukder. Sanjeev Kumar, I. R. Das. (2024a). Implications of Blockchain Technology- Based Cryptocurrency in the cloud for the Hospitality Industry. In *Emerging Trends in Cloud Computing Analytics, Scalability, and Service Models* (p. 19). https://doi.org/DOI: 10.4018/979-8-3693-0900-1.ch018

Mohammad Badruddoza Talukder. Sanjeev Kumar, I. R. Das. (2024b). Perspectives of Digital Marketing for the Restaurant Industry. In *Advancements in Socialized and Digital Media Communications* (p. 17). https://doi.org/DOI: 10.4018/979-8-3693-0855-4.ch009

Mohammed, A., & Sookram, S. (2015). The Impact of Crime on Tourist Arrivals A Comparative Analysis of Jamaica and Trinidad and Tobago. *Social and Economic Studies*, 64(2), 153–176.

Moin, S. M. A. (2020). *Brand storytelling in the digital age – theories, practice and application*. Palgrave-Macmillan. DOI: 10.1007/978-3-030-59085-7

Moraga, E. T., Rodríguez-Sánchez, C., & Esper, F. S. (2021). Understanding Tourist Citizenship Behavior at the Destination Level. *Journal of Hospitality and Tourism Management*, 49, 592–600. Advance online publication. DOI: 10.1016/j.jhtm.2021.11.009

Moragas, M. (1996). *Olympic villages: a hundred years of urban planning and shared experiences: International Symposium on Olympic Villages*. In Centre d'Estudis Olímpics i de l'Esport Universitat Autònoma de Barcelona; Olympic Museum (Ed.), Olympic Villages Hundred Years of Urban Planning and Shared Experiences. Lausanne.

Morgan, N., & Pritchard, A. (1998). *Tourism promotion and power: creating images, creating identities*. John Wiley & Sons.

Morgan, N., & Pritchard, A. (1998). *Tourism Promotion and Power: Creating Images, Creating Identities*. Wiley.

Morgan, N., Pritchard, A., & Pride, R. (2014). *Destination Branding: Creating the Unique Destination Proposition*. Elsevier Butterworth-Heinemann.

Moscardo, G. (2008). *Building community capacity for tourism development*. CABI. DOI: 10.1079/9781845934477.0000

Mossberg, L., Therkelsen, A., Huijbens, E., Björk, P., & Olsson, A. K. (2010). Storytelling and destination development - Possibilities and drawbacks of using storytelling as a means of developing and marketing Nordic tourism destinations. Nordic Innovation Centre (NICe) Project. Retrieved January 11, 2022, from http://www.nordicinnovation.org/Global/_Publications/Reports/2010/201012_StorytellingAndDestinationDevelopment_report.pdf

Mousavi, R., Najafabadi, M. O., Mirdamadi, S. M., & Hosseini, S. J. F. (2022). Rural sports and local games: Missing link between sports tourism development and sustainability. *Journal of Sport & Tourism*, 26(3), 201–223. DOI: 10.1080/14775085.2022.2058069

Moyo, S., & Tichaawa, T. M. (2017). Community involvement and participation in tourism development: A Zimbabwe study. *AJHTL*, 6, 1–15.

Muñoz, F. (1996). Historic evolution and urban planning typology of Olympic Village. Hundred years of urban planning and shared experiences, International Symposium on Olympic Villages. IOC

Mu, Q. (2022). Understanding Heritage-Led Development of the Historic Villages of China: A Multi-case Study Analysis of Tongren. *The Historic Environment*, 13(2), 216–241. DOI: 10.1080/17567505.2021.1940575

Musavengane, R. (2019). Understanding tourism consciousness through habitus: Perspectives of 'poor' black South Africans. *Critical African Studies*, 11(3), 322–347. DOI: 10.1080/21681392.2019.1670702

Mydłowska, E. (2023). Geocoaching Adventure Lab–The Innovative Tool for Exploring and Creating Tourism Space. *Studia Maritima*, 36(1), 1–22. DOI: 10.18276/sm.2023.36-02

Nachimias, D., & Nachimias, C. F. (1987). *Research methods in the social sciences*. St. Martin's Press.

Nag, A. (2024). Local Development and Tourism Competitiveness: Analyzing the Economic Impact of Heritage Tourism Initiatives. In *Gastronomic Sustainability Solutions for Community and Tourism Resilience* (pp. 160-190). IGI Global.

Nag, A., & Mishra, S. (2023). Destination Competitiveness and Sustainability: Heritage Planning From the Perspective of the Tourism Industry Stakeholders. In *Cases on Traveler Preferences, Attitudes, and Behaviors: Impact in the Hospitality Industry* (pp. 1-32). IGI Global.

Nag, A., & Mishra, S. (2024). Sustainable competitive advantage in heritage tourism: Leveraging cultural legacy in a data-driven world. In *Review of Technologies and Disruptive Business Strategies* (Vol. 3, pp. 137-162). Emerald Publishing Limited.

Nascimento, F. M. (2009). *Cineturismo*. Aleph.

Ndivo, R. M., & Cantoni, L. (2016). Rethinking local community involvement in tourism development. *Annals of Tourism Research*, 57, 275–278. DOI: 10.1016/j.annals.2015.11.014

Neacşu, M.-C., Neguţ, S., & Vlăsceanu, G. (2016). Place Branding – Geographical Approach. Case Study: Waterloo. *Amfiteatru Economic*, 18(10), 944–959.

Newland, B. L., & Yoo, J. J. E. (2021). Active sport event participants' behavioural intentions: Leveraging outcomes for future attendance and visitation. *Journal of Vacation Marketing*, 27(1), 32–44. DOI: 10.1177/1356766720948249

Ng, S. L., & Feng, X. (2020). Residents' sense of place, involvement, attitude, and support for tourism: A case study of Daming Palace, a Cultural World Heritage Site. *Asian Geographer*, 37(2), 189–207. DOI: 10.1080/10225706.2020.1729212

Nguyen, K. T. T., Murphy, L., Chen, T., & Pearce, P. L. (2024). Let's listen: The voices of ethnic villagers in identifying host-tourist interaction issues in the Central Highlands, Vietnam. *Journal of Heritage Tourism*, 19(2), 263–286. DOI: 10.1080/1743873X.2023.2259512

Niekerk, M., & Coetzee, W. (2011). Utilizing the VICE model for the sustainable development of the Innibos arts festival. *Journal of Hospitality Marketing & Management*, 20(3-4), 347–365. DOI: 10.1080/19368623.2011.562422

Njoya, E. T., & Seetaram, N. (2018). Tourism contribution to poverty alleviation in Kenya: A dynamic computable general equilibrium analysis. *Journal of Travel Research*, 57(4), 513–524. DOI: 10.1177/0047287517700317 PMID: 29595836

Novelli, M., Cheer, J. M., Dolezal, C., Jones, A., & Milano, C. (Eds.). (2022). *Handbook of Niche Tourism*. Edward Elgar Publishing. DOI: 10.4337/9781839100185

Nugroho, A. W., Prasetyo, S. I., Candra, I. A., Saputra, R. A., & Putra, A. S. (2023). Community-Based Tourism: Strengthening understanding and assistance in establishing tourism awareness group. *Journal of Community Service and Empowerment*, 4(2), 271–282. DOI: 10.22219/jcse.v4i2.26389

numbeo.com. (2024). Crime Index by Country 2024. Retrieved May 28, 2024, from https://www.numbeo.com/crime/rankings_by_country.jsp

Nunes, F. (1999), *Processo de Planeamento de Marketing Territorial Estratégico- Um instrumento de operacionalização de estratégias de política para Área Metropolitana do Porto*, Dissertação de Mestrado apresentada à Faculdade de Arquitetura e Engenharia do Porto, Porto. 160 p.

Nunes, E. (2011). *Fatores de sucesso em marketing territorial: desafios de desenvolvimento na região Alentejo*. Instituto Superior de Ciências Sociais e Políticas.

Nurhayati, A., Herawati, T., Handaka, A. A., Pamungkas, W., Akbarsyah, N., & Sudarmono, A. (2023). Sustainable marine ecotourism governance based on tourism preferences. *IOP Conference Series. Earth and Environmental Science*, 1289(1), 012012. DOI: 10.1088/1755-1315/1289/1/012012

Nwankwo, E. A. (2020). *Exploring the Three-Way Destination Safety Solution to Crisis Management in Tourist Destinations in Rural Nigeria*. DOI: 10.5772/intechopen.89727

O'Reilly, A. M. (1986). Tourism carrying capacity: Concept and issues. *Tourism Management*, 7(4), 254–258. DOI: 10.1016/0261-5177(86)90035-X

Obiol, E. (2002). Marcas turísticas y territorio: Un análisis geográfico del turismo valenciano. *Cuadernos de Turismo*, 9, 85–101.

OCDE. O. (2014). *OECD Tourism trends and policies 2014*. OECD Publishing.

Ochieng, J., Knerr, B., Owuor, G., & Ouma, E. (2018). Strengthening Collective Action to Improve Marketing Performance: Evidence from Farmer Groups in Central Africa. *Journal of Agricultural Education and Extension*, 24(2), 169–189. Https://Doi.Org/10.1080/1389224x.2018.1432493. DOI: 10.1080/1389224X.2018.1432493

OECD. (2009). *The Impact of Culture on Tourism*. OECD Publishing.

Oh, C., Kim, K.-B., Lee, H., & Nam-Jo, S. K. (2024). Beaches for Everyone? World's First Water Wheelchair with Smart Safety Features for Barrier-Free Tourism. *Journal of Coastal Research*, 116(sp1). Advance online publication. DOI: 10.2112/JCR-SI116-097.1

Oh, H., Fiore, A. M., & Jeoung, M. (2007). Measuring experience economy concepts: Tourism applications. *Journal of Travel Research*, 46(2), 119–132. DOI: 10.1177/0047287507304039

Oh, H., Parks, S. C., & Demicco, F. J. (2002). Age- and Gender-Based Market Segmentation. *International Journal of Hospitality & Tourism Administration*, 3(1), 1–20. DOI: 10.1300/J149v03n01_01

Ojha, A. K. (2022). Strategies for sustainable tourism business development: A comprehensive analysis. Retrieved from https://dx.doi.org/DOI: 10.55529/jsrth.24.25.30

Okrainec, K., Booth, G. L., Hollands, S., & Bell, C. M. (2014). Impact of Language Barriers on Complications and Mortality Among Immigrants With Diabetes: A Population-Based Cohort Study. *Diabetes Care*. Advance online publication. DOI: 10.2337/dc14-0801 PMID: 25028526

Oktay, K. (2006). Kırgızistan'daki Tuketicilerin Giyim Tercihleri Uzerine Bir Arastırma. *Manas Universitesi Sosyal Bilimler Dergisi.*, 15, 197–211.

Okumus, F., Van Niekerk, M., Koseoglu, M. A., & Bilgihan, A. (2018). Interdisciplinary research in tourism. *Tourism Management*, 69, 540–549. DOI: 10.1016/j.tourman.2018.05.016

Olbrich, R., Jansen, H. C., & Teller, B. (2015). Quantifying Anti-Consumption of Private Labels and National Brands: Impacts of Poor Test Ratings on Consumer Purchases. *The Journal of Consumer Affairs*. Advance online publication. DOI: 10.1111/joca.12084

Oliveira, S. (2007). O Turismo Gastronómico e o Enoturismo como Potenciadores do Desenvolvimento Regional. Comunicação apresentada no III Congresso Internacional de Turismo. Disponível em http://cassiopeia.ipleiria.pt/esel_eventos/files/3902_12_SimaoOliveira_ 4bf5103dd97f6.pdf)

Omar, N. A., Nazri, M. A., Alam, S. S., & Ali, M. H. (2017). *Consumer Retaliation to Halal Violation Incidents: The Mediating Role of Trust Recovery*. Jurnal Pengurusan., DOI: 10.17576/pengurusan-2017-51-09

Ortega, E., Mora, P., & Rauld, L. (2006). El eslogan en el sector turístico español. *Cuadernos de Turismo*, 17, 127–146.

Osogbo, Nigeria. (2023). The effect of informal economy on human capital development. *Izvestiya Journal of the University of Economics – Varna, 67*(3), 182–195. DOI: 10.56065/IJUEV2023.67.3.182

Ozanne, L. K., & Ballantine, P. W. (2010). Sharing as a Form of Anti-consumption? An Examination of Toy Library Users. *Journal of Consumer Behaviour, 9*(6), 485–498. Advance online publication. DOI: 10.1002/cb.334

Özdemir, G., & Adan, Ö. (2014). Film tourism triangulation of destinations. *Procedia: Social and Behavioral Sciences*, 148, 625–633. DOI: 10.1016/j.sbspro.2014.07.090

Pahrudin, P., Chen, C.-T., & Liu, L. (2021). A Modified Theory of Planned Behavioral: A Case of Tourist Intention to Visit a Destination Post Pandemic Covid-19 in Indonesia. *Heliyon*, 7(10), e08230. Advance online publication. DOI: 10.1016/j.heliyon.2021.e08230 PMID: 34708160

Palomeque, A. T.-D. (2014). Measuring sustainable tourism at the municipal level. *Annals of Tourism Research*, 49(C), 122–137.

Panagiotopoulou, M., Somarakis, G., & Stratigea, A. (2020). Smartening up participatory cultural tourism planning in historical city centers. *Journal of Urban Technology*, 27(4), 3–26. DOI: 10.1080/10630732.2018.1528540

Pan, S., & Ryan, C. (2009). Tourism Sense-Making: The Role Of The Senses And Travel Journalism. *Journal of Travel & Tourism Marketing*, 26(7), 625–639. DOI: 10.1080/10548400903276897

Papadopoulou, N. M., Ribeiro, M. A., & Prayag, G. (2022). Psychological Determinants of Tourist Satisfaction and Destination Loyalty: The Influence of Perceived Overcrowding and Overtourism. *Journal of Travel Research*. Advance online publication. DOI: 10.1177/00472875221089049

Papageorgiou, M. (2016). Coastal and marine tourism: A challenging factor in Marine Spatial Planning. *Ocean and Coastal Management*, 129, 44–48. DOI: 10.1016/j.ocecoaman.2016.05.006

Papp-Váry, Á. (2021). Mitől jó egy szlogen? 2. rész – A legfontosabb marketingszempontok, amiket aztán mégis mindig elfelejtenek a marketingesek (What makes a good slogan? Part 2 – The most important marketing aspects that marketers always forget). *Márkamonitor Magazin*, 2021(3-4), 46–50.

Papp-Váry, Á. F. (2020). *A márkanév ereje – A sikeres brandépítés alapjai (The power of brand names – the basics of powerful brand building)*. Dialóg-Campus Kiadó.

Park, D.-B., & Yoon, Y.-S. (2009). Segmentation by motivation in rural tourism: A Korean case study. *Tourism Management*, 30(1), 99–108. DOI: 10.1016/j.tourman.2008.03.011

Pasanchay, K., & Schott, C. (2021). Community-based tourism homestays' capacity to advance the sustainable development goals: A holistic sustainable livelihood perspective. *Tourism Management Perspectives*, 37, 100784. DOI: 10.1016/j.tmp.2020.100784

PATA. (2023). *Sustainable Tourism Online: Destinations and Communities*. Available online: https://www.pata.org/blog/sustainable-tourism-online-destinations-and-communities (accessed on 20 March 2023).

Patton, M. Q. (2015). *Qualitative research & evaluation methods: Integrating theory and practice* (4th ed.). Sage Publications.

Paul, J., & Criado, A. R. (2020). The art of writing literature review: What do we know and what do we need to know? *International Business Review*, 29(4), 101717. DOI: 10.1016/j.ibusrev.2020.101717

Paul, J., & Rosado-Serrano, A. (2019). Gradual internationalization vs born-global/international new venture models: A review and research agenda. *International Marketing Review*, 36(6), 830–858. DOI: 10.1108/IMR-10-2018-0280

Payne, M. (2007). A Gold-Medal Partnership. *Strategy & Business*.

Pellowski, A. (1990). *The World of Storytelling*. Wilson.

Peräkylä, A. (2010). Two traditions of interaction research. *British Journal of Social Psychology*. PMID: 15035695

Pera, R., Viglia, G., & Furlan, R. (2016). Who am I? How compelling self-storytelling builds digital personal reputation. *Journal of Interactive Marketing*, 35(1), 44–55. DOI: 10.1016/j.intmar.2015.11.002

Persson-Fischer, U., & Liu, S. (2021). What Is Interdisciplinarity in the Study of Sustainable Destination Development? *Sustainability (Basel)*, 13(7), 3639. Advance online publication. DOI: 10.3390/su13073639

Peterson, C., Ortiz, R., & Rocconi, L. (2022). Community food security: The multi-level association between social capital, economic capital, and diet quality. *International Journal of Community Well-being*, 5(3), 571–585. DOI: 10.1007/s42413-022-00170-w

Petr, C. (2002). Tourist apprehension of heritage: A semiotic approach to behaviour patterns. *International Journal of Arts Management*, •••, 25–38. https://www.jstor.org/stable/41064753

Petr, C. (2009). Fame is not always a positive asset for heritage equity! Some clues from buying intentions of national tourists. *Journal of Travel & Tourism Marketing*, 26(1), 1–18. DOI: 10.1080/10548400802656694

Petr, C. (2015). How heritage site tourists may become monument visitors. *Tourism Management*, 51, 247–262. DOI: 10.1016/j.tourman.2015.05.018

Pham, K., Andereck, K. L., & Vogt, C. (2024). Stakeholders' involvement in an evidence-based sustainable tourism plan. *Journal of Sustainable Tourism*, •••, 1–24. DOI: 10.1080/09669582.2023.2259117

Phomsiri, S. (2015). Film tourism and destination marketing: Case studies of inbound and out-bound in Thailand. *Review of Integrative Business and Economics Research*, 4(3), 241.

Pike, S. (2004). Destination brand positioning slogan: Towards the development of a set of accountability criteria. *Acta Turística*, 16(2), 102–124.

Pike, S. (2007). *Destination marketing organizations and destination marketing: A narrative analysis of the literature*. Elsevier Science Publishers. DOI: 10.4324/9780080494463

Pike, S., & Mason, R. (2010). Destination competitiveness through the lens of brand positioning: The case of Australia's Sunshine Coast. *Current Issues in Tourism*, 14(2), 169–182. DOI: 10.1080/13683501003797523

Pine, B. J.II, & Gilmore, H. J. (1999). *The Experience Economy: Work isTheatre & Every Business a Stage*. Harvard Business School Press.

Pisula, E. (2021). Informative, educational, and promotional role of geocaching in the region. *ToSEE – Tourism in Southern and Eastern Europe*, Vol. 6, pp. 623-635

Pisuła, E., Florek, M., & Homski, K. (2023). Marketing communication via geocaching–When and how it can be effective for places? *Journal of Outdoor Recreation and Tourism*, 42, 100622. DOI: 10.1016/j.jort.2023.100622

Polletta, F., Chen, P., Gardner, B. G., & Motes, A. (2011). The sociology of storytelling. *Annual Review of Sociology*, 37(1), 109–130. DOI: 10.1146/annurev-soc-081309-150106

Popesku, J. (2016). *Menadžment turističke destinacije* (5. Izdanje). Univerzitet Singidunum, Beograd, Srbija, str. 98-104. (In Serbian)

Popp, L., & McCole, D. (2016). Understanding tourists' itineraries in emerging rural tourism regions: The application of paper-based itinerary mapping methodology to a wine tourism region in Michigan. *Current Issues in Tourism*, 19(10), 988–1004. DOI: 10.1080/13683500.2014.942259

Poria, Y., Butler, R., & Airey, D. (2004). Links between tourists, heritage, and reasons for visiting heritage sites. *Journal of Travel Research*, 43(1), 19–28. DOI: 10.1177/0047287504265508

Poria, Y., Reichel, A., & Biran, A. (2006). Heritage site perceptions and motivations to visit. *Journal of Travel Research*, 44(3), 318–326. DOI: 10.1177/0047287505279004

Porter, B. A., Orams, M. B., & Lück, M. (2018). Sustainable Entrepreneurship Tourism: An Alternative Development Approach for Remote Coastal Communities Where Awareness of Tourism is Low. *Tourism Planning & Development*, 15(2), 149–165. DOI: 10.1080/21568316.2017.1312507

Power, S. (2022). Enjoying your beach and cleaning it too: A Grounded Theory Ethnography of enviro-leisure activism. *Journal of Sustainable Tourism*, 30(6), 1438–1457. DOI: 10.1080/09669582.2021.1953037

Pradhan, D., Malik, G., & Vishwakarma, P. (2023). Gamification in tourism research: A systematic review, current insights, and future research avenues. *Journal of Vacation Marketing*, •••, 13567667231188879. DOI: 10.1177/13567667231188879

Prefeitura Municipal de Pelotas. "Ministério do Turismo garante verba para quatro pórticos em Pelotas" (2019, May, 9) https://bit.ly/2EcUM28

Preuss, H. (2000). *Economics of The Olympic Games: Hosting the Games 1972 – 2000. Walla Walla Press*. The University of Germany.

Prial, A., Zhu, X., Bol, L., & Williams, M. R. (2023). The impact of moderate physical activity and student interaction on retention at a community college. *Journal of American College Health*, 71(1), 154–161. DOI: 10.1080/07448481.2021.1881103 PMID: 33734951

Priatmoko, S., Kabil, M., Akaak, A., Lakner, Z., Gyuricza, C., & Dávid, L. D. (2023). Understanding the complexity of rural tourism business: Scholarly perspective. *Sustainability (Basel)*, 15(2), 1193. DOI: 10.3390/su15021193

Pride William, M. ve Ferrell, O. C. (2000). *Marketing Concepts and Strategies,* Houghton Mifflin Compony. U.S.A.

Priyatmoko, R., & Maulana, A. (2022). *Halal Tourism and Its Misconceptions: A Study on the Rejection of Indonesian Non-Muslim Destinations.* Dinar Jurnal Ekonomi Dan Keuangan Islam., DOI: 10.21107/dinar.v9i1.13976

Prokopenko, O., Järvis, M., Saichuk, V., Komarnitskyi, I., Glybovets, V., & Troian, M. (2023). International Marine Tourism: Trends and Prospects for Sustainable Development. *Pomorstvo*, 37(1), 23–31. DOI: 10.31217/p.37.1.3

Proos, E., & Hattingh, J. (2022). Dark tourism: Growth potential of niche tourism in the Free State Province, South Africa. *Development Southern Africa*, 39(3), 303–320. DOI: 10.1080/0376835X.2020.1847636

Pulido-Fernández, J. I., Andrades, L., & Marcelino Sánchez, R. (2014, November). Is sustainable tourism an obstacle to the economic performance of the tourism industry? Evidence from an international empirical study. *Journal of Sustainable Tourism*, 23(1), 47–64. DOI: 10.1080/09669582.2014.909447

PwC. (2010). *Cities of Opportunity*.

PwC. (2010). *Public-Private Partnerships: The US Perspective*.

Quinn, B. (2005). Arts Festivals and the City. *Urban Studies (Edinburgh, Scotland)*, 42(5-6), 927–943. DOI: 10.1080/00420980500107250

Quinn, B. (2006). Problematising 'festival tourism': Arts festivals and sustainable development in Ireland. *Journal of Sustainable Tourism*, 14(3), 288–306. DOI: 10.1080/09669580608669060

Qu, L., & Hyunjung, H. (2011). A model of destination branding : Integrating the concepts of the branding and destination image. *Tourism Management*, 32(3), 465–476. DOI: 10.1016/j.tourman.2010.03.014

Rainisto, S. (2003). *Sucess factores of Place Marketing: a Study of Place Marketing Practices in Northern Europe and Unite States.* Helsinki University of Technology, Finland: Institute of Strategy and International Business, Doctoral Dissertations.

Ramkissoon, H., Nunkoo, R., & Gursoy, D. (2009). How consumption values affect destination image formation. In: Woodside, A. G., Megehee, C. M., & Ogle, A. (eds.), Perspectives on Cross-Cultural, Ethnographic, Brand Image, Storytelling, Unconscious Needs, and Hospitality Guest Research (Advances in Culture, Tourism and Hospitality Research, Volume 3). Emerald, 143–168. DOI: 10.1108/S1871-3173(2009)0000003008

Ramkissoon, H., & Uysal, M. S. (2018). Authenticity as a value co-creator of tourism experiences. In Prebensen, N. K., Chen, J. S., & Uysal, M. S. (Eds.), *Creating experience value in tourism* (pp. 98–109). CABI., DOI: 10.1079/9781786395030.0098

Ramsey, D., & Everitt, J. (2008). If you dig it, they will come!: Archaeology heritage sites and tourism development in Belize, Central America. *Tourism Management*, 29(5), 909–916. DOI: 10.1016/j.tourman.2007.11.002

Ramshaw, G. (2020). *Heritage and sport: An introduction.* Channel View Publications.

Rather, R. A. (2019). Customer experience and engagement in tourism destinations: The experiential marketing perspective. *Journal of Travel & Tourism Marketing*, 37(1), 15–32. DOI: 10.1080/10548408.2019.1686101

Redondo, I. (2012). Assessing the appropriateness of movies as vehicles for promoting tourist destinations. *Journal of Travel & Tourism Marketing*, 29(7), 714–729. DOI: 10.1080/10548408.2012.720156

Reinhold, S., Beritelli, P., Fyall, A., Choi, H.-S. C., Laesser, C., & Joppe, M. (2023). State-of-the-art review on destination marketing and destination management. Retrieved from https://dx.doi.org/DOI: 10.3390/tourhosp4040036

Reisinger, Y. (2015). *Transformational tourism: host perspectives*. CAB International. DOI: 10.1079/9781780643922.0000

Renzi, M. F., Loureiro, S., Toni, M., & Panchapakesan, P. (2018). Relationship between destination affect and intention to visit: the case of destination dislike. *In 47th International EMAC conference-People Make Marketing.*

Revista News. "Pelotas ganha novo pórtico de entrada no Simões Lopes" (2020, April, 25) https://bit.ly/3kwpnY5

Ribeiro, E. (2010). Análise financeira. Portal Gestão. Disponível em www.portal-gestao.com

Richards, G. (2001). The experience industry and the creation of attractions. In *Cultural attractions and European tourism* (pp. 55–69). Cabi Publishing., DOI: 10.1079/9780851994406.0055

Richards, G. (2011). Creativity and Tourism: The State of the Art. *Annals of Tourism Research*, 38(4), 1225–1253. DOI: 10.1016/j.annals.2011.07.008

Richards, G. (2018). Cultural tourism: A review of recent research and trends. *Journal of Hospitality and Tourism Management*, 36, 12–21. DOI: 10.1016/j.jhtm.2018.03.005

Richards, G., & Wilson, J. (2006). Developing creativity in tourist experiences: A solution to the serial reproduction of culture? *Tourism Management*, 27(6), 1209–1223. DOI: 10.1016/j.tourman.2005.06.002

Richards, L. (2014). *Handling Qualitative Data*. SAGE Publications. Ritchie, B., & Crouch, G. (2003). *The Competitive Destination: A Sustainable Tourism Perspective*. CABI.

Ries, A., & Trout, J. (1991). *Posicionamento: a batalha pela mente*. Pioneira.

Ries, L. (2015). *Battlecry – Winning the battle for the mind with a slogan that kills*. Ries Pieces.

Riis, T., Kelly-Quinn, M., Aguiar, F. C., Manolaki, P., Bruno, D., Bejarano, M. D., Clerici, N., Fernandes, M. R., Franco, J. C., Pettit, N., Portela, A. P., Tammeorg, O., Tammeorg, P., Rodríguez-González, P. M., & Dufour, S. (2020). Global overview of ecosystem services provided by riparian vegetation. *Bioscience*, 70(6), 501–514. DOI: 10.1093/biosci/biaa041

Rinaldi, C., & Beeton, S. (2015). Success in Place Branding: The Case of the Tourism Victoria Jigsaw Campaign. *Journal of Travel & Tourism Marketing*, 32(5), 622–638. DOI: 10.1080/10548408.2014.953288

Risitano, M., Tutore, I., Sorrentino, A., & Quintano, M. (2017). The Influence of Tourists' National Culture on Their Behaviors in a Sport Mega-Event. *International Journal of Culture, Tourism and Hospitality Research*, 11(2), 193–210. Advance online publication. DOI: 10.1108/IJCTHR-07-2015-0077

Ritchie, B., & Crouch, G. (2011). A model of destination competitiveness and sustainability.

Ritchie, J. B., & Smith, B. H. (1991). The impact of a mega-event on host region awareness: A longitudinal study. *Journal of Travel Research*, 30(1), 3–10. DOI: 10.1177/004728759103000102

Roberts, K. D.-B. (n.d.). Attempting rigour and replicability in thematic analysis of qualitative research data; a case study of codebook development . *BMC Medical Research Methodology*.

Robinson, M., & Novelli, M. (2005). In Sheldon, P. J., Wöber, K. W., & Fesenmaier, D. R. (Eds.), *Niche Tourism: Contemporary issues, trends and cases. Elsevier publishers* (pp. 294–302). Information and Communication Technologies in Tourism.

Roche M. (2003). The Olympics and the Development of "Global Society", in M. De Moragas, C. Kennett, N. Puig (a cura di), *The Legacy of the Olympic Games*, Document of the Olympic Museum, International Olympic Committee, Losanna.

Roche, M. (1992). Mega-Events and Micro-Modernisation: On the Sociology of the New Urban Tourism. *The British Journal of Sociology*, 43(4), 563–600. DOI: 10.2307/591340

Roche, M. (2000). *Mega-events and Modernity: Olympics and Expos in the Growth of Global C*. Routledge.

Roche, M. (2002). Olympic and Sport Mega-Events as Media-Events: Reflections on the Globalisation paradigm. *Symposium A Quarterly Journal in Modern Foreign Literatures*, pp. 1–12.

Roche, M. (2006). Mega-Events and Modernity Revisited: Globalization and the Case of the Olympics. *The Sociological Review*, 54(2, suppl), 27–40. DOI: 10.1111/j.1467-954X.2006.00651.x

Rodriguez, M. (2020). *Brand storytelling: Put customers in the heart of your brand story*. Kogan Page.

Rosalina, P. D., Dupre, K., Wang, Y., Putra, I. N. D., & Jin, X. (2023). Rural tourism resource management strategies: A case study of two tourism villages in Bali. *Tourism Management Perspectives*, 49, 101194. DOI: 10.1016/j.tmp.2023.101194

Rose, A. K., & Mark, M. Spiegel (2009). The Olympic Effect. *National Bureau of Economic Research*, October 2009.

Rose, F. (2011). The art of immersion: How the digital generation is remaking Hollywood, Madison Avenue, and the way we tell stories. *International Journal of Advertising*, 30(5), 915–919. https://www.academia.edu/download/35025431/Resena_The_art_of_inmersion.pdf. DOI: 10.2501/IJA-30-5-915-916

Rosengren, S., & Dahlén, M. (2006). Brand–slogan matching in a cluttered environment. *Journal of Marketing Communications*, 12(4), 263–269. DOI: 10.1080/13527260600714700

Royo, V. M. (2009). Rural-cultural excursion conceptualization: A local tourism marketing management model based on tourist destination image measurement. *Tourism Management*, 30(3), 419–428. DOI: 10.1016/j.tourman.2008.07.013

Rumiantseva, I. (2023). Systematization of tourist market development factors. *Ukrainian Journal of Applied Economics and Technology*, 8(4), 250–257. DOI: 10.36887/2415-8453-2023-4-41

Ryan, C., & Higgins, O. (2006). Experiencing cultural tourism: Visitors at the Maori arts and crafts institute, New Zealand. *Journal of Travel Research*, 44(3), 308–317. DOI: 10.1177/0047287505279002

Saarinen, J. (2019). Communities and sustainable tourism development: Community impacts and local benefit creation in tourism. In McCool, S. F., & Bosak, K. (Eds.), *A Research Agenda for Sustainable Tourism* (pp. 206–222). Edward Elgar Publishing Limited., DOI: 10.4337/9781788117104.00020

Salgado-Barandela, J., Barajas, Á., & Sánchez-Fernández, P. (2021). Sport-event portfolios: An analysis of their ability to attract revenue from tourism. *Tourism Economics*, 27(3), 436–454. DOI: 10.1177/1354816619884448

Salma, Wijaya, A. A. M., Basir, M. A., and Lawelai, H. (2022). Community Based Tourism in The Development of Sustainable Tourism in Baubau City. *APLIKATIF: Journal of Research Trends in Social Sciences and Humanities*, 1(1), 28–38. DOI: 10.59110/aplikatif.v1i1.32

Sampaio, S., Vidal, F., & Lourenço, I. (2021). Desafios do "turístico" na atualidade: Uma introdução surpreendida por uma pandemia. *Etnográfica (Lisboa)*, 25(1), 119–129. DOI: 10.4000/etnografica.9851

Sandıkçı, Ö., & Ekici, A. (2009). Politically Motivated Brand Rejection. *Journal of Business Research*, 62(2), 208–217. Advance online publication. DOI: 10.1016/j.jbusres.2008.01.028

Sands Lee M. (2008). The 2008 Olympics' Impact on China, *The China Business Review*, July August 2008.

Sanfilippo, F., Pomeroy, C., & Bailey, D. N. (2023). Crisis Management. In F. Sanfilippo, C. Pomeroy, & D. N. Bailey, *Lead, Inspire, Thrive* (pp. 99–102). Springer Nature Switzerland. DOI: 10.1007/978-3-031-41177-9_16

Santos, A. C. S. C, M. J. & Eusébio, C. (2012). *Avaliação de festivais: O caso da Viagem Medieval de Santa Maria da Feira.* Revista Turismo e Desenvolvimento 1645- 9261. 1597-1609. https://www.ua.pt/file/30716

Santos, V. R., Sousa, B. B., Ramos, P., Dias, Á., & Madeira, A. (2022). Encouraging wine storytelling in the tourist experience: a preliminary study. In *Advances in Tourism, Technology and Systems: Selected Papers from ICOTTS 2021* (Vol. 1, pp. 235–242). Springer Nature Singapore. DOI: 10.1007/978-981-19-1040-1_20

Santos, V., Sousa, B., Ramos, P., & Valeri, M. (2022). Emotions and involvement in tourism settings. *Current Issues in Tourism*, 25(10), 1526–1531. DOI: 10.1080/13683500.2021.1932769

Saputro, K. E. A. (1835). Hasim, Karlinasari, L., & Beik, I. S. (2023). Evaluation of Sustainable Rural Tourism Development with an Integrated Approach Using MDS and ANP Methods: Case Study in Ciamis, West Java, Indonesia. *Sustainability (New Rochelle, N.Y.)*, 15(3).

Saraniemi, S., & Komppula, R. (2017). The development of a destination brand identity: A story of stakeholder collaboration. *Current Issues in Tourism*, 31(17), 1116–1132.

Sárközy, I. (2009). Szlogenmeghatározások (Slogan definitions). Retrieved November 10, 2017, from www.szlogenek.hu/szlogenmeghat.php

Sato, S., Kim, H., Buning, R. J., & Harada, M. (2018). Adventure tourism motivation and destination loyalty: A comparison of decision and non-decision makers. *Journal of Destination Marketing & Management*, 8, 74–81. DOI: 10.1016/j.jdmm.2016.12.003

Saufi, A., O' Brien, D., & Wilkins, H. (2014). Inhibitors to host community participation in sustainable tourism development in developing countries. *Journal of Sustainable Tourism*, 22(5), 801–820. DOI: 10.1080/09669582.2013.861468

Saunders, M. L. (2009). *Research Methods for Business Students*. Pearson.

Sautter, E. T., & Leisen, B. (1999). *Managing stakeholders: A tourism planning model. Annals of Tourism*

Savery, J., & Ghezzi, A. (2022). Applying Sustainable Development Goal 14. In *The Routledge Handbook of Sport and Sustainable Development* (pp. 364-367). Routledge.

Schneider, I. E., Silverberg, K. E., & Chavez, D. (2011). Geocachers: Benefits sought and environmental attitudes. *LARnet*, 14(1), 1–11.

Šegota, T., Mihalič, T., & Perdue, R. R. (2024). Resident perceptions and responses to tourism: Individual vs community level impacts. *Journal of Sustainable Tourism*, 32(2), 340–363. DOI: 10.1080/09669582.2022.2149759

Shah, S., & Corley, K. (2006). Building Better Theory by Bridging the Quantitative–Qualitative Divide. *Journal of Management Studies*, 43(8), 1821–1835. DOI: 10.1111/j.1467-6486.2006.00662.x

Sharma, A., Lesjak, M., & Borovčanin, D. (2024). *Sport Tourism, Events and Sustainable Development Goals: An Emerging Foundation.* Taylor & Francis. DOI: 10.4324/9781003384786

Sharpley, R. (2020). Tourism, sustainable development and the theoretical divide: 20 years on. *Journal of Sustainable Tourism*, 28(11), 1932–1946. DOI: 10.1080/09669582.2020.1779732

Sharpley, R., & Vass, A. (2006). Tourism, farming and diversification: An attitudinal study. *Tourism Management*, 27(5), 1040–1052. DOI: 10.1016/j.tourman.2005.10.025

Sharrock, W., Anderson, B., & Anderson, R. (1986). The ethnomethodologists. Taylor & Francis.

Shore, S. (2010). Cultural and heritage tourism-international. *Travel & Tourism Analyst*, •••, 8.

Silva, J., Sousa, B., & Abreu, J. (2023). Place Marketing and Destination Management: A Study in the "Quadrilátero do Minho". In *Advances in Tourism, Technology and Systems: Selected Papers from ICOTTS 2022* (Vol. 2, pp. 567–577). Springer Nature Singapore. DOI: 10.1007/978-981-19-9960-4_49

Silverman, D. (2006). Interpreting Qualitative Data: Methods for Analysing Talk, Text and Interaction (éd. 3). Sage.

Silverman, D. (2010). Doing Qualitative Research: A Practical Handbook (éd. 3rd). London: Sage Publication.

Simeoni, F., & De Crescenzo, V. *Walking tourism: opportunities and threats for sustainable development.The case of the 'Va' Sentiero' project.* In Proceedings of the XXII International conference excellence in services, Thessaloniki, Greece, 29-30 August 2019.

Skinner, H., Sarpong, D., & White, G. R. (2018). Meeting the needs of the Millennials and Generation Z: gamification in tourism through geocaching. *Journal of tourism futures*, 4(1), 93-104.

Škrabić Perić, B., Šimundić, B., Muštra, V., & Vugdelija, M. (2021). The role of unesco cultural heritage and cultural sector in tourism development: The case of EU countries. *Sustainability (Basel)*, 13(10), 5473. DOI: 10.3390/su13105473

Slusariuc, G. (2020). Health tourism – evolutions and perspectives. *Journal of Tourism*, 29, 1–4. http://revistadeturism.ro/rdt/article/view/471

Smit, A. J. (2010). The competitive advantage of nations: Is Porter's Diamond Framework a new theory that explains the international competitiveness of countries? *Southern African Business Review*, 14(1).

Smith, A. (2005). Reimaging the city: The value of sport initiatives. *Annals of Tourism Research*, 32(1), 217–236. DOI: 10.1016/j.annals.2004.07.007

Smith, B., & General, S. (2008). Towards a 'City Model' for Heritage-Led Regeneration and Tourism Development. *Epoch*.

Smith, M. (2003). *Issues in Cultural Tourism studies*. Routledge. DOI: 10.4324/9780203402825

Snyder, H., Witell, L., Gustafsson, A., Fombelle, P., & Kristensson, P. (2016). Identifying categories of service innovation: A review and synthesis of the literature. *Journal of Business Research*, 69(7), 2401–2408. DOI: 10.1016/j.jbusres.2016.01.009

Sohel Ahmed, S. M.Sohel Ahmed, S. M. (2019). Risks of Climate Change at Coastal Tourism in Bangladesh: A Study on Cox's Bazar. *Information Management and Business Review*, 11(3(I)), 1–12. DOI: 10.22610/imbr.v11i3(I).2942

Sölvell, Ö. (2015). The Competitive Advantage of Nations 25 years–opening up new perspectives on competitiveness. *Competitiveness Review*, 25(5), 471–481. DOI: 10.1108/CR-07-2015-0068

Soroker, S., Berger, R., Levy, S., & Nebenzahl, I. D. (2023). Understanding consumer sophistication and the moderating role of culture in the tourism context. *International Journal of Hospitality & Tourism Administration*, 24(1), 29–64. DOI: 10.1080/15256480.2021.1938781

Sousa, B., Malheiro, A., Liberato, D., & Liberato, P. (2021). Movie tourism and attracting new tourists in the post-pandemic period: a niche marketing perspective. In *Advances in Tourism, Technology and Systems: Selected Papers from ICOTTS20, Volume 1* (pp. 373-384). Springer Singapore. DOI: 10.1007/978-981-33-4256-9_34

Sousa, B., & Liberato, D. (2022). Film induced Tourism. In *Encyclopedia of Tourism Management and Marketing* (pp. 1–3). Edward Elgar Publishing. DOI: 10.4337/9781800377486.film.induced.tourism

Sousa, B., Machado, A., de Oliveira, F. F., de Abreu Rocha, A. M., & Ribeiro, M. (2023). Promoting Favela Storytelling in the Tourist Visitation: An Exploratory Study. In *Advances in Tourism, Technology and Systems: Selected Papers from ICOTTS 2022, Volume 2* (pp. 343-351). Singapore: Springer Nature Singapore. Pisula, E., Florek, M., & Homski, K. (2023). Marketing communication via geocaching–When and how it can be effective for places? *Journal of Outdoor Recreation and Tourism*, 42, 100622.

Sousa, B., Silva, A., & Malheiro, A. (2020). Differentiation and Market Loyalty: An Approach to Cultural Tourism in Northern Portugal. In Rocha, Á., Abreu, A., de Carvalho, J., Liberato, D., González, E., & Liberato, P. (Eds.), *Advances in Tourism, Technology and Smart Systems. Smart Innovation, Systems and Technologies* (Vol. 171, pp. 681–690). Springer., DOI: 10.1007/978-981-15-2024-2_58

Speck, J. (2012). *Walkable city: how downtown can save America, one step at a time*. Macmillan Publishers.

Stamboulis, Y., & Skayannis, P. (2003). Innovation strategies and technology for experience-based tourism. *Tourism Management*, 24(1), 35–43. DOI: 10.1016/S0261-5177(02)00047-X

Stepchenkova, S., & Li, X. R. (2014). Destination image: Do top-of-mind associations say it all? *Annals of Tourism Research*, 45, 46–62. DOI: 10.1016/j.annals.2013.12.004

Stepchenkova, S., Su, L., & Shichkova, E. (2018). Marketing to Tourists From Unfriendly Countries: Should We Even Try? *Journal of Travel Research*. Advance online publication. DOI: 10.1177/0047287517752883

Stepchenkova, S., & Zhan, F. (2013). Visual destination images of Peru: Comparative content analysis of DMO and user-generated photography. *Tourism Management*, 36, 590–601. DOI: 10.1016/j.tourman.2012.08.006

Štetić, S. & Šimičević, D. (2017). *Menadžment turističke destinacije*. Visoka turistička škola strukovnih studija, Beograd, Srbija. (In Serbian).

Štetić, S., & Trišić, I. (2018). *Strengthening the tourism offer–case study Braničevo District. In Modern Management Tools and Economy of Tourism Sector in Present Era*, (3rd Ed.). Bevanda, V. & Štetić, S., Eds. Association of Economists and Managers of the Balkans, Belgrade, Serbia, Volume 3, 637-650.

Supphellen, M., & Nygaardsvik, I. (2002). Testing country brand slogans: Conceptual development and empirical illustration of a simple normative model. *Brand Management*, 9(4–5), 384–395. https://link.springer.com/article/10.1057/palgrave.bm.2540085

Su, Y. W., & Lin, H. L. (2014). Analysis of international tourist arrivals worldwide: The role of world heritage sites. *Tourism Management*, 40, 46–58. DOI: 10.1016/j.tourman.2013.04.005

Su, Y., Mei, J., Zhu, J., Xia, P., Li, T., Wang, C., Zhi, J., & You, S. (2022). A global scientometric visualization analysis of rural tourism from 2000 to 2021. *Sustainability (Basel)*, 14(22), 14854. DOI: 10.3390/su142214854

Szabó, D. R. (2015). *Sustainable tourism destination management strategies: using the EVIDENCES model for evaluating TDM tenders*. In some current issues in economics; Karlovitz, J. T., Ed.; International research institute sro., Komárno, Slovakia, 249-258.

Taheri, B., & Gannon, M. (2021). Contemporary Issues and Future Trends in Food Tourism. *International Journal of Tourism Research*, 23(2), 147–149. Advance online publication. DOI: 10.1002/jtr.2446

Tait, M., Gaughen, K., Tsang, A., Walton, M., Marcoux, S., Kekoa, L., Kunz, M., & Vaughan, M. (2024). Holomua Marine Initiative: Community-generated sociocultural principles and indicators for marine conservation and management in Hawai'i. *Ecology and Society*, 29(1), art4. DOI: 10.5751/ES-13640-290104

Tajeddini, K., & Ratten, V. (2017). The moderating effect of brand orientation on inter-firm market orientation and performance. *Journal of Strategic Marketing*, •••, 1–31.

Taliouris, E., & Trihas, N. (2017). Public Policy for Corporate Social Responsibility and Governance for Sustainable Tourism Development in Greece. *Business Ethics and Leadership*, 1(4), 49–57. DOI: 10.21272/bel.1(4).49-57.2017

Talukder, M. B. (2020). An Appraisal of the Economic Outlook for the Tourism Industry, Specially Cox's Bazar in Bangladesh. *i-manager's Journal on Economics & Commerce*, 2(1), 23-35. DOI: 10.26634/jecom.2.1.17285

Talukder, M. B., & Kumar, S. "The Effect of Food Service Quality on Customer Satisfaction in the Hotel Industry: A Conceptual Paper," StudyGate, Jun.10, 2023. [Online]. Available: https://www.studygate.net/publication/371503829_The_Effect_of_Food_Service_Quality_on_Customer_Satisfaction_in_the_Hotel_Industry_A_Conceptual_Paper

Talukder, M. B., Kabir, F., Kaiser, F., & Lina, F. Y. (2024). Digital Detox Movement in the Tourism Industry: Traveler Perspective, In *Business Drivers in Promoting Digital Detoxification* (pp. 91-110). IGI Global. DOI: 10.4018/979-8-3693-1107-3.ch007

Talukder, M., Shakhawat Hossain, M., & Kumar, S. (2022). Blue Ocean Strategies in Hotel Industry in Bangladesh: A Review of Present Literatures' Gap and Suggestions for Further Study. SSRN Electronic Journal. DOI: 10.2139/ssrn.4160709

Talukder, M.B., & Kumar, S. (2024). Revisiting intention in food service outlet of five-star hotels: A quantitative approach based on food service quality. Sport i Turystyka. Środkowoeuropejskie Czasopismo Naukowe, 7(1), 137–156. DOI: 10.16926/sit.2024.01.08

Talukder, M. B. (2020b). The Future of Culinary Tourism: An Emerging Dimension for the Tourism Industry of Bangladesh. I-Manager's. *Journal of Management*, 15(1), 27. DOI: 10.26634/jmgt.15.1.17181

Talukder, M. B. (2021). An assessment of the roles of the social network in the development of the Tourism Industry in Bangladesh. *International Journal of Business, Law, and Education*, 2(3), 85–93. DOI: 10.56442/ijble.v2i3.21

Talukder, M. B. (2024). Implementing Artificial Intelligence and Virtual Experiences in Hospitality. In *Innovative Technologies for Increasing Service Productivity* (pp. 145–160). IGI Global., DOI: 10.4018/979-8-3693-2019-8.ch009

Talukder, M. B., & Hossain, M. M. (2021). Prospects of Future Tourism in Bangladesh: An Evaluative Study. I-Manager's. *Journal of Management*, 15(4), 1–8. DOI: 10.26634/jmgt.15.4.17495

Talukder, M. B., & Kaiser, F. (2023). Economic Impact of River Tourism: Evidence of Bangladesh. *i-manager's. Journal of Management*, 18(2), 47–60. DOI: 10.26634/jmgt.18.2.20235

Talukder, M. B., Kumar, S., & Das, I. R. (2024). *Food Wastage on the Economic Outcome: Evidence From the Hotel Industry. Sustainable Disposal Methods of Food Wastes in Hospitality Operations*. IGI Global., DOI: 10.4018/979-8-3693-2181-2.ch005

Talukder, M. B., Kumar, S., & Das, I. R. (2024). Mindfulness of Digital Detoxification: Healthy Lifestyle in Tourism. In *Contemporary Management and Global Leadership for Sustainability* (pp. 56–71). IGI Global., DOI: 10.4018/979-8-3693-1273-5.ch004

Talukder, M. B., Kumar, S., Sood, K., & Grima, S. (2023). Information Technology, Food Service Quality and Restaurant Revisit Intention. *International Journal of Sustainable Development and Planning*, 18(1), 295–303. DOI: 10.18280/ijsdp.180131

Talukder, M., Kumar, S., Misra, L., & Kabir, F. (2024). Determining the role of ecotourism service quality, tourist satisfaction, and destination loyalty: A case study of Kuakata Beach. *Acta Scientiarum Polonorum. Administratio Locorum*, 23(1), 133–151. DOI: 10.31648/aspal.9275

Tasci, A., & Gartner, W. (2007). Destination image and its functional relationships. *Journal of Travel Research*, 45(4), 25–413. DOI: 10.1177/0047287507299569

Terzić, A., Petrevska, B., & Bajrami, D. D. (2022). Personalities Shaping Travel Behaviors: Post-Covid Scenario. *Journal of Tourism Futures*. DOI: 10.1108/JTF-02-2022-0043

Thiele, J., Albert, C., Hermes, J., & von Haaren, C. (2020). Assessing and quantifying offered cultural ecosystem services of German river landscapes. *Ecosystem Services*, 42, 101080. DOI: 10.1016/j.ecoser.2020.101080

Thu Huong, D. T., Lan, T. D., & Le, D. T. (2024). Environmental Conflicts with Tourist Beach Uses along the Northeastern Vietnam Coast. *Journal of Coastal Research*, 40(1). Advance online publication. DOI: 10.2112/JCOASTRES-D-23-00002.1

Tight, M. (2017). *Understanding Case Study Research-Small-scale Research with Meaning*. SAGE Publications. DOI: 10.4135/9781473920118

Timothy, D. J. (2011). *Cultural heritage and tourism: An introduction* (Vol. 4). Channel View Publications. DOI: 10.21832/9781845411787

Timothy, D. J., & Boyd, S. W. (2003). *Heritage tourism*. Pearson Education.

Tjiptono, F., & Yang, L. (2018). To go or not to go: a typology of Asian tourist destination avoidance. *Asian cultures and contemporary tourism*, 183-200.

Tkalec, M., Zilic, I., & Recher, V. (2017). The effect of film industry on tourism: Game of Thrones and Dubrovnik. *International Journal of Tourism Research*, 19(6), 705–714. DOI: 10.1002/jtr.2142

Tomić, S., Leković, K., & Tadić, J. (2019). Consumer behaviour: The influence of age and family structure on the choice of activities in a tourist destination. *Ekonomska Istrazivanja*, 32(1), 755–771. DOI: 10.1080/1331677X.2019.1579663

Tomka, D. (2014). On the Balkans – History, Nature, Tourism and Dilemmas Faced by Researchers. *American Journal of Tourism Management*, 3(1B).

Tosun, C. (2006). Expected nature of community participation in tourism development. *Tourism Management*, 27(3), 493–504. DOI: 10.1016/j.tourman.2004.12.004

Tranter, P., & Tolley, R. (2020). *Slow cities: conquering our speed addiction for health and sustainability* (1st ed.). Elsevier.

Trihas, N., Perakakis, E., Venitourakis, M., Mastorakis, G., & Kopanakis, I. (2013a). Destination Marketing using Multiple Social Media: The Case of 'Visit Ierapetra'. *Tourism Today (Nicosia)*, 13, 114–126.

Trihas, N., Perakakis, E., Venitourakis, M., Mastorakis, G., & Kopanakis, I. (2013b). Social Media as a Marketing Tool for Tourism Destinations: The Case of Greek Municipalities. *Journal of Marketing Vistas*, 3(2), 38–48. DOI: 10.26215/tourismos.v11i3.486

Trihas, N., Vassakis, K., Kopanakis, I., Nikoloudakis, Y., Kefaloukos, I., Pallis, E., & Markakis, E. (2023). The impact of COVID-19 on travel behavior and holiday intentions. Evidence from Greece. In Sharp, B., Finkel, R., & Dashper, K. (Eds.), *Transforming Leisure in the Pandemic: Re-imagining Interaction and Activity during Crisis* (pp. 42–56). Routledge.

Trišić, I., Milojković, D., Ristić, V., Nechita, F., Maksin, M., Štetić, S., & Candrea, A. N. (2023a). Sustainable tourism of Important Plant Areas (IPAs)—A case of three protected areas of Vojvodina Province. *Land (Basel)*, 12(7), 1278. DOI: 10.3390/land12071278

Trišić, I., Nechita, F., Milojković, D., & Štetić, S. (2023b). Sustainable tourism in protected areas—Application of the Prism of sustainability model. *Sustainability (Basel)*, 15(6), 5148. DOI: 10.3390/su15065148

Trišić, I., Privitera, D., Ristić, V., Štetić, S., Milojković, D., & Maksin, M. (2023c). Protected areas in the function of sustainable tourism development—A case of Deliblato sands special nature reserve, Vojvodina Province. *Land (Basel)*, 12(2), 487. DOI: 10.3390/land12020487

Tsartas, P., Despotaki, G., & Sarantakou, E. (2015). New trends for tourism products: the issue of tourism resources. 10. 194-204. https://www.researchgate.net/publication/322055295_New_trends_for_tourism_products_The_Issue_of_tourism_resources

Tuclea, C. E., & Nistoreanu, P. (2011). How film and television programs can promote tourism and increase the competitiveness of tourist destinations. *Cactus Tourism Journal*, 2(2), 25–30.

Tung, V. W. S., Tse, S., & Chan, D. C. F. (2021). Host-guest relations and destination image: Compensatory effects, impression management, and implications for tourism recovery. *Journal of Travel & Tourism Marketing*, 38(8), 833–844. DOI: 10.1080/10548408.2021.1883499

Ullah, N., Khan, J., Saeed, I., Zada, S., Xin, S., Kang, Z., & Hu, Y. (2022). Gastronomic Tourism and Tourist Motivation: Exploring Northern Areas of Pakistan. *International Journal of Environmental Research and Public Health*, 19(13), 7734. Advance online publication. DOI: 10.3390/ijerph19137734 PMID: 35805393

Universidade Federal de Pelotas. "Concurso para a marca de Pelotas" (2017a, July, 7) https://bit.ly/3c8fHjx

Universidade Federal de Pelotas. "Votação para a marca de Pelotas" (2017b, July) https://bit.ly/3mtU7KN

UNWTO. (2010). *World Tourism Barometer January 2010*. UNWTO.

UNWTO. (2017). *Tourism and the Sustainable Development Goals – Journey to 2030*. UNWTO.

UNWTO. (2023). *Tourism Statistics Database*. Available at UNWTO.

UNWTO. (2023a). *Tourism and the Sustainable Development Goals – Journey to 2030*. Available online: https://www.e-unwto.org/doi/book/10.18111/9789284419401 (accessed on 7 June 2023).

UNWTO. (2023b). *Product Development*. Available online: https://www.unwto.org/tourism-development-products (accessed on 10 June 2023).

UNWTO. (2023c). *Indicators of Sustainable Development for Tourism Destinations*. Available online: https://www.e-unwto.org/doi/epdf/10.18111/9789284407262?role=tab (accessed on 3 June 2023).

Valachis, I. (2021). Photographic Tourism. In Agarwal, S., Busby, G., & Huang, R. (Eds.), *Special interest tourism* (pp. 249–270). Broken Hill Publishers Ltd. (in Greek)

Valachis, I., & Giouzepas, D. (2006). Mould tourists into environmental friendly visitors: 'Interactive architecture' and eco-educating parks. 2nd *International Scientific Conference Progress in Tourism and Hospitality: Present & Future Challenges*, Thessaloniki, Greece

Van Assche, K., Beunen, R., & Oliveira, E. (2020). Spatial planning and place branding: Rethinking relations and synergies. *European Planning Studies*, 28(7), 1274–1290. DOI: 10.1080/09654313.2019.1701289

Van Den Berg et al. (2002). *Sports and City Marketing in European Cities. European Institute for Comparative Urban Research*. Ashgate.

Van Rheenen, D., Naria, O., Melo, R., & Sobry, C. (2024). *Sport Tourism, Island Territories and Sustainable Development*. Springer. DOI: 10.1007/978-3-031-51705-1

Vassiliadis, C. A., Mombeuil, C., & Fotiadis, A. K. (2021). Identifying service product features associated with visitor satisfaction and revisit intention: A focus on sports events. *Journal of Destination Marketing & Management*, 19, 100558. DOI: 10.1016/j.jdmm.2021.100558

Veal, A. (2018). *Research Methods for Leisure and Tourism*. Pearson.

Vela, E.. (2017). The visual landscape as a key element of the local brand. *Journal of Place Management and Development*, 10(1), 23–44. DOI: 10.1108/JPMD-09-2016-0060

Viehoff, V. G. P. (2018). *Mega-event Cities: Urban Legacies of Global Sports Events* (1st ed.). Routledge.

Vieira, J. S., Araújo, C. A., & Sousa, B. B. (2022). Film-Induced Tourism and Selling Storytelling in Destination Marketing: The Legend of the Rooster of Barcelos (Portugal). In J. Santos (Ed.), *Sales Management for Improved Organizational Competitiveness and Performance* (pp. 290-302). IGI Global. https://doi.org/DOI: 10.4018/978-1-6684-3430-7.ch015

Visit Britain (2013). *Post-Games Tourism Performance Report*.

Visuwasam, L. M. M., Srinath, M., Raj, V. S. A., Sirajudeen, A., Sudhir Maharaaja, S., & Raja, D. (2023). Tourist Behaviour Analysis Using Data Analytics. In Singh, S., Rajest, S. S., Hadoussa, S., Obaid, A. J., & Regin, R. (Eds.), (pp. 343–355). Advances in Business Information Systems and Analytics. IGI Global., DOI: 10.4018/979-8-3693-2193-5.ch023

Volo, S., & Irimias, A. (2016). Film tourism and post-release marketing initiatives: A longitudinal case study. *Journal of Travel & Tourism Marketing*, 33(8), 1071–1087. DOI: 10.1080/10548408.2015.1094000

Vuković, M. & Štrbac, N. (2019). *Metodologija naučnih istraživanja*. Tehnički fakultet u Boru Univerziteta u Beogradu, Bor, Srbija, str. 32-41. (In Serbian)

Wang, P. (2014). *The Influence of Tourists' Safety Perception During Vacation Destination-Decision Process: An Integration of Elaboration Likelihood Model and Theory of Planned Behavior*. DOI: 10.1007/978-3-319-10211-5_23

Wang, F., Feng, Y., & Wang, Z. (2022). Inspiring Desirability or Ensuring Feasibility: Destination Image and Psychological Distance. *International Journal of Tourism Research*, 24(5), 667–676. Advance online publication. DOI: 10.1002/jtr.2529

Wang, S., & Gu, K. (2020). Pingyao: The historic urban landscape and planning for heritage-led urban changes. *Cities (London, England)*, 97, 102489. DOI: 10.1016/j.cities.2019.102489

Wang, Y., Huang, L., Li, J., & Yang, Y. (2019). The mechanism of tourism slogans on travel intention based on Unique Selling Proposition (USP) theory. *Journal of Travel & Tourism Marketing*, 36(4), 415–427. DOI: 10.1080/10548408.2019.1568950

Wani, M. D., Batool, N., Dada, Z. A., & Shah, S. A. (2024). Investigating the impact of community-based tourism on the residents' quality of life and their support for tourism. *Community Development (Columbus, Ohio)*, 55(1), 138–159. DOI: 10.1080/15575330.2023.2272271

Wani, M. D., Dada, Z. A., & Shah, S. A. (2022). Building peace through tourism: The analysis of an ongoing Siachen Glacier dispute between India and Pakistan. *Asian Journal of Comparative Politics*, 7(4), 836–848. DOI: 10.1177/20578911221118730

Wani, M. D., Dada, Z. A., & Shah, S. A. (2024). The impact of community empowerment on sustainable tourism development and the mediation effect of local support: A structural equation modeling approach. *Community Development (Columbus, Ohio)*, 55(1), 50–66. DOI: 10.1080/15575330.2022.2109703

Ward, S. (1998). Selling places: the marketing and promotion of towns and cities, 1850-2000.

Weed, M. (2009). Progress in sports tourism research? A meta-review and exploration of futures. *Tourism Management*, 30(5), 615–628. DOI: 10.1016/j.tourman.2009.02.002

Wen, J., Goh, E., & Yu, C. E. (2023). Segmentation of physician-assisted suicide as a niche tourism market: An Initial Exploration. *Journal of Hospitality & Tourism Research (Washington, D.C.)*, 47(3), 574–589. DOI: 10.1177/10963480211011630

Wen, J., Wang, W., Kozak, M., Liu, X., & Hou, H. (2020). Many brains are better than one: The importance of interdisciplinary studies on COVID-19 in and beyond tourism. *Tourism Recreation Research*, 46(2), 310–313. DOI: 10.1080/02508281.2020.1761120

Wicker, P. (2019). The carbon footprint of active sport participants. *Sport Management Review*, 22(4), 513–526. DOI: 10.1016/j.smr.2018.07.001

Wilson, S., Fesenmaier, D. R., Fesenmaier, J., & Van Es, J. C. (2001). Factors for success in rural tourism development. *Journal of Travel Research*, 40(2), 132–138. DOI: 10.1177/004728750104000203

Witell, L., Snyder, H., Gustafsson, A., Fombelle, P., & Kristensson, P. (2016). Defining service innovation: A review and synthesis. *Journal of Business Research*, 69(8), 2863–2872. DOI: 10.1016/j.jbusres.2015.12.055

Wong, P. P. W. (2015). Role of components of destination competitiveness in the relationship between customer-based brand equity and destination loyalty. *Current Issues in Tourism*, 21(5), 504–528. DOI: 10.1080/13683500.2015.1092949

Wood, L. E., Vimercati, G., Ferrini, S., & Shackleton, R. T. (2022). Perceptions of ecosystem services and disservices associated with open water swimming. *Journal of Outdoor Recreation and Tourism*, 37, 100491. DOI: 10.1016/j.jort.2022.100491

World Economic Forum. (2019). The travel and tourism competitiveness report. Consulté le June 26, 2020, sur https://www.weforum.org/reports/the-travel-tourism-competitiveness-report-2019

World Economic Forum. (2020). *Global Risks 2020: A Global Risk Network Report*.

WTO. World Tourism Organisation (2009), "Handbook on Tourism Destination Branding." Europe-World Tourism Organization.

Wu, M. Y., Tong, Y., Li, Q., Wall, G., & Wu, X. (2022). Interaction rituals and social relationships in a rural tourism destination. *Journal of Travel Research*, •••, 00472875221130495.

Wyer, R. S. (1995). *Knowledge and memory: The real story*. Lawrence Erlbaum Associates.

Xie, L., Shahzad, M. F., Waheed, A., Ain, Q. U., Saleem, Z., & Ali, M. A. (2022). Do Meat Anti-Consumption Opinions Influence Consumers' Wellbeing?–The Moderating Role of Religiosity. *Frontiers in Psychology*, 13, 957970. Advance online publication. DOI: 10.3389/fpsyg.2022.957970 PMID: 36312138

Yanes, A., Zielinski, S., Cano, M. D., & Kim, S. I. (2019). Community-based tourism in developing countries: A framework for policy evaluation. *Sustainability (Basel)*, 11(9), 2506. DOI: 10.3390/su11092506

Yang, Y., Nan, L., Meijian, L., & Li, S. (2011). Study on the Effects of Logistics Service Quality on Consumers' Post-Purchase Behavior of Online Shopping. *International Journal on Advances in Information Sciences and Service Sciences*. DOI: 10.4156/aiss.vol3.issue11.30

Yang, C. H., Lin, H. L., & Han, C. C. (2010). Analysis of international tourist arrivals in China: The role of World Heritage Sites. *Tourism Management*, 31(6), 827–837. DOI: 10.1016/j.tourman.2009.08.008 PMID: 32287732

Yang, Y., Zhang, H., & Chen, X. (2020). Coronavirus pandemic and tourism: Dynamic stochastic general equilibrium modeling of infectious disease outbreak. *Annals of Tourism Research*, 83, 102–913. DOI: 10.1016/j.annals.2020.102913 PMID: 32292219

Yen, C. H., & Croy, W. G. (2016). Film tourism: Celebrity involvement, celebrity worship and destination image. *Current Issues in Tourism*, 19(10), 1027–1044. DOI: 10.1080/13683500.2013.816270

Yin, R. (2009). Case study research: Design and methods (éd. 4). Thousand Oaks, CA: SAGE.

Yin, R. K. (2015). Estudo de caso: Planejamento e métodos. *The Bookman*.

Youssef, K. B., Leicht, T., & Marongiu, L. (2019). Storytelling in the context of destination marketing: An analysis of conceptualisations and impact measurement. *Journal of Strategic Marketing*, 27(8), 696–713. DOI: 10.1080/0965254X.2018.1464498

Yuan, Q., Song, H. J., Chen, N., & Shang, W. (2019). Roles of tourism involvement and place attachment in determining residents' attitudes toward industrial heritage tourism in a resource-exhausted city in China. Sustainability (Switzerland), 11(19).

Yung, R., Khoo-Lattimore, C., & Potter, L. E. (2021). Virtual reality and tourism marketing: Conceptualizing a framework on presence, emotion, and intention. *Current Issues in Tourism*, 24(11), 1505–1525. DOI: 10.1080/13683500.2020.1820454

Zamani-Farahani, H., & Musa, G. (2012). The relationship between Islamic religiosity and residents' perceptions of socio-cultural impacts of tourism in Iran: Case studies of Sare'in and Masooleh. *Tourism Management*, 33(4), 802–814. DOI: 10.1016/j.tourman.2011.09.003

Zaman, U., Aktan, M., Agrusa, J., & Khwaja, M. G. (2022). Linking Regenerative Travel and Residents' Support for Tourism Development in Kaua'i Island (Hawaii): Moderating-Mediating Effects of Travel-Shaming and Foreign Tourist Attractiveness. *Journal of Travel Research*. Advance online publication. DOI: 10.1177/00472875221098934

Zavattaro, S. (2014). *Place Branding through Phases of the Image* (1a Ed). New York: Palgrave Macmillan

Zehrer, A., & Hallmann, K. (2015). A stakeholder perspective on policy indicators of destination competitiveness. *Journal of Destination Marketing & Management*, 4(2), 120–126. DOI: 10.1016/j.jdmm.2015.03.003

Zenker, S. (2011). How to catch a city? *The concept and measurement of place brands.Journal of Place Management and Development*, 4(1), 40–52. DOI: 10.1108/17538331111117151

Zenker, S. B. E., & Petersen, S. (2017). Branding the destination versus the place : The effects of brand complexity and identification for residents and visitors. *Tourism Management*, 58, 15–27. DOI: 10.1016/j.tourman.2016.10.008

Zeydan, İ., & Gürbüz, A. (2023). Examining tourists' travel intentions in Türkiye during pandemic and post-pandemic period: The mediating effect of risk reduction behavior. *Journal of Multidisciplinary Academic Tourism*, 8(2), 171–183. DOI: 10.31822/jomat.2023-8-2-171

Zhandilla, B. (2023). Conceptual Foundations of the Category of Tourist Destination. *Bulletin of the Karaganda University Economy Series*. DOI: 10.31489/2022ec4/135-143

Zhang, G., & Xing, L. (2023). Study on tourism economic effect under the threshold of new-type urbanization in coastal cities of China: From the perspective of development economics. *Ocean and Coastal Management*, 239, 106587. DOI: 10.1016/j.ocecoaman.2023.106587

Zhang, T., Chen, J., & Hu, B. (2019). Authenticity, quality, and loyalty: Local food and sustainable tourism experience. *Sustainability (Basel)*, 11(12), 3437. DOI: 10.3390/su11123437

Zhang, Y., Zou, Y., Zhu, Z., Guo, X., & Feng, X. (2022). Evaluating pedestrian environment using DeepLab models based on street walkability in small and medium-sized cities: Case study in Gaoping, China. *Sustainability (Basel)*, 14(22), 15472. DOI: 10.3390/su142215472

Zhang, Z., Fisher, T., & Wang, H. (2023). Walk score, environmental quality and walking in a campus setting. *Land (Basel)*, 12(4), 732. DOI: 10.3390/land12040732

Zhao, C., Shang, Z., & Pan, Y. (2023). Beauty and tourists' sustainable behaviour in rural tourism: A self-transcendent emotions perspective. *Journal of Sustainable Tourism*, •••, 1–20.

Zhou, B., Liu, S., Wang, L., Wang, L., & Wang, Y. (2022). COVID-19 Risk Perception and Tourist Satisfaction: A Mixed-Method Study of the Roles of Destination Image and Self-Protection Behavior. *Frontiers in Psychology*, 13, 1001231. Advance online publication. DOI: 10.3389/fpsyg.2022.1001231 PMID: 37035511

Zhou, Y., Maumbe, K., Deng, J., & Selin, W. (2015, July). Resource-based destination competitiveness evaluation using a hybrid analytic hierarchy process (AHP): The case study of West Virginia. *Tourism Management Perspectives*, 15, 72–80. DOI: 10.1016/j.tmp.2015.03.007

Zhu, C., Fong, L. H. N., Li, X., Buhalis, D., & Chen, H. (2024). Short video marketing in tourism: Telepresence, celebrity attachment, and travel intention. *International Journal of Tourism Research*, 26(1), e2599. DOI: 10.1002/jtr.2599

Zhu, H., Guan, H., Han, Y., & Li, W. (2019). A Study of Tourists' Holiday Rush-Hour Avoidance Travel Behavior Considering Psychographic Segmentation. *Sustainability (Basel)*, 11(13), 3755. Advance online publication. DOI: 10.3390/su11133755

Ziakas, V., Tzanelli, R., & Lundberg, C. (2022). Interscopic fan travelscape: Hybridizing tourism through sport and art. *Tourist Studies*, 22(3), 290–307. DOI: 10.1177/14687976221092169

Zouganeli, S., Trihas, N., Antonaki, M., & Kladou, S. (2012). Aspects of Sustainability in the Destination Branding Process: A Bottom-up Approach. *Journal of Hospitality Marketing & Management*, 21(7), 739–757. DOI: 10.1080/19368623.2012.624299

Zupic, I., & Čater, T. (2015). Bibliometric methods in management and organization. *Organizational Research Methods*, 18(3), 429–472. DOI: 10.1177/1094428114562629

About the Contributors

Romina Alkier Tomić, PhD. is a Full Professor at the Faculty of Tourism and Hospitality Management Opatija, University in Rijeka, specialised in the field of tourism. She graduated at the Faculty of Tourism and Hospitality Management Opatija, University of Rijeka. At the same institution she finished her Master of Science and Doctoral studies and got her PhD in tourism. She teaches Introduction to Tourism, International tourism, Safety in Tourism, and Rural Tourism. She published numerous scientific and professional papers in relevant scientific journals and conference proceedings, as well as 2 books. As a researcher she participated in several scientific and professional projects. She was the leader of the scientific project „New security paradigm and valorisation of a tourist destination". Currently she is the leader of a scientific project titled "Perception of Kvarner as a Tourist Destination for Beauty and Health". Numerous students got their Bachelor and Masters degrees under her supervision. She reviews papers for scientific journals and conferences, participates in organization of scientific conferences, as well as in programs of lifelong learning. Her research topics are: International Tourism, Safety in Tourism and Rural Tourism.

Giuseppe Catenazzo is the Dean of Academics at Helvetic Business School and the Head of Research at AUS American Institute of Applied Sciences in Switzerland. He also teaches Market Research, Operations Management, and Statistics at several institutions in Switzerland. Giuseppe is an Italian and Swiss citizen. He studied in France, Italy, Switzerland, and the United Kingdom and speaks several languages. Dr Catenazzo is also an editor of international research books; his research on quality perceptions, service recovery, and complaining behaviour has been published in Production Planning and Control, International Journal of Quality and Reliability Management, and the Journal of Consumer Satisfaction, Dissatisfaction & Complaining Behavior.

Vedran Milojica, univ. mag. oec. is a PhD Candidate at the Faculty of Tourism and Hospitality Management, University of Rijeka, Republic of Croatia. His career spanned from tourism and hospitality, to finance, and higher education. Vedran was a Lecturer at a private university of applied sciences, where he taught multiple courses in tourism and hospitality, marketing and methodology of scientific research. He participates actively in various scientific and professional education programmes and contributes regularly to the organising committees of scientific conferences and congresses as an external associate. He is also the secretary of the Journal of Economics, Management and Informatics BizInfo (Blace) and reviews scientific papers for scientific journals. He published a significant number of scientific papers in scientific journals and proceedings of international conferences. His areas of research include specific forms of tourism, such as Health Tourism, Rural Tourism, Nautical Tourism, Event Tourism, Gastronomic Tourism, Cultural Tourism, Religious Tourism, Urban Tourism, Beach Tourism, as well as International Tourism, Tourist behaviour, and safety and security in tourism.

Aleksandra Zając is a social scientist specialising in security studies. She holds master degrees in International Relations and in Philosophy. She earned her PhD in 2019 based on a dissertation about customer orientation and improvement of services of the Polish Police. From 2016 until 2021 she worked as an Assistant Professor at the State University of Applied Sciences in Racibórz, Poland, teaching both security professionals (policemen, prison and border guards, soldiers) and civilians. From 2022 to 2024 she worked as Researcher at the American Institute of Applied Sciences in Switzerland, building research capacities of the school. In May 2024 she became Chancellor of Swiss Institute of Management and Sciences. Beyond academia her professional experience include Anti Money-Laundering and paralegal services for business. She also served as United Nation Junior Legal Expert on Poland (2021).

***

Jiyoon An (Ph.D., University of Rhode Island) is an Assistant Professor of Marketing at Fayetteville State University (FSU), a constituent institution of The University of North Carolina System. She researches the intersection of digital transformation, innovation, and marketing strategy. Her research has appeared in peer-reviewed journals, including the Social Responsibility Journal, Consumer Behavior in Tourism and Hospitality, and Maritime Business Review. She is a recipient of the Best Research Presentation Award, National Conference of Creativity, Innovation, and Technology (NCCiT) and Best Abstract Award, SCM & Logistics Track, Atlantic Marketing Association (AtMA) Conference.

Valerio Della Sala is an Adjunct Professor in the Department of Geography at the Autonomous University of Barcelona; member of the Organizing Committee of the Sport Research Institute (IRE-UAB) of the Universitat Autonoma de Barcelona, and of OMERO (University of Turin). Academic research covers general topics on urbanism, human geography, environment, landscape and urban culture, including applied projects on the sport, spatial policy and the retrofitting of urban space and cultural-led regeneration programs.

Ahmad Hajeer earned his Ph.D. with a summa cum laude distinction, focusing on the decision-making process of readers of promotional materials. His work spans complex qualitative and quantitative research methodologies, leading to publications in high-ranked journals. Dr. Hajeer has international teaching experience and conducts training sessions in intercultural competence. His research areas include the marketing of education, intercultural sensitivity, and discourse analysis.

Mushfika Hoque, a distinguished figure in the field of tourism and hospitality management, serves as an esteemed lecturer in the department of Tourism and Hospitality Management at Daffodil Institute of IT. With a wealth of academic expertise and a passion for cultivating the next generation of industry leaders, Mushfika Hoque's career has been defined by her commitment to merging theoretical knowledge with practical applications. Her groundbreaking research on sustainable tourism and experiential hospitality has earned her recognition in academic circles and her engaging teaching style has left an indelible mark on countless students. A trailblazer in her field, Mushfika continues to inspire and shape the future of tourism and hospitality education through her innovative approach and dedication to excellence.

Ali İnanir is assoc. Prof. and head of Depertment of Travel Tourism and Leisure Services in School of Ağlasun Vocational at Mehmet Akif Ersoy University. His research interests are destination management and marketing, hotel management, organizational behavior in tourism, alternative tourism and sustainable tourism.

Firoj Kabir is an accomplished author, researcher and Lecturer and Coordinator of the Department of "Tourism and Hospitality Management" of Daffodil Institute of IT (DIIT), Dhaka, Bangladesh with a strong academic background in BBA and MBA majoring in Tourism and Hospitality Management from the University of Dhaka. His passion lies in exploring the intersection of travel and culture. His diverse areas of interest include archaeological tourism, sustainable tourism, and the unique characteristics of Generation Z travelers. Through his extensive research and insightful writing, he sheds light on the intricate connections between historical sites, responsible tourism, and the evolving preferences of the next generation of travelers. His work not only enriches the field of tourism but also inspires readers to engage with the world around them in meaningful and responsible ways.

Fahmida Kaiser is a distinguished academic figure in the field of tourism and hospitality management. As a Lecturer at the Department of Tourism and Hospitality Management at Daffodil Institute of IT, she has dedicated her career to advancing knowledge in the intersection of tourism and sustainability.With a passion for exploring the multifaceted relationship between tourism and sustainable practices, Her research has not only contributed to the academic community but also holds significant implications for the global tourism industry. Her commitment to shedding light on the importance of responsible and eco-conscious tourism practices has garnered recognition from both peers and students alike.Her academic journey has been marked by a relentless pursuit of knowledge and a desire to bridge the gap between theory and practical application in the realms of tourism and sustainability.

Yusuf Karakuş completed his undergraduate studies in Tourism and Hotel Management at Erciyes University. He was awarded a Doctorate in 2017 by Nevşehir Hacı Bektaş Veli University upon successfully defending his Ph.D. thesis entitled "New product development model for tourism destinations: The case of Nevşehir". In 2021, he commenced his academic career as an Assistant Professor at Recep Tayyip Erdoğan University, Ardeşen Vocational High School. Since 2023, he has been serving as an Associate Professor at the Ardeşen Tourism Faculty, where he also holds the position of Vice Dean. His research interest areas: Tourism product, Destination marketing and management, Decision making in tourism research.

Danka Milojkovic (1971), an Assistant Professor in the scientific field of Management at the Singidunum University in Belgrade Faculty of Tourism and Hospitality Management and Faculty of IT, is a Graduate Management Engineer from the Faculty of Organizational Science of the University of Belgrade – Program in Management (1997). She defended her master's thesis entitled "Possibilities for Applying Strategic Management to Serbian Enterprises" at the Faculty of Organizational Science of the University of Belgrade (2008) becoming a Master of Engineering Science in the field of Organizational Science for Management. She defended a doctoral dissertation entitled "Application of Mathematical Methods in Planning Cluster Organizations' Development in the Republic of Serbia" at the Faculty of Economics of the University of Nis becoming a Ph.D. in Economic Science (2015). She started her professional career as a scholarship holder of the Serbian Ministry of Science and Technology, an intern gifted for scientific research and educational work at the Faculty of Organizational Science in Belgrade. For more than two decades, he has been performing development, research, and educational-promotional work in the business sector, domestic and international organizations, and academic institutions. She was a member of the Board of Directors of the Institute for Innovation, Competitiveness and Clusters "Global TCI Network" in Barcelona (2014/19), a member of EU / ECCP & ESCA working groups (since 2017), a president of the Serbian Chamber of Commerce Cluster Council (2011/15), and a member of the working group of the National Training Incubation Training Program supported by the SINTEF/ENTRANSE program in Serbia (2005/6). Since 1997 she has been an author and a participant in a large number of SME development projects, a speaker at international conferences, and a guest lecturer at academic institutions and professional gatherings at the University "Cyril and Methodius" in Skopje, Faculty of Economics in Nis, University of Transylvania in Brasov (Romania), Kazan (Russia), Daegu (South Korea), Eindhoven (Netherlands) and Puerto Vallarta (Mexico). She is an author of the original business development model "Cluster House" for a cluster approach to local economic development in the Balkans, with the transcontinental application of the model in Egypt and Peru. She is an author/co-author of 18 journal articles, 23 conference papers, and the 3 chapters of thematic monographs. She is a winner of the following national awards: "The Flower of Success" for the promotion of women's entrepreneurship in Southern Serbia (2012), and "The Captain Misa Anastasijevic" for entrepreneurship development in the Year of Entrepreneurship in Serbia (2016).

Smriti Mishra, an Architect and Urban Planner, is currently working as an Associate Professor in the Department of Architecture and Planning, Birla Institute of Technology, Mesra, Ranchi, India and heading the department. She specializes in the field of urban and regional planning and has research interests in perception studies, tourism heritage management, vulnerability of peri-urban areas, vernacular architecture, indigenous planning, energy conservation and has few publications in her records.

Aditi Nag is an Architect and Urban Planner, pursuing a Ph.D. in the Department of Architecture and Planning, Birla Institute of Technology, Mesra, Ranchi, India. She has done research in the field of urban and rural planning and has a few publications in her record. She is the 1st to have been awarded the DST Inspire Fellowship in the field of Architecture and Planning by the Ministry of Science and Technology, Govt. of India.

Árpád Ferenc Papp-Váry (PhD) is the Head of the Marketing MSc programme at the biggest Hungarian business university, Budapest Business School. In addition to that, he is a senior research associate at the Economic Geography and Urban Marketing Centre of John von Neumann University, Kecskemét, Hungary, and he leads the Marketing and Tourism Programme at the Doctoral School of the Faculty of Economics of the University of Sopron, Hungary. Árpád is the author of several well-known marketing and branding books, the most recent of which is "Country Branding – Creating a Competitive Identity and Image". A large part of his publications is also available on his website in pdf format: http://papp-vary.hu/ Besides university education, he regularly holds training sessions and provides branding consultancy, and his company, Márkadoktor Kft., is an accredited consultant of the Hungarian Multi Program. He is a jury member of more than ten marketing, advertising and PR competitions. He has been Vice President of the Hungarian Marketing Association (MMSZ) for three terms.

Lara Santos completed her Ph.D. in Marketing and Strategy in 2019 from the University of Aveiro, the University of Beira Interior, and the University of Minho. She is an Assistant Professor at the Lusófona University - Centro Universitário do Porto - Faculty of Economic, Social and Business Sciences, Guest Assistant Professor at the Polytechnic Institute of Bragança - School of Administration, Communication and Tourism, and Guest Assistant at the Polytechnic Institute of Cávado and Ave - Higher School of Hospitality and Tourism. Published eight articles in specialized journals and has eight book chapters. Works in Social Sciences with an emphasis on Economics and Management. She developed his research activity at the Intrepid Lab, which was recently integrated as a hub of CETRAD - Center for Transdisciplinary Studies for Development.

Štetić Snežana is working in Tourism more than 40 years and in education for Tourism. She finished her PhD in economics, tourism and hotel management, her main fields of scientific research are Tourism, Sustainable tourism, Specific forms of tourism, Tourist destinations, Crises and Tourism. As a recognized expert in tourism, in addition to teaching in Serbia she is (was) a visiting professor in many European countries. Published 35 books about tourism, geography, management of tourist destination, rural tourism, travel agencies and tour operators, event management. More than hundred articles in field of tourism. Participated in over 40 tourism development projects in the regional plans for Tourism, master plans destinations and development studies of cross-border cooperation. Author of specialized business schools in Tourism and Hotel management, and organizer, administrator and instructor. Lecturer at numerous seminars for tour operator representatives and tourist guides. Founder, Board Member of many societies in Tourism. Editor and member of Editorial Board of the international professional magazine for tourism and boards of publishing Houses. She is highly regarded for her work

Bruno Barbosa Sousa is Adjunct Professor of Marketing at Polytechnic Institute of Cávado and Ave (IPCA), Portugal and PhD in Marketing and Strategy in Universidade do Minho, Portugal. Head of Masters Program - Tourism Management and Marketing Tourism (IPCA); CiTUR – Center for Tourism Research, Development and Innovation and UNIAG research member. He has published in the Journal of Enterprising Communities, Tourism Management Perspectives, Current Issues in Tourism, Journal of Organizational Change Management, World Review of Entrepreneurship, Management and Sust. Development, among others..

Mohammad Badruddoza Talukder is an Associate Professor, College of Tourism and Hospitality Management, International University of Business Agriculture and Technology, Dhaka, Bangladesh. He holds Ph.D. in Hotel Management from Lovely Professional University, India. He has been teaching various courses in the Department of Tourism and Hospitality at various universities in Bangladesh since 2008. His research areas include tourism management, hotel management, hospitality management, food & beverage management, and accommodation management, where he has published research papers in well-known journals in Bangladesh and abroad. Mr. Talukder is one of the executive members of the Tourism Educators Association of Bangladesh. He has led training and consulting for a wide range of hospitality organizations in Bangladesh. He just became an honorary facilitator at the Bangladesh Tourism Board's Bangabandhu international tourism and hospitality training institution.

Nikolaos Trihas is an Associate Professor in the Department of Business Administration and Tourism at the Hellenic Mediterranean University in Greece, and a tutor at the Hellenic Open University, where he lectures courses on marketing, management and tourism.

Ioannis Valachis is an Affiliate Lecturer in Tourism Management at Hellenic Open University. He works at the Tourism Department of the Municipality of Veria and runs a family hotel in Halkidiki, Greece.

Index

B

Brand Identity 10, 16, 148, 149, 157, 231, 253, 297
Branding Strategies 6, 10, 90, 228, 232, 233, 295

C

Community engagement 87, 191, 201, 202, 286, 287, 288, 290, 296, 297, 298, 309, 312, 313, 314, 324
Cultural Advancement 83
Cultural Identity 4, 17, 27, 28, 46, 52, 249, 292, 307
Cultural preservation 13, 95, 96, 97, 286, 287, 293, 295, 298, 299, 305, 306, 308, 309, 311
Cultural Studies 227, 229, 248
Culture and Heritage Tourism 27, 28, 35

D

Destination Appeal 2, 5
Destination Branding 8, 9, 10, 15, 17, 40, 53, 81, 118, 162, 163, 227, 228, 229, 233, 246, 247, 248, 251, 252, 254
Destination competitiveness 6, 27, 33, 35, 36, 38, 39, 40, 42, 50, 51, 52, 54, 55, 182, 253, 254, 285, 289, 290, 313, 322
destination management 2, 5, 6, 7, 9, 15, 24, 28, 35, 38, 42, 43, 62, 121, 126, 153, 165, 170, 173, 175, 176, 191, 192, 193, 194, 201, 202, 203, 205, 213, 214, 215, 216, 217, 219, 226, 258, 260, 263, 275, 281, 285, 286, 287, 289, 295, 298, 306, 312, 324
Destination Marketing 1, 2, 3, 8, 9, 18, 19, 21, 22, 23, 24, 25, 36, 80, 118, 119, 125, 128, 134, 135, 138, 139, 165, 166, 167, 168, 170, 171, 172, 173, 175, 176, 178, 179, 180, 181, 182, 208, 209, 228, 251
destination rejection 205, 206, 208, 209, 210, 212, 213, 214, 215, 216, 221, 226
Dissonant heritage 27, 42, 45

E

Economic Growth 83, 84, 85, 92, 94, 97, 155, 174, 193, 213, 214, 248, 249, 257, 286, 287, 288, 289, 298, 299, 301, 302, 304, 306, 311
Environmental Sustainability 35, 93, 189, 203, 301, 302

F

film-induced tourism 125, 126, 127, 135, 137, 139

G

geocaching 105, 106, 107, 108, 109, 110, 111, 112, 113, 114, 115, 117, 118, 119, 120, 121, 122

H

Heritage-led tourism 285, 287, 289, 290, 299, 305, 306, 307, 308, 309, 310, 311, 312, 313, 314, 315

L

Legacy planning 191, 192, 194, 201, 202
local community 57, 58, 59, 62, 63, 64, 65, 66, 70, 71, 73, 74, 78, 150, 159, 195, 256, 259, 260, 263, 275, 276, 306
local development 75, 77, 105, 142, 319, 322

M

Marine Tourism 83, 84, 85, 86, 87, 88, 89, 90, 91, 92, 93, 94, 95, 96, 97, 98, 101
Mega-events 180, 185, 186, 187, 198, 199, 201, 202

N

niche marketing 106, 107, 115, 126, 136, 137, 138
niche tourism 106, 107, 115, 119, 120, 122, 126, 138

O

Olympic Games 186, 187, 188, 189, 190, 191, 192, 194, 196, 197, 198, 201, 202

P

Place Branding 25, 150, 161, 162, 163, 164, 227, 228, 230, 231, 232, 244, 245, 246, 247, 250, 251, 252, 253, 254, 317

R

Responsible tourism 85, 87, 89, 96, 209, 288, 293, 295, 296, 299, 304, 305, 306, 309, 310, 311, 312, 314

S

Service Innovation 165, 172, 175, 176, 182
Social inclusion 88, 195, 196, 201
socio-economic 255, 256, 257, 264
Sport Tourism 165, 166, 168, 172, 173, 174, 175, 176, 178, 179, 181, 182, 183
Storytelling 1, 2, 3, 4, 5, 6, 9, 12, 18, 19, 20, 21, 22, 23, 24, 25, 48, 121, 137, 139, 295, 300, 301, 303, 312, 315
Storytelling Strategies 20, 25
Strategic Planning 62, 93, 141, 142, 144, 145, 146, 147, 151, 160, 202, 302
Sustainable tourism 6, 20, 23, 33, 42, 51, 52, 53, 54, 57, 58, 59, 63, 72, 73, 74, 75, 76, 77, 79, 80, 88, 92, 100, 106, 115, 117, 122, 132, 178, 179, 181, 183, 194, 213, 214, 215, 218, 222, 226, 255, 260, 276, 277, 279, 280, 281, 282, 283, 287, 289, 290, 304, 305, 306, 309, 310, 311, 312, 314, 316, 317, 318, 320, 322
sustainable tourism development 57, 58, 59, 63, 72, 73, 74, 77, 79, 80, 282

T

Territorial Brand 148, 150, 227, 228, 229, 231, 232, 233, 234, 235, 236, 238, 242, 243, 244, 245, 246, 247, 248, 249, 250, 251
territorial management 105, 141, 142, 144
tourism awareness 57, 58, 60, 62, 64, 65, 71, 73, 74, 78
Tourism Slogans 1, 8, 9, 10, 14, 15, 18, 21, 24
Tourism strategy 27, 30, 32, 41, 191, 306

U

Urban transformation 187, 188, 203

V

VICE model 255, 260, 263, 273, 276, 277, 280

W

World Cup 165, 166, 168, 169, 177, 179, 180, 202, 243

www.ingramcontent.com/pod-product-compliance
Lightning Source LLC
LaVergne TN
LVHW081432140225
803711LV00016B/16